China – The New Developmental State?

Hohenheimer Volkswirtschaftliche Schriften

Herausgegeben von
Prof. Dr. Michael Ahlheim, Prof. Dr. Thomas Beißinger, Prof. Dr. Ansgar Belke,
Prof. Dr. Rolf Caesar, Prof. Dr. Harald Hagemann, Prof. Dr. Klaus Herdzina,
Prof. Dr. Walter Piesch, Prof. Dr. Ingo Schmidt, Prof. Dr. Ulrich Schwalbe,
Prof. Dr. Peter Spahn, Prof. Dr. Jochen Streb, Prof. Dr. Gerhard Wagenhals,

Band 60

PETER LANG
Frankfurt am Main · Berlin · Bern · Bruxelles · New York · Oxford · Wien

Nicola Meier

China – The New Developmental State?

An Empirical Analysis of the Automotive Industry

PETER LANG
Frankfurt am Main · Berlin · Bern · Bruxelles · New York · Oxford · Wien

Bibliographic Information published by the Deutsche Nationalbibliothek
The Deutsche Nationalbibliothek lists this publication in the Deutsche Nationalbibliografie; detailed bibliographic data is available in the internet at <http://www.d-nb.de>.

Zugl.: Hohenheim, Univ., Diss., 2008

D 100
ISSN 0721-3085
ISBN 978-3-631-58284-8

www.peterlang.de

To my family

Acknowledgements

It is a delightful opportunity to thank the people who helped in the preparation of this study. I want to express my deepest appreciation and respect to Prof. Dr. Ansgar Belke, and my second supervisor, Prof. Dr. Sonja Opper. They were wonderful Ph.D. advisers who complemented each other perfectly. They devoted enormous amounts of their time and intelligence and took great efforts to help me expand my knowledge on the subject and spurred on the completion of the thesis. I am also thankful to them for carefully reading and commenting on countless revisions of this manuscript.

I am extremely grateful for the assistance, generosity and encouragement I received from my colleagues and friends in the *Economic and Market Intelligence* team at Daimler AG, especially, Dr. Peter-Ruediger Puf, Juergen W. Mueller and Dr. Ingo Konrad. They have always supported this study, and given me advice and support. Furthermore, they constantly encouraged my business career within the company. My special thanks go to Ingo, whose influence on this study cannot be overstated. He spent hours reading parts of the thesis and discussing various issues with me.

I wish to thank my dearest friends who proof-read this thesis, and constantly motivated me, supported me morally, and always understood the time stress I was suffering from. I thank them all for giving me their friendship, as deep and as rich as friendship can be.

I reserve my most profound thanks for my family, whose trust and belief in me have been endless. They have always enthusiastically taken part in my life, and helped with words and deeds at all times. From the bottom of my heart, I thank Tim for his continuous understanding and energetic support during the last years. He sacrificed a great deal for my academic career, endured with serenity and selflessness every emotion, and suffered long hours of neglect during the preparation of this thesis.

I thank the Stiftung Landesbank Baden-Württemberg for the financial support.

Stuttgart, November 2007

Nicola Meier

Table of contents

List of figures

List of tables

List of tables in the appendix

List of abbreviations

ACEA	Association des Constructeurs Européens d'Automobiles
AMC	American Motor Corporation
BAIC	Beijing Automotive Industry Company
BBDCA	Beijing Benz-DaimlerChrysler Automotive Ltd.
CAAM	Chinese Association of Automotive Industry
CAGR	Compound Annual Growth Rate
CBU	Completely Built Up
CCC	China Compulsory Certification
CCP	Communist Party of China
CKD	Completely Knocked Down
df	degrees of freedom
e.g.	for example (*exempli gratia*)
EU	European Union
FAW	First Auto Works
FDI	Foreign Direct Investment
ff	following pages
FFE	Foreign-Funded Enterprise
GATT	General Agreement on Tariffs and Trade
GDP	Gross Domestic Product
GIC	Delegation of German Industry and Commerce
GM	General Motors
IPR	Intellectual Property Right
JV	Joint Venture
MITI	Ministry of International Trade and Industry
MNC	Multinational corporation
NAFTA	North American Free Trade Area
n	number
n.d.	no date
NDRC	National Development and Reform Commission
NIC	Newly Industrialized Country
No.	Number
NPL	Non-Performing Loan
OECD	Organization for Economic Cooperation and Development
OEM	Original Equipment Manufacturer
p	probability
p.	page
pp.	pages
PNE	Production Networks for Exports
PRC	People's Republic of China
R&D	Research and Development
RMB	Renminbi
SAIC	Shanghai Automotive Industry Corporation
SASAC	State-owned Assets Supervision and Administration Commission
SAW	Second Auto Works

SCM	Subsidies and Countervailing Measures
SKD	Semi Knocked Down
SOE	State-Owned Enterprises
SPSS	Statistical Package for Social Sciences
S&T	Science and Technology
SVW	Shanghai Volkswagen
TAIC	Tianjin Automotive Industry Group Corporation
TRIMs	Trade-Related Investment Measures
TRIPs	Trade-Related Intellectual Property Rights
TVE	Township-Village Enterprise
UK	United Kingdom
US	United States
USA	United States of America
USD	United States Dollar
VDA	German Association of Automobile Manufacturers (*Verband der Automobilindustrie)*
Vol.	Volume
VW	Volkswagen Group
WFOE	Wholly Foreign-Owned Enterprise
WTO	World Trade Organization

1 Introduction

"The extent to which the state was responsible for the economic 'miracles' of East Asia is a matter of considerable debate, of course, but what is more important [...] is that a great number of Chinese policy-makers believed it to be true in the early 1990s." (Eric Thun)[1]

1.1 The context - putting China in perspective

"Beijing, not Washington, increasingly takes the decisions that affect workers, companies, financial markets and economies everywhere." [2] This statement can be found at the be-ginning of a special report on China and the world economy issued in *The Economist.* Not every economist would agree with this statement, especially if it is to be interpreted literally. However, there exists broad agreement that during the last two decades, China has become one of the key players in the world economy.

In 1978, the Chinese government began to shift its focus from political struggle to economic development. Compared with the economic transitions initiated in the early 1990s in several states of Eastern Europe and in parts of the former Soviet Union, China's approach to economic reform appears to offer crucial advantages. Since the introduction of its opening up strategy China has experienced rapid economic growth. The compound annual growth rate (CAGR) of China's Gross Domestic Product (GDP) was 16.3 percent between 1986 and 2006.[3] Its robust economic growth, which brought the country to the status of the fourth largest economy in the world in 2005, has dramatically reduced poverty.[4] More than 400 million people have been lifted above the 1 United States Dollar (USD) a day poverty level in the last 20 years.[5]

Chinese companies are competitive global players in many industries, especially those that are labor intensive. According to Shenkar (2005), *"China-based factories make 70 percent of the world's toys, 60 percent of its bicycles, half of its microwave ovens and one-third of its television sets and air conditioners etc."* [6] In some other product categories, such as textile and garments, China's share has been held back by quotas and tariffs. However, these barriers to trade have been released after

1 Thun (2004a), p. 457.

2 The Economist (2005), "From T-Shirts to T-bonds", Internet Edition, reviewed 18.09.2006.

3 Refer to China Statistical Yearbook (2007).

4 In 2007, the Economist Intelligence Unit wrote: *"China will very soon (if it has not done so already) overtake Germany as the world's third largest economy at market exchange-rates".* Refer to Economist Intelligence Unit (2007), "China Economy: Pushing Past Germany", Internet Edition, reviewed 02.11.2007.

5 The net per capita income of rural residents increased at 6 percent during 2001-2006. Refer to World Bank (2007), "China Quick Facts", Internet Edition, reviewed 21.09.2007.

6 Refer to Shenkar (2005), p. 3.

China joined the World Trade Organization (WTO) in 2001. Concerning the product mix, China is increasingly leaving the state of the world's workbench – a rising share of capital- and technology-intensive production indicates China's march up the value chain. To give an example, at the International Motor Show in Germany in 2005, Chinese automotive (later: auto) manufacturers presented their models for the first time.

1.2 The state of research and aim of the study

After the collapse of communism in Eastern Europe and subsequently in the Soviet Union, political democratization and economic liberalization were widely regarded as recipes for prosperity by neoliberals in the West during the 1980s. However, the economic success of the East Asian states (which were almost all former Stalinist countries) challenges the fundamental principles of liberal political economy which emphasizes minimum state intervention for economic development. The East Asian development path has posed the question of why some states such as Japan, South Korea (later: Korea) and Taiwan have been able to play a more effective role than others (such as Eastern Europe and Russia) in coordinating industrial change.[7]

Various economists and political scientists, among them advocates of statism (statists) such as Johnson (1987), as well as neoliberal institutions like the World Bank (1993), argue that an activist state has underpinned the growth of the East Asian miracles. Government policies and bureaucracies have not only promoted economic growth, but have been essential to it.[8] However, as most poorly performing economies in Latin America, Africa and also Asia have activist states too, state activism per se does not contribute to growth. If governmental activism has supported the economic growth of the East Asian *developmental states*, one has to ask how governments do effectively promote growth, and which industrial policy instruments they use.

A range of studies analyze the positive role of the state in economic transformation. Stiglitz (2002) has analyzed how the governments of developing countries can improve the outcome of economic transformation by well-chosen interventions. White and Wade's (White and Wade 1988; Wade, 1990) concepts of the *"strong state"*, Johnson's (1987) study of *"administrative guidance"*, Amsden's (1989) approach to *"getting prices wrong"* and Evans' (1995) analysis of *"embedded autonomy"* have become classics in the field of East Asian transformation.[9]

---

7 In some analyses also Singapore, Hong Kong, Malaysia and Thailand are regarded as East Asian developmental states.

8 For further information refer to Johnson (1987) and the World Bank (1993).

9 For further information refer to Stiglitz (2002), White and Wade (1988), Wade (1990), Johnson (1987), Amsden (1989a) and Evans (1995).

While the economic slowdowns and the financial crises in much of Asia in the late 1990s abated some of the blind admiration of the "East Asian Miracle", China's economic growth in the post-Mao period has revived attention on the positive role of the state in promoting transformative economic development. China's industrialization has been in the focus of academics and policy-makers alike; however, the reasons behind its economic development are still poorly understood. China's current industrial policies have various unique features. The country has confounded free-market theorists' expectations in many ways, because its economic policies and public institutions do not conform to orthodox prescriptions for creating the conditions for high growth such as minimal government intervention and private companies. The clear overlap of economic and political spheres in China inevitably goes back to the centuries-old theoretical debate on the appropriate role of the state. Accordingly, one of the most interesting questions in the field of economics and political economy, and the central interest in this analysis, is whether the rapid growth of transforming China can be attributed to the emulation of certain mechanisms of the East Asian transformation. This results in the research question: *Is China the new developmental state?*

As China's development, similar to that of the East Asian Newly Industrialized Countries (NICs) (Korea, Taiwan, Singapore and Hong Kong, often referred to as "four little dragons"), contradicts the expectations of neoutilitarian arguments, and is in measurable terms of economic development and social change unprecedented in speed, scale and scope, it is surprising that almost no analysis of China has been conducted within the context of the East Asian developmental state theory. The studies that have analyzed the developmental role of the Chinese state are, among others, Breslin (1996), Nee et al. (2005), So (2003), Unger and Chan (1995, 1996), White (1988, 1991), Xia (2000) and Zhu (2004).[10] While these studies have paid attention to China incorporating the East Asian developmental state concept, none of them provides a clear-cut specification of the defining institutional features and economic policies of a (Chinese) developmental state. They rather focus on specific criteria and single determinants of China's transformation approach.

This study's focus is on China's development path and the role of the state in its transformation process. China's economy can only be understood if the concomitance of economic development (industrialization) and economic transformation (from planned- to market-economy) is taken into consideration. This is done by specifying conditions and measures that a developmental state has to fulfill in order to transform its backward domestic companies into internationally competitive players. As a point of reference, the Japanese, Korean and Taiwanese models of development are examined. China's development approach is compared with these former developing countries' transformation in order to come to an assessment of the

10 For further information refer to Breslin (1996), Nee et al. (2005), So (2003), Unger and Chan (1995, 1996), White (1988, 1991), Xia (2000) and Zhu (2004).

uniqueness of the Chinese model of economic development and thus fill the academic gap. Hence, the study is relevant to the "transformation theory", general questions on development economics, and the current policy debate about a role model for transforming countries' reform approaches.

Moreover, not only the *uniqueness* of the Chinese model of economic development is in the focus of this study, but also its *effectiveness*. In order to gain insight into the *effectiveness* of the Chinese model of economic development, the study uses the auto industry as a means of understanding the performance outcome of state-guidance. The development of the auto industry is a classic example of China's efforts to transform inefficient and technologically backward Chinese companies into powerful national and international champions. This effort began in the 1980s, long before similar efforts in other industries, when the auto sector was chosen as a "pillar" industry and became a primary target of government industrial policy.

Until 1978 there had been almost no passenger car production in China, and cars were the prerogative of a relatively small number of high-ranking officials. Since then, many of the world's most powerful original equipment manufacturers (OEMs) and suppliers have staked their future on the Chinese auto industry. It is thus important to understand its evolution in the context of China's economic development and transformation:

- The auto industry has traditionally spearheaded organizational and industrial change affecting all other industries, because sophisticated products have to be manufactured in high volumes.
- The auto industry is playing an important and unique role as a system integrator of a number of important other industries (electronics, steel, glass). Products manufactured by these and other industries are used in the design and production of modern autos.
- Although the analysis is sector specific, it is representative of sectors that are technology- and capital-intensive, and in which foreign direct investment (FDI) is motivated by market access rather than cost-cutting. It is possible to investigate problems not only of industrialization in general, but also of economic integration and technology transfers, because the Chinese auto industry has encompassed domestic and foreign economic and decision processes.

This is not the first empirical analysis based on the Chinese auto industry. Studies on the Chinese auto industry have been conducted by Mann (1989), Harwit (1995, 2001), Thun (2004a, 2004b, 2006), and Noble et al. (2005).[11] However, none has pursued a comprehensive analysis of the Chinese auto industry, examining its

[11] For further information refer to Mann (1989), Harwit (1995, 2001), Thun (2004a, 2004b, 2006) and Noble et al. (2005).

development approach according to the criteria that characterize the East Asian developmental states' economic transformation.

1.3 Methodology and available sources

The underlying premise of this study on China is that industrial development is multi-faceted. It is well known that focusing on only one aspect of the process of industrial development may result in misleading conclusions and simplistic policy recommendations. It is hence essential to consider multiple dimensions of industrial development in order to discover whether China is the new developmental state. Accordingly, various methods are applied within this study:[12] First, the study uses a secondary analysis approach to gain general information on the Chinese model of economic development, evaluating secondary statistical data as well as abundant material of Chinese and international authors, institutions and organizations. Second, an empirical analysis of the Chinese auto industry is conducted. Insights into state-guidance in the auto sector come from secondary analysis, as well as qualitative and quantitative analysis. Thus, theoretical arguments can be underpinned by empirical evidence. The period of examination is from China's early reform years (late 1970s) until November 2007.

(1) Secondary analysis of the Chinese model of economic development:

Secondary analysis is the (re-)analysis of data. Pre-existing data is used either to investigate new research questions or to re-examine primary study questions for purposes of corroboration.[13] Information is gained from the (re-)analysis of the following sources with special focus on the subject:

- *Official documents of Chinese political agencies and leaders:* The research is based on the examination of official documents from Chinese sources. Most official regulations, laws and statements are available in English. Due to the evaluation of these documents, political and economic indicators that are decisive for China's reform process can be isolated. Furthermore, the review of official documents from the beginning of the reform process until 2007 provides an insight into the characteristics of the Chinese transformation approach in the course of reform. Among those documents are statements from China's political leadership, five-year plans and industrial policy documents of the National Development and Reform Commission (NDRC), regulations of the Ministry of Commerce, and the homepage of the Chinese central government etc. Furthermore, on the local government level,

12 The theoretical foundation of this study, the state's role in (East Asian) economic development, is based on literature review. The review describes, summarizes, evaluates and clarifies this literature. It gives a theoretical base for the research. Works which are irrelevant are discarded and those which are peripheral are looked at critically.

13 Refer to Glass (1976), pp. 3-8.

documents on foreign investment schemes which are available on the homepages of e.g. the municipalities of Beijing and Shanghai, are evaluated.

- *Official statistics of the National Bureau of Statistics of China:* The evaluation of statistical yearbooks provides relevant information. Various issues of the "China Statistical Yearbook", the "China Compendium of Statistics", the "China External Economic Statistical Yearbook" and the "China Statistical Yearbook on Science and Technology", as well as the "Beijing Statistical Yearbook" and the "Shanghai Statistical Yearbook" are used. China's membership in international organizations such as the World Bank and the International Monetary Fund since the beginning of the 1980s, has generally contributed to the qualitative improvement of statistical data. Moreover, international classifications have been adopted successively and an approach towards international standards can be registered.[14] Nevertheless, different reports (such as Holz 2001, 2005) are skeptical of the quality of Chinese official statistical data.[15] The problem of official data inconsistency has directly affected the results of commercial, academic and policy studies alike. Due to these reasons, this study covers national development trends. The inaccuracy of specific data may be accepted, because the reliability of official data can be verified by comparing it with alternative sources. In consequence, the data used is suitable for the method and aim of this study.
- *Articles from the national and regional Chinese daily press:* The freedom of the press is still restricted by the Chinese central government. Accordingly, articles from the Chinese national press might be colored by political statements. Qualitative improvements of press statements can be seen in recent years, however. Furthermore, the daily press is the only medium which allows the researcher to incorporate up-to-date developments as well as the latest reform results. For this reason, the researcher uses various internet publications from relevant Chinese and other daily presses.

---

14 Refer to Opper (1999), p. 28.

15 First, some data such as data on GDP may have been intentionally misreported. Second, a quantity of data is of dubious economic meaning due to the way in which it is constructed (for example, data on fixed assets and farm employment). Third, economic variables and enterprise categories have frequently been re-defined without revision of the variables or category names. This has caused statistical breaks, as in 1993 and 1998 for reference and severe comparability problems in both time series and cross-sectional data. Fourth, detailed data that is in line with Western national income accounting standards is available for the 1990s. However, inconsistencies due to periodic adjustments still abound. While far less data is available for the 1980s, when industrial statistics were constructed in accordance with the Material Product System, this data is somewhat more consistent. Fifth, enterprises and local governments alike have varying incentives to manipulate and misreport data which obviously resticts its quality. Enterprises for reference may underreport value added in order to avoid tax payments. However, the National Bureau of Statistics is working hard to reduce its reliance on questionable data provided by other government departments, and to bridge the central-local divide. Refer to Holz (2002), p. 52 and Holz and Lin (2001), p. 30 ff. For further information refer to Rawski (2001).

Although remarkable information can be gained from the evaluation of these sources, the basis of the analysis is extended by sources from various international authors, institutions and organizations. The analysis concentrates on scientific publications such as books, reports, review articles and other reference-type materials.[16] International secondary literature is analyzed to complement Chinese secondary statistics in English language and to counter biased, politically or ideologically colored interpretation of Chinese sources.

(2) Empirical analysis of the auto sector (incorporating a mixed methods approach):

In social research, the term "triangulation" [17] (or mixed methods approach) is used to refer to the observation of the research issue from at least two different points.[18] The application of different methods becomes essential in the study of complex fields of investigation. Triangulation allows one to exceed the limitations of a single method by combining several methods and giving them equal relevance. Thus, a highly synergistic combination of data types can be achieved. Only the variety of different methods reveals the necessary range of information to gain a complete picture, and to validate all items of information.[19] Triangulation allows multiple confirmation of the findings of secondary analysis, as well as qualitative and quantitative analysis (refer to Figure 1).

Figure 1: Triangulation.

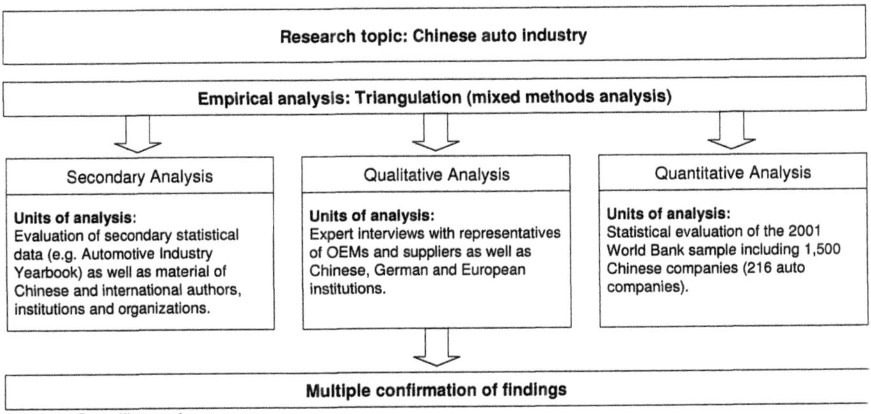

Source: Own illustration.

---

16 This mainly applies to data and regulations from the early reform period.

17 For information on "triangulation" refer to Webb et al. (1966), Smith (1975) and Denzin (1978).

18 Refer to Flick (2004b), p. 179. For further information refer to Flick (2004a) and Jick (1979).

19 Refer to Flick (2005), Internet Edition, reviewed 05.02.2006.

Figure 1 shows that the empirical analysis of the auto sector uses a secondary analysis approach that concentrates on the re-analysis of industrial policy documents, laws and regulations with special focus on state-guidance in the sector. Moreover, secondary statistics from the China Automotive Industry Yearbook 2006 and various issues of the China Statistical Yearbook provide a fact base for conclusions about the sector's development since the early reform years.

In addition to secondary analysis, qualitative analysis reveals the dynamic process of industrial development as well as the role of changing government policies and institutional settings. Expert interviews were conducted in China. Interviews provide targeted and directly-focused approaches, and give insightful causal details on the research topic.[20] Among the experts are managers of foreign auto companies (OEMs and suppliers) as well as experts from German, Chinese and European (government) institutions located in Beijing and Shanghai. The qualitative researcher uses complex reasoning that is multifaceted, iterative, and simultaneous.[21] The qualitative analysis focuses on the institutional framework and the national industrial policy design for the auto sector.

The quantitative analysis uses data from the World Bank survey "Competitiveness, Technology and Firm Linkages in Manufacturing Sectors" (2001). The sample includes 1,500 Chinese firms (of which 216 are auto companies). The statistical evaluation of the survey data bases conclusions on the state-directed development approach in the auto sector on quantitative evidence.

1.4 Line of action

The analysis of the Chinese development path is presented in five chapters. The state's role in economic transformation with respect to the East Asian developmental states is analyzed in Chapter 2. This serves as the theoretical foundation for the analysis of the Chinese economic transformation approach (Chapter 3) and also provides a benchmark to assess its effectiveness on the basis of the Chinese auto industry (Chapter 4). Chapter 5 answers the question of research, and gives lessons on other transforming countries' development paths.

The study analyzes the subsequent details: *Chapter 2* outlines the theoretical debate on the appropriate role of the state, and thus establishes the theoretical groundwork for this study. The chapter examines the economic and institutional arrangements for development in three East Asian countries, namely Japan, Taiwan and Korea. The analysis is based on the classic works on the state's role in economic development in general, and the most influential studies on the developmental state theory in particular. The rapid economic growth of the East Asian economies raises the question of the policies and institutional factors that contributed to growth. The

---

20 Although the interviews are essential evidence, interview data can be corroborated with additional information when necessary. Refer to Eisenhardt (1989b), p. 538 and Yin (1994), p. 86.

21 Refer to Creswell (2003), p. 182.

analysis of the three East Asian states suggests that their development approach should not be perceived as a unique, cultural or regional phenomenon, but as an alternative model of development that offers an important policy option for developing countries. From this, a model of East Asian development is created. The East Asian Developmental State Model serves as an analytic research framework. The model includes conditions and measures a developmental state has to have and implement, respectively, in order to accelerate economic growth and transformation.

In *Chapter 3* the model of East Asian development is used as a basis to analyze China's development path. First, the question of whether China fulfills the conditions "dictated" by the East Asian Developmental State Model is explored. As this can be confirmed, the Chinese transformation path since 1978 is analyzed with respect to each criterion of the model. The focus is on determining the defining elements of the Chinese development strategy. The mechanisms used by the Chinese government to promote transformative economic growth are clarified and specified using a secondary analysis. Thus, the question is answered as to whether China is a mere follower of the best practices of the East Asian states or whether the Chinese model of economic development is unique.[22] The distinctiveness and innovative character of the Chinese model of economic reform unveils similarities and differences between the East Asian developmental states' and China's approach to economic development.

The empirical analysis of *Chapter 4* focuses on the development of the Chinese auto industry, and uses a mixed methods research approach. The chapter examines whether the development of the auto sector reflects the uniqueness of China's transformation strategy. The policy and bureaucracy framework of the auto industry is analyzed to identify the inherent characteristics of the Chinese model of economic development in the auto industry. Only by starting from a full picture at the macro level of the auto industry in China (analysis of the institutional settings and the policy documents guiding the sector's development), can appropriate in-depth analyses at lower levels (expert interviews, World Bank sample, secondary analysis on firm performance etc.) be conducted in order to obtain convincing evidence. The chapter, moreover, analyzes the performance outcome of China's development approach to the sector. Secondary statistics, as well as information gathered from qualitative and quantitative research, form the basis of evidence. The study intends thus to fill the gap between theoretical and empirical approaches and increases the "persuasiveness" of evidence.

---

[22] When analyzing development strategies as the object of analysis, the following methodological problems arise: First, "strategy" is usually associated with clearly intended state action. As strategies may also emerge by default, trial-and-error or compromise, imputing a central design requires caution. "Strategies" often take years to crystallize and are often plagued by internal inconsistency. Second, strategies generally consist of *packages* of policies, and different policies involve different political cleavages and conflicts. It is thus useful to disaggregate "strategies" where possible. Third, development strategies are not unambiguously given by factor endowments, but also by natural endowments such as interest groups seeking to maximize their rents. Those usually influence the decisions of policy-makers. These limitations of analyzing strategies have to be considered when conducting this study. Refer to Haggard (1990), p. 23.

Chapter 5 draws conclusions from the previous analysis on China's economic development, and assesses whether its development path corresponds to that of the three East Asian states. Answers are given as to whether China is the new developmental state, and whether China's distinctiveness has been conducive to economic growth. The findings seek to help economists and political scientists, policy-makers and businessmen to understand China's transformation process with its conditions, institutional settings, industrial policy mechanisms and limitations. This contributes to fact-based decision-making at both the industrial and national level. The analysis concludes with broader lessons for the role of an activist government concerned with economic development and the transition from a socialist economy. The study's line of action with its detailed design is illustrated in Figure 2.

Figure 2: Line of action.

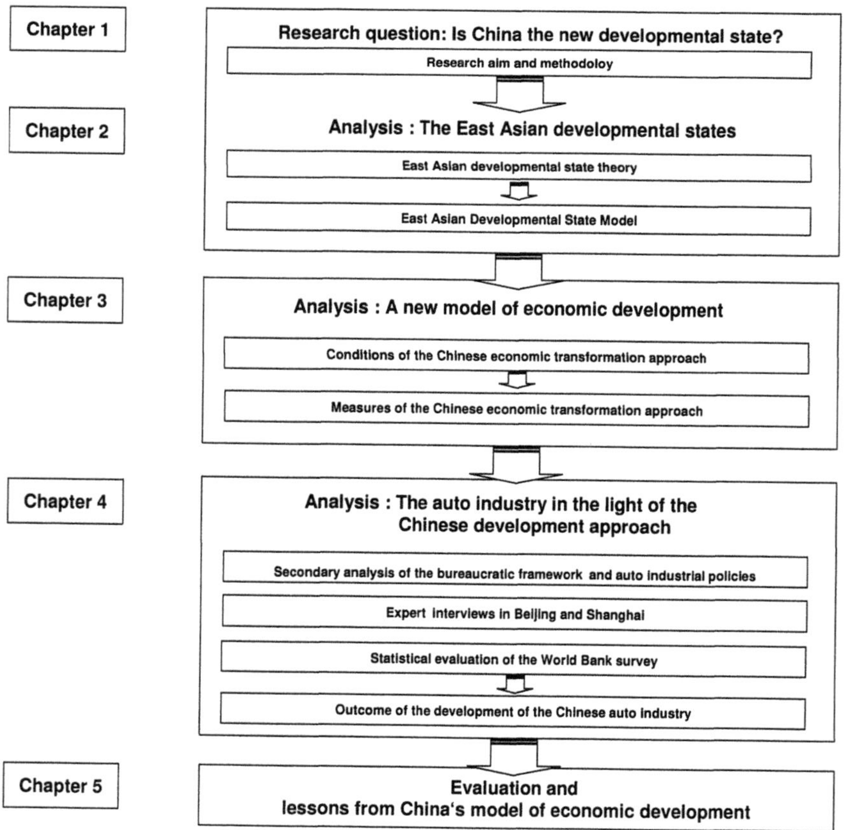

Source: Own illustration.

2 The East Asian developmental states

In the post-World War II period, the leading economies of the East Asian region have experienced a historically unprecedented rate of economic growth and commercial expansion. Some of the emerging economies in the region achieved higher growth rates than those of Western economies in comparable periods of the development process. Today, Japan and the East Asian NICs have levels of GDP per capita comparable to those of the richest nations of the world. Their largest companies are engaged in a phase of dramatic regional and, in some cases, global expansion. The "recent" cases from East Asia have come to exemplify the modern concept of the developmental state. Knowledge of the developmental state is largely derived from a number of descriptive studies which each focus on one case or another rather than a general model. Although it might be questionable whether it is possible to treat the East Asian countries as a whole, for the purpose of this study, the similarities between Japan, Taiwan and Korea are highlighted, while still acknowledging that there are significant differences between them. From this, a distinct model of East Asian development can be derived.

2.1 Debate on the beneficial role of the state

By the end of the 1970s, statists acknowledged the economic success of Japan, Korea, Taiwan, Singapore and Hong Kong, as the result of proactive state involvement.[23] Except for Hong Kong, the governments of all these states have actively used industrial policy to accelerate and direct economic development.[24] Distinct from trade policies, industrial policy is defined as *"government efforts to alter industrial structure to promote productivity-based growth"*.[25] Industrial policy aims to promote technological innovation and to catch up with international best practices.[26] Far from being a novelty of East Asia, industrial policy has been an integral part of the economic policies of many advanced capitalist countries during the post-war period.[27] In the United Kingdom (UK), industrial policy was discussed controversially when the Labor government introduced industrial policy programs in the late 1970s.[28] The de-industrialization debate in the UK perceived industrial policy as one way to stop the progress of de-industrialization and revive the economy.[29] During the 1980s, studies of various European countries' policy approaches to overcome the industrial

23 Refer to Evans (1989), p. 563.

24 Refer to Robins (2002), p. 293.

25 Refer to World Bank (1993), p. 304.

26 Refer to Naseem (2003), p. 636.

27 Refer to Chang (1994), p. 56.

28 For further information refer to Blackaby (1979) and Matthews and Sargent (1983).

29 For further information refer to Singh (1977) and Rowthorn and Wells (1987).

crisis of the late 1970s emerged.[30] The issue of industrial policy, however, was debated most strongly in the United States of America (USA). In the early 1980s, the Harvard Business Review served particularly as the major forum.[31] Strategic-trade policy literature has also been influenced by (and has influenced) the industrial policy debates.[32]

Despite successful state-led growth in the East Asian countries, by the end of the 1970s, economic theorists as well as practioners demanded free market and laissez-faire policies which soon became the dominant view of international bodies such as the International Monetary Fund and the World Bank.[33] For the neoclassicals, economic success is achieved by the efficiency of market mechanisms and policies emphasizing openness, private enterprise and the minimal role of government.[34] Since Smith (1776), liberal political economy has contended that the government should not directly intervene in firm's decisions, but monitor and enforce the regulatory environment in which firms compete for survival and profits. Public choice theory adds that politicians and bureaucrats should not directly intervene in firms' business activities, because they will use their power to further their personal interests, such as the maximization of political support and re-election, rather than the firm's efficiency.[35] Kornai (1980) furthermore warns that risk-sharing between government and enterprises (via state ownership and state guarantees) may lead to inefficiencies, as state officials might impose political interests (such as job creation) on the firm. The firm expects external financial assistance from the state (subsidies, preferential credit, and reduced tax rates) and builds it firmly into its behavior. This is known as the "soft budget constraint" problem.[36]

Consequently, the neoliberals contend that governments should only intervene in the economy to overcome inherent market failure. Hayek (1945) argues that it is impossible for governments to have the necessary information to plan and coordinate economic activities effectively, even if their bureaucrats possess the best knowledge

---

30 For further information refer to Pinder (1982), Jacquemin (1984), Cox (1986) and Duchêne and Sheperd (1987).

31 For reviews of the debate refer to Norton (1986) and Thompson (1989).

32 For further information refer to Kirzkowski (1984) and Krugman (1988).

33 For further information on the recent politics of the World Bank refer to e.g. Easterly (2001). His book combines modern growth theory with experiences from his fieldwork for the World Bank.

34 For further information refer to Ricardo (1817).

35 For further information refer to Buchanan (1980) and Shleifer and Vishny (1994). Krueger furthermore postulates that political decision-makers tend to pursue rent-seeking activities instead of maximizing societal welfare. Rents are defined as excess returns over opportunity costs. Rent-seeking is the attempt to redistribute the rights or entitlements to such returns through political action. Refer to Krueger (1974).

36 Kornai differentiates between the hardness and softness of budget constraint. For further information refer to Kornai (1986, 1990, 1998, 2001).

available.[37] The government's proper role is to help create and maintain an environment in which resource allocation is effectively determined by price signals. This entails a policy regime that sets the framework for the functioning of the market and a small public sector. Influenced by this line of argumentation, government failures in the 1980s led to deregulation, liberalization and privatization in a large number of developing economies.[38]

The World Bank, being an adherent of the neoclassical theory, has been tardy in extending praise to the East Asian model. In 1992, however, it emphasized for the first time the role of the state and its institutions in general, and good governance in particular. However, not until the World Bank's publication of *"The East Asian Miracle: Economic Growth and Public Policy"* in 1993, was the decisive role of the governments of East Asia with their active state interventionism acknowledged by some neoclassicals.[39]

In 1997, the debate on the beneficial role of the state revived as the Asian financial crisis revealed an institutional shortcoming of Asian capitalism.[40] Despite ample evidence of decisive government industrial policy in the region of East Asia, economists remained divided in their interpretation of the developmental role of East Asian governments for a long time. The economists disagreed on whether it is government initiatives or market forces which have constituted the primary causal factor in stimulating modern economic development and productivity growth.[41] Accordingly, the development debate was mostly framed in terms of stark, simplistic alternatives, as a kind of contest between the power of the state versus the power of the free market.

The Asian financial crisis cannot be used to discredit the whole model of East Asian development. While the crisis revealed the risks of politicizing the economic system, this does not imply that economists and politicians cannot learn from the East Asian experience. The questions that must be addressed are: under what circumstances is

---

37 For further information refer to Hayek (1945). Nee et al. add that it does not make any difference whether the government unit is a central ministry or local government bureau. No individual government official has the requisite knowledge to outperform the market mechanism in general. Refer to Nee et al. (2007), p. 22.

38 Refer to Yue (1995), pp. 76-79 and Minns (2001), pp. 1025-1026.

39 The World Bank (1993) study "The East Asian Miracle" had to be sponsored by the Japanese themselves as they wanted to highlight the role of the state behind the miracle. Additionally, at the annual meeting of the World Bank/International Monetary Fund in the fall of 1991, Attila Karaosmanoglu, at this time vice president and managing director of the World Bank, said that the East Asian NICs and their successful emulators are a powerful argument that a more activist, positive governmental role can be a decisive factor in rapid industrial growth. He added, what is replicable and transferable must be brought to light and shared with others. Refer to Stiglitz (2002), p. 91. The view of the World Bank is manifested in the "World Development Report 1997: The State in a Changing World".

40 Refer to Edin (2000), p. 19.

41 Refer to Robins (2002), p. 292.

state intervention likely to be successful, and which factors determine the effectiveness of industrial policy? More specifically, how can the state remove the privileges of particular firms, and ensure that the rents created by state intervention encourage productive activities? What is needed is clarification of the quality of state involvement in industry promotion. Therefore, the necessary conditions and measures for successful state-led economic growth have to be specified. The key issue then becomes not whether, or how much, states should intervene, but rather what makes some states more effective than others in developing their economy.

2.2 The developmental state theory

The growth of some East Asian states has exemplified the active role of the state in economic transformation. The principal idea behind it may yet be traced to much earlier times. A long tradition of scholarship has focused on the historical role of the state in industrialization, and defended the proposition that an active and effective state apparatus is an essential element in successful industrialization.[42]

2.2.1 Early recognition of the state's role in industrialization

List (1885) emphasized the strategic role of the state in harnessing domestic and international market forces in the national interest. He examined how Germany had been able to develop a manufacturing industry at a time when British manufacturers were far in advance.[43] He was one of the pioneers of the infant industries conception.[44] Even more important was his idea of a national system of political economy.[45] It attacked Smith's unlimited freedom of trade and the liberal principle of laissez-faire.[46] List and the German Historical School essentially argued, based on the concept of historicism, that universal economic laws were non-existent, and thus states had the right to intervene in the economy.[47] Especially in the case of late-developing countries, the promotion of national economic development was regarded as being critical to their success in "catching-up" with the industrialized, developed

---

42 Refer to Evans (1989), p. 566.

43 Refer to List (1885), p. 39 ff.

44 The infant industry argument says that developing sectors of the economy need protection against international competition in order to establish themselves. Refer to List (1885), p. 224 ff.

45 Refer to List (1885), p. 259 ff and p. 347 ff.

46 Decisive for Smith's laissez-faire approach is the following quotation: *"The statesmen who should attempt to direct private people in what manner they ought to employ their capitals, would not only load himself with a most unnecessary attention, but assume an authority which could safely be trusted to no council and senate whatever, and which would nowhere be so dangerous as in the hands of man who had folly and presumption enough to fancy himself fit to exercise it."* Quoted in Hayek (1976, reprinted in 1994), p. 63 and Smith (1776), Book Four, Chapter V, p. 540 ff.

47 Refer to List (1885), p. 172 ff.

world.[48] On a theoretical level, not simply mere exchangeable value, but productive forces account for the wealth of a country. List formulated a theory of economic development that was based on the promotion of *"productive powers"* [49] through the state which contrasted with Smith's free enterprise system.

Weber (1911) called attention to established market societies, and argued that the operation of large-scale capitalist enterprises depended on the existence of the kind of order that only a modern bureaucratic state could provide. Weber emphasized that capitalism and the bureaucratic state apparatus belong intimately together.[50] He argued for the fundamental value of bureaucracy as one of the institutional foundations of capitalist growth.[51] Weber pointed out that bureaucrats were only concerned with fulfilling their assignments and contributing to the achievement of the goals of the apparatus as a whole. For him, use of the privileges of office for maximizing private interests was a feature of earlier prebureaucratic forms. The bureaucracy needs to be a corporately coherent entity in order to support markets and capitalist accumulation. In this coherent entity, individuals see the promotion of corporate goals as the best means of maximizing their individual self-interest. Individual incumbents have to be insulated to some degree from the demands of society in order to achieve corporate coherence. The enhancement of insulation is achieved by conferring a distinctive and rewarding status on bureaucrats. Also central to the bureaucracy's effectiveness is its concentration of expertise through meritocratic recruitment and the provision of opportunities for long-term career rewards.[52] Altogether, Weber stressed the fundamental role of an authoritative bureaucracy as a prerequisite to the operation of markets, and thus as one of the institutional foundations of capitalist growth.

Polanyi (1957) too elaborated on the positive attributes of state intervention in economic life and addressed state intervention in the economy from a sociological point of view. He discussed Smith's *"natural propensity to truck, barter and exchange one thing for another"* [53] and criticized the proposition that exchange was a "natural" activity that required only minimal institutional underpinnings. As he conceived it, the

---

48 List was a liberal nationalist and his concept of economic nationalism - which was often but unjustifiably regarded as "neo-mercantilist" - together with the ideas of the German Historical School, provided an intellectual stimulus for Meiji Japan. Consequently, Japan's leadership systematically fostered economic growth and industrialization, and turned Japan into a state where national economic development was the prime objective. Refer to Sohn (1998), p. 17.

49 List takes up Smith's expression of "productive powers" which in sum, according to Smith, causes the condition of nations and develops this term further. Refer to Smith (1776), Introduction, p. XXIV ff and List (1885), p. 133 ff and p. 163 ff.

50 Refer to Weber (1911), p. 973 ff and pp. 1394-1395.

51 This thesis always had to contend with the historically prior and ideologically powerful classical view of Smith's laissez-faire government role.

52 Refer to Weber (1911), pp. 958-960, p. 974 and pp. 978-979.

53 Refer to Smith (1776), Book One, Chapter II, p. 14 ff.

successful rise of the market in the UK required intervention by the state: *"The road to the free market was opened and kept open by an enormous increase in continuous, centrally organized and controlled interventionism".*[54] From the beginning, the market was intertwined not just with different kinds of social ties, but with the interventionist policies of the state.

Gerschenkron's work (1962) on late developers complemented Weber. Asserting that late developers faced different conditions than the early industrializers,[55] Gerschenkron illustrates why a strong state is likely to push industrialization forward in particularly backward countries.[56] Whereas individual entrepreneurs largely contributed to the industrialization and development of the UK, in the first "late" industrializers – Germany, Switzerland, Italy, France, Austria, the Austrian-Hungarian Empire and Belgium[57] – universal banks played the major role in kickstarting industrial expansion. Banks stepped in, because entrepreneurs in these countries had little capital with which to build up large firms. The banks provided not only funding for industrialization, but also took key investment decisions in the firms in which they invested, and limited competition among their financial offspring. In the even more backward Hungarian and Russian states, the state stepped in as the chief investor in industry due to the weak financial system. The state incorporated the role of entrepreneur and banker alike. The state created, funded and directed much of the new industrialization. In order to catch up in their economic development, late industrializers were forced to rely on the power of the state.[58] While in Weber's model, the government simply provides a suitable environment, Gerschenkron's state is actively organizing a crucial aspect of the market.

Altogether, in Gerschenkron's reasoning, the more backward a country, the greater the role played by the state in increasing the supply of capital to the nascent industries and in providing guidance. As a consequence, active state involvement is seen to be of little importance to early developers, or once a country has industrialized.[59]

Hirschman (1958) analyzed the state's entrepreneurship. Based on his observations of the *"late late"* developers of the 20th century Third World, entrepreneurship in the sense of willingness to risk the available surplus by investing it in productive activities is lacking, namely, *"the ability to make and carry out development decisions"* and *"the*

---

54 Refer to Polanyi (1967), p. 140.

55 According to Gerschenkron, *"...[I]n several very important respects the development of a backward country may, by the very virtue of its backwardness, tend to differ fundamentally from that of an advanced country."* Gerschenkron (1962), p. 7.

56 Ibidem, pp. 5-30.

57 Ibidem, p. 16.

58 Ibidem, p. 11 ff, p. 14 ff and p. 19 ff.

59 Refer to Weiss and Hobson (1995), p. 2.

perception of investment opportunities and transformation into actual investments".[60] The state therefore has to lead entrepreneurial activities in order to transform (potentially) existing savings into available productive activities. By providing *"disequilibrating"* incentives the state induces private capitalists to invest and, at the same time, to be ready to alleviate bottlenecks that are creating disincentives to investment.[61]

Altogether, by puncturing the myth of the original industrial revolution as a purely private process, these interpretations have brought the state to the fore in the analysis of European industrialization.[62] The outlined comparative historical visions were the beginnings of a positive vision of how an effective state might act and be organized.

2.2.2 Origin of the East Asian capitalist developmental state theory

Developing these visions of an active state further and laying special focus on East Asia, in 1981, Johnson introduced what was to become a focal point in future debates over the role of the state in industrialization.[63] It was only with the publication of his work on the East Asian states and Japan in particular that the phrase "developmental state" made its formal debut, and that a serious attempt was made to conceptualize it.

Johnson argued that Japan's developmental state and its changing of industrial structure was a central element in explaining the country's post-World War II economic miracle.[64] Johnson traced the emergence of Japanese industrial development back to 1868 and the Meiji era (1868–1912), where Japan first began to be *"plan rational and developmental".*[65] He distinguished the *"developmental orientation"* of such a *"plan rational"* state from both the *"plan ideological"* state of the Soviet-type command economies and from the *"regulatory orientation"* of typical liberal-democratic or even social-democratic states.[66]

Johnson can be regarded as the "father" of the developmental state approach. He discussed in detail the attributes and qualities of the developmental state,[67] but did not, however, offer an isolated definition. As this seems necessary at the beginning

60 Refer to Hirschman (1958), pp. 35-36 ff.

61 Ibidem, p. 65 ff.

62 Refer to Rueschemeyer and Evans (1985), p. 44.

63 Refer to Johnson (1981).

64 Refer to Johnson (1982), pp. 9-10, p. 3 ff and p. 31 ff.

65 Ibidem, p. 23.

66 Ibidem, pp. 18-19.

67 Ibidem, p. 17 ff.

of the analysis, the definition of Leftwich (1995), who examined features of different developmental states,[68] delivers insight:

> *"Developmental states may be defined as states whose politics have concentrated sufficient power, autonomy and capacity at the center to shape, pursue and encourage the achievement of explicit developmental objectives, whether by establishing and promoting the conditions and direction of economic growth, or by organizing it directly, or a varying combination of both."*[69]

Developmental states are mainly the states in East Asia, above all Japan, and additionally Taiwan, Korea, Hong Kong and Singapore. Japan, Korea and Taiwan are the most typical cases in terms of wide state intervention among Asian countries, compared with more laissez-faire Hong Kong and, to a lesser degree, Singapore, and the resource-rich countries of Southeast Asia. Hence, as Hong Kong and Singapore are special cases of developmental states,[70] here, only Japan, Taiwan and Korea are examined.

The developmental state's capacity refers to the ability of policy-making authorities to pursue domestic adjustment strategies. These strategies are set up in cooperation with organized economic groups and intend to upgrade or transform the industrial economy.[71] Accordingly, the idea of the developmental state is indicative of the role of the state and its policies as well as the internal relationships that constitute the state itself. The state has an important legitimate part to play in determining the course and content of national economic development. In addition, the developmental state is suggestive of a particular constellation of political and economic relations. This implies relations amongst the personnel that constitute the state, and between the state and society and the business sector, respectively.

The East Asian capitalist developmental states - although they are neither communist nor laissez-faire - exhibit characteristics of the neoclassical minimalist state and the centrally planned Leninist state.[72] Neither a pure state-centered nor market-centered explanation takes into consideration the East Asian experience. The developmental state plays an activist, rather than minimalist, role and is characterized, above all, by the synergy of state and market, or "guided markets" (refer to Figure 3).

---

68 Leftwich is one of the few authors who attempted to build a general model of the developmental state which is not confined to the East Asian region. In his model, six major components define the developmental state model: a determined developmental elite; relative autonomy; a powerful, competent and insulated economic bureaucracy; a weak and subordinated society; the effective management of non-state economic interests; and repression, legitimacy and performance. As developmental states Leftwich includes Botswana, Korea, Taiwan, Singapore, China, Indonesia, Thailand and Malaysia. Refer to Leftwich (1995), p. 405.

69 Leftwich (1995), p. 401.

70 For further reading refer to Perkins (1994).

71 Refer to Weiss (1998), p. 4.

72 Refer to Oi (1995), p. 1132.

Figure 3: The state's role in development.

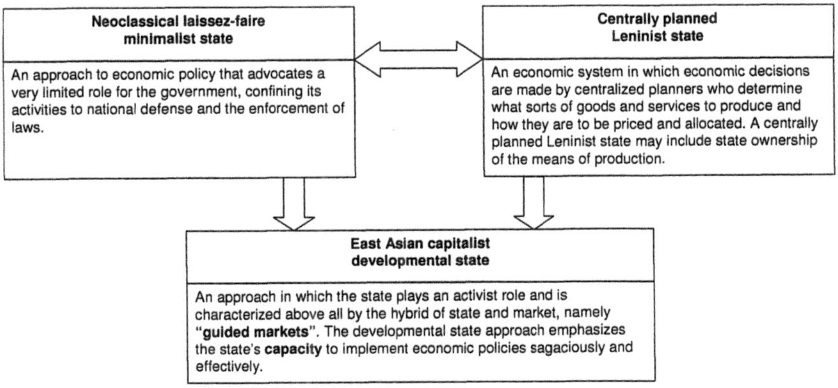

Source: Own illustration.

2.2.3 Different developmental state approaches

Various scholars have based their analysis of developing countries' transformation processes on the developmental state theory. The three most influential concepts are Johnson's developmental state approach as well as its enhancement by Amsden (1989) and Wade (1990).[73]

Johnson's "capitalist developmental state":

As Johnson (1982, 1987) analyzed, the foremost and single-minded priority of state action is economic development in terms of growth, productivity and competitiveness.[74] In order to avoid a conflict of goals, no commitment to equality and social welfare is made.[75] The developmental states' goals are rendered concrete by comparison with external reference economies which provide state elites with models for emulation. State intervention is firmly committed to private property and the rules of the market. Johnson contends that

> *"[S]erious industrial policy must be long-run in focus, consistent in its various aspects (monetary, regulatory, environmental and so forth), and operated through mutually supportive policy instruments."*[76]

---

[73] For further information refer to Amsden (1989) and Wade (1990).

[74] For further information refer to Johnson (1982, 1987).

[75] Refer to Johnson (1982), p.19 and p. 306.

[76] Johnson (1987), p. 151.

Industrial policy has to be aimed at cost and price competitiveness in world markets, not just the domestic market. As it directs some resources to high-priority sectors, industrial policy must have the power to demand from these high-priority sectors to meet performance goals. In addition to his concept of industrial policy, Johnson bases his approach of the *"capitalist developmental state"* [77] on institutional arrangements common to high growth East Asian capitalist countries.

According to Johnson, the combination of strategic industrial policy with a specific institutional setting leads to the successful economic transformation of the developmental state. Johnson established crucial features of the developmental state such as market-conforming state intervention in the economy and a small depoliticized elite bureaucracy organized in a pilot organization.[78]

Amsden's approach of "getting prices wrong":

Amsden (1989) suggests that Korea grew rapidly because it got prices wrong, but in ways that nurtured firm-level learning and innovation.[79] Her analysis runs parallel to Johnson's, however, she introduces new aspects of the developmental state approach.

In line with Gerschenkron and Hirschman, she conceives that in backward countries, the level of international competition, the technology gap, the investment barriers and savings deficiencies, are so problematic that government intervention is needed to address these hurdles.[80] She adds that *"late industrialization"* [81] East-Asian style requires state intrusion beyond Gerschenkron's state that has the role of an investment banker or Hirschman's *"disequilibrating investments'*[82]. According to Amsden,

> *"The first industrial revolution was built on laissez-faire, the second on infant industry protection. In late industrialization the foundation is subsidy which includes both protection and financial incentives. The allocation of subsidies has rendered the government not merely a banker, as Gerschenkron conceived, but an entrepreneur, using the subsidy to decide what, when and how much to produce."* [83]

---

77 Johnson (1982), p. 312.

78 Ibidem, pp. 19-23 and pp. 315-324.

79 For further information refer to Amsden (1989).

80 Refer to Amsden (1989), p. 148.

81 It should be noted that what Amsden labels *"late industrialization"* is the mid-twentieth-century industrialization that Hirschman called *"late late industrialization"*, as distinct from Gerschenkron's nineteenth- and twentieth-century *"late industrialization"*.

82 Hirschman (1958), p. 65 ff.

83 Amsden (1989), p. 145.

In late industrializing countries, the state is to mediate between market forces. Its role is to intervene in order to address the needs of both savers and investors, and of exporters and importers, by creating multiple prices. For reference, some interest rates are higher than others and importers and exporters face different prices for currency. Hence, in striking contrast to the logic of neoclassical development theory *("getting prices right")*, a high degree of government intervention occurred in the developmental states to distort relative prices *("getting prices wrong")* in favor of economic growth.[84] By this policy, the desired level of investment was directed towards greater investment and was able to materialize in the strategic sectors.[85] "Getting prices wrong" therefore contributes to a successful industrial policy and rapid economic development.

Wade's "governed market" theory:

Wade (1990), like Amsden, builds upon the original formulation of Johnson. He brings into focus the Taiwanese industrial policy.[86] Wade makes significant contributions towards understanding the nature of strategic industrial policy and its impact on industrial performance. He proposes a *"governed market theory of East Asian success"* [87] which specifies Johnson's model of the developmental state.[88] Taiwan's industrial success can be ascribed to the "governed market", a series of policies that

> *"enabled the government to guide – or govern – market processes of resource allocation so as to produce different production and investment outcomes than would have occurred with either free market or simulated free market policies."*[89]

Subsequently, the role of the state in Taiwan's development has been to guide the market, rather than "follow" it.[90] The essence of the governed market theory can be ascribed to three proximate causes: very high levels of productive investment, making for fast transfer of newer techniques into actual production; more state investment in certain key industries than would have occurred in the absence of

---

84 Refer to Amsden (1989), p. 8 and pp. 13-14.

85 Due to these price distortions, the state generated an industrial structure different from what the market would have produced on its own. Refer to Amsden (1989), p. 14 ff.

86 For further information refer to Wade (1990).

87 Wade (1990), pp. 24-29.

88 Wade bases his findings on case studies.

89 Refer to Wade (1990), pp. 26-27.

90 Ibidem, p. 303.

government intervention and the exposure of domestic firms to international competition (in foreign markets if not at home).[91]

Altogether, the classic case studies, using the developmental state approach, focused on different aspects of government-led economic transformation. It is thus important to elaborate on the institutional organization in the developmental states as well as the measures of state-led growth, and build an integrative model of East Asian development.

2.3 The developmental states' institutional and bureaucratic organization

The developmental states' industrial policy was supported by specific political, institutional and organizational arrangements pertaining to the state apparatus, private businesses and their mutual interaction. The political elites in the developmental states aimed at rapid economic development and had far-reaching power and authority to plan and implement efficient policies.

2.3.1 Depoliticized elite bureaucracy

As Public Choice Theory states, politicians tend to seek popular support in the short run as their goal is to win the next election; and there will never be a shortage of private claimants on the government, regardless of their economic performances and prospects.[92] Industrial policy and the state's abstaining from social welfare are thus difficult to implement by politicians. If political leaders want to pursue a successful long-term industrial policy, they have to depoliticize in part their key economic decisions. Hence, in the developmental states, a nonpolitical elite was appointed which was to some degree sheltered from direct political pressures.[93]

Depoliticization was achieved through an implicit division of labor within the polity: *"The politicians reign and bureaucrats rule"*.[94] In the East Asian developmental states, the politicians set broad goals and provided the space and power for the bureaucrats. They legitimated and ratified the decisions taken by the bureaucrats. In addition, they took the heat when corruption scandals were uncovered (according to Johnson, *"such scandals are unavoidable when government plays any role in economic affairs"*).[95] It was the official bureaucracy that did the actual planning,

91 These proximate causes were the result of the government's deliberate economic policies of market guidance which in their turn, were supported by authoritarian and corporatist arrangements. Refer to Wade (1990), p. 26.

92 Refer to Buchanan and Tullock (1962), Olson (1965) and Downs (1957).

93 Refer to Johnson (1987), pp. 151-152.

94 Refer to Johnson (1982), p. 316.

95 Refer to Johnson (1987), p. 152.

intervention and guiding of the economy. Only by this separation, could *"a political system in which the bureaucracy is given sufficient scope to take initiatives and operate effectively"* be provided.[96]

The role performed by the executive or the political elites in the context of postwar Japan was similar to the task performed by the military in Korea and Taiwan. The (military) elites were committed to developmental goals as an instrument of securing national survival and independence.[97] This was a key factor in ensuring the effective deployment of bureaucratic power.

2.3.2 Cohesiveness and autonomy of the elite bureaucracy

A prerequisite for successful economic transformation is an elite bureaucracy which is able to produce sizeable effects on the economy and control the direction of the effects.[98] According to Weber, the bureaucracy needs to be able to act as a corporate entity with broadly collective goals, rather than as the sum of the individual strategies of the functionaries. They are thus able to support markets and capitalist accumulation and promote development. This internal cohesiveness secures the state's capacity to carry out stringent policies, and is therefore a crucial precondition for successful industrial transformation.[99]

Furthermore, the bureaucracy needs to follow the goal of economic transformation rather than personal gain. The politicians, even when they are public-minded, have no more power than to monitor the bureaucracy according to the criterion that the total costs of state expenditure should not exceed total benefits. Bureaucrats, however, might act as selfish agents.[100] Generally, the theory of self-seeking bureaucrats is based on the postulate that bureaucrats are in no sense different from other individuals in pursuing their own interests. It is assumed that bureaucrats are budget-maximizers, following Niskanen's (1971) argument that

> *"[A]mong the several variables that may enter the bureaucrat's utility function are the following: salary, perquisites of the office, public reputation, power, patronage, output of the bureau, ease of making changes and ease of managing the bureau. All except the last two [...] are a positive monotonic function of the total budget of the bureau during the bureaucrat's tenure in office".*[101]

96 Refer to Johnson (1982), p. 315.

97 Refer to Önis (1991), p. 115.

98 Refer to Wade (1990), p. 343. For further information refer to Tullock (1985).

99 For further information refer to Weber (1911).

100 Refer to Cullis and Jones (1987), p. 127.

101 Refer to Niskanen (1971), p. 38. For further information also refer to Niskanen (1973).

In the three developmental states, norms of comportment for state functionaries and structural organization ensured state cohesiveness and a reputable, rule-committed civil service:

- *Rules:* The bureaucracy and its functionaries had to follow clearly specified rules. The institutional framework of the bureaucracy ensured that the functionaries' decisions were guided by such rules instead of individualistic and predatory interests.[102]
- *Merit-based recruitment:* The commitment to rule-following was compounded by a mechanism crucial for state cohesiveness, namely, the adherence to precise norms of recruitment. Functionaries thus pursued their work duties rather than personal gain. Bureaucrats recruited according to meritocratic criteria generated a kind of "esprit de corps" within the bureaucracy. The knowledge that they belonged to a highly selected "club", with similar qualifications and rare skills, created a corporate culture among functionaries. This in turn ensured state cohesiveness which would not be possible through meritocracy alone.[103] Common educational backgrounds of the bureaucratic and business elites and their significant cross penetration played a key role in generating extraordinary degrees of elite unity.[104]
- *Career prospects:* One requirement for a successful bureaucracy is a well-defined, competitive career path with a substantial prize for those who make it to the top.[105] In the East Asian developmental states, the top decision-makers in industrial policy generally reached their positions after they had gained work experience from several agencies or public enterprises. In these years, they also built close working relationships with a stable core of colleagues.[106] In Japan, retirement comes early, and the rewards to a successful bureaucrat are substantial, extending beyond the pay, perks, and prestige.[107]
- *Remuneration:* The institutionalization of meritocratic recruitment patterns and predictable career paths was accompanied by the provision of sufficient resources, such as remuneration, to make careers in the state competitive with careers in the private sector.[108] In general, the more favorably the total public sector compensation package compares with compensation in the private sector, the better the quality of the bureaucracy. In economies where public sector wages are at least decent, prestige, job security and other

---

102 The predatory state is a state in which the bureaucracy is not immune to rent-seeking and state-society relations do not happen between organized groups and the state as an institution, but between individuals. There is no functioning bureaucracy in a Weberian sense. Refer to Evans (1995), pp. 29-30 and 48-49.

103 Refer to Evans (1995), p. 49.

104 Refer to Õnis (1991), p. 115.

105 Refer to World Bank (1993), p. 178.

106 Refer to Wade (1990), pp. 224-225.

107 Refer to World Bank (1993), p. 178.

108 Refer to Evans (1989), p. 582.

advantages of public employment will persuade some talented individuals to forgo higher earnings in the private sector. By the beginning of the 1990s, the World Bank (1995) also acknowledged that high-performing East Asian economies (in contrast to the Philippines, Uruguay, Argentina and Somalia) all provided their bureaucrats with wages comparable to those in the private sector. The World Bank analysis showed that bureaucratic salaries in the state sector in East Asia were as high as, or even higher than, in the private business sector, particularly at the senior level.[109] Lower salaries in the bureaucrat sector than in the private sector aggravate the danger of rent-seeking in states, where salaries cannot prevent bureaucrats from predatory behavior.

- *Size of the bureaucratic apparatus:* As in the developmental states, the functions of the elite bureaucracy were carried out by only a small economic general staff. There is no obvious correspondence between effective market-augmenting state intervention, on the one hand, and the size of the bureaucratic apparatus or the public sector on the other. The East Asian developmental states testified that highly effective forms of market-augmenting intervention could be consistent with relatively small bureaucratic structures and public sectors. Small public sectors had nevertheless embodied highly productive and profitable public enterprise sectors. Economic policy-making in Taiwan was dominated by scarcely more than a dozen people.[110]

Economic policy-making in Taiwan was intensely centripetal, carried out entirely in Taipei within the executive branch. Only some input from the top of the party occurred. Few individuals dominated this process of economic policy-making. They ranged from the president, to a number of relevant cabinet ministers, to senior people in several government ministries or commissions, to managers of the largest public enterprises, to a few private businessmen who were well connected to the party.[111] Indeed, from the early 1960s to the mid-1980s, just five men had a preponderant voice in economic policy, including monetary, fiscal, industrial and trade policy.[112] Most of the personnel graduated from the same two or three elite universities, mostly Taiwan National University in Taipei.[113] Almost all belonged to the Nationalist Party and many held concurrent party posts. Mostly, they held the latter because of their positions in the economic hierarchy. The combination of party ties, common educational background and, most importantly, long-standing working relationships with colleagues, resulted in high personal and professional empathy among top

109 Refer to World Bank (1993), pp. 176-177.

110 Refer to Önis (1991), pp. 122-124.

111 Refer to Wade (1990), p. 195.

112 Ibidem, p. 217.

113 An examination of personnel records suggests that at the "lowest" ranks (not further defined) of the Ministry of Economic Affairs about 40 percent are graduates of Taiwan National University. About 80 percent of Japan's higher-level civil service in the 1960s graduated from Tokyo University. Refer to Wade (1990), p. 217.

officials. This helped to create a broad consensus among them on the general growth-oriented goals of Taiwan's economic policies. A highly competitive examination had to be passed for recruitment to the economic bureaucracy. A sizeable proportion of the graduates who passed the government examination actually joined the government or public enterprises. Government service attracted a substantially higher proportion of university graduates than college graduates. As Taiwan's educational system was intensely meritocratic, this implied a higher proportion of the more able students.[114]

Overall, in the developmental states, startling post-war economic growth occurred with the help of this powerful, talented and prestige-laden economic bureaucracy. However, none of the East Asian developmental states was immune to clientelism and corruption. Bureaucrats used some of the social surplus for the benefit of incumbents and their friends rather than those of the citizenry as a whole. In certain periods, their regimes appeared more rapacious than developmental (e.g. the KMT in Taiwan, the Rhee regime in Korea). The exploitation of personal gain by state functionaries, however, happened less than in other transformation states. In addition, the consequences of their actions promoted rather than impeded transformation. This was essential to the bureaucracy's effectiveness.[115]

2.3.3 The pilot agency

Within the bureaucracy of the East Asian developmental states, "pilot agencies" played a key role in policy formulation and implementation. For Johnson (1982), the pilot agency was the *"greatest concentration of brain power"*.[116] It was a powerful and autonomous agency able to solely formulate industrial policy and coordinate economic development. The authoritative pilot agencies were charged with the task of planning, guiding and coordinating industrial policies.

The most well known government institution of this kind is Japan's Ministry of International Trade and Industry (MITI). MITI is the classic example of a pilot agency functioning like a superministry.[117] Evans (1989) acknowledges MITI and its policies by contending that *"the administrative apparatus that oversaw Japan's industrial transformation was as impressive as the transformation itself"*.[118]

MITI held several functions to promote the industrial structure and enhance the nation's international competitiveness. It performed think-tank functions, decided over strategic industries and high-priority sectors and prepared the environment for

[114] Refer to Wade (1990), pp. 217-218.

[115] Refer to Evans (1989), p. 563 and p. 571 and Evans (1995), p. 49.

[116] Refer to Johnson (1982), p. 26.

[117] Compared with the pilot agencies of Taiwan and Korea, MITI has been the most powerful and the Taiwanese counterparts the least so. Refer to Chan (1990), p. 49.

[118] Refer to Evans (1989), p. 572.

economic development.[119] It obtained a consensus for its plans from the private sector, acted as a "gatekeeper" for contacts with foreign markets and investors and provided positive government support for private economic initiatives.[120]

Korea's Economic Planning Board and Taiwan's Council for Economic Planning and Development followed Japan's blueprint of a pilot agency.[121] Before its restructuring in 1994, the Korean Economic Planning Board had planning, budgetary and economic management functions. The Economic Planning Board was able to provide a strong coordinating role, as it stood outside and astride the individual ministries. Individual economic ministers were required to consult with the head of the Economic Planning Board, the deputy prime minister, before they could initiate major policies. The Economic Planning Board resisted having close identification with any particular sector or group and thus protected its institutional insulation and its broad political mandate. During its 33 years of existence, it never had direct relationship with the private sector. However, conflict and confusion over the structure and role of Korea's system of national economic management within the bureaucracy emerged which finally led to the dismantling of Korea's key pilot agency in late 1994.[122] This subsequently comprised the state's transformative capacity.

The Council for Economic Planning and Development in Taiwan also operated independently of the ministerial bureaucracy and similarly had its own planning and budgetary functions. The Council for Economic Planning and Development integrated the leadership of the individual ministries. In this way, they were forced to act as a unit rather than to represent client interests. The Council for Economic Planning and Development acted relatively insulated from special interests and fulfilled its coordinating role. Although its importance as center of economic decision-making was unquestioned, its power relative to that of particular ministries varied over time and across issue areas.[123]

2.4 State-led economic growth

The developmental states have been doing more than the neoclassical accounts recognize to increase supply responsiveness and steer the direction of industrial growth. State-led economic growth includes strategic industrial policy to promote "winner industries", a dualistic trade policy that protects certain infant industries and encourages domestic companies to export on a large scale, as well as the controlled inflow of foreign investment.

---

[119] Refer to Johnson (1982), p. 19.

[120] Refer to Wade (1990), p. 195.

[121] Of these, MITI has been the most powerful and the Taiwanese counterparts the least so.

[122] At this time, bureaucrats were often trained in a neoclassical perception in the US.

[123] Refer to Weiss (1998), p. 53.

2.4.1 East Asian industrial policy

Like most developing countries, the East Asian developmental states had multiyear development plans. In Taiwan, the first plan, covering four years from the beginning of 1953 was called "The Plan for Economic Rehabilitation".[124] Industrial policy in the East Asian developmental states has been strategically targeted towards the long-term development of selected industries. These have enjoyed competitive advantage through state support.

Industrial policy directed towards long-term development goals:

According to the developmental statists, the elite bureaucrats in the pilot agencies can have an advantage over the private sector when it comes to information and data-gathering due to excessive resources such as personnel and money to conduct research on market development.[125] Subsequently, they might have good overall and long-term views of the economy. Furthermore, as governments pool and disseminate technical, commercial and market information, they can help to improve private sector decision-making and minimize their investment risks.[126] Scholars, however, have applied relatively little research to the question of how individual sectors are chosen for high-priority treatment in particular countries and times.[127] Consequently, there is only a little information available. In Taiwan, domestic and international research institutes and consultancy firms have worked on identifying sectors and products of interest for foreign investors.[128] Moreover, particular industries were chosen for special attention by looking at outside reference economies. Japan looked to the USA and Europe, Korea and Taiwan to Japan and to each other.[129] Sometimes policies were even copied in detail.

Generally, in the developmental states, the basic criteria for the choice of strategic industries involved high income elasticity of demand in world markets and the potential for rapid technological progress and labor productivity growth. Sectoral industrial policy was adjusted to the long-term goal of industrialization rather than short-term profit maximization on the basis of current comparative advantage.[130] The

---

[124] Refer to Wade (1990), p. 81.

[125] Hayek, however, argued that planners will never have enough information to carry out allocation of ressources reliably. The efficient exchange and use of resources, Hayek claimed, can be maintained only through the price mechanism in free markets. For further information refer to Hayek (1945).

[126] Refer to Yue (1995), p. 86.

[127] This aspect is further elaborated in Chapter 2.7.1.

[128] Refer to Edin (2000), p. 26 and Wade (1990), pp. 188, 211 ff.

[129] Refer to Wade (1990), p. 334.

[130] The essence of Japan's, Taiwan's and Korea's industrial policy was that they all were cases of a guided market economy in which market rationality has been constrained by the priorities of industrialization.

economic bureaucrats acted in anticipation of future comparative advantages rather than in accordance with them. Thus, the governments of the developmental states have *"made the winners".*[131]

Japan's MITI shifted from labor intensive light (textile) to capital intensive heavy industry (steel works, harbors, dockyards, airports, autos etc.) already in the early 1950s, although this was contrary to their comparative advantage, cheap labor, at that time.[132] This may be considered as one of MITI's most important decisions. MITI officials believed that products with higher income elasticities of demand like appliances and electronics offered a way out for Japan from its position of dependency. In the 1960s, before the period of liberalization, synthetic textiles, plastics, petrochemicals, autos and electronics were nurtured and supported.[133] Even after the economy had been liberalized, the economic officials continued to identify such new strategic industries as semiconductors, numerically controlled machine tools and advanced consumer goods like videotape recorders and computers.[134]

In this way, Japanese firms were encouraged to move up the ladder of technology and pass the less desirable industries where their international competitiveness was already declining (those with low technology content, high labor intensity, environmental pollution hazards) to follower nations such as Taiwan and Korea.[135] As Japan's economy was strongly dependent on exports, these steps were clearly designed to encourage continuous industrial adjustment and to stimulate dynamic trade competitiveness. In this respect, MITI controlled not only foreigners' access to the Japanese economy, but also Japanese producers' access to foreign markets.[136]

Preferential treatment only for selected industries:

Strategic industrial policy implied that preferential treatment of enterprises was channeled on a selective basis according to the state's long-term development plan. Only certain enterprises of "upstream" industries with the most favorable environment for growth were targeted. Protection and assistance such as preferential allocation of key production inputs and bureaucratic support for promotion, were given primarily to

---

131 For information on Taiwan's promotion of the heavy and chemical industries during the 1960s and 1970s, refer to Wade (1990), p. 110 and p. 334.

132 Similar to the developments in Japan and Taiwan, Korea's transformation from light to heavy industry came at the state's command. For a detailed analysis refer to Amsden (1989), p. 81, Wade (1992), p. 287, Johnson (1982), p. 31 and p. 240.

133 Refer to Edin (2000), p. 26.

134 With regard to MITI refer to Johnson (1982), p. 302.

135 Taiwan's development path looks very similar, moving up from light to heavy and chemical industry. In the early stage, textiles, plastics and the synthetic fiber industry were treated. Preferential treatment was later given to petrochemicals, machinery, computer terminals, machine tools, semiconductors, computers, telecommunications, robotics and biotech. Refer to Wade (1990), pp. 90-99. Korea followed suit with a big push in heavy machinery and chemicals in the late 1970s, and targeted, among others, the electronics and the auto industries. Refer to Amsden (1989), p. 81.

136 Refer to Chan (1990), p. 50.

infant industries and to those industries perceived to be "sunrise industries" with potential future competitiveness. Downstream or "sunset" industries have been left much freer.[137] This was contrary to the general policies of mercantilism where the domestic industry as a whole was protected.

The Japanese state, after experimentation with direct and detailed intervention in the pre-World War II period, limited itself to strategically selected economic involvement. The industries apart from the priority sectors experienced policy intervention only from time to time, while the remaining industries were exposed unaided to the rigors of market competition. Subsequently, the centerpiece of industrial policy was a high degree of selectivity.[138]

Instruments of the pilot agency:

The policy tools the pilot agency's bureaucrats used were manifold: tax incentives and breaks, subsidies, preferential bank loans and selective credit allocations, tariffs on imported goods, foreign investment screening, foreign technology licensing as well as government sponsored research and development (R&D).[139] In addition, the pilot agencies provided administrative guidance that regulated competition in an industry.[140] Control of foreign exchange together with export incentives were the link between industrial policy and international trade.[141] The use of selective subsidies based on performance was probably the most important of the different policy tools MITI had. In this line, in accordance to the neoclassical approach, MITI encouraged specialization according to Japan's comparative advantage. At the same time, it tried to minimize the country's dependence on, and therefore vulnerability to, external suppliers (as advised by the dependency theorists) by import substitution of certain products. Besides regulating imports and allocating export quotas, MITI officials influenced the geographic location of particular plants. They also issued advisory directives *("administrative guidance")* that attempted to steer firms toward, and to prepare them for, future "sunrise" industries like electronics or information systems, and to persuade them to abandon unprofitable "sunset" industries like textiles or petrochemicals.[142]

Through all these measures, the developmental states sought, not always successfully however, to bring about mergers or collaboration among firms in order to

---

137 Refer to Wade (1990), p. 73.

138 Among others, refer to Amsden (1989), p. 243 ff.

139 In Taiwan for reference, in the 1960s, in order to promote technological and managerial upgrading in industry additionally to those established in the 1950s, the government established several more research and service organizations. For an analysis of these institutions refer to Wade (1990), p. 95.

140 Refer to Edin (2000), pp. 26-27.

141 MITI in 1952 informally advised ten large cotton spinners to reduce production by 40 percent and those who did not heed this advice were told that foreign currency for the following months supply of raw cotton might not be available. Refer to Johnson (1982), pp. 224-225.

142 Refer to Chan (1990), p. 49.

profit from economies of scale and pool resources. In this way, the pilot agencies aimed to enhance the international competitiveness of selected industrial sectors in order to spur the state's economic transformation.

Overall, the difference between what happened in East Asia and elsewhere cannot be ascribed to industrial policy instruments not known elsewhere.[143] Many other developing nations have at one time or another tried most of the policy tools used in East Asia. What differentiates their efforts, above all, are the pilot agency's consistent and coordinated attentiveness to the problems and opportunities of particular industries in the context of a long-term perspective of the economy's evolution. Another key message is that a powerful pilot agency such as MITI provided important strategic guidance in the selection of key industries to be encouraged and also in the provision of a stable and predictable environment for private investors to undertake risky, long-term investment projects.[144] Hence, sector-specific forms of indicative planning can be an essential complement of market-oriented growth in the initial phase of transformation.

2.4.2 Trade policy – import substitution and export promotion

The developmental states protected strategic infant industries from international competition. Pursuing this goal, the Japanese government attracted only specific imports like production ingredients that Japan either lacked or did not have in sufficient quantity or quality. Specifically, these were raw materials and certain advanced technology from external markets such as in the aerospace and computer sectors. Simultaneously, the government hindered the import of e.g. foreign capital. The goal was to encourage national autonomy in strategic industries such as computer, telecommunications steel and energy. At the same time, foreign penetration and domination of these sensitive sectors was to be avoided.[145]

The initial phase of build-up protection in the East Asian developmental states was combined with an export-oriented free trade regime which initially paralleled and later displaced the previous import substitution policy. The developmental states have exposed national companies to international competition by encouraging them to export. In general, export-promotion was based on the following arguments:

- Continued import substitution in the form of protectionism in narrow domestic markets requires the production of commodities that involve higher domestic costs per unit of foreign exchange saved. Exporting, by contrast, involves the

143 Refer to Wade (1990), p. 343.

144 Refer to Önis (1991), p. 122.

145 Refer to Chan (1990), p. 49.

production of commodities in which the country has a comparative advantage. This implies low domestic resource costs per unit of foreign exchange.

- Exports enable fuller capacity utilization and allow reduction in unit costs through the exploitation of economies of scale contributing thereby to efficient import substitution.
- Export orientation not only provides an engine of growth, it also encourages domestic industries to become and remain internationally competitive. By exporting, enterprises are disciplined because they have to fulfill standards set by export markets in order to be internationally competitive. Exposure to foreign competition is decisive as it provides the stimulus needed for technological change.[146]

The protection of infant industries in the East Asian developmental states was unlike the policy approaches of other late developers such as Latin America. In East Asia, the period of "pure" import substitution industrialization (that is without a significant manufactured goods export drive) was generally shorter: in Korea only for a short spell in the 1950s and in Taiwan only between 1953 and 1957. Korea and Taiwan adopted an outward-oriented strategy in the early sixties, emulating the industrial strategy of Japan.[147]

Akamatsu's (1962) *"flying geese pattern"* implies that there is a broad similarity in the types of export industries in which countries specialize in comparable development stages.[148] All developmental states started with a focus on technologically simple labor-intensive goods such as clothing, toys, processed foods and so forth, and advanced to exports of more capital-intensive, technologically sophisticated items.[149] Obviously, the speed of graduation has varied; however, the moves have been the same.[150]

---

146 A number of indirect, but positive effects also result from export promotion. Export expansion will ease the foreign exchange constraint, thereby permitting increases of materials and machinery imports. For further positive indirect effects refer to Balassa (1981a), p. 15.

147 In Korea, the share of exports in manufactured output rose from 1 percent in 1960 to 41 percent in 1973. In Taiwan, the share of exports rose from 9 percent in 1960 to 50 percent in 1973. Despite their poor natural resource endowment, the East Asian countries had the highest growth rates of primary exports and thus of total exports, compared to the developing Latin American countries, which had mostly chosen an import-substitution strategy of development. Refer to Balassa (1981a), pp. 14-15.

148 The center of gravity of industries shifts from first movers of industrialization to the second-tier group, and then to a third group of countries. Refer to Akamatsu (1962), pp. 3-25.

149 Refer to Weiss (2005), p. 3 and Ito (2001), p. 61.

150 The move of the ladder of comparative advantage can be illustrated with data from Korea. In 1961, the single largest export item was iron ore (13 percent of total exports), in 1980 it was textiles and garments (29 percent of the total) and in 1989 it was electronics (also 29 percent). Refer to Weiss (2005), p. 3.

Since the 1990s, there has been much less emphasis on increasing and coordinating investment for the purpose of export promotion and industry creation in Japan, Korea and Taiwan. Instead, stress has been laid on developing and disseminating new products and technologies. The developmental states have focused on the R&D side of industry policy, namely the promotion and diffusion of technologies instead of sectoral promotion of export via investment allocation.[151] In this line, trade policy in Korea has shifted from import substitution (prevalent in the 1950s) towards export promotion (starting in the 1960s) and high-tech industrialization (since the late 1980s). At the same time, policy instruments have changed from import protection, export subsidization and policy loans to investment incentives for R&D and eventual financial sector liberalization (refer to Table 1).

Table 1: Timing of shifts in Korea's trade policy.

Period	**Priority activities**	**Main instruments**
1960 - 1973	Initial export take-off: Promotion of exports in general - key sectors labor-intensive manufacturers.	Import protection, export subsidies including duty drawbacks, subsidized credit allocation, export targeting.
1973 - 1980	Heavy and chemical industry drive: selective promotion - priority sectors steel, petrochemicals, non-ferrous metals, shipbuilding, electronics and machinery; priority firms selected large enterprises.	Import protection, export subsidies including duty drawbacks, subsidized credit allocation, export targeting. Widespread use of policy loans to channel funds to priority firms and sectors. Investment incentives through tax credits.
1980 - 1990	Gradual trade liberalization and move to less selectivity. Priority on high technology activities.	Phased import liberalization, ending of policy loans. Still government influence over allocation of credit. Investment incentives for R&D. Easing of restrictions on FDI.
1990 - onwards	Trade liberalization and high-tech exports. Private sector-led development; restructuring of chaebol after financial crisis in 1997.	Financial sector liberalization; open capital account.

Source: Refer to World Bank (1993), p. 124 and Weiss (2005), pp. 3-4 and p. 19.[152]

In the East Asian developmental states exports generated "learning-by-doing". Exports also improved the quality of capital stock because of the need for products to compete in export markets. This in turn raised overall productivity, which then led to an increase in average profit rates across the whole economy (not just in exports). Real wages could thus rise without inflation.[153] The developmental states used various measures in order to stimulate exports.[154] Among those have been export promotion schemes, performance tracking as well as the devaluation of the developmental states' currencies.[155]

151 Refer to Weiss (1998), p. 33.

152 For further information refer to Kim and Leipziger (2000).

153 Refer to Wade (2004), p. 10.

154 The policy instruments used certainly changed over different periods.

155 For further information on export incentives refer to Wade (1990), p. 119.

Export promotion schemes:

In order to give positive discrimination in favor of export sales, several export promotion schemes were introduced in the East Asian developmental states.[156] Exporting enterprises were free to choose between domestic and imported inputs. Exporting enterprises, as well as the producers of domestic inputs used in export production, were granted several privileges, such as exemption from indirect taxes on their output and in inputs, they were not obliged to pay duty on imported inputs, and were entitled to retain a large proportion of their foreign exchange.[157] Moreover, the broadest functional targeting of credit in the developmental states has been to exporters.[158]

Taiwan introduced fiscal incentives, such as a five-year tax exemption for a wide range of industrial goods. The state granted tax reliefs only if companies' exports equaled 50 percent or more of production. Furthermore, only a small percentage of a firm's export earnings was made tax exempt.[159] The state granted these privileges to all enterprises, as a differentiation among individual export commodities did not take place.[160] Altogether, subsidies in the form of tax exemptions and credits at low

---

156 One of the most influential models of strategic export policy is the Brander - Spencer model, in which it is shown that the home government has a unilateral interest in adopting an export subsidy policy if the home firm competes with a foreign firm in quantities (they refer to the example of the American and European aircraft manufacturers Boeing and Airbus). The central motive for these types of strategic policies is to shift profits from foreign firms to the home country. Refer to Brander and Spencer (1985).

157 Refer to Balassa (1981a), p. 12.

158 The East Asian developmental states had different characteristics of export credit schemes.

Japan: Between 1946 and 1972, the Bank of Japan rediscounted export bills at low rates of interest (1 to 2 percentage points lower than that applicable to general trade bills). During this period, the Bank of Japan directed 10 percent of its loans to export finance (which financed 50 percent of total export-related bank lending).

Korea: The Korean Export-Import Bank offered concessional rediscounting of preshipment credit based on letters of credit. The differential between loan rates of this export credit and general loan rates was between 3 and 20 percentage points until 1982, when this difference was eliminated. In 1984, the differential was restored at 1.5 percentage points. The Korean Export Import Bank also provided longer-term post-shipment finance and export credit insurance.

Taiwan: Banks offered firms short-term preshipment loans based on letters of credit. After products were shipped, firms were eligible for loans based on letters of credit, documents against acceptance of payment, and shipment documents. In addition, the Central Bank provided a special discount rate to designated domestic banks for export loans, usually at 1 percentage point lower than the usual discount rate. The export loan rate was about 3 to 5 percentage points below the minimum interest rate for secured loans between 1970 and 1980, and it dropped to 1 to 2 percentage points after 1980. Refer to World Bank (1993), p. 281.

159 Refer to Wade (1990), p. 119.

160 There is evidence that the system of incentives applied affects the country's export performance. Econometric estimates made for a number of countries show that increase in export prices due to export incentives are associated with a rise in the volume of exports. In addition, export incentives positively correlate with the share of exports in domestic output and with the contribution of exports to increases in output in an inter-industry framework. Refer to Balassa (1981a), pp. 13-14. For further information refer to Balassa (1981b).

interest rates were one of the main incentives the developmental states offered their exporting firms. Thus, the disadvantage faced by national firms in international competition was offset, and the industrial structure moved up the value-chain toward more technology-intensive activities.

The Korean textile industry gave the national economy its initial push to significant growth and it largely accounted for the country's impressive export performance. In the late 1960s, subsidies, at that time a new policy instrument, were implemented to guide the textile industry.[161] Subsidies were introduced because the cost position of Korean manufacturers of cotton textiles was less favorable than that of their Japanese counterparts although the income level in Korea was lower. Amsden (1989) observed,

> *"Subsidies in Korea were necessary not because of 'distortions' [in particular, the exchange rate was not much distorted] but because the Koreans could not, initially, compete against the Japanese, even in industries such as cotton spinning and weaving in which the least developed, most labor-intensive countries supposedly have a comparative advantage".*[162]

Only with the state's subsidies, could the Korean textile industry enter export markets on a sizable scale.[163] Subsidized credit for working capital was available to any exporter, but long-term capital at favorable interest rates was allocated only to targeted firms and industries.[164] At the same time, import restrictions were applied by the government in order to exclude foreign competition. The state also initiated mergers of small firms to encourage productive manufacturing and improve competitiveness. Drastic growth of exports followed only after the May 1961 military coup, and was hence a direct consequence of the new military regime's policies. The share of textile and clothing exports in Korea's gross national product rose from 1.8 percent in the mid-1950s to 7.7 percent in the early 1970s. The share of textiles in manufacturing exports grew from less than 5 percent in 1963 to more than 47 percent in 1973.[165] At that time, the cotton textile industry had become internationally competitive in a system of free trade and could be weaned off subsidies.[166]

Performance tracking:

In addition to the government's support for exporting companies, it exerted strong discipline on businesses to which it granted subsidies. Firms had to fulfill certain performance standards in exchange for subsidies.[167] The performance had to be

---

161 Refer to Levi-Faur (1998), pp. 77-78.

162 Amsden (1989), p. 88.

163 Refer to Wade (1992), p. 286.

164 For examples refer to Amsden (1989), p. 73.

165 Refer to Levi-Faur (1998), p. 77.

166 Refer to Wade (1992), p. 287.

167 Refer to Amsden (1989), p. 8.

accomplished whether the targeted enterprises were public or private.[168] The businesses in the developmental states that used subsidies "well" were rewarded with further help, and support was withdrawn from those that did not.[169] This suggests a reciprocal relationship between governments and firms. The conditional performance which was imposed on firms located in strategic sectors and the discipline exercised by them led to price distortions, such as heavily subsidized rates of interest on long-term credits. However, resources were not wasted as in the case of many other middle income economies which made extensive use of subsidies to declining firms or industries experiencing financial difficulties. As subsidization was not dependent on business performance in those countries, subsidies emerged as a major avenue for rent-seeking.[170] In the developmental states, the government has deliberately refrained from bailing out firms which were badly managed.

In order to hold enterprises accountable for achievements, the developmental states formulated performance criteria. In line with the outward-oriented development strategy of the developmental states, success in export markets became the main criterion of good use of subsidies, and of the distribution of further subsidies. In Taiwan, a firm was entitled to concessional credit on the basis of the previous year's export performance and the planned exports for the current year.[171] In similar ways protection was made conditional. In 1982, an import ban on videocassette recorders was granted by the Taiwanese government in order to assist two domestic electronics companies to build up their capacity. Eventually, after eighteen months, as their prices were still substantially above those of Japan, the ban was lifted.[172] At this time the government announced that it was allowing Sony to form a joint venture (JV) with a local firm (not one of the two which had already started). The only condition was that 50 percent of production should be exported after three years.[173]

---

168 The distinction between public and private ownership is of subordinate importance, as ownership structure has varied from country to country in East Asia. Governments chose which type of enterprises they use to implement their economic policies. Taiwan has seen one of the largest public enterprise sectors outside the communist bloc, complemented by a large number of small family firms. In comparison, most of the enterprise conglomerates, *zaibatsu* in Japan and *chaebol* in Korea, are private businesses.

169 Refer to Wade (1992), p. 285 and Amsden (1989), p. 116.

170 Refer to Önis (1991), pp. 112-113 and Amsden (1989), p. 145.

171 Refer to Wade (1990), p. 142.

172 Sony was subsequently allowed to form a JV with another domestic firm on condition that, after a 3 year period, 50 percent of production was exported. Refer to Wade (1990), pp. 132-133.

173 Refer to Wade (1990), p. 133. With regard to the Korean developmental state, Amsden delivers insight from fairly detailed case studies of approximately thirty-five Korean enterprises not only in the textile industry, but also in the cement, paper, steel, shipbuilding, general machinery, auto and construction industries. Several subsidiaries within a business group were studied (five in the case of Hyundai, three in the case of Samsung) to analyze, among other issues, whether repeated patronage by the government was justified on efficiency grounds. Refer to Amsden (1989a), p. 16.

Exchange rate devaluation:

The East Asian developmental states also maintained an undervalued and thereby "distorted" exchange rate against the currency of the main export market, mostly the USD.[174] This undervaluation, combined with export-exhorting national campaigns and competitions like "Japan's Trade Promotion Monthly", provided incentives to seek out export markets. The undervalued exchange rate not only provided a general incentive to exports, but also provided a measure of protection against imports. In the East Asian developmental states, despite the resulting increase of economic growth, the undervalued exchange rate remained credible, because it was linked to fiscal conservatism. Latin American states, in contrast, often pegged exchange rates, which became overvalued through domestic inflation. The loss in credibility then resulted in a financial crisis. In East Asia, the profitability of the companies, rising real wages and the credibility of the currency peg, attracted additional domestic savings and more foreign investments. The quality of capital stock and labor stock rose again, due to high rates of investment and re-investment.[175]

Altogether, while encouraging exports and simultaneously protecting key infant industries, the developmental states strategically pursued a dualistic approach of regulating international competition according to its needs. The central role of the government's guiding hand is obvious. According to Haggard (1990), export promotion is one decisive factor which explains the accomplishments of Asia-Pacific industrialization compared with less successful transformation states.[176] A short period of import substitution led to a less intensive development of industrial-societal forces, which demanded protection of the domestic industry in the East Asian developmental states. Unlike the East Asian developmental states, in Latin America, a long period of import substitution industrialization allowed a strong lobby for inefficient firms to develop.[177]

2.4.3 Foreign capital

One element within the development approaches of the East Asian states appears to be contradictory. Japan has been *"close to paranoid on the subject of the dangers of an invasion of foreign capital"* [178] and has eagerly tried to prevent foreign participation in its economy. Unlike the Japanese approach, Korean and Taiwanese bureaucrats have used foreign and multinational capital extensively. Yet, what is important is that they attracted the needed foreign capital without at the same time becoming obsequious to it.

---

174 On exchange rate regimes in East Asia, refer to Collignon et al. (1999).

175 Refer to Wade (2004), pp. 9-10.

176 Refer to Haggard (1990).

177 Refer to Thompson (1996), p. 631.

178 Johnson (1987), p. 163.

Postwar Japan did not totally exclude foreign investment or foreign borrowings. It imported loans from the World Bank and from American commercial banks during the 1950s, and made use of American offshore procurement contracts and military expenditures. It was concerned to separate foreign money and technology, both of which it needed from foreign ownership-rights and manufacturing facilities, because it aimed to preserve its large domestic market for its new industries. The Japanese state aimed to restrict foreign investment. Due to its larger size (in comparison with Korea and Taiwan) the domestic market was used for national companies to prove their competitiveness, and then successfully export in international markets. Thus, high economic growth could be achieved.

The domestic markets of Korea and Taiwan were too small to generate enough domestic savings needed for fast industrialization. Subsequently, they had to attract foreign capital extensively. While in Korea and Taiwan, firms exported and developed overseas markets, bureaucrats additionally aimed at attracting foreign firms. Foreign firms investing in Korea and Taiwan were largely producing for export.[179] At the same time, however, Korea and Taiwan exercised broad controls over foreign investments (such as "unrealistically" high local content requirements) which were decisive in avoiding domination of more powerful countries.[180] Essentially, despite different strategies of letting foreign capital participate in its economies, none of the East Asian developmental states has become "subservient" to it, as the inflow of capital has been intensively controlled by the state.

2.5 Financial system

The governments of the developmental states were able to wield instruments capable of discriminating between industrial sectors in order to lead industrial restructuring. One instrument has been the financial sector.

Generally, financial systems may be capital market-based or credit-based. Each has different implications for the influence of governments and banks on business. In a capital market system such as the American and British financial systems, securities (stocks and bonds) are the main source of long-term business finance. There is a wide range of capital and money-market instruments. Furthermore, a large number of specialized financial institutions compete strongly in terms of price and service, and actively contribute to the financing of particular firms.[181] In a credit-based system, the capital market is usually weak. Thus, besides retained earnings, firms heavily depend on credit. The allocation of credit can be actively controlled either by relatively autonomous banks, as in Germany or by banks dependent on the government.

[179] Refer to Johnson (1987), p. 163.

[180] Refer to Wade (1990), p. 137 and Johnson (1987), pp. 162-164.

[181] Refer to Wade (1988a), p. 131.

The East Asian developmental states had bank- and credit-based financial systems,[182] and the banks were virtually all owned or controlled by the government throughout their transition periods.[183] In the developmental states, the financial authorities adopted a grading system to ensure that money was directed to productive investments. Bank loans were approved for business plans in priority sectors (e.g. producing textiles for export markets) and were hindered for businesses in low priority sectors (e.g. noodle production for domestic consumption).[184] In this, the attention of the business groups was diverted towards capital accumulation.

As governments in the developmental states Japan, Korea and Taiwan had control over the financial system, they were able to allocate credit at low interest rates to strategic industries. The three developing countries, however, had different institutional roots and forms of how to mobilize capital:[185]

- In Japan, the banks were mostly privately owned. However, in order to expand their lending, they depended on the central bank for access to supplementary deposits.[186] The central bank, the Bank of Japan, has been controlled by the government's Ministry of Finance, and the public postal savings system has been a key component of the entire system.[187] Subsequently, until the 1970s, MITI and the Ministry of Finance were able to re-cycle Japan's high levels of domestic savings to targeted domestic industrial sectors and businesses. Selected businesses received capital at "artificially" low interest rates. This gave them an advantage over established rivals elsewhere.[188] Already in 1982, the Japanese postal savings system controlled more assets than the Bank of America, which was the world's largest commercial bank at that time.[189] The sources of funds for large Japanese companies showed almost

182 Refer to Whitley (1999), pp. 159 and 171.

183 In Korea, one of the first acts of the government of Park Chung Hee (since 1961) was to nationalize the banking system. (The government of Syngman Rhee had to denationalize it a decade earlier to appease American pressures.) Although pressures to liberalize in the 1980s led the government to privatize commercial banks, thereby strengthening aggregate economic concentration and income inequality, the government maintained its control over commercial banking. However, the government still reaches far down into the officially denationalized banks in terms of personnel policies, appointment of senior managers, range of services and the like. Refer among others to Amsden (1989), p. 16 and Wade (1988a), p. 133.

184 Refer to Clifford (1994), pp. 40-41.

185 Refer to Pempel (1999), p. 149.

186 Refer to Wade (1988a), p. 133.

187 Refer to Pempel (1999), pp. 149-150. For further information on the postal savings system refer to Amyx (2005), "Reforming Government-Backed Financial Institutions, Internet Edition, reviewed 01.05.2007.

188 Refer to Beeson (2004), p. 6.

189 In 2001, the Japanese postal savings system accounted for 34 percent of household deposits and held about USD 2.2 trillion in deposits. Still in 2005, it is the largest financial institution in the world. Of course, the Japanese save so heavily in postal savings accounts, because, by law, these accounts offer the highest rate of interest available to small savers. Refer to FRBSF Economic Letter (2001), "Japan's New Prime Minister and the Postal Savings System", p. 1, Internet Edition, reviewed 22.10.2006 and Frankfurter Allgemeine Sonntagszeitung (2005), p. 11.

no change during the period 1972-1981. In 1972, companies obtained 75 percent of their funds through loans from banks, and only 19 percent from shares, and the figures for 1981 were 68 percent and 21 percent.[190] Government control of the domestic banking system ensured that indigenous financial institutions cooperated in providing funds to industry. This in turn helped to consolidate the close ties between industrial and financial capital that was characteristic of Japan during the boom years.[191] Although some measures of financial "internationalization" have taken place, the government's postal savings system is still intact and functioning as one of Japan's most important institutional inventions.

- In Taiwan, only 5 percent of deposits as well as the branches of all commercial banks were under private ownership in 1980. Moreover, banks' chairmen were either former Ministry of Finance employees or central bank officials appointed by the government. Bank boards had little autonomy: all transactions had to be reported once a week to the central bank, and all foreign exchange transactions had to be reported daily.[192]
- In Korea, although almost all banking was privatized, government oversight was critical in directing capital to desired sectors.[193] The Korean Economic Planning Board exerted extensive financial control. It effectively controlled Korea's banking sector and credit allocation decisions, as it had supervision over the Ministry of Finance. Its authority encompassed several different functions such as the appointment of personnel and foreign exchange allocations. Since the 1960s when the commercial banks were also nationalized, they have had to deposit their funds in the Korean Development Bank and to purchase long-term bonds issued by the Korean Development Bank. In addition, they were required to extend credit to firms with loan guarantees from the Korean Development Bank. The government used policy loans to support exports and promote the industrialization of the heavy and chemical industries in the 1970s, or to re-structure Korea's auto industry. Foreign loans were also channeled via government which implied that all firms needed approval from the Economic Planning Board in order to obtain loans from foreign banks. As foreign credit constituted an important source of capital to Korean firms, the Economic Planning Board had an important leverage over Korean firms through foreign credit control. However, as the debt/equity ratio in Korea reached 300 percent, the government's credit control was an important policy instrument for the bureaucracy.[194]

---

190 Refer to Johnson (1987), p. 148.

191 Refer to Beeson (2004), p. 6.

192 Refer to Wade (1990), p. 161 and p. 264.

193 Refer to Pempel (1999), p. 150.

194 Refer to Huang (2002a), pp. 552-553.

The developmental states' bank- and credit-based financial system enabled policy leaders to support selected industries by credits at below market interest rates through the banking system. Japan, during its postwar reconstruction, and Korea, during the 1970s, directed large amounts of credit to specific sectors and firms, mostly in heavy and chemical industries.[195] The Fiscal Investment and Loan Program of the Japanese government accounted for about one third of new equipment lending in the 1950s. Korea's policy loans were almost 60 percent of the total loans of its deposit money banks between 1973 and 1981. Most of Japan's priority lending through the early 1960s targeted industries associated with large optimum scales and increasing returns to scale. This is in accordance with Korea's lending behavior during the heavy and chemical industries period.[196]

A well documented industrial policy success relates to the government-sponsored Japan Electronic Computer Company. In 1960, MITI decided that Japan should establish a domestic computer industry. Between 1961 and 1981, USD 2 billion were invested in this sector, because the Japanese government offered low-interest loans only for investments in this sector.[197] Thus, it decisively helped create Fujitsu, as it is known today. The policy mechanisms used have their parallels in the East, but are unknown in the West.

Directed credit in the East Asian developmental states has generally gone to the private sector, unlike many other developing economies, where directed credit often went to public and quasi-public enterprises. Although the developmental states have also directed credit to state enterprises, the proportions of total credit were not persistently high, the parastatal banks tended to perform better financially, and the interest rate subsidies were not large. Korea can be regarded as an exception, because its lending to the public steel plant, POSCO, was substantial, and widely considered a success story.[198]

The analysis revealed that in countries where capital is channeled largely through banks, the state is in a position to extend a visible and vigorous hand in the operation of the economy. The system of external indirect financing gives the state the power to ration credit to banks and channel capital to targeted sectors. This enables the state to influence the direction of industrial change. Since capital is the "lifeblood" of industrial activity, the state's capacity to set the supply and channel the flow of capital, constitutes one of the most effective tools of industrial policy.[199]

---

195 Refer to Okimoto (1989), p. 142 ff.

196 Refer to World Bank (1993), p. 280.

197 Refer to Robins (2002), p. 294.

198 Refer to World Bank (1993), pp. 280-281.

199 Refer to Okimoto (1989), pp. 142-143.

2.6 State-society and government-business relations

As the economic bureaucracy is itself an elite body *"occupying a position of preeminence in the society",*[200] it is important to examine external ties with the rest of society. In the following, the connections of the state with the public are divided into an analysis of the state's relations to societal groups, and government agencies' interaction with industrial capital, namely the private business sector.

2.6.1 State-society relations

The strong developmental states were characterized by authoritarian governance. An authoritarian regime can be defined by the cooptation of important interest groups ("limited pluralism"), the renunciation of militant forms of ideology and mobilization of the masses, and therefore the promotion of political apathy and passivity.[201]

Japan was termed "soft authoritarian", meaning the prewar authoritarianism of the Meiji and early Showa eras, and the postwar pattern of the monopolization of political power by a single party. This form of organization made possible the implementation of a set of economic priorities that seemed unattainable under true political pluralism. This also applies to Taiwan and Korea in later phases of their development: Korea was ostensibly a democratic country, however, actually had a military dominated single-party regime which was close in form, if not in ideology, to Japan during the 1930s and 1940s. Taiwan differed from both Japan and Korea, as it did not even claim to be a democracy. Publicly, Taiwan justified the single-party rule of the Kuomintang in terms of the threat from communist China, the political crisis caused by its international isolation and the need to maintain stability on the island. Taiwan was the most explicitly authoritarian of the three countries.[202]

Essentially, democratization in the East Asian developmental states has taken place only after substantial economic development was already achieved.[203] In Korea and Taiwan, authoritarian regimes raised living standards before democratic transition took place. When both countries democratized, this political transformation had been long delayed.[204]

---

200 Refer to Wade (1990), p. 195.

201 Refer to Linz (1995), pp. 40-43. For further information refer to Duckitt (1989) and Kemmelmeier et al. (2003).

202 Refer to Johnson (1987), p. 137 ff and pp. 143-145.

203 Refer to Thompson (1996), p. 637.

204 With respect to Taiwan, Wade conceives: *"... what is striking, I think, is how late this (political) softening comes – long after the regime was well formalized and institutionalized, long after the mainland receded, long after the period of economic breakthrough, long after living standards began to rise for everyone".* Refer to Wade (1990), p. 254.

In the developmental states, the characteristic of authoritarianism was combined with a weak society.[205] Thus, the authoritarian state organization enabled the ruling elite to pursue a strategy of minimizing commitments to the few existing groups and preventing counter-elites from defining their opposition in politically relevant terms.[206] The governments prevented emerging groups from acquiring autonomy from the state and hindered the formation of independent interest aggregation. Moreover, the governments spread threats of adverse consequences should a private party refuse to conform to a "suggestion or recommendation" of the government. MITI is well-known for having accomplished this with great skill.[207] The elite bureaucracy therefore had the necessary autonomy to define, and the power to implement, national goals.[208] In 1993, the World Bank also stressed the importance of the bureaucracy's insularity from society for strategic, long-term policy implementation:

> *"Without it [technocratic insulation], technocrats in the high-performing Asian economies would have been unable to introduce and sustain rational economic policies, and some vital wealth-sharing mechanisms would have been neutralized soon after their inception, as was land reform in the Philippines."*[209]

In this respect, the nation-building strategies of the ruling elites in the East Asian developmental states differed from those used in Latin America. Their ruling group (from 1949 onwards for Taiwan, and from the arrival of Park Chung Hee in 1961 for Korea) had clear principles of industrialization. The process of industrialization was seen and understood in a comprehensive, rather than piecemeal, perspective from the beginning. Both countries were under threat from powerful external enemies, which made industrialization even more vital.[210] The implementation of a comprehensive industrial policy by the elite bureaucracy was possible because the state was strong enough to turn away demands of different interest groups. Thus, these groups were not in a position to pick industrial policy to pieces.

Some bureaucratic-authoritarian regimes in Latin America strived to acquire similar autonomy, but came to power in situations where many existing groups already had

---

205 In none of these countries were peasants united or politically organized, partly because small-holder agriculture predominated. In non of these countries were labor movements able to challenge state authority. Only in Korea and Singapore was labor strong enough to provoke repressive measures from the state in the early phases of export development. In addition, in neither case was labor's resistance sustained effective. Refer to Deyo (1987), pp. 233-234.

206 According to Skocpol, the interest-group approach is about *"the allocations of benefits among demanding groups"*. Refer to Skocpol (1985), p. 4. The argument goes, since the most powerful groups will be most able to affect the decisions of the state, state economic policies will be inevitably biased towards them. The most representative of these theories is the "regulatory-capture" theory of the Chicago school. Refer to Stigler (1975).

207 Refer to World Bank (1993), p. 186.

208 Evans (1989), p. 574 and White and Wade (1988), p. 10.

209 World Bank (1993), p. 167.

210 Refer to White and Wade (1988), p. 10.

considerable autonomy from the state. The states of Latin America were confronted with bargaining and shifting alliances of strong interest groups. These groups influenced the policy process of those countries. Macroeconomic populism has become a regular part of the Latin American economic environment. Due to the missing autonomy, the state operated under constant duress.[211] The Latin American states became unable to realize their long-term vision for their countries. These are examples of such political economies of the "predatory state", in which close government-society cooperation has materialized in the context of "weak" states, which lack autonomy from powerful groups in society.

The industrialized countries and the developing countries in East Asia and Latin America can be categorized according to their state's and society's strength or weakness: the industrialized countries are characterized by strong states and a strong society; the East Asian developing countries exhibit a strong state and a weak society, whereas the developing countries of Latin America represent the combination of a weak state and a strong society (refer to Figure 4).

Figure 4: A framework for state-societal interaction.

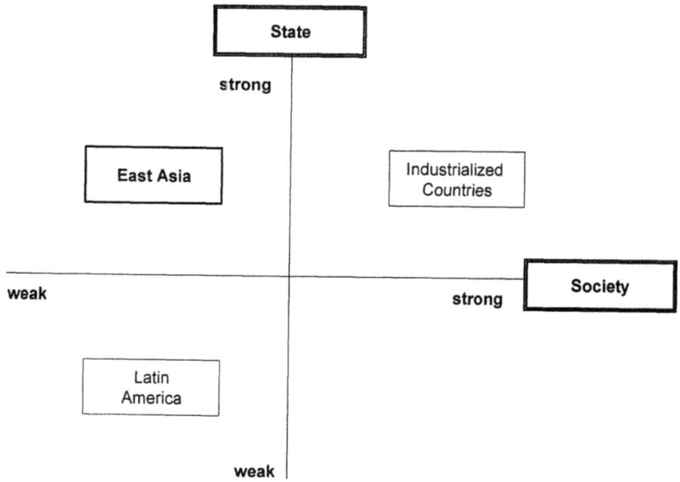

Source: Refer to Luiz (2000), p. 232.

Altogether, in neither Taiwan, nor in Japan and Korea, were organized groups an important factor in shaping economic and social policy, and their disruptive potential was under control. Industrial associations were not important centers of autonomous

[211] Luiz (2000), p. 239.

influence on the state. Additionally, in none of those countries was an elected legislature important in policy-making.[212] The strong and cohesive elite bureaucracy was insulated from external demands and was not captured by their interests. Thus, the constellation of a strong state and a weak society is a crucial factor for cohesive policy-implementation by the bureaucracy.

2.6.2 Government-business relations

Okimoto (1989) contends that informational asymmetry between the state and other agents can be reduced through institutional design. The willingness of Japanese firms to reveal the necessary information to the state and thus reduce informational asymmetry, is often attributed to the tradition of a close government-business relationship.[213] "Business" essentially implies the massive conglomerates in the developmental states.[214] "Government" in this context, refers primarily to a number of key ministries in the state bureaucracy, like MITI in Japan.

Governments can improve private sector decision-making by minimizing risks as they collect, pool and disseminate technical, commercial and market information. Nevertheless, they usually do not have a comparative advantage at the micro-level. In consequence, while governments may provide special support based on the infant industry argument, they are not capable of actually picking national "winners".[215] Therefore, close institutionalized links between the elite bureaucracy and private businesses for consultation and cooperation between government and business are decisive.[216] It enables state actors to base long-term development goals on up-to-date information gained from direct involvement with key economic agents.[217] Consequently, the state can obtain information on how changing economic realities affect entrepreneurial interests.

---

212 Refer to White and Wade (1988), p. 10-11.

213 Refer to Okimoto (1989), p. 156.

214 Conglomerates in Japan, prewar *zaibatsu* and post-war, vertical integrated *keiretsu*, were large corporate holding groups. The *zaibatsu* were closely linked with the military-bureaucratic complex of the 1920s and 1930s and were a key element in building the economy's industrial and military base. Most of the leading electronics firms in Japan, such as Nippon Electric Corporation, Fujitsu, Hitachi and Toshiba, belong to a major *keiretsu*. For *keiretsu* firms, membership actually means extensive intra-keiretsu stockholding, reliance on the main *keiretsu* bank for external indirect financing, and stable but by no means exclusive business transactions. For further information on the Sumitomo *keiretsu* which incorporates Nippon Electric Corporation, refer to Okimoto (1989), p. 133 ff.

215 Refer to Yue (1995), p. 86.

216 Refer to Johnson (1982), p. 23.

217 Refer to Nee et al. (2005), pp. 7-8.

2.6.2.1 Information exchange

In the East Asian states, there has been far-reaching public-private cooperation. In Japan, bureaucrats regularly invited representatives from private industry to discuss policy and market trends. Private actors could exchange information with economic bureaucrats in "deliberation councils", which were attached to the respective ministries.[218] Deliberation councils were organized either along functional or thematic lines, such as pollution and finance or according to industry, such as autos or chemicals. The councils were established by government ministries and were generally associated with a specific bureau within the ministry. The private sector was represented by people from business, labor, consumers, academia and the press. The success of MITI's policy implementation was only achieved with a consensus from the relevant deliberation council.[219] Through discussions in the councils, economic bureaucrats obtained crucial market information from industry representatives. At the same time, economic bureaucracies had considerable in-house expertise.[220] Thus, state officials could profit from their extensive linkages with industry, and use the knowledge and business experience from private entrepreneurs for their policy considerations. They obtained information about specific sectors and products from industry representatives. This information was then incorporated in their own research.

In Korea, from the mid-1960s to the early 1980s, government and private sector relations were close and cooperative, although some might argue that the government was too strong handed or even dictatorial. Government and business leaders met frequently although less formally than in Japan. Until the early 1980s, the most important communication channels were monthly export-promotion meetings presided over by Korea's president, at which businessmen expressed their opinions on markets, regulations and potential plans. The president then instructed the responsible ministers to attend to each important issue and present, at the next meeting, a progress report on their assigned tasks.[221]

The Korean bureaucracy also established special intermediate organizations such as trade associations and industry promotion societies. These were responsible for fostering new industries and supporting the private sector in its development. In 1967, the government established the Korea Electronics Industry Promotion Society to promote the electronics sector. Its members were drawn from the leading electronics producers. The Korea Electronics Industry Promotion Society was authorized by the then Ministry of Trade and Industry as the exclusive body representing the interests of the industry. Thus, it became the major link between bureaucracy and firms. The Korea Electronics Industry Promotion Society interacted

---

218 Refer to Johnson (1982), p. 47.

219 Refer to World Bank (1993), p. 182.

220 Refer to Edin (2000), p. 109.

221 Refer to World Bank (1993), p. 183.

with the Economic Planning Board, the Ministry of Trade and Industry and other government agencies through its specially constituted deliberation council. Thus, it was best informed to fashion and implement development strategies for the sector.[222]

Essentially, the councils enabled the bureaucracy to gather information about world markets, technology trends and the impact of regulations domestically and abroad. The government could then synthesize the information into an action plan. This plan was communicated back to the private sector. The repeated nature of the collaboration restricted more or less self-interested behavior, and in part helped to establish the bureaucrats' credibility. Politically, these councils served as proto-democratic institutions, because they provided direct channels for business, labor and academia to the seat of power. Moreover, because the rules of governing industry were established in the council, every member was assured that the rules could not be altered arbitrarily.[223]

Developmental statists also call attention to the construction and execution of joint projects between the state and nascent industrial groups.[224] This relationship was beneficial to both parties, as Okazaki (1997) elaborates, referring to Japan's reestablishment efforts of its heavy-industry base. In the 1950s, MITI attempted to abandon Japan's textile industry, which was unskilled-labor-intensive and challenged by developing countries, and move towards heavy industry.[225] The Council for Industrial Rationalization (an advisory organization for the Minister of International Trade and Industry) was a body wherein co-operation between government and private enterprises could create a path to escape coordination failure, which resulted from complementarity among industries, economies of scale and incomplete information.[226] The Council developed the plans for simultaneous investment in related industries, helped companies to raise funds, and coordinated industrial enterprises with financial institutions. This process can be interpreted as a coordinated experiment by the government and private enterprise, which was one of the essential aspects of the government-firm relationship in postwar Japan.[227] The intimacy of interaction was possible in Japan for several reasons:

- MITI officials were viewed as impartial and supportive.
- There was no tradition of ideological bias against public-private interpenetration.

---

222 Refer to Weiss (1998), pp. 57-58.

223 Refer to World Bank (1993), p. 187.

224 The idea of "joint projects", which is central to the visions of Gerschenkron, Hirschman, Amsden and Wade, makes close ties of key social groups fundamental to developmental efficiency.

225 Refer to Okazaki (1997), p. 95.

226 The Council was composed of representatives from the industrial associations and leading enterprises of each industry. Refer to Okazaki (1997), pp. 94-95.

227 Refer to Okazaki (1997), pp. 92-95.

- Government and industry shared overriding interests.
- Most industries looked to MITI for some kind of support.
- The private sector, on balance, was satisfied with MITI's industrial policy.
- The advantages of long-term cooperation were perceived to outweigh any incentives for industry to engage in rent-seeking behavior.[228]

In order not to fall captive to specific industrial interests, MITI officials in the vertical bureaus and divisions could not develop a strong sympathy for the interests and needs of industries under their jurisdiction. Only those businesses that would not damage higher-priority sectors and harm the economy were able to pass through MITI's policy-making channels without opposition or fundamental revision. However, because MITI's horizontal divisions had to find ways of integrating policies advocated by all units, the needs and interests of one industry had to be balanced against others. This provided built-in safeguards against responding politically to short-term industrial demands.[229]

Overall, the analysis indicates that the industrial transformation in the developmental states was enhanced not by a strong state acting over or against capital from the business sector, but by a project-oriented state that has worked in coalition with a well-organized private sector.

2.6.2.2 Embedded autonomy

Evans (1995) also discusses how bureaucracies provide institutional channels for continual negotiation with external groups, regarding economic development goals and policies. Evans argues that states which aim to transform economically have to be sufficiently *autonomous* from special interests to formulate their own goals, and at the same time also adequately *embedded* in particular industrial networks between bureaucrats and organized business to implement them. *"Embedded autonomy"*, as Evans conceives, *"is precisely the mirror image of the incoherent absolutist domination of the predatory state"*.[230] According to Evans, the logic of the developmental state rests precisely on embedded autonomy, namely of bureaucratic autonomy, with an unusual degree of embeddedness in the sense of public-private cooperation. Embeddedness links the state intimately and aggressively to particular social groups, with whom the state shares the goal of development and transformation. Thus, the success of the developmental state depends on the highly developed bureaucratic apparatus with interventive capacity that is built on historical

228 Refer to Okimoto (1989), pp. 156-157.

229 Ibidem, p. 157.

230 Evans (1989), p. 574.

experience, and well organized private actors who can provide useful intelligence and the possibility of decentralized implementation.[231]

The embedded autonomy approach intends to solve the puzzle of why highly interventionist states like Korea have successfully translated their developmental goals into practice, while others like India and Brazil have been less effective in economic management.[232] Evans' explanation is not based on the form of governance such as authoritarian versus democratic, but on the equal importance of embeddedness and autonomy. Either autonomy or embeddedness may produce perverse results without the other.[233] According to Evans, in Korea, a strong and coherent bureaucratic apparatus and close ties to private industrial capital were an efficient combination in high technology, just as it had been in other industrial sectors. The complex ties between the Ministry of Communication, the Electronics and Telecommunications Research Institute and the *chaebol* were used to nurture technological entrepreneurship and epitomized embedded autonomy.[234]

Unlike Korea, neither the state of Brazil nor India was able to pursue economic transformation successfully, as both lacked either autonomy or embeddedness. In Brazil, despite the pervasive presence of the state, its apparatus was badly divided, and lacked the overall coherence and cohesiveness it needed. This lack of coherence made it hard to use ties with local firms effectively. In India, bureaucracy was designed to avoid the pitfalls of being too closely tied to society with its contradictionary demands. Because of this, however, it was difficult to promote new industrial entrepreneurship from the private sector necessary for dynamic industrialization.[235]

The question remains, whether embedded autonomy is simply a property of successful late industrializers, as Evans suggested. While pre-industrial states were almost entirely disconnected from their surrounding society, embedded autonomy applies, to some degree, to most contemporary industrial states. No modern state lacks multiple linkages and connectedness with its civil society, and only few modern states are without some degree of organizational autonomy from special interests. However, only a few states have also developed these features in a form and degree of particular benefit to the industrial economy. In the developmental states, although state-economy linkages have sometimes been tight, they have always been highly selective, with structured access points for particular groups, and the exclusion of

231 Refer to Evans (1995), p. 59.

232 For further information on Brazil refer to Evans (1979).

233 Without autonomy, embeddedness might turn into capture. However, autonomy by itself does not necessarily predict an interest in development, either in the narrow sense of economic growth or in the broader sense of improved welfare. Refer to Evans (1995), p. 59.

234 Refer to Evans (1995), p. 209. *Chaebol* refers to a Korean form of business conglomerate, in its core features comparable to the Japanese *keiretsu* business groups. For further information on *chaebols* refer to Amsden (1989), Fields (1995), Janelli (1993) and Steers et al. (1989).

235 Refer to Evans (1995), p. 209.

others from this access. Hence, the core feature has been selective embeddedness.[236]

Despite the fruitfulness in Evan's work, the notion of embedded autonomy suffers from ambivalence. Evans' empirical evidence of embedded autonomy as a prerequisite of successful industrial policy is vague, regardless of the right balance between insulation and direct intervention.[237] The state has to be sufficiently autonomous from society in order not to be captured by rent-seeking groups and be able to coordinate development. At the same time, the state has to be sufficiently embedded in society and be able to established links and ties with social groups. Such a state would constantly be in danger of being too little insulated and too tightly embedded.[238]

Political institution-bound factors in the East Asian region have effectively bolstered industrial growth. It is extremely difficult, though, to engineer equilibrium between the two apparently contradictory conditions of bureaucratic autonomy and public-private cooperation, and to sustain it over time. The equilibrium can easily be disturbed by the more rapid growth of private vis-à-vis public power.[239] Therefore, embedded autonomy, as Evans defined it, is important, but not compelling. Even Evans together with Rauch (1999) stresses in later works the bureaucracy's characteristic of "Weberianess" for successful economic development and neglects the factor of embedded autonomy.[240]

The analysis showed that, in essence, effective market-augmenting forms of state intervention require both bureaucratic autonomy and close public-private cooperation. Both have to be built up gradually through a process of institutional reform. Hence, bureaucratic capacity and autonomy, as well as organized and institutionalized forms of information-sharing, and cooperation between public and private spheres for targeting and prioritizing certain sectors, are important for improving the effectiveness of state intervention in a market-oriented setting.

Political institutions are not the unique product of a particular cultural environment. Factors such as traditions of social and political hierarchy and group solidarity have played an important role in East Asian industrialization. However, the degree of social consensus and cooperation linked to the East Asian developmental state cannot be associated purely with cultural explanations. In Japan, the key institutions

---

236 Refer to Weiss (1998), p. 36.

237 Refer to Nee et al. (2005), p. 30.

238 For further information refer to Weiss and Hobson (1995).

239 Refer to Liao (2001), p. 38 and Önis (1991), p. 122.

240 "Weberianness" implies the bureaucracy's characteristics as Weber defined and which were examined in the beginning of this chapter. Refer to Evans and Rauch (1999), p. 748 ff. For detailed information refer to Evans and Rauch (1999) and Evans and Rauch (2000).

underlying rapid economic growth are of relatively recent origin. Similarly, the developmental state's characteristics of consensus and cooperation are a specific post-war phenomenon. The rejection of the culturalist explanation implies that bureaucratic capability and public-private cooperation can be built up over time through a process of institutional reform.[241]

2.7 Assessment of the East Asian developmental state approach

Extracting the relevant elements of the institutional context and formulating them at a level of generality appropriate for possible transfer to societies with different cultures and histories is a formidable challenge. It has to be answered what features of the multifaceted East Asian institutional context constitute prerequisites for successful policy implementation. This, in turn, requires a characterization of the successful policies themselves and an assessment of possible short-comings of the East Asian developmental state approach.

2.7.1 Subjects unaddressed by the developmental state theory

Among the weaknesses the developmental state's transformation approach might have, two aspects need to be pointed out: crony capitalism and the selection of priority sectors. These aspects become relevant after the initial stage of transformation and endanger the long-term strategic development approach and the future stability of the developmental state.

Crony capitalism:

The state controlled financial system helps bureaucrats to promote the chosen priority sectors and contain the ones which are expected to have no profitable future. Yet, a state controlled financial system only has positive results if the state possesses a functioning, strict bank regulation system and full transparency of business activities. The developmental states have not always been able to do this. In Korea, high private savings (amounting to 35 percent of gross savings in the 1990s) were deposited in banks. The banks in turn lent these savings to large *chaebols*. Especially to the ones which were supported by the government and thus had easy access to credits.[242] While in the early periods of Korea's development, strong discipline was exerted on cheap credits, during the 1990s the supervision diminished. Creditworthiness was not anymore determined by the soundness of firms - their books were laxly examined - but by the government's political decision of supporting the industrial sectors in which the borrowers were active. As the *chaebols*

---

241 Refer to Önis (1991), pp. 122-123.

242 Korean firms in general had been allowed to operate with 20 percent of equity borrowing at 4/1 ratio.

produced for the domestic and the international market, they borrowed heavily and used large amounts of funds in their foreign market ventures. Yet, their profitability was often low. Loans thus frequently turned into non-performing ones.[243] Krugman (1998) even claimed that

> *"The success of too many Asian businessmen depended less on what they knew than on whom they knew"* and *"dubious investments [...] were cheerfully funded by local banks, as long as the borrower had the right government connections"*.[244]

Within a state-controlled banking system, the relationship between governments, banks and firms may insulate business from market forces. This can lead to an encouragement of excessive borrowing despite a weak equity basis. A wasteful use of resources is the result. Structural weaknesses such as inadequate bank regulation,[245] and a lack of transparency in business, together with excessive borrowing, may turn into dead debt. Moreover, due to the bank's soft budget constraints, the state's deficit spending increases steadily.[246]

During the Asian financial crisis in 1997, the negative consequences of dense ties between the state and private businessmen came to light. The form of Asian capitalism, namely the link between state officials and key families, the military and various individuals who have built huge conglomerates is unique. These arrangements are called *"crony capitalism"*.[247] Crony capitalism consists of close business-government networks that are based on trust and patron-client relations, which are effective in capital accumulation and development. Policy networks that existed between states and societies became a critical channel to drive various industries to an investment decision.[248]

Despite powerful government institutions, the close coordination between the state and the private sectors gave rise to serious problems in corporate governance and regulatory forbearance. This experience showed that certain institutional arrangements that were effective at earlier stages of development, became destructive as market-based arrangements expanded.[249] As the state's selection and intervention in particular "sunrise" industries is decisive for the successful transformation of the developmental state in its early stages, the state depends on

---

243 Refer to Carreno (2001), p. 2.

244 Krugman (1998), p. 70.

245 Stiglitz conceives that the *"The crisis was caused in part by too little government regulation (or perverse or ineffective government regulation)"*. Refer to Stiglitz (1998), Internet Edition, reviewed 25.5.2006.

246 Refer to Kornai (1992a), p. 140 ff.

247 Refer to Krugman (1998), p. 70.

248 Refer to Liao (2001), pp. 38-39 and p. 41.

249 Refer to Elson (2006), p. 40.

information sharing with private enterprises on future trends. Thus the key to successful interactive negotiation on policies and goals must be an organized and, above all, institutionalized form of cooperation that can hardly turn into the capture of the state by private businesses. In this sense, it is quite obvious that, unless "autonomy" and "cooperation" requirements are satisfied, attempts to implement developmental state style industrial policies will prove to be counterproductive: In such an environment, bureaucratic elites will lack the capability to identify dynamic industries to be targeted in the first place, and will be in a weak position in terms of monitoring and regulating the activities of firms located in strategic industries.

In the initial phase of the state's development, a state-controlled and bank-based financial system may positively support the state's industrial policy. Strict regulation, transparency and hard budget constraints are of importance. In the long-run, however, a private banking system needs to be implemented gradually, so that credit issuing is based on commercial criteria. In addition, cooperation and information sharing between the state and private businesses has to happen in an institutionalized manner.

Long-term selection of priority sectors:

The long-term selection of priority sectors is largely unaddressed in the developmental state theory. The state's information problem (the state "does not know better" about the future course of events, and such an informational deficiency can only be corrected at a prohibitive cost) is a point that was already made by the Austrian school in the central planning debate in the 1930s.[250] In a market economy, the profit and loss system which is based on market prices provides the necessary information, as to which industries should expand, and which should contract, in a market economy. In the developmental states, this function was largely fulfilled by the state. Thus, the question arises how the pilot agencies gained the knowledge that was assumed to be superior to the free market. Moreover, once anticipated profitable industries are selected, how are the planners' interests to promote only those industries that best generate economic growth to be sustained?

With state industrial planning, the problem emerges that due to the synergism of state and market, the market is not replaced with complete central planning, because the state requests the information needed for an efficiently functioning economy that is guaranteed by the market. The interference with, and distortion of, price signals by selectively promoting individual industries undermines, in turn, the process by which the necessary market information is generated.[251] In this respect, bureaucratic elites

---

[250] For further information refer to Lavoie (1985) for a discussion of the debate. Another important dimension of the information problem is the existence of informational asymmetry, the principal-agent problem. Refer to Stiglitz (1987).

[251] Refer to Powell (2003), pp. 10-11.

are incapable of guiding the developmental process beyond a certain critical point. As Gerschenkron (1962) conceived, in the initial phase of development, the "late developer", that has enough autonomy and capacity, can "catch up" with the existent industrial power by replicating successful strategies, borrowing key technologies and generally accelerating the course of industrialization. In the East Asian developmental states, the successful and rapid catching-up process was evidence of the effectiveness of their industrial policy approaches. At the time when countries reach the "technological frontier", and are confronted by fundamental uncertainty which characterizes the course of technological evolution, the benefits and capacities of the state-led approach diminish.[252] State planners are clearly not infallible, when it comes to deciding which future industry sectors are likely to be at the technological cutting edge, and therefore worthy of government support.[253]

Thus, while governments may provide special support based on the flying geese argument in the initial phase of development, they are not well equipped, and thus do not have the ability to pick national champions in the long run.[254] In a later period of development, only the free powers of the market can decide on profitable investments, and only private enterprises are flexible and efficient enough to be competitive in profitable sectors.

Future stability of the developmental state:

The stability of the developmental state in the long run is questionable. The successful developmental state that accelerates income and the standard of living might be "its own gravedigger":[255]

- Stronger private firms are in a position to better resist government direction. Once the private business sector has accumulated industrial capital, it becomes less dependent on resources provided by the state. The relative dominance of the state diminishes, and government industrial policies are more conditioned by negotiations with private firms and industry associations.[256] In the 1980s, powerful emerging domestic forces hampered the operations of the Korean developmental state, thus threatened its state autonomy, and forced it to retreat step by step. The very success of the Korean developmental state undermined the basis of its power.[257]
- The general weakness and control of civil society appears to have been a general condition for the constitution and continuity of developmental states. However, as it did in Japan in the early 1970s, the very success of Taiwan and

252 For further information refer to Fong (1998).

253 For further information refer to Callon (1995), p. 147 ff.

254 Refer to Yue (1995), p. 86.

255 The unsuccessful developmental state, the one that cannot accelerate economic growth, loses the legitimation for its authoritative ruling in the long run as well.

256 Refer to Wade (2003b), p. 343.

257 Refer to Minns (2001), p. 1031.

Korea caused fundamental changes in the relationship of states with society.[258] The government's economic achievements have promoted the growth of an active civil society. Regular participation in modern economic life, rising levels of consumption, expanding education provision, the strengthening of labor and capital organizations and the functional requirements of economic growth have all been achievements of developmental states.[259] Rising affluence and education make for large middle classes, which demand participation in the form of democracy.[260]

- The applicability of the developmental state approach to other than authoritarian national settings is questionable. Is the East Asian developmental state approach desirable and practicable in environments where democratic values and institutions, as well as widespread political participation, have already emerged as central objectives? Indeed, in countries which have experienced a long trajectory of democratic development, it would be impossible for the state to withdraw entirely from participation and social welfare, and focus solely on growth and productivity objectives. In this respect, the question arises, whether the developmental state is compatible with emerging political liberalization and participation demands, namely a liberal western type political system, as a form of governance in the long-run. Thus, while not possible in this study, it would be interesting to examine whether, and to what extent, the institutions of the developmental state have survived and will survive in the future under conditions of popular participation and democratic governance in Japan, Taiwan and Korea.

Despite the shortcomings the developmental state theory exhibits, economists allege that only few societies in the modern world will achieve high economic growth rates and thus make successful transitions from poverty without states which approximate to the model of a developmental state.[261] From this arises the question about the culture-free lessons to be learned from the examined developmental states.

2.7.2 The East Asian Developmental State Model

The focus of the developmental state theory has generally been on East Asia, with only few analyses concentrating on Southeast and South Asia.[262] Some even argue that the developmental state is a product of East Asia's unique historical

[258] Refer to Wade (2003b), p. 343.

[259] Refer to Leftwich (1995), p. 416.

[260] Refer to Wade (2003b), p. 343.

[261] Refer to Leftwich (1995), p. 421.

[262] For further information on Southeast Asia refer to Hawes and Liu (1993) and on South Asia refer to Chibber (2003).

circumstances.[263] The knowledge about developmental states is based on case study research. The main objective of statists such as Johnson, Amsden and Wade was to describe the economic policies that led to success in each of the respective countries they studied.[264] They integrated the findings of earlier studies on the active state, bureaucratic organization and state-society relations from scholars like List, Polanyi, Weber, Gerschenkron, Hirschman, Skocpol and others into their own research (refer to Figure 5).

Figure 5: Highlighted features of developmental states by different scholars.

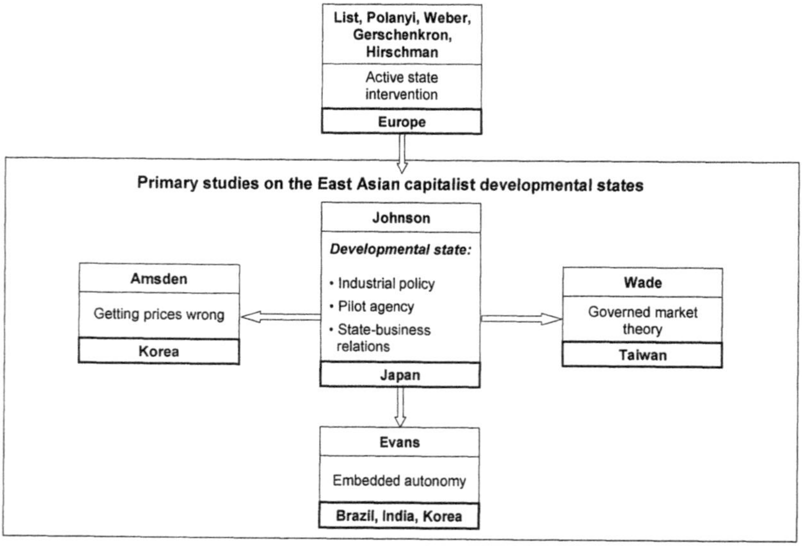

Source: Own illustration.

The analysis showed that the examined works of developmental statists not only focused on different countries, but also set different focal points. In addition, although the East Asian developmental states have all played a developmental role, there are important differences between them. Looking for shared features is the best starting point for an understanding of the state's industrial policy, and the organizational and structural characteristics that allow the state to play a developmental role. In the following, similarities between the three examined developmental states are categorized by conditions to be historically given, and measures (policy indicators and institutional setting) to be implemented by the authorities.

263 Refer to Leftwich (1995), p. 405.

264 Refer to Edin (2000), p. 24.

(1) Conditions:

- The state's stringent developmental approach could only be implemented because of the states' authoritarian structure. Authoritarianism enabled the state to contain civil society in the form of public interest groups. Labor was disciplined and dissent quickly suppressed. Subsequently, society in the developmental states was usually weak, and did not actively participate in policy formation. The state's capacity and autonomy from strong societal groups was important to East Asia's economic development, and was often lacking in Latin America. The developmental states were able to ensure insulation of the central decision-makers from interest groups by their authoritative state structure.[265]
- The developmental states' intense and almost unequivocal commitment on the part of government to build up the international competitiveness of the domestic industry arises from their economic backwardness. Japan, Korea and Taiwan were all industrial backward states (so called "late developers").This can mostly be attributed to geopolitical pressures and national security issues.[266] Thus, economic growth has been increased, yet sometimes at the expense of other objectives, like social welfare.[267]

(2) Measures:

a) Bureaucracy:

- Decision-makers all pursued growth-oriented goals and had centralized structures through which to decide and coordinate relative priorities. In the various East Asian economies, there was generally close coordination between various ministries. The bureaucracy was depoliticized (separated from politicians) which enabled it to implement "unfavorable" policies.
- The decision-making process was streamlined in a leading government agency (pilot agency) which had a strong coordinating authority. The pilot agency "translated" national strategic visions of economic development into specific policy actions.[268]
- Asian governments fostered the development of a professional, merit-based civil service tradition. Thus, the decision-making structure was staffed by the best administrative and managerial talents. Remuneration of management and career paths in the public sector were competitive with those offered by the private sector.

265 These interest groups might for example be the legislature, a farm lobby, a trade union or entrepreneurs which tried to lay pressure on the government. Refer to So (2003), p. 18, Wade (1988a), pp. 129-163 and Yue (1995), p. 81.

266 Refer to Weiss and Hobson (1995), p. 184.

267 Refer to Wade (1990), p. 7.

268 Refer to Elson (2006), p. 40.

- Clearly defined norms of comportment (with regards to recruitment, career, remuneration) helped to contain rent-seeking.
- The East Asian bureaucracies were generally characterized by unity, competence and efficiency. Government interventions had a high degree of policy and implementation coherence. Interventions pulled in the same direction and had cumulative impacts.[269]

b) State:

- The developmental states' economic development was state-led. The bureaucracy used strategic industrial policy mechanisms to influence the economic development of particular sectors. National bureaucrats identified existing market failures, and devised appropriate policy responses.
- The state only supported selected industries. Protection and assistance were given primarily to infant industries, and to those industries perceived to be economies with potential competitiveness ("sunrise industries") rather than those which had already lost their competitiveness ("sunset industries").
- The developmental states in East Asia initiated a dualist trade regime with significant focus on exports. The outward industrialization strategy is the principal difference between the developmental states in East Asia and those in Eastern Europe and Latin America.[270] The regimes of the developmental states *"made exports a compulsion rather than a choice"* for private companies.[271] At the same time, specific nascent industries have been protected.[272] To ensure that protected industries became competitive, the economic bureaucracy used different ways to do so.[273] Often, exports were used as an instrument to measure performance, and bureaucrats linked subsidies to performance. Subsidies were cut down if no longer needed, or if performance expectations were not fulfilled after a certain period of time.
- Although the developmental states' approach towards foreign capital and participation differed in its intensity, FDI inflow has been limited. The state strictly controlled inflowing investments, and encouraged domestic companies

269 Activities that received help through trade controls were also assisted through financial subsidies and fiscal incentives. Refer to Wade (1988a), p. 157 and Wade (1988b), p. 139 ff.

270 Refer to Kim (1998), p. 9.

271 Refer to Amsden (1989), p. 69.

272 Hence, the import substitution policy was not totally abandoned. The state continuously provided financial subsidies to the private firms for the development of domestic technology to substitute for imported intermediate goods. Nevertheless, Korea and Taiwan show high levels of export dependency in their economic growth. During the 1980s the average trade dependency ratio was almost 65 percent in Korea and 83 percent in Taiwan. Putting this in perspective, it was 36 percent in France, 47 percent in Germany, and 16 percent in America. Refer to Kim (1998), p. 9.

273 The Korean government strongly encouraged infant industries to export. They were directly exposed to international competition, even when exports had to be sold at a loss. Subsequently, import substitution did not saddle Korea with inefficient and non-competitive industries.

to compete in foreign markets and gain international expertise. None of the states has become subservient to foreign capital, and all have strictly controlled inflowing investments.

c) Financial system:

- The developmental state's financial system played an important role in the state's development process. It was largely government-controlled and bank- and credit-based.
- The financial system enabled the government to directly influence the sectoral and firm-level allocation of credit to promote strategic industries. The developmental states had state-owned banks as well as private banks. Yet, both types operated under close government-business guidance. The state used the banks as conduits for development and fiscal policies.[274]

d) Government-business relations:

Complementing insulation, the success of the state required a high degree of public-private cooperation and information sharing. In the East Asian setting, the careful construction of policy networks, namely, the organizational and particularly institutional links between the bureaucrats of the pilot agency and major private sector firms were crucial in order to generate a consensus on goals and to exchange information; both of which constitute essential components of the process of policy formulation and implementation. Government-business cooperation was institutionalized in a variety of forms, including state-sponsored industrial associations, export cartels and policy consultation bodies. Subsequently, the key to successful cooperation was an institutionalized form of information exchange.

Altogether, policy consistency and bureaucratic autonomy in East Asian societies during their post-war development compensated for the lack of well-developed market-based institutions and legal frameworks on which economic development in the advanced countries is based.[275] Accordingly, the East Asian developmental states had an institutional advantage at the governmental level.

According to the flying geese pattern, developing countries can catch up with advanced economies which point to the "right industries" to promote. Comparative advantages can be used and the necessary technology can be imported. Korea and Taiwan followed the pattern of Japanese industrialization, and moved up the value chain starting from light industries to heavy and chemical industries, then to electronics, and to high-tech industries. Thus, the difficulty in industrial policy of backward countries in the development stage lies not in identifying the right

274 Refer to Liao (2001), p. 39.

275 Refer to Elson (2006), p. 40.

industries to promote, but in designing a system of transformation that is less subject to moral hazard.[276] This is exactly what defines the required conditions and measures of the developmental state in order to be able to conduct industrial policies which lead to internationally competitive industries and fast national economic growth (refer to Figure 6).

Figure 6: The East Asian Developmental State Model.

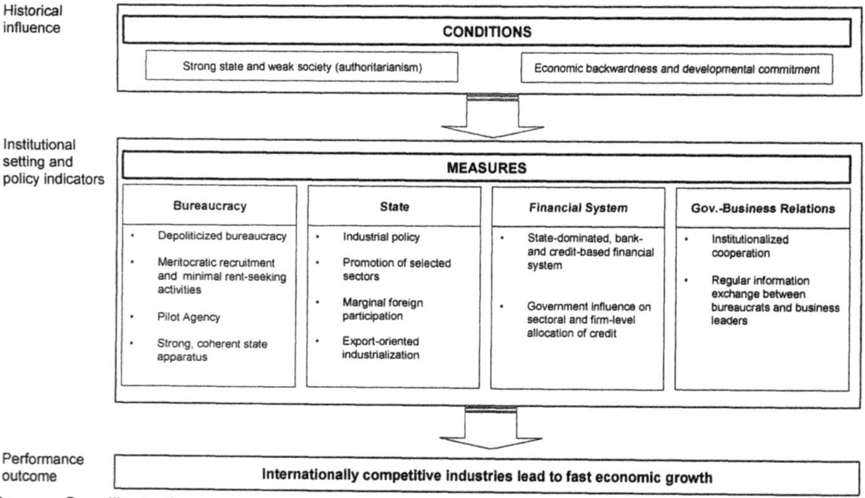

Source: Own illustration.

Developmental states vary with respect to distinct specifications of the major factors outlined above. They have in common, however, that the state is a key factor which determines economic development in the region. For a developmental state to be successful, not all of the above conditions and measures have to be adopted to an equal extent.

The central lesson that emerges from the examined literature on East Asian development is that the transfer of specific policies to new environments will be self-defeating in the absence of the political and institutional conditions and measures required for their effective implementation. Without such states, transitions may be slow, and the social costs (rent-seeking, unemployment, low education levels etc.) immense.[277] The corollary of this proposition is that the same set of policies will be counterproductive, or at least ineffective, in the absence of the associated set of

[276] Refer to Ito (2001), p. 63.

[277] Refer to Leftwich (1995), p. 421.

institutional and political structures or contexts. Hence, the developmental state approach points towards the importance of certain interaction between government, market and society in the development process. The experiences from the growth model of the East Asian developmental states raises the question of the repeatability of the developmental state model for transforming countries.

2.7.3 Emulation of the developmental state model by other developing countries?

The last fifty years have shown both the benefits and the limitations of state actions, especially in the promotion of development. Even where governments have successfully promoted economic development in the past, the question remains whether they will be able to adapt to the demands of a globalizing world economy. Along with globalization, developing countries need to integrate their economies into the international economy. With integration into the world economy in turn, external pressure from industrialized countries arises, which urges the developmental states to open their markets to international goods and services, and to stop their "export extravaganza". Accordingly, many of the policy instruments of the developmental states (used in the 1950s through the 1970s) such as protection, export promotion, foreign investment and exchange controls are being marginalized. Japan and Korea were welcomed as members of the General Agreement on Tariffs and Trade (GATT),[278] although they were still violating the free trade principles of GATT at that time.[279] In consequence, developing countries today are being increasingly constrained in their national development strategies by proliferating regulations formulated and enforced by international organizations.[280]

From this, the question arises as to whether the less industrialized countries can mimic the developmental states and use similar policy measures to accelerate growth in a liberal economic environment under the guidance of the WTO.[281] Is the developmental state concept an option available to other countries regardless of the integration level in the world economy?[282]

States which are more integrated into the international economy may yet still influence the development of their domestic economies, and implement industrial policy. There continues to be considerable scope for state guidance in national economic management, and for government-business cooperation, even – or perhaps especially – as economies restructure to meet the new conditions of economic openness.[283] In essence, the developmental states' ability to foster

278 Japan became a GATT member in 1955 and Korea in 1967. Refer to WTO, "The 128 countries that had signed GATT by 1994", Internet Edition, reviewed 23.09.2007.

279 Refer to Perkins (2001), p. 248.

280 Refer to Wade (2003a), p. 621.

281 Refer to Amsden (2000), p. 105.

282 Refer to Pempel (1999), p. 147.

283 Refer to Weiss (2003), p. 246.

economic transformation is mostly dependent on the nature of domestic linkages and national strategies, and less on the level of economic integration. With economic integration, the tasks of developmental states have to change from export promotion and industry creation to the coordination of innovation and technology diffusion, as well as the management of trade disputes, currency realignments and economic integration. The state thereupon constantly creates new tools of industrial policy for its new tasks along with the changing domestic and international circumstances.[284]

Altogether, what makes for an effective state differs enormously across countries at different stages of development. Even among countries at the same level of income, differences in size, ethnic makeup, culture and political systems exist. This does not, however, imply that each transforming country has to "invent" its own development strategy.

[284] Refer to Weiss (1998), pp. 7-8.

3 A new model of economic development

The analysis of China's economic development applies the East Asian Developmental State Model as a benchmark model. The chapter contains the following cluster:

- Exploration of whether the conditions set by the East Asian Developmental State Model were present in China at the beginning of its economic reforms in the late 1970s.
- Analysis of China's development approach, and the measures used to transform its economic system and advance economic growth, with regard to the criteria of the East Asian Developmental State Model.
- Elaboration of whether China has adopted or adapted the measures of the East Asian developmental states.

3.1 Applicability of the East Asian Developmental State Model to China

China has been attempting to transform its economic system from a planned to a market economy since 1978. As in the East Asian developmental states, China's development strategy has been characterized by state-guided development. In 1997, the World Bank Development Report stated that *"the state is central to economic and social development, not as a direct provider of growth but as a partner, catalyst and facilitator".*[285] For decades, China has been the fastest growing present-day late-developing country. China might have learned from the positive experiences of the East Asian developmental states and adopted their development model, or followed a different, "new" development path and created a distinct Chinese model of economic transformation. Whether the conditions of the East Asian Developmental State Model were present in China on the eve of economic reform is analyzed in the following section.

3.1.1 Conditions of the Chinese economic development approach

The East Asian Developmental State Model defined two criteria as conditional for a country to apply the model's measures necessary for state-led economic growth. The criteria are strong state and weak society (authoritarianism) as well as economic backwardness and developmental commitment. The following analysis concentrates on each criterion, highlighting China's political, societal, economic and industrial situation on the eve of economic reform.

285 Refer to World Bank (1997), "World Development Report 1997: The State in a Changing World", Internet Edition, reviewed 27.11.2006.

(1) Strong state and weak society (authoritarianism):

The structure of power in the Chinese system prior to 1978 can be characterized as authoritarian. Authoritarianism in a Chinese context means the retention of ultimate, unlimited authority by the central party state.[286] Some scholars even regard the Chinese system prior to 1978 as totalitarian, because the influence of the bureaucracy encompassed culture, religion and various aspects of family life such as the number of children.[287] In addition, the power of the bureaucracy was totalitarian, as it permeated the whole society and influenced every citizen. Account was kept of every resident and employee by the state apparatus, party branches, mass organizations, and police authorities of each locality and place of work.[288]

The Chinese Communist Party (CCP) dominated the political system, which was formally organized on Marxist-Leninist principles. Top leaders, among them Mao Zedong[289], wielded enormous power and "ruled by law" (law as an instrument of government) as no institutional checks existed to guard against the exercise and abuse of this power. Although China had a constitution, its bureaucracy was not subordinate to any stable legal system. Laws were formally passed by parliament (the National People's Congress), but in practice the party organization and the party apparatus decided what the law should stipulate.[290]

The public security apparatus maintained social order through the threat and use of force. After the land reform in the late 1940s and the early 1950s, the strong landlord class had been wiped out, labor unions were restricted, and the military was tightly controlled by party and senior leaders. Thus, at the outset of reform, senior leaders did not foresee an imminent (internal) threat from strong interest groups, as society at large was weak.[291] No encompassing organizations had yet emerged, which could represent and "deliver" their membership in a comprehensive transition bargain with a reform government.[292]

The strong Leninist party-state has remained largely intact in the reform era, and the Chinese central government has had the power to introduce economic programs, to vary the speed and the sequence of reform, and to make corrections or even reverse its policy if necessary. Altogether, bureaucratic authoritarian institutions in China

---

286 Refer to Hamrin and Zhao (1995), p. xxvi and Lieberthal and Oksenberg (1988), p. 4.

287 For further information on totalitarianism refer to Arendt (1951) and Brzezinski and Friedrich (1965).

288 Refer to Kornai (1992a), p. 47.

289 Mao Zedong (26.12.1893 – 09.08.1976) was the chairman of the Politburo of the CCP from 1943 and the chairman of the Central Committee of the CCP from 1945 until his death in 1976. Under his leadership, the CCP became the ruling party of mainland China as the result of its victory in the Chinese Civil War. On 01.10.1949, Mao declared the formation of the People's Republic of China.

290 Refer to Kornai (1992a), pp. 46-47.

291 Refer to Li and Lian (1999), p. 174.

292 Refer to Kornai (1992a), p. 4.

have had the power to process and implement economic policies like governments in the developmental states.[293]

(2) Economic backwardness and developmental commitment:

For the first 30 years of the People's Republic of China, the government practiced an economically isolated, planned economy system adhering to Marxist economic principles.[294] Markets and private ownership of productive assets were eliminated, and replaced by non-market, bureaucratic allocation through annual and five-year plans.[295] The CCP and the central government relied on political controls and managed all dimensions of production and distribution. In consequence, apart from the existence of a few rural markets, the market as a coordinating mechanism of production and distribution was virtually nonexistent on the eve of economic reform in 1978.[296]

In addition, fiscal revenues and expenditure were centralized in the Chinese state bureaucracy. Profits and taxes collected by local governments were handed over to the central government.[297] The expenditure of local governments depended less on local revenue-generating efforts, and more on bargaining with higher authorities for budgetary slack. Local governments would not hesitate to bail out unprofitable enterprises because shortfalls in one year became the rationale for bargaining for larger allocations the next year.[298] This cycle gave rise to the classic soft budget constraint syndrome.[299] On the macro-level, soft budget constraints led to overinvestment and shortages; on the firm level, they caused ex ante and ex post inefficiency.[300]

---

293 Refer to So (2003), p. 18 and Shirk (1993), p. 14.

294 The economic isolation that results from its self-sufficiency approach was furthermore completed by China's scientific and cultural isolation. Refer to Kornai (1992a), p. 18ff and p. 335 and Editorial Board of the Progress of China Industry Modernization (1999), p. 139.

295 For a detailed analysis of the causes of poor plan performance refer to Killick (1976), p. 164. For further information on development planning refer to Dobb (1960) and Griffin and Enos (1970).

296 Refer to Nee and Opper (2007), p. 94. For further information refer to Schurmann (1968), Whyte and Parish (1984) and Walder (1986).

297 Refer to Peng (2001), p. 1343.

298 For further information refer to Walder (1995).

299 Kornai saw this as an incurable disease inflicting SOEs because the state, as the owner, also has objectives (e.g., maintaining employment and political stability) other than financial performance. Refer to Kornai (1992a), pp. 489–497.

300 Bailing out poor-performance firms ex post means that the mechanism of "constructive destruction" is not at work. Furthermore, because unprofitable companies expect government bailouts, firm managers have little incentive to improve productivity and efficiency. Refer to Peng (2001), p. 1343.

The deficiencies in the system had the result that China's economic development was retarded by low micro-economic efficiency.[301] The central government did not achieve its intended goal of accelerating development, and could not overcome the country's economic backwardness.

Also, China's Great Leap Forward Strategy had left it with poor overall economic performance.[302] Essentially, the ineffectiveness of the socialist centrally-planned economy limited China's growth before the reform in 1978.[303]

At the late 1970s, the planning system had been practiced in China for three decades. Market mechanisms adopted in neighboring economies, such as Japan and the four little dragons, had brought them double-digit annual growth for decades. Particularly, the sharp contrast in performance between mainland China and Taiwan, between North and South Korea, and between East and West Germany confirmed the superiority of the market mechanism over the planning system.[304] The backwardness of China's industries, in comparison with some of its East Asian counterparts, the inefficiencies of the centrally planned economy, agricultural stagnation and the need to accelerate growth and provide jobs to reduce widespread poverty, propelled the reformers among the senior members of the CCP in the early 1980s.[305]

The Third Plenary Session of the 11th CCP Central Committee, held in December 1978, decided to shift the focus of the party's work from *"class struggle to economic development".*[306] It started the socialist modernization drive and set the reform and opening-up policy. It thereby rejected the Maoist model of development (heavy industry-oriented development; leap forward development strategy). This allowed a shift of ideology within the CCP and initiated economic reforms. The accepted

301 Refer to Lin et al. (1996), p. 60.

302 The Great Leap Forward was the name given to the Second Five Year Plan which was scheduled to run from 1958-1963, though the name is now generally limited to the first three years of this period. Chairman Mao Zedong started the Great Leap Forward in 1957 to rapidly advance the country's economic development and transform China into a leading industrial power. Mao's plan was to massively increase both agricultural and industrial production. Peasants had already started farming the land co-operatively in the 1950s. During the Great Leap Forward, they joined large communes consisting of thousands of people. Large-scale irrigation schemes were undertaken to improve agricultural productivity. Mao furthermore pushed for the construction of steel plants across the country. With local governments' rush to recruit labor for work in steel production, agricultural tasks were neglected, leading to a widespread famine in the years 1959-61. The government also plunged the country into debt by increasing spending on the development of heavy industry.

303 Refer to Chinese Government (2005), "Economic System", Internet Edition, reviewed 28.03.2006.

304 Refer to Li and Lian (1999), p. 173. For further information refer to Nee and Lian (1994) on why communist rulers initiated economic reforms.

305 Refer to Yusuf and Nabeshima (2006a), p. 4.

306 Refer to Editorial Board of the Progress of China Industry Modernization (1999), p. 36.

ideology at the beginning of reform was the idea of *"planning as a principle and market as a supplementary part"*.[307] Chinese leaders envisioned accelerating economic transformation under strong state leadership, as their East Asian counterparts had done.[308] Rather than accept the division of labor dictated by comparative advantage, China sought to develop industrial sectors and firms that would foster entrepreneurial activity and create positive spillovers in the economy as a whole.[309]

Altogether, China, like the East Asian developmental states, had similar conditions when it started its reform policy and maintained these throughout the reform period. Similar to the East Asian developmental states, China has been an authoritarian state. The CCP has solely reigned and tightly controlled and suppressed all political demands. This has hindered the establishment of a strong civil society. In 1978, China was an economically backward country, a so-called "late developer", with a distorted industrial structure and an inward-looking economy. Furthermore, the Chinese bureaucracy, similar to that of the East Asian developmental states, has continuously committed itself to economic growth and transformation. The conditions of the developmental state model are thus fulfilled.

3.1.2 Characteristics that distinguish China from the developmental states

Despite the similarities between China and the East Asian developmental states, there are at least three characteristics that differentiate China from its East Asian neighbors:

- *Geographical vastness:* Not only is China's territory more than eighteen times larger than that of the four little dragons and Japan combined, its population (1.3 billion) is also almost six times greater.[310] Due to its size, the central government had already decentralized decision-making to local governments during the Great Leap Forward.[311] As many of these firms obtained most of their inputs from, and also produced for, their jurisdictions, Mao decentralized

307 Refer to Qian (2000), p. 153.

308 For understanding the Chinese reform process, it is important to note that according to the self-conception of the central leadership, China is no transformation country like the Central and East European Countries, but rather a developing country. Accordingly, the transformation experiences of the Central and East European countries have had less impact on China's economic policy than the development path of its successful East Asian neighbors.

309 Refer to Thun (2006), p. 3.

310 Refer to Xia (2000), p. 2.

311 Mao implemented decentralization, because the central government in Beijing did not have the information needed to centrally control an industrial sector that included 30,000 large and medium-size firms and nearly 150,000 small firms at that time. Refer to Qian and Weingast (1996b), p. 11.

decision-making to the individual provinces, counties and villages.[312] Although in the early 1960s, after the failure of the Great Leap Forward, the central government aimed to recentralize some controls, much planning and control activity remained at the provincial level. The Cultural Revolution almost paralyzed the central government, and again strengthened decentralization tendencies. The rural small-scale industry program in the 1970s also devolved further industrial planning rights and control to the county and commune levels.[313] Along with decentralization, the political system has been disaggregated into several constituent levels. Accordingly, China has a multilevel political system with five major territorial levels: first, the central government, which covers the entire country; second, 22 provinces[314] and five autonomous regions and four centrally administrative municipalities (administratively, they have province-level status); third, 333 cities and prefectures; fourth, 2,816 counties; and fifth, 44,016 township level units. The townships are themselves divided into villages or neighborhoods and communities.[315]

- *Communist legacy:* Unlike the East Asian developmental states, China's economic and political transition process has been carried out under a communist leadership. The CCP came to power in 1949 intent on eradicating private ownership. Economic reform has thus been guided by the legacies of the Mao era and its set of ideological socialist political and economic norms like egalitarism, Stalinist bureaucracy and a centrally-planned economy.[316] These Maoist ideological legacies have imposed constraints upon the transitional process in the post-Mao reform period.
- *International environment*: The Cold War provided an unusually benevolent context for the East Asian states (and not for China in the 1980s). As part of its effort to contain the Soviet Union, the USA donated extensive foreign aid to its allies in East Asia. The East Asian states could hence focus solely on economic development. Moreover, the USA unilaterally opened its markets to goods from East Asia and granted them protection from security threats. At that time, the USA did not perceive the rapid rise of Japan, Korea and Taiwan as a threat to its economic supremacy. It was even the explicit objective of the United States' (US') strategy in the decades following World War II.[317]

These characteristics do not debilitate the conditions a transforming country has to fulfill for application of the East Asian Developmental State Model. The following analysis on China hence concentrates on the *measures* of the East Asian

---

312 This type of decentralized planning began around 1957.

313 Refer to Yusuf and Nabeshima (2006b), pp. 49-50.

314 China considers Taiwan its 23rd province.

315 Refer to OECD (2006a), p. 6 and Shambaugh (2000), p. 168.

316 Refer to Xia (2000), p. 2.

317 Refer to Thun (2006), pp. 4-5.

Developmental State Model. Accordingly, the various factors (institutional setting and policy indicators) of the model are analyzed with respect to China:

- *Bureaucracy:* depoliticized bureaucracy; meritocratic recruitment and minimal rent-seeking; pilot agency; coherent state apparatus.
- *State:* industrial policy; promotion of selected sectors; marginal foreign participation; export-oriented industrialization.
- *Financial system:* state-dominated, bank- and credit-based financial system; government influence and firm-level allocation of credit.
- *Government-business relations:* institutionalized cooperation; regular information exchange between bureaucrats and business leaders.

From the analysis of the four categories of the East Asian Developmental State Model, one can infer whether the Chinese central government has been committed to emulate the developmental state model, which was capitalist in nature, and originated primarily in small countries.

3.2 Bureaucracy

In economic literature, bureaucratic organization and performance are typically addressed by using a principal-agent model. Its origins can be found in the new economics of organization as a theoretical construct devised to examine relations within the firm.[318] Since then, the principal-agent model has become the dominant framework for examining the difficulties that arise from contracting.[319] Agency relationships are created when the principal enters into a contractual agreement with an agent, and delegates to the latter responsibility for carrying out a function or set of tasks on the principal's behalf.[320] The principal delegates responsibility to the agent in order to economize on transaction costs, and thus pursue its goals that would otherwise be too costly.[321] Governments (the principal) delegate authority to the public administration, subnational jurisdictions, and private actors (the agents) in

318 For further information refer to Moe (1984). For a number of applications refer to Alt and Shepsle (1990) and Brobak and Nye (1997).

319 Refer to Eisenhardt (1989a,b), Grossman and Hart (1983) and Jensen and Meckling (1976).

320 The principal can be any individual or organization. In the classic representation, the principal is the shareholder of a company that contracts an executive to manage the business on a day-to-day basis.

321 As suggested by Coase and developed by Williamson, the organization of hierarchies may minimize transaction costs. Coase (1937, 1960) introduced the concept of transaction costs to explain the size of firms and suggests that well-defined property rights could overcome the problems of externalities. Williamson (1975, 1985) suggests that transaction costs include both the direct costs of the transaction and the possible opportunity costs of inferior governance decisions. North (1981) explains the political conditions that give rise to efficient property rights favorable to economic growth.

order to exploit specialization advantages and cope with the complexity of structural reforms.[322] Delegation, however, might create principal-agent problems that arise from the asymmetric distribution of information that favors the agent, including adverse selection and moral hazard.[323] Delegation bears subsequently the risk that the agent does not act in the interest of the principal (the government) and pursues its own interests.[324] In consequence, governments need to implement systematic control over public officials, policy and institutional reforms in order to ensure successful economic transformation.[325] As in the East Asian developmental states, organizations might design appointment and promotion rules to deal with these problems.

3.2.1 Bureaucratic organizational structure

In the Chinese system, every office usually has a bureaucratic rank assigned to it.[326] One territorial level of government contains several bureaucratic ranks within its organs.[327] The top of the political hierarchy consists of the Politburo and the State Council. The Politburo is the supreme decision-making body which makes all major strategic decisions. The State Council translates those into concrete policies. Commissions and ministries are below the State Council.[328] Commissions are one step down and ministries are another step down. Bureaus within ministries are yet another step down and so forth. Provincial governments are the same bureaucratic rank as their ministerial counterparts.[329]

While the commissions have responsibility for the entire national economy, ministries are accountable for particular sectors or regions.[330] Ministries are therefore organized by sector (e.g. agriculture, coal, machinery) or function (education, culture, public security).[331] Although each ministry's actual influence varies not only with the

322 Refer to Ahrens and Mengeringhaus (2006), p. 79.

323 For further information refer to Kiewiet and McCubbins (1991), Holmstrom (1979), Pollack (1997) and Ross (1973).

324 Economists have focused on incentive structures that discourage opportunistic behavior on the part of the agent. The agent might exploit the principal's costs of measuring the agent's performance and act contrary to the preferences of the principal. Contractual restrictions on the agent's operational purview or monitoring the agent are possibilities, but can be costly. Their effectiveness is limited by the extent to which the agent's actions can be observed. Refer to Doleys (2000).

325 Refer to Ahrens and Mengeringhaus (2006), p. 79.

326 Refer to Lieberthal (1997), p. 3 and Shirk (1993), p. 93 ff.

327 Here, government also applies to the CCP's governing structure.

328 The CCP's Politburo ranks higher than the State Council. Refer to Huang (2002b), p. 66.

329 Refer to Lieberthal and Oksenberg (1988), p. 143 and Lieberthal (1997), p. 3.

330 Refer to Shirk (1993), p. 93 and Lieberthal and Oksenberg (1988), p. 63.

331 Ministries are expected to articulate the interests of their particular sector. When ministers or vice-ministers are called together to discuss a policy proposal, they are expected to represent the perspective of their particular ministries. Refer to Shirk (1992), pp. 69-70 and Shirk (1993), p. 93.

prestige of its minister, but also with its function, its control over subordinate enterprises and its financial contribution, the formal status of each ministry is the same. According to the commissions' higher rank they give instructions to ministries, however, only within their respective spheres of competence. Commissions take a more comprehensive view of policy approaches than do the narrowly focused line ministries. Commissions thus have to equilibrate the ministries' competing efforts in favor of the overall national situation.[332]

In correspondence to the administrative structure, industrial policies are level by level filtered down through plans. Accordingly, the central government assigns local governments to draw up their own plans on the basis of national plans and appropriate to local conditions. The governments' duties at the local level, however, are always to be performed on behalf of the central government. Units of the same rank cannot issue binding orders to each other. Accordingly, ministries cannot issue binding orders to provinces, even though on an organizational chart it appears that the ministries sit above the provinces.[333] Consequently, consensus-building is often needed in order to operate effectively, and negotiations aimed to find agreements have become a core feature of the Chinese system.[334]

Assuming that staff numbers are correlated with administrative functions, the central government is unusually small in China: the central ministries and agencies account for only about 2 million employees, or 6 percent, of the nearly 33 million in total public employment.[335] The rest - 31 million of them - are employed in sub-national governments and institutions (refer to Figure 7). The central government is too small to be able to exert detailed control over the huge number of subordinates. The structure of administration in China puts burdens on the core-ministries and state agencies at the central level which add up to about 50,000 employees just after the 1998 downsizing campaign. Besides running the central government businesses, the central ministries and state agencies must manage the services provided by central public service units that have nearly 2 million employees, and provide a management framework for the provision of these services at the sub-national levels by some 23 million employees.[336]

332 Refer to Shirk (1992), p. 71 and Lieberthal and Oksenberg (1988), p. 63.

333 The same rule means that ministries cannot issue binding orders to other ministries, provinces cannot issue binding orders to other provinces and so forth. Refer to Lieberthal (1997), p. 3.

334 Refer to Edin (2000), p. 86.

335 The OECD offers some benchmark numbers: central government employees in Germany (1993): 0.6 million, Japan (1993): 1.2 million, and the UK (1995): 1.0 million. Refer to OECD (2006a), p. 25.

336 The decentralized administrative structure is also split up into core governments and public service units. Public service units are publicly owned institutions. They provide a variety of services such as education and health. They are subordinate to the government and account for about 30 percent of budgetary expenditures. Refer to OECD (2006a), p. 26.

Figure 7: The distribution of public employment.

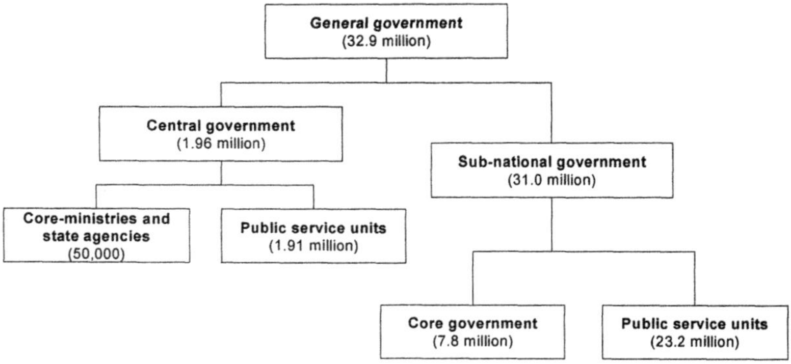

Source: Organization for Economic Cooperation and Development (OECD) (2006a), p. 25.
Note: Number of employees in brackets.

Embedded within Chinese organizations and missing from the formal organizational structure charts are the personal ties that interconnect different agencies.[337] In China, interpersonal connections are called *guanxi.* Virtually every Chinese person is connected to at least one *guanxi* network, arising from family connections, common geographical origin, joint experience (school or military service ties) or shared loyalty toward the same higher-ranking bureaucrat.[338]

Walder (1986) notes that "the concept is by no means culturally unique".[339] Personal connections are particularly important in countries without a stable legal and regulatory environment.[340] In China, *guanxi* networks particularly function as substitutes for formal institutional regulations. Particularly businessmen cultivate personal connections to substitute for a reliable government and an established rule of law.[341] *Guanxi* networks can be seen as clubs that may lower transaction costs for their members (in the form of contact, and especially control costs) in China's institutionally disorderly environment. Thus, *guanxi* networks guarantee their members the enforceability of available property rights.[342] *Guanxi* limits the state's

[337] Moreover, at the top, in many respects power is vested more in individuals than in specific institutions. Refer to Lieberthal and Oksenberg (1988), p. 63.

[338] The Chinese *guanxi* networks can be understood as institutions that arose centuries ago to secure trade relations in an environment that was only insufficiently covered by the formal legal system. For further information refer to Carr and Landa (1983) and Posner (1980).

[339] Refer to Walder (1986), p. 179.

[340] Some form of *guanxi* exists in every society, but it has different manifestations in different societies. Refer to Liu and Dicken (2006), pp. 1237-1238.

[341] Refer to Xin and Pearce (1996), p. 1642.

[342] Refer to Schramm and Taube (2002), "The Institutional Economics of Legal Institutions, Guanxi, and Corruption in the PR China", Internet Edition, pp. 5-6, reviewed 22.11.2006.

capacity for autonomous action, and interpenetrates the state and society, especially at the lower levels of the Chinese state.[343] Politically ambitious bureaucrats try to place people with whom they have *guanxi* in other agencies to extend their influence. Bureaucrats initiate contacts across bureaucratic boundaries through someone with whom they have *guanxi*. The person serves as the entrée into another organization, and acts as the guarantor of one's merit and seriousness.[344]

3.2.2 The civil service system

Since the 1980s, the term "civil servant" has been used to describe China's administrative officers in governmental organizations, known as "state cadres". Civil servants are those employed by the state (at central, regional and local level) who manage social public goods, exercise administrative power, and carry out public functions on behalf of the state.[345] Employees of legislative bodies are included in government personnel.[346]

3.2.2.1 Depolitization of civil servants?

An important determinant of China's civil service system has been the political environment in which it is embedded. The relationship between party and government can also be described as a principal-agent relationship in which the party has the function of the principal and government agencies represent diverse agents.[347] Although separating party and state functions was one motivation of the reform, the leadership rejected the concept of a politically neutral civil service from the beginning.[348] Instead, according to the "Provisional Regulations for State Civil

343 Refer to Nee (2000), pp. 34-35.

344 Refer to Lieberthal and Oksenberg (1988), pp. 156-157.

345 Refer to Cooke (2003), p. 382.

346 Employees of state enterprises and state institutions (including educational, research, sports, health and cultural institutions) are not civil servants. Refer to Chew (1990), p. 773.

347 Refer to Nee and Opper (2007), p. 109.

348 In Deng's speech "On the Reform System of Party and State Leadership" in August 1980, he stressed that it was time *"for us to distinguish between the responsibilities of the party and those of the government and to stop substituting the former for the latter. [...] This will [...] promote a better exercise of government functions and powers"*. Deng (1984), p. 303. In 1986, Deng Xiaoping made the separation of work of party and government the core of his political reform. Although separation was promoted in order to improve the quality of decision-making by putting the government on a longer leash, authority of the party over the government was never questioned. In the same light can Zhao Ziyang's approach at the Thirteenth Party Congress be seen: Even while he urged greater autonomy for government, he emphasized that the CCP Central Committee would retain its leadership over the government in political principles and in major policy decisions and would continue to appoint leading cadres for central state organs. Refer to Shirk (1993), pp. 62-63.

Servants" of 1993, civil servants are required to adhere to Marxist ideology, support socialism and accept the party's leadership.[349]

The CCP has always been the source of both civil service empowerments and control. According to Chan (2007), the 2005 Civil Service Law affirms the principle of party control of cadres. The 2005 Civil Service Law reconfirms that the CCP holds a tight control over leadership change and management at various levels.[350] According to Article 4 of the Civil Service Law, the civil service system shall follow the basic premises of the primary stage of socialism; follow the party's line, guiding principles, and policies concerning cadres; and adhere to the principle of party control of cadres.[351] The article in effect provides party committees and their organizational departments at various levels with the legal authority to manage cadres.[352]

The party's authority over the government is based primarily on *nomenklatura* power: The central government, specifically CCP organs, appoints almost all of the leading positions in government and administration institutions, among them the top provincial officials.[353] This *nomenklatura* system is an instrument of party control.[354] It is therefore assured that government institutions principally follow party instructions when making decisions.[355] The percentage of cadres in the rank of ministers and deputy ministers that were CCP members in 1990 (97.3 percent) reveals the unity of party, state and civil service.[356] The Chinese bureaucracy has thus not been depoliticized as the bureaucracy in the East Asian developmental states.

3.2.2.2 Meritocratic recruitment

Public sector reforms have been considered by researchers and practitioners of economic development as one of the major factors contributing to successful economic development. Public sector reforms refer not only to market liberalization

---

349 Refer to Tong et al. (1999), p. 196 and Cooke (2003), p. 392.

350 Refer to Chan and Suizhou (2007), p. 390.

351 Ibidem.

352 For further information on the 2005 Civil Service Law and the effort to modernize China's state bureaucracy, refer to Chapter 3.2.2.2.

353 Refer to Huang (1996), p. 28.

354 Furthermore, e.g. directors of SOEs are at the same time party members and are appointed and recalled according to the cadre system by the party. Refer to Huang (1996), p. 89 and Breslin (1996), p. 697. Fur further readings regarding the Chinese *nomenklatura* system refer to Burns (1987, 1989b).

355 Refer to Heilmann (2002), p. 88.

356 The political influence on leadership cadres did not change throughout the reform period. In 1998, 97.7 percent of the mister level cadres were members of the CCP. Refer to Heilmann (2002), pp. 96-97.

and privatization, but also to reforms of the civil service system. For developing countries, public sector reforms are especially important, because the reforms need to emphasize efforts to promote professional values and norms on the one hand, and to reduce bureaucratic corruption and political influence on the other.[357]

As Evans and Rauch (2000) elaborate, making entry to the bureaucracy conditional on passing a civil service exam or attainment of a university degree, and paying salaries comparable to those for private positions requiring similar skills and responsibility, should produce a capable pool of officials. The stability provided by internal promotion allows the formation of stronger ties among them. This improves communication, and therefore effectiveness. When officials enter the bureaucracy on the basis of merit, performance is likely to be a valued attribute among them. The long-term career rewards generated by a system of internal promotion should reinforce adherence to codified rules of behavior. Ideally, a sense of commitment to corporate goals and "esprit de corps" develops.[358]

The Chinese transformation path has been characterized by strong economic growth under one-party monopoly.[359] For the time being, political liberalization toward representative democracy and the "rule of law" have been limited. Despite the deficiencies of political liberalization, China has benefited from a transformation of its bureaucratic system. Since the start of economic reform, administrative reform in the form of rebuilding and modernizing China's bureaucracy has been the government's priority. In 1979, Deng promulgated:

> *"If we want to do our work according to economic law, we should train people to act accordingly. [...] We have 18 million cadres but lack technical cadres, technicians, managerial staff, and other professionals."*[360]

When China entered the post-Mao reform period, procedures for recruitment, promotion and appraisal were vague, administrative proficiency low and the leadership aged throughout all ranks.[361] The bureaucracy's scant expertise became an obstacle to continued development along economic reforms in the late 1970s and 1980s. The government's ability to spur economic growth was decelerating and administrative corruption growing.[362] In order to promote the process of economic

---

357 For further information on the civil service system and its reforms refer to Burns (1989a, 1993); Cabestan (1992), Aufrecht and Li (1995), Liou (1997).

358 Refer to Evans and Rauch (2000), p. 52.

359 Refer to Li (1998), p. 393.

360 Deng (1979), "Some Comments on Economic Work", Internet Edition, reviewed 19.03.2006.

361 Refer to Nolan (1995b), p. 165 and Nee et al. (2007), p. 24. The decade-long tumultuous upheaval of Mao's Cultural Revolution had demoralized and crippled China's state apparatus.

362 Refer to Tsao and Worthley (1995), p. 169.

reform, the professionalization of the Chinese bureaucracy became essential.[363] In 1980, major changes in the Chinese bureaucracy were initiated.

While at the time of the Cultural Revolution political loyalty to the CCP and appropriate social class background were more important than expertise (borrowed from the Soviet Union in the 1950s), this changed dramatically in the post-Mao reforms. Political loyalty was emphasized, but it acquired adherence to the party's reform policies. Unqualified party officials in the government administration were retired, and political qualities and activities diminished as recruitment criteria.[364] New selection criteria of the bureaucracy emphasized not only competence, such as educational credentials, but also age.[365]

As a result of Deng's retirement policy, the leadership structure in various institutions and different ranks changed. While in 1980, only 36.2 percent of the leadership cadres[366] in the rank of ministers and deputy ministers had an academic degree, ten years later, 87.7 percent had one. In the same period, the average age dropped from 64 to 57.[367] In 1994, according to a national survey of 55,509 interviewed civil servants, civil servants from office staff to division chiefs had attended school for more than 11 years. Moreover, while the average age of division chiefs was 51 years in 1994, it was 57 in 1990 and 63 in 1980 (refer to Table 2).[368]

Table 2: Basic conditions of civil servants, 1994.

	Number of interviewed civil servants	Average wage (RMB)	Average years of education (year)	Average age (year)	Average seniority (year)	Average post-holding (year)
National	55,509	5,823	11.8	42.0	19.7	4.9
Division Chief	374	8,263	12.7	50.8	32.0	4.9
Section Chief	15,239	6,452	11.8	48.6	26.8	4.8
Office Staff	36,895	5,338	11.8	35.0	14.3	5.9

Source: China Statistical Yearbook (1996).

363 Qualified personnel was needed to e.g. make decisions about technology transfer and absorption, the expansion of foreign trade etc.

364 Refer to Howell (1991), p. 131 and Li (1998), p. 3 ff. For further information refer to Manion (1985) and Burns (1987).

365 Refer to Zhou (2001), p. 1042. Also refer to Deng (1979), "Some Comments on Economic Work", Internet Edition, and Deng (1992), "Excerpts From Talks Given in Wuchang, Shenzhen, Zhuhai and Shanghai", Internet Edition, both reviewed 19.03.2006. This effort parallels those of Bismarkian Germany and Meiji Japan in the late nineteenth century, or Taiwan and Korea in the 1950s, in which a key point of the modernisation drive was the creation of a professional government administration which was responsible to an unelected executive authority rather than to an elected parliament. Refer to Nolan (1993a), p. 77.

366 Leadership cadres are e.g. leading officials of country leadership level and above in organs of the CCP, the People's Congresses, the People's Governments, the Political Consultative Conference, the judical organs, the All-China Federation of Trade Unions, the Communist Youth League, the All-China Women's Federation, as well as other state-controlled associations. Refer to Heilmann and Kirchberger (2000), p. 12 and Li (1998), p. 394.

367 Refer to Heilmann (2002), p. 96.

368 Data for the years 1990 and 1980 are from Heilmann and Kirchberger (2000), p. 12.

The government officials' education, age and expertise further improved under Zhu Rongji's leadership.[369] In 1998, 99.1 percent of the leadership cadres (in the rank of ministers and deputy ministers) had a college-level education.[370] The average age of bureaucrats dropped further and bureaucrats shifted from revolutionary cadres to party technocrats (study field: engineering and natural sciences) whose representation rose dramatically in all high-level leadership categories.[371] Among ministers, provincial secretaries and governors as well as among central committee full members, more than 50 percent of the members were technocrats in 1997 (compared with less than 2 percent in 1982).[372] Provincial governors had the largest share of technocrats in 1997 (77 percent) (refer to Table 3).[373] The younger and better educated leaders were generally more supportive of reforms, more adaptable, and more pragmatic.

Table 3: Technocrats' representation in high-level leadership, 1982-1997.

	Ministers		Provincial Secretaries		Provincial Governors		Central Committee Full Members	
Year	No.	%	No.	%	No.	%	No.	%
1982	1	2	0	0	0	0	4	2
1987	17	45	7	25	8	33	34	26
1997	28	70	23	74	24	77	98	51

Source: Li (2001), p. 41.

In October 1993, the central government adopted the "Provisional Regulations on State Functionaries" (inaugurated in March 1994).[374] The central government officially defined civil servants as those 5.3 million cadres or administrators, managers and professionals who worked for government agencies.[375] The 1993 act intended to provide substantive advancement of routines, rationality and professionalism in the Chinese civil service. Chapter 1 articulated the intent of the Provisional Regulations:

369 Refer to Xia (2000), pp. 82-83 and Cooke (2003), pp. 389 ff.

370 Refer to Heilmann (2002), pp. 96-97.

371 The elite transformation from revolutionary veterans to technocrats during the post-Mao era has been the largest peaceful elite turnover in Chinese history. It is even the most massive, rapid change of elites within any regime in human history. Refer to Li (2001), p. 41. For further information refer to Fewsmith (2001a,b,c), Lee (1991), p. 268 and Lieberthal (1995), p. 236.

372 Among these were not only graduate students from China's prestigious universities, but also returned students from the Soviet Union, Eastern Europe and from the USA and other Western countries. Refer to Xia (2000), p. 82.

373 Refer to Li (2001), p. 41.

374 Permanent Mission of the People's Republic of China to the United Nations Office at Geneva and Other International Organizations in Switzerland (2005), "Building of Political Democracy in China", Internet Edition, reviewed 17.11.2006.

375 Refer to China Daily (2003), "Focus: China embarks on civil service reforms", Internet Edition, reviewed 23.03.2006.

> *"[T]o facilitate the scientific management of state functionaries, ensure honesty and enhance administrative efficiency"; "to the purpose of hiring people [...] to the principle of openness, equality, competition and selecting the best";* and *"that state functionaries perform their duties according to the law and be protected by the law".*[376]

The Provisional Regulations promulgated entry through open, competitive examinations and the civil service to be managed according to law. The regulations set forth strict and rule-governed performance guidelines with respect to appropriate conduct. The reform successfully attained its objective of regularizing performance reviews: over 96 percent of the civil servants underwent annual performance appraisals between 1994 and 1998.[377] The Provisional Regulations furthermore enforced public announcement of openings, reliance on scores in civil service examinations to recruit candidates, competitive examinations in routine promotions, and monitoring by the personnel department. All procedures were institutionalized at all levels of the national bureaucracy.[378] Yet, the selection of civil servants continued to be based on talent and virtue in terms of political and ideological values (*"hiring people with both political integrity and ability"*[379]), because the Provisional Regulations promulgated that the party and the state formed a single, integrated authority to which civil servants were politically responsive. No distinction was made between politicians and civil servants. Elected senior officials such as the Premier, Vice Premiers, State Councillors, Ministers and provincial Governors were also counted as civil servants.[380] Therefore, the civil service was still politicized to the extent that political loyalty was a criterion for selection.

The open selection of leading cadres was introduced gradually from coastal to inland areas, from local to central government departments and from section to department levels. Aspects of the open selection are open posts and requirements as well as open examination and public promulgation of results. Among commissions and ministries, examinations decide on the recruitment of new personnel.[381] From 1994

---

376 See Article 1, 2 and 4 of the Provisional Regulations on State Functionaries. Refer to Tsao and Worthley (1995), p. 170 and Tong et al. (1999), p. 197.

377 Refer to Chou (2005), pp. 45-46.

378 Refer to Nee and Opper (2007), p. 98.

379 See Article 2 of the Provisional Regulations on State Functionaries. Refer to Tsao and Worthley (1995), p. 170 and Tong et al. (1999), p. 197.

380 Refer to China Daily (2003), "Focus: China embarks on civil service reforms", Internet Edition, reviewed 23.03.2006.

381 The Ministry of Personnel for reference held a recruitment examination for 22 central level ministries and public corporations, including the Ministry of Agriculture and the State Statistics Bureau in March 1991. These administrative organs selected 280 from about 10,000 candidates. By late 1990, 35 ministries or commissions of the State Council staffed 70 percent of their vacant positions through examination. Moreover, until 1993, 61 ministries or commissions and their subordinated organizations of the State Council, and 29 provinces, regions and municipalities recruited 67,000 state civil service cadres out of 440,000 plus applicants through recruitment with examinations. Refer to Liu (2001), p. 131.

until 2003, China employed more than 700,000 civil servants from 2.4 million candidates through the annual civil service examinations.[382] Party and government institutions have also taken competition as the main form for the promotion of cadres since 1998. In 2002, about 180,000 government officials were promoted and filled posts via competition, making up 59.8 percent of the total cadres promoted in that year.[383]

Salaries are one component of attracting the best skilled to jobs in the state sector. In the East Asian developmental states, the positions of bureaucrats were the best paid compared with the ones in the business sector. In China, the well-educated had several job opportunities due to the country's integration with the global economy. Lower-paid government jobs were no longer the most attractive.[384] While government administrative cadres were the highest paid of all occupation groups in the mid-1950s, jobs in the private sector (particularly those that require higher education such as a master degree) had become better paid than jobs in government organs until 1994.[385] According to survey results published in the China Statistical Yearbook (1996), among 8,050 interviewees at the rank of division chief, the average monthly wage in enterprises was Renminbi (RMB) 8,718 and in government organs RMB 8,283 in 1994. The wage difference between enterprises and government organizations becomes clear when grouped according to educational background: the interviewed persons who had a master degree (n=258) stated to earn RMB 9,538 in an enterprise, and RMB 6,138 in a government organ. The same applies to section chiefs and office staff, as well as to bachelor and college graduates (refer to Table 4). However, civil servants enjoy insurance and welfare benefits in addition to their salary. The state implements a labor insurance system to provide material aid to civil servants who have temporarily or permanently lost the ability to work. Civil servants are also granted benefits in free medical service, pay during sickness and maternity leave, home-visiting holiday and welfare subsidies, as well as pension and compensation payment.[386] Furthermore, secure permanent employment by the state as well as high social status serve as incentives for a career within the civil service.[387] Accordingly, the state has been able to employ well educated civil servants, despite lower remuneration.

382 Alone in Jiangxi Province, more than 600 people nationwide applied to participate in an open recruitment examination for the posts of 13 deputy directors of various provincial government departments, and 114 of them applied for the post of the deputy director of the provincial party committee's policy research office in 1999. Refer to Mu (2001), pp. 20-21 and People's Daily (2003), "Exam-based Civil Service Prevails in China", Internet Edition, reviewed 03.10.2006.

383 People's Daily (2003), "Promotion Through Competition – A Major Way for Party & Government Officials", Internet Edition, reviewed 03.10.2006.

384 Refer to Zheng (1997), p. 214.

385 This is based on net income of fixed salaries.

386 Refer to China Gate (n.d.), "The System of Civil Servant", Internet Edition, reviewed 13.07.2007.

387 Refer to Nee and Opper (2007), p. 99 and Chan and Suizhou (2007), p. 395 ff.

Moreover, in the Chinese bureaucratic system, the duration of a bureaucrat's tenure has been reduced.[388] Rotation and turnovers are indirect mechanisms that serve the functions of simultaneously overcoming information imperfections and maintaining controls in the country's large and complex political system. Educated and well-trained civil servants combined with rule-governed performance guidelines such as public announcements of open positions, annual performance reviews and competitive examinations (affirmed by the Civil Service Law of 2005) have gradually improved the transparency and predictability of regulations and helped the implementation of economic reform.[389]

Table 4: Monthly wage levels in enterprises and government organizations, 1994.

	Number of civil servants interviewed		Average wage (RMB)	
	Enterprises	Government Organs	Enterprises	Government Organs
Grouped by post				
Division Chief	4,676	3,374	8,718	8,283
Section Chief	18,105	15,239	7,540	6,452
Office Staff	43,131	36,895	6,185	5,338
Grouped by educational background				
Master	105	153	9,538	6,138
Bachelor	6,011	5,293	7,782	6,048
College Graduates	17,213	19,197	6,883	5,711

Source: China Statistical Yearbook (1996).

Notwithstanding national reform measures, the quality of the Chinese civil service is characterized by a high degree of geographical heterogeneity. The development between provinces, autonomous regions and municipalities is uneven. In the center and in the richer coastal areas, civil servants are usually selected by meritocratic recruitment, rewards are linked to their performance, and corruption is controlled and pursued by the judiciary. In the 2006 World Competitiveness Yearbook, the IMD ranked Zhejiang province 17th out of 61 countries and economic regions worldwide with regard to bureaucratic efficiency - ahead of China's overall average (rank 35).[390] In the less developed hinterland, however, not only position and organization determine political power, but also prestige and seniority, as well as loyalty of protégés and clever political manipulation.[391] Thus, formal power of meritocratic party- or ministry-positions is often undermined by informal hierarchies of influence.

---

388 Tenure in top provincial positions typically is shorter than the mandated term of office for those positions. Refer to Huang (1996), p. 115 ff and Lieberthal (1997), p. 6.

389 Refer to Nee and Opper (2007), pp. 97-98.

390 Refer to IMD World Competitiveness Yearbook (2006), Survey question 2.3.15 (*"Does bureaucracy hinder/not hinder business activity?"*), p. 376.

391 Refer to Heilmann (2002), p.57.

As the civil service sometimes operates as an "employer of last resort", such provinces exhibit relatively high levels of indiscipline and corruption among its bureaucrats.[392]

To sum up, unlike the East Asian developmental states, there is no separation between the CCP and the state, and furthermore no separation between the state and the bureaucracy, as civil servants are usually party cadres. On the basis of the *nomenklatura* system, important bureaucratic positions are filled by CCP members that exert a control system over all levels. Thus, clear depolitization as in the East Asian developmental states cannot be found in China. The roles of politicians and bureaucrats have been fused. Similar to the East Asian developmental states, in the reform period, the average age of civil servants has been reduced and the average years of education increased through meritocratic recruitment. This new group of officials was eager and able to steer economic reforms.[393] This resembles the practices of the East Asian developmental states, where the elite bureaucrats were graduates of the top universities. However, party- or ministry-positions are still often filled according to network and loyalty systems.

3.2.3 A Chinese pilot agency?

Developmental statists attribute the success of governments in achieving economic growth and industrial transformation to the quality of the bureaucracy in general, and to the developmental states' powerful and autonomous pilot agencies in particular. The most powerful was the Japanese MITI, which served Korea and Taiwan as a benchmark model. The developmental states' pilot agencies had the overall responsibility of managing industry, including planning and financing, as well as domestic and foreign trade. There were no industrial ministries and industrial bureaus.[394] In the East Asian developmental states, top-down industrial planning was pursued with a high degree of independence of the elite bureaucrats to realize

---

392 While the importance of *school and blood ties* diminishes gradually, school and blood ties were important aspects of the recruitment and promotion of civilian and military elites during the reform era. Qinghua University could be regarded as China's leading engineering school and was known as the *"cradle of technocrats"*. Graduates of Qinghua University occupied a significant portion of top party and state leadership posts. Li (2001) contends *"belonging to an elite university network is even far more essential for politicians than having an elite university degree"*. Not only school ties, but also blood ties (e.g. being the child of a high-ranking official) were important for the career advancement of elite cadres: The children or relatives of veteran elite cadres of the CCP and the army are called "party princelings". They usually graduate from elite universities and are part of a tight network of other princelings of these universities. They advanced quickly with the help of their parents or their parents' comrades in arms. As during the nineties, many princelings had political or economic leading positions in the coastal areas, political resistance to the careers of the princelings became manifested. Refer to Li (2001), p. 16 ff and p. 82 ff and Heilmann (2002), pp. 59-60. Also refer to OECD (2006a), p. 28.

393 Refer to Shirk (1993), p. 64.

394 Refer to Unger and Chan (1995), p. 42.

industrial policy. Unlike the East Asian developmental states, in its strategic approach to economic development and interaction with the business sector, China's central government relies on various agencies.

3.2.3.1 The State Planning Commission and its successors

Among the various commissions, it was the State Planning Commission which came closest to an East Asian pilot agency in the reform period.[395] The "Outline of State Industrial Policies for the 1990s" confirmed the planning institutions of the Mao era in office. The outline prescribed that national industrial policy is decided by the State Council and that the State Planning Commission was the government agency responsible for the promulgation and harmonization of national industrial policies (five-year and annual plans).[396] On the basis of the "Outline of State Industrial Policies", the State Planning Commission promulgated a series of industrial policies for different sectors. It approached its task from a long-term, strategic and comprehensive viewpoint which meshed with the state's long-term interests.[397] It concentrated solely on macro-economic coordination instead of micro-managing the economy and specific industries. The State Planning Commission was mainly responsible for general overseeing and forecasting long-term policies for the national economy.[398] The implementation of various industrial policies was carried out by the administrative agencies of different industries. The government agencies responsible for economic management had to coordinate with the State Planning Commission before adopting any important policy measures which would influence industrial development.[399]

The State Planning Commission also guided and organized the production and distribution of commodities. It controlled the production level and allocation of goods which were considered crucial for national economic growth (such as petroleum, electricity, cement and steel). Through its control of bank credits and prices it could influence material supplies, and thus the growth rate of industrial sectors. The State Planning Commission provided financing for domestic projects according to its national industrial plan, and the Construction Bank released investment funds accordingly. The State Planning Commission, however, was not primarily responsible for assuring that the government in fact had sufficient funds or supplies to cover the cost of the projects in the plan. These tasks fell instead to the Material Supply Bureau and the Ministry of Finance. The latter did not always agree with the State Planning

---

395 Refer to Lieberthal and Oksenberg (1988), p. 64.

396 Refer to State Council of China (1994), "Outline of State Industrial Policies for the 1990s", Internet Edition, reviewed 31.03.2006. For further information refer to Wang and Fewsmith (1995), p. 52.

397 Refer to Lieberthal and Oksenberg (1988), p. 64.

398 Refer to Xia (2000), p. 86.

399 Economic management includes planning, public financing, central banking, taxation, international and domestic trade, tariff, securities market regulation, administration of industry and commerce as well as state-owned asset management.

Commission over investment levels. Meetings between these two ministries to coordinate their decisions were often needed.[400]

The State Planning Commission also played a crucial role in selecting which of the numerous proposed capital construction projects were accepted and acted upon. In considering new investments, the State Planning Commission determined not only the size of investment funds but also their overall geographical and sectoral distributions. It also decided on major JVs and key projects in the economy. As a supra-ministerial body, it directed the activities of a range of ministries and other bodies in bringing new projects to fruition.[401]

In the energy sector,[402] the State Planning Commission formulated mid-term and long-term energy plans that included construction, production and conservation; it decided which projects to construct, conducted appropriate technical and other feasibility studies and determined the project's size, its speed of development and the year in which each effort should begin; and it coordinated the actual construction of energy-related projects. The planning effort itself required that the State Planning Commission forecast future energy supplies and demands, both sectorally and geographically. The Ministry of Coal Industry and the Ministry of Water Resources and Electric Power planned the development of their sectors separately. However, since most of China's electricity was generated in coal-fired thermal plants, the development of both sectors had to be closely coordinated, based on the future need for electricity. The State Planning Commission performed this task of coordination.[403]

The State Planning Commission relied on the line ministries and the provincial bodies to generate most requests for new projects, and to buttress those requests. These requests were part of the plans that each of the four energy-sector line ministries (Ministry of Coal Industry, Ministry of Petroleum Industry, Ministry of Water Resources and Electric Power, and Ministry of Nuclear Industry) and the provinces submitted to the State Planning Commission. The plans were supposed to be based on the broad guidelines for long-term development promulgated by the State Planning Commission. However, most of the times requests exceeded the country's capacities for new construction. Thus, the State Planning Commission had to determine which proposals were desireable and both technically and economically feasible.[404] The State Planning Commission finally drew upon an overall balance based on repeated consultations with the ministries and provinces in the process of

400 Refer to Lieberthal and Oksenberg (1988), p. 64 and pp. 69-70.

401 Refer to Wang and Fewsmith (1995), p. 61 ff.

402 The energy sector is taken as an example to illustrate the functions of the State Planning Commission. It is representative for other sectors.

403 Refer to Lieberthal and Oksenberg (1988), pp. 64-66.

404 Ibidem, pp. 67- 68.

turning their aspirations into a national plan.[405] When the draft of the final plan was completed, it was sent to the State Council for approval.[406]

After the Ninth National People's Congress in March 1998, along with the restructuring of government, which included a radical retrenchment of government organizations and employees both at the central and local levels,[407] the State Planning Commission (which was always resistant to marketization)[408] was renamed State Development Planning Commission.[409] The commission's new name indicates the weakened function of state planning and the increased importance of state-coordinated development along economic structural reform. The State Development Planning Commission's members often included the ministers from the Ministry of Finance, the Ministry of Labor, the State Commission of Science, the President of the People's Bank of China and the directors of the State Bureau of Statistics and the State Bureau of Prices. It issued directives to the ministries and provinces and was the most powerful and most comprehensive Chinese economic policy-making organ of its time like its predecessor the State Planning Commission.[410] Even during the process of marketization it did not lose its relevance to the Chinese national economy.

Despite its influence, the State Development Planning Commission's power was limited and its macro-economic control restricted. Hence, it never reached the status

405 Coordination and construction was a critical task because all ministries have the same rank and therefore do not have formal leverage over each other. It requires either the State Council itself or a commission, which is higher than a ministry, to make various ministries and provinces (which have the same bureaucratic rank) coordinate their efforts.

406 In general, the State Council in turn submits it to the National People's Congress for examination and approval. This gives the plan a legal character.

407 In March 1998, the number of ministries was cut from from 40 to 29 in order to concentrate "power" in a few agencies with broad authority. Moreover, in order to turn SOEs into independent legal entities, with operation mostly in the hands of professional managers, many of the ministries that managed industries were abolished. The abolished functions of the former ministries were overseen by the State Economics and Trade Commission. Refer to Lan (1999), p. 30, Unger and Chan (1995), p. 42 and Zhu (2003), p. 157.

408 The State Planning Commission was established in 1952, according to the Soviet model of the centrally planned economy. Planning theory, planning methods, planning content and planning organizations were all copied; even the planning tables were imported from the Soviet Union. As the organization charged with overall control of the planned economy, the State Planning Commission had a strong institutional interest in resisting, deflecting, and enervating the market-oriented reform policies put forth by reform-minded leaders. Refer to Wang and Fewsmith (1995), p. 52.

409 Refer to Ministry of Science and Technology (1998), "Reform Program for State Council Departments", Internet Edition, reviewed 22.01.2007.

410 Often, the State Development Planning Commission was referred to as "the Little State Council". Refer to Wang and Fewsmith (1995), p. 52.

of a pilot agency like the MITI in Japan.[411] The State Development Planning Commission had to consult with the Ministry of Finance over the annual budget plans and long-term financial balances and with the Ministry of Foreign Trade and Economic Cooperation[412] for the foreign trade balance.[413] In addition, in order to determine the national industrial plan, the State Development Planning Commission had to coordinate closely with the State Economics and Trade Commission, which traditionally served as a counterweight to the State Development Planning Commission.[414] The State Economics and Trade Commission was concerned less with long-term planning and more with coordinating day-to-day enterprise operations. The State Development Planning Commission's responsibility was furthermore restricted as it had to pass on large-scale projects to the State Council for decision. In addition, China's decentralized economic management limited the State Development Planning Commission's power. Due to the system of bottom-up planning, the State Development Planning Commission simply aggregated requests from different ministries. Furthermore, the projects that were below a certain scale could be initiated by the line ministries or local governments without item approval by the State Development Planning Commission. Thus, the State Development Planning Commission was only one part of a large web of organizational relationships.[415]

In 2003, the State Development Planning Commission was transformed into the NDRC. With the new name, the State Council eliminated the word "planning", which indicates a further renunciation of planning mechanisms in favor of market mechanisms. The NDRC took over the major functions of its predecessor, and was assigned new responsibilities along with overall government reorganization.

411 Refer to Huang (2002a), p. 553.

412 The Ministry of Foreign Trade and Cooperation was the Ministry of Economic Relations and Trade before 1993. The Ministry of Economic Relations and Trade was established in March 1982.

413 Refer to Lieberthal and Oksenberg (1988), pp. 64-65.

414 The State Economics and Trade Commission was the "final incarnation" of a body that has existed throughout most of the reform period (indeed, throughout much of the history of the People's Republic of China), namely, the State Economic Commission. The State Economic Commission pleaded for expanded enterprise rights and autonomy, and thus became a force in favor of industrial reforms during the 1980s. The State Economic Commission was merged with the State Planning Commission, but subsequently separated again under a variety of different names, including the State Economics and Trade Commission in the late 1990s. Refer to Naughton (2003a), p. 4.

415 Refer to Huang (2002a), p. 553-554 and Lieberthal and Oksenberg (1988), p. 65.

3.2.3.2 Streamlined government structure

In March 2003, following the 10th National People's Congress, China restructured its key economic ministries.[416] The State Council scrapped the approval formalities on more than 1,000 items since China's entry into the WTO and thus loosened its grip on the economy.[417] Unlike the reform of 1998, which mainly focused on downsizing, the reform of 2003 (refer to Figure 8) intended to reduce the overlap of the government departments' responsibilities, strengthen the coordination between them, and define the scope of their duties.

Figure 8: The restructuring of government in 2003.

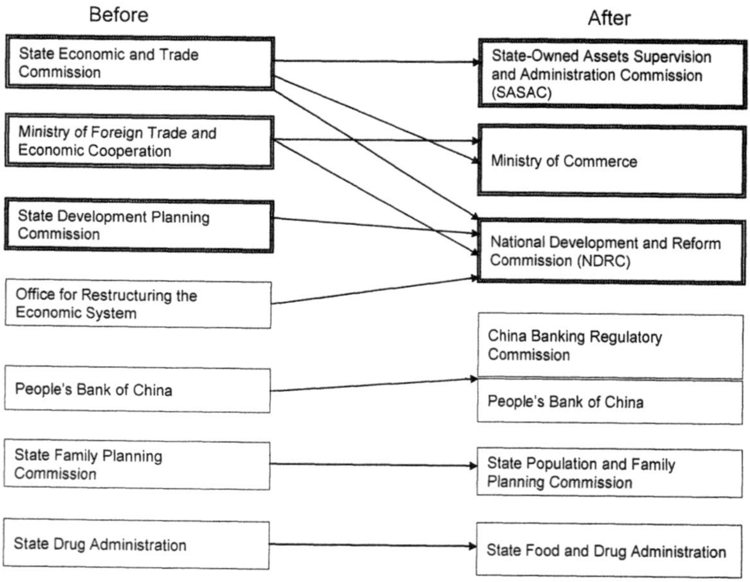

Source: Fan and Zhang (2003), p. 30.

The three most important reorganizations (illustrated in Figure 8), that aimed to increase the government's efficiency in line with the market system and China's WTO accession, are:

---

416 Refer to Ministry of Commerce (2004), "Analysis on the Current Situation of Government Management System Adapting Itself to the Market Economy", Internet Edition, reviewed 23.03.2006.

417 Refer to Fan and Zhang (2003), pp. 28-29.

- *Bundling different functions in the NDRC:* The NDRC took on the duties of the State Council Office for Economic Restructuring and some functions of the State Economics and Trade Commission and the Ministry of Foreign Trade and Economic Cooperation.[418] The NDRC is the macro-economic regulatory department under the State Council. It reports on the national economy and social development to the National People's Congress and guides the overall economic system restructuring. The NDRC was established in order to improve macroeconomic control by merging the functions of development and reform. It has the sole authority for the planning and implementation of industrial policy in order to accelerate the move from interventionist to vision-based industrial policy.[419]
- *Creation of the State*-owned Assets *Supervision and Administration Commission (SASAC):* According to the "Interim Regulations on Supervision and Management of State-owned Assets of Enterprises" (2003), the SASAC was created as a special ministerial level institution directly under the State Council.[420] Its establishment represented a departure from the previous situation, where multiple government ministries and other bureaucratic entities had a say in state-owned enterprises' (SOEs) daily operations.[421] SASAC is responsible for the micro-economic coordination and regulation of the big domestic state-owned companies.[422]

---

418 Refer to NDRC (2007), "Main Functions of the NDRC", Internet Edition, reviewed 16.01.2007.

419 Refer to Ken'ichi (2003), p. 2.

420 Refer to SASAC (2007), "Main Functions and Responsibilities of SASAC", Internet Edition, reviewed 16.01.2007 and to SASAC (2003), Decree of the State Council of the People's Republic of China, No. 378, "Interim Regulations on Supervision and Management of State-owned Assets of Enterprises", Internet Edition, reviewed 23.03.2006.

421 The Ministry of Finance was responsible for the administration of capital, for example, the definition and registration of property rights of state assets and the supervision of state asset evaluations and transactions, along with the supervision of revenue collection. The Special Inspector's Commission was responsible for financial auditing. The State Economics and Trade Commission and the State Development Planning Commission were responsible for the supervision and control of enterprises' business activities, including financing, investment, the sale of assets and internal restructuring. Refer to Tenev et al. (2002), p. 27 and Fernandez-Stembridge and Huchet (2006), p. 32-33 and Taube (2005), p. 4.

422 Its task is to separate the government's functions as investor and owner of state assets from its function as the public manager of society as a whole. In particular, SASAC was created as an instrument to address the problems of debt-ridden SOEs, which by then represented almost 200,000 companies worth about RMB 10 trillion. As of mid-2006, it oversaw a portfolio of 165 of the biggest and centrally controlled SOEs – including those involved in critical sectors of the economy such as telecommunications, civil aviation, oil, steel and auto manufacturers – with combined assets of about RMB 6 trillion. The overseeing of all remaining SOEs was left to local state-asset organizations. Refer to SASAC (2003), "China State-owned Assets Management System Reform Entering New Stage", Internet Edition, reviewed 23.03.2006. For further information refer to Fernandez-Stembridge and Huchet (2006), p. 33 and Xinhuanet (2006), "Rule will require SOEs to submit dividends to government", Internet Edition, reviewed 03.10.2006.

- *Establishment of the Ministry of Commerce:* Some of the functions of the State Economics and Trade Commission[423] and the Ministry of Foreign Trade and Economic Cooperation were combined in a new agency, the Ministry of Commerce.[424] In addition, functions of the former State Development Planning Commission were integrated. After China's entry into the WTO, some of the functions of the Ministry of Foreign Trade and Economic Cooperation have become less important or even futile. The Ministry of Commerce was established to reduce the overlap of responsibilities between the departments that used to oversee foreign and domestic trade regulations, and thus to increase administrative efficiency. For instance, the State Economics and Trade Commission originally determined whether foreign imports had harmed domestic firms, and the Ministry of Foreign Trade and Economic Cooperation determined whether anti-dumping or safeguarding measures would be implemented. These two functions relevant to China's WTO accession were to be combined into one ministry.[425] The Ministry of Commerce shares its responsibility for FDI-related policies with the NDRC.

The assignment of tasks to various commissions and ministries shows that China has no pilot agency in the sense of the Japanese MITI. Although each ministry and commission is responsible for a special sector, they have to work closely together. Economic policy-making, and particularly the implementation of industrial policies, is organized along different central level commissions and ministries, and along central and local-level state institutions.[426] The developmental states were far more centralized, and policy functions were entirely carried out by the elite bureaucracy of the pilot agency. Although the State Planning Commission and its successors can be regarded as the most influential superministry throughout the reform period, authority has been fragmented by function, territory and rank.[427]

New policy initiatives affect various bureaucratic officials with vaguely defined and sometimes overlapping jurisdictions, conflicting interests, and complex, distinct structures of authority.[428] In addition, the decentralized structure of the Chinese bureaucracy has intensified the need for coordination among bureaucratic agencies in Beijing.[429] A number of functions of an East Asian pilot agency are performed by

423 As the industrial ministries were abolished in 1998, the State Economics and Trade Commission took over most of their remaining functions. Refer to Naughton (2003a), p. 4.

424 Refer to Ministry of Commerce (2007), "Mission - Main Mandate of the Ministry of Commerce", Internet Edition, reviewed 15.01.2007.

425 Refer to Fan and Zhang (2003), p. 30.

426 In a system with multiple principals, monitoring costs are likely higher, because of co-ordination costs. Refer to Kassim and Menon (2003), p. 124. Also refer to McCubbins et al. (1989).

427 Refer to Lieberthal (1997), p. 4.

428 For further information refer to Lampton (1987a, 1987b), Lieberthal (1991, 1992, 1995, 1997) and Lieberthal and Oksenberg (1988).

429 Refer to Shirk (1985), pp. 216-217.

local leaders at each level of government.[430] According to Singh (1992), policy-making institutions are fragmented and proliferation of independent policies at the various levels of government is common.[431] This questions the capacity of the central state and its autonomy to implement a coherent economic reform policy during its transition.

The fragmented structure of authority means that it is often necessary to achieve consensus among several bureaucratic bodies.[432] If policies are to move forward, all involved agencies have to be consulted and supportive.[433] In the telecom sector, to give an example, at least ten organizations (including the Ministry of Information Industry and the Ministry of State Security) retain a regulatory stake regarding telecom decisions.[434] Key decisions are therefore often the result of a series of reinforcing compromises made in a number of loosely co-ordinated decision-making bodies over a long period.[435] The consequence is that any major project or policy requires a gradual and protracted process of consensus and alliance building among competing bureaucracies at each level to gain support both vertically and horizontally in the bureaucratic system.

3.3 State

Johnson (1987) contends that industrial policy can be distinguished from general economic policy by *"its penetration to the micro-level, meaning government attempts to influence economic sectors [...], whole industries [...] and individual enterprises within industries".*[436] Industrial strategists maintain that industrial policy and selective state intervention ("picking winners") is necessary to enable industries in developing countries to gain dynamic efficiency in the sense of achieving international competitiveness within a reasonable period of time. International competitiveness is achieved when these industries can compete in international markets without state support. Successful state intervention promotes infant industries and rationalizes industries that encounter difficulties in competing. The role of government is to improve the technological capability of firms by moving them down their learning curve.[437]

---

430 This is further elaborated in Chapter 3.3.2.

431 Refer to Singh (1992), p. 101.

432 Literature on "fragmented authoritarianism focuses on the shift from bureaucratic central command through the planning apparatus to interunit bargaining in economic governance. Refer to Lieberthal and Oksenberg (1988), pp. 22-23, Lieberthal (1995), p. 169, Hamrin and Zhao (1995), p. xxvii, Lieberthal (1992), p. 2 ff and Heilmann (2004), p. 64.

433 For further information refer to Zhao (1995).

434 Refer to Pearson (2006), p. 18.

435 For further information refer to Lieberthal and Oksenberg (1988).

436 Refer to Johnson (1987), p. 159.

437 For further information refer to Pack and Westphal (1986) and Poulson (1994), p. 388 ff.

3.3.1 Industrial policy

Like the East Asian developmental states, the Chinese government applies industrial policy to promote economic development by readjusting the industrial structure and the product mix and helping to improve the competitive standing of Chinese firms.[438] Industrial policy - measures that favor one or more industries (or firms) over others - can take a range of forms, such as export subsidies and preferential loans. The positive example of the East Asian developmental states and their execution of industrial policy in the form of selective state intervention have influenced China's industrial policy-making. The Chinese government has instrumentalized industrial policy (which was close to planning in the command economy) in order to maintain extensive competencies of economic planning and intervention, at least temporarily. In consequence, not only has change of demand been responsible for structural transformation, but also economic policy measures of the CCP. Direct intervention in the market mechanism, and also the time and sequence of the reform process, have influenced structural adjustment processes.[439]

Chinese leaders' commitment to economic openness in combination with strong state intervention has continued throughout the reform period.[440] Central authorities still continue to issue five-year and single-year plans which cover strategically important aspects of the Chinese economy. With these policies, the central government aims to develop industry, guide foreign investment and foreign trade, and establish large enterprise groups. The first explicit and detailed official guideline for a national industrial policy was the "Decision on the Gist of Current Industrial Policy" that the State Council issued in 1989.[441] The decision testifies the central government's ambitions to guide the process of modernization and correction of China's industry structure. The Eighth Five-Year Plan (1991-1995) also confirmed the central role of industrial policy for economic development. The plan contends:

> *"[Industrial] planning plays the major role in setting targets for economic growth, controlling total supply and demand, readjusting economic structure and geographical distribution of major sectors of the economy, and controlling other important economic activities. [...] Most production activities and operations in enterprises, ordinary technological upgrading and small-scale construction projects are to be regulated by market forces."*[442]

438 Refer to Rosen (1992), p. 79.

439 Refer to Opper (1999), p. 69.

440 Refer to Unger and Chan (1995), p. 32 and Zhu (2003), p. 157.

441 Refer to Zhang and Long (1997), pp. 264-265 and Lu (2000a), p. 356.

442 Li (1991), "Report on the Outline of the Ten-Year Program and of the Eighth Five-Year Plan for National Economic and Social Development", p. XVII.

The scope and role of planning substantially changed during the reform era. In the Eighth Five-Year Plan, the central government confirmed its ambition to combine *"the planned economy with market regulation"* and gradually replace mandatory plans of the Mao era by guidance plans.[443] The central government used *"economic, administrative and legal means, especially price control, taxation, interest rates and exchange rates"* to promote economic development.[444] The state's responsibility to govern resource allocation by economic-political interventions arises from the central government's mistrust of the functioning of markets. Its intervention aims to induce changes of the production structure necessary for economic transformation. The CCP's and the central government's legitimacy are thus based on the assumption that government intervention in the form of industrial policy is a necessary precondition for economic transformation. The CCP's legitimation of power could thus be retained and even strengthened.[445]

In 1993, after Deng's "Southern Inspection Tour",[446] the National People's Congress issued an amendment to the Constitution of the People's Republic of China, promulgating the "socialist market economy".[447] The emphasis of the "Decision of the CCP Central Committee on Some Issues Concerning the Establishment of a Socialist Market Economic Structure" [448] was on the changing role of the government from a central planning and controlling function for a planned economy to a supporting role for a market economy, but without losing its function as a regulator.[449]

With the promulgation of the socialist market economy, the central leaders emphasized their intention to transform the economic system by an unprecedented path of development, and promulgated a new version of the market economy,

---

443 Ibidem, p. XVII.

444 Ibidem, p. XVI.

445 Refer to Opper (1999), p. 74.

446 Along his tour Deng recommended that China should learn from the Asian four little dragons and proceed in its transformation path. Refer to Deng (1992), "Excerpts From Talks Given in Wuchang, Shenzhen, Zhuhai and Shanghai", Internet Edition, reviewed 19.03.2006.

447 Refer to National People's Congress, "Constitution of the People's Republic of China", Amendment Two, Approved on 29.03.1993 by the 8th NPC at its 1st Session. In his political report to the congress, Jiang Zemin, General Secretary of the CCP, stated that *"the objective of the reform of the economic structure will be to establish a socialist market economy that will further liberate and expand the productive forces."* Beijing Review (1992), "Party Congress Introduces Market Economy", p. 6.

448 In November 1993, the CCP passed the "Decision of the CCP Central Committee on Some Issues Concerning the Establishment of a Socialist Market Economic Structure". Refer to Beijing Review (1992), "Party Congress Introduces Market Economy", pp. 5-6 and Li (1993), "Report on the Work of the Government", p. VIII.

449 Refer to Cooke (2003), pp. 388-389.

namely a "socialist" one.[450] The socialist market economy incorporates aspects of a planned economy as well as market regulations which correspond to the East Asian developmental states (market regulations under the rule of a strong state). The State Council confirmed in 1993, that *"state planning"* was *"an essential means of macro-control"* in order to *"optimize the economic structure".*[451] In a country that detaches itself from socialism, state intervention is needed in order to build new, capitalist institutions and regulations and abandon the central planning institutions of the pre-reform era.[452] The state's economic policies intended to shape the macro incentive structure that firms in the economy face.

With the "Outline of State Industrial Policies for the 1990s", which was promulgated by the State Council in 1994, the central government confirmed that industrial policy remains an important instrument of economic policy:

> *"The formulation of industrial policies is to work as one of the important means of the state in its strive to strengthen and improve macro-economic control, effectively adjust and optimize the industrial structure, improve the quality of industries and promote a sustainable, fast and healthy development of the national economy [...]."*[453]

Unlike industrial policy in the 1980s and early 1990s, which lacked clear priorization of industries (the 1989 Decision specified solely in the category "encouraged production" more than 200 products without order of priority),[454] the 1994 Outline of State Industrial Policies focused on priority industries and key enterprises. Similar to the East Asian developmental states, the outline emphasized to accelerate the development of "pillar industries" which were to promote national economic

[450] A major shift in ideology underpins the reforms, with the CCP moving from a dogmatic emphasis on the Maoist version of Marxism-Leninism to a pragmatic, market-oriented approach with its emphasis on "establishing a unified and open market system". Although the rhetoric on socialism and the dominance of the public sector have been retained, the staunch anti-market, anti-private initiative, anti-private gain focus has been removed. Since then property reforms in the state-sector have accelerated. Moreover, the central government emphasized that in the socialist market economy prices are set by the marketplace and public ownership dominates but coexists with private ownership. Indeed, in 1992, the government freed the prices of 600 industrial producer goods. Refer to National People's Congress (1982), "Constitution of the People's Republic of China", Article 6, Internet Edition, reviewed 11.09.2006 and Chinese Government (2005), "Economic System", Internet Edition, reviewed 28.03.2006. For further information refer to Montionola and Weingast (1995), p. 52, Qin (2004), p. 872 and Yusuf et al. (2006), p. 70.

[451] Refer to Li (1993), "Report on the Work of the Government", p. X.

[452] Refer to Nee and Opper (2007), p. 93.

[453] State Council (1994), "Outline of State Industrial Policies for the 1990s", Implementation, Internet Edition, reviewed 31.03.2006.

[454] Refer to Li (1996), "Report on the Outline of the Ninth Five-Year Plan for National Economic and Social Development and the Long-Range Objectives to the Year 2010", pp. I-XVI. For further information refer to Opper (1999), p. 85 and Singh (1992), p. 1 ff.

development. These include the machinery industry, the electronic industry, petroleum processing and the raw chemical materials industry, the auto industry and the construction industry. Growth of the pillar industries was promoted through government funds and preferential access to resources and materials.[455] The central government allowed large enterprise groups to directly raise funds abroad. Products of the pillar industries were declared as *"infant industrial products"* and protected from international competition through quotas and tariffs. The central government moreover declared it would open part of the domestic market so that companies in the pillar industries were able to import needed technology and equipment.[456] In this regard, the central government used the same policy instruments to promote selected industries with the aim of increasing their international competitiveness.[457]

In order to strengthen market mechanisms, in the Ninth Five-Year Plan (1996-2000), the central government replaced guidance plans, that included enterprise-specific requirements, by indicative plans, that set general goals and suggestions.[458] In the plan, the CCP completely gave up formulating detailed planning targets, but provided an overview of the expected developments of particular sectors and businesses.[459] Already in 1993, the proportion of the mandatory industrial production plan in total industrial output value, under the charge of the State Planning Commission, dropped from 12 percent to 7 percent.[460] Since then, plans have mostly formulated development goals and informed economic agents on economic developments that have been envisioned by the CCP and the central government. Nonetheless, through five-year plans, the central government continues to exert impact on the top management of China's leading enterprises.[461]

In its "Report on the Outline of the Tenth Five-Year Plan for National Economic and Social Development (2001-2005)", the Chinese government confirmed its support for the declared pillar industries.[462] Unlike former five-year plans, in the Tenth Five-Year Plan the government no longer supervised all matters, but focused its attention on

455 Refer to State Council (1994), "Outline of State Industrial Policies for the 1990s", Chapter III, Internet Edition, reviewed 31.03.2006. For further information refer to Zhu (2003), p. 150 and Oi (1999), pp. 117-118.

456 Ibidem, Chapter IV.

457 State promotion of selected sectors is further elaborated in Chapter 3.3.3.

458 Refer to Opper (1999), p. 70 and Taube (2005), p. 3.

459 Refer to Kennedy (2005), p. 47.

460 Also materials distributed under the unified state plan decreased from prereform figures of 256 kinds to 19 kinds. State planning control was manifested mainly in the examination and approval of investment projects, the use of foreign exchange as well as the planned distribution of bank loans. Refer to Su (1993), p. 110.

461 Refer to Taube (2005), p. 3.

462 Refer to NDRC (2006), "Strengthen the Integration of Science, Technology and Economy Enhance Independent Innovation Capability", Internet Edition, reviewed 18.12.2006.

working out development strategies and plans.[463] The Tenth Five-Year Plan became simpler and shorter. The number of indices of the Tenth Five-Year Plan was reduced to 39 from 105 in the Ninth Five-Year Plan, and with only 1,500 characters devoted to industry.[464] The Tenth Five-Year Plan stressed market requirements, and attached greater importance to the efficiency of economic development.[465] The Tenth Five-year Plan did not include any directives, but relied on indicative planning and indirect means of control and regulation.

In the context of the Eleventh Five-Year Plan, NDRC stated that the government's *"general guidance and coordination of reform"* will persist, and even be strengthened, throughout the next five years.[466] The new economic plan includes more than just the general outline of economic development goals.[467] The plan for the period 2006-2010 is much more flexible than the directives issued in former periods. The promulgation of the Eleventh Five-Year Plan indicates that, despite the expansion of free market mechanisms - completion of price reform in 2003,[468] domination of the private sector (about two thirds of China's GDP) and the prevalence of foreign-funded enterprises (FFEs) which contribute about one third to China's gross industrial output[469] - the state's influence on the market through industrial policy is still prevalent. China is reviewing and formulating new industrial policies which are mainly divided into two categories: directional industrial policy (e.g. "Outline of State Industrial Policies for the 1990s") and differentiated industrial policy for specific industries (such as the auto industry, the electronic industry, and the telecommunications industry).

Overall, according to Taube (2005), the central government sees itself as the strategic mastermind of national (economic) development, although at the same time upholding the premise that market forces should be the dominant coordination mechanism for day-to-day business interaction.[470] The central government is still not

---

463 Refer to People's Daily (2001), "NPC Deputies, CPPCC Members Interpret New Five-Year Plan", Internet Edition, reviewed 04.08.2006.

464 Refer to Ken'ichi (2003), p. 2.

465 Refer to People's Daily (2001), "NPC Deputies, CPPCC Members Interpret New Five-Year Plan", Internet Edition, reviewed 04.08.2006.

466 Refer to Ma (2006), "The Eleventh Five-Year Plan: Targets, Paths and Policy Orientation", 19.03.2006, Internet Edition, reviewed 14.11.2006.

467 Refer to Taube (2005), p. 3.

468 In 2003, price reform was nearly completed, leaving only a few strategic goods in the control of state agencies.

469 Precise measurement of the size of the private sector is difficult. Defining as private all companies that are controlled neither by state nor collective shareholders suggests that the private sector was responsible for 57 percent of the value-added produced by the non-farm business sector in 2003. Refer to OECD (2005), "Economic Survey of China 2005: Improving the productivity of the business sector", Internet Edition, reviewed 02.01.2007.

470 Refer to Taube (2005), p. 3.

abandoning its function of formulating economic targets, and does not leave the development of the economy to market forces, because in China - even more than in the East Asian developmental states - economic growth is the basis of state power. China's transition strategy safeguards the power and privileges of the political elite, and implements wide-ranging economic reforms that both reduce the scope of state managerial controls over production and distribution and expand the role of the market as a mechanism to motivate and guide economic growth at the same time.[471] The central government follows the East Asian industrial policy approach of guiding the market and active state intervention through industrial policy in order to enhance economic development.

Before analyzing more recent industrial policy implementation and focusing on the criteria of the East Asian Developmental State Model such as promotion of selected sectors, usage of foreign investment and trade policy, specific Chinese institutional innovations have to be highlighted. Fiscal federalism and collective ownership at the local level have particularly shaped industrial policy-making and have influenced the country's economic transformation since the early reform years.

3.3.2 Institutional reforms – drivers of and obstacles to economic growth

As the previous analysis indicates, in the 1980s, the relative scope of market institutions in coordinating the economy expanded, and the property rights structure changed. An incremental shift from a redistributive to a regulatory state happened gradually. These changes are key factors explaining the rapid growth of hybrid governance structures and private enterprises. These structural changes in combination with local bureaucrats' fiscal incentives resulted in economic performance improvements and subsequently economic growth.[472]

3.3.2.1 Fiscal federalism

Qian and Roland (1998) contend that two mechanisms may particularly constrain predatory political interference in the economy.[473] First, under the assumption of factor mobility, fiscal decentralization can prompt more efficient provisions of local public goods if individuals can freely move across localities.[474] Competition between localities thus increases opportunity costs of bailouts and any activities leading to inferior enterprise performance. Second, in a federal system, local governments

---

[471] Refer to Nee and Opper (2007), p. 95.

[472] For further information refer to Nee (1989) and Nee and Su (1990).

[473] For further information refer to Qian and Roland (1998).

[474] Tiebout argues that in a system with fiscal decentralization and interjurisdictional competition, citizens can *"vote with their feet"* by moving to the locality that provides their optimal bundle of public goods and taxes. For further information refer to Tiebout (1956) and Bardhan (2002).

compete in building a business environment favorable to private capital. Only local governments that manage to provide a hospitable business environment will attract the resources needed to enhance economic growth. This may harden budget constraints of jurisdictions and provide incentives for efficiency-oriented local activities. In a federalist system, interjurisdictional competition may consequently constrain discretionary authority, predatory behavior, and rent-seeking.[475]

Fiscal decentralization may, however, also cause allocative inefficiency. According to Riker (1964), the central design problem of federalism is how to create institutions that grant the central government enough authority to provide central goods and police subunits, but not so much that it usurps all public authority.[476] The two dilemmas are difficult to solve because institutional mechanisms designed to mitigate one might exacerbate the other. To control subnational governments, the federal government must have the power to punish them. This power, however, allows a non-benevolent federal government to abuse states. Sustaining federalism therefore requires a careful balance between the two dilemmas. The central government must have sufficient power to prevent states from free-riding; yet not be so powerful as to be able to overawe them.[477]

In China, the most important of the fiscal reforms was the tax responsibility system. By the mid-1980s, provinces, municipalities, prefectures, counties and townships were subject to a bottom-up revenue-sharing system. The central state and each of its provinces signed fiscal contracts to formalize revenue sharing. In the same manner, each province and its prefectures, each prefecture and its counties, and each county and its townships signed respective fiscal contracts.[478] Only certain taxes such as taxes on state and collective industries were subject to share contracts, and collected by localities, as they constituted the core of the locality's "within-budget revenues". The other major items that made up the within-budget revenues included agricultural tax and profits from state-run enterprises within the locality. Most of the other revenues that a locality collected were considered as "extrabudgetary revenues" which were not subject to revenue sharing.[479] As Figure 9 shows, the extrabudgetary revenue of local governments increased from RMB 3.1 billion in 1978 to RMB 14.0 billion in 1994.

---

475 Refer to Weingast (1995) and Nee and Opper (2007), p. 100-101.

476 For an elaboration on his general theory of federalism refer to Riker (1964).

477 De Figueiredo and Weingast argue that the center and the states must have incentives to fulfill their obligations within the limits of federal bargains. For further elaboration on self-enforcing federalism refer to de Figueiredo and Weingast (2005).

478 Not all areas have instituted the tax responsibility system to the township. Some places used an overall ratio, such as 70:30, where the locality kept 70 percent and 30 percent was sent to the next higher level. In other cases the locality payed a set quota to the next higher level, but once that quota was met, the locality retained all or at least the bulk of the remaining tax revenues.

479 In addition, there were some taxes designated as "central taxes". These were not subject to revenue sharing. Central taxes were the sole property of the central state. Localities collected but received nothing from central taxes. Refer to Oi (1992), p. 104.

Figure 9: Extrabudgetary revenue of local governments, 1978-1994.

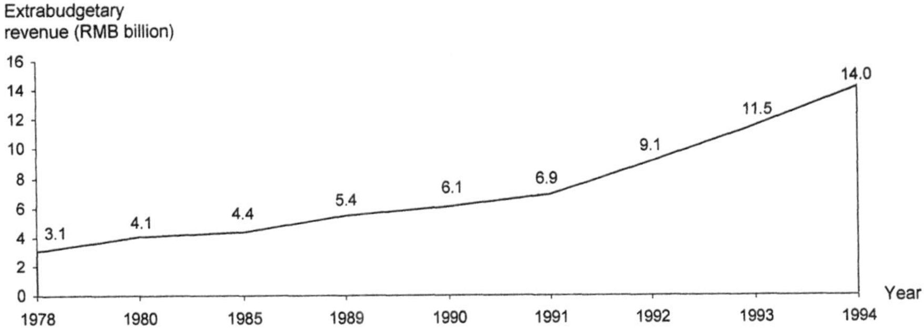

Source: China Statistical Yearbook (2006).

Due to the tax responsibility system, localities became independent fiscal entities that had both responsibility for local expenditures and the unprecedented right to use the revenue they retained.[480] As tax revenue is positively correlated with firm performance, local bureaucrats started to support the growth and profitability of their locality's enterprises.[481] Fiscal decentralization gave local governments the incentive to choose the policy that appeared to be the most successful according to local characteristics.[482] In order to attract private investors and entrepreneurs, localities offered indirect incentives that did not interfere with the market mechanism. They provided enterprises within their locality well developed infrastructure and services, and the reduction of county-level tax and local fees.[483] Additionally, local governments attempted to have efficient and timely bureaucratic procedures in order to achieve and enhance local competitiveness. In this way, local authorities attracted inward investment from abroad and promoted the sale of their localities' goods in international markets.[484]

480 Ibidem, p. 103.

481 Previously, the central government took away all the locally generated revenue. In consequence, the local government did not have any ince ntive to support productive local businesses because it could not benefit from their efforts. Conversely, if local governments' expenditures are closely linked to the revenue they generate, the local governments will more likely support productive local businesses as they benefit directly from their efforts. Refer to Qian (2003), pp. 27-30 and Nee and Opper (2007), p. 101. For a useful summary of the evolution of fiscal policies and variations in the formal system, refer to Oksenberg and Tong (1991), Tong (1989) and Wong (1991, 1992).

482 Refer to Thun (2006), pp. 16-17.

483 Refer to Nee et al. (2005), p. 31 and Edin (2000), pp. 105-106.

484 Refer to Nolan (1995b), p. 178.

On January 1, 1994, the central government introduced major tax and fiscal reforms.[485] The reform included a clear distinction between national and local taxes, and established a national tax bureau and local tax bureaus, each responsible for its own tax collection.[486] The reform also set up fixed rules between the national government and local governments. It included the introduction of an indirect value-added tax which has to be shared by the national and local government at a fixed ratio of 75:25 in order to assure adequate revenues for the central government.[487] With the adoption of the new reform, local governments can hardly extract tax revenues at the expense of the central government (refer to Figure 10).

Figure 10 shows that while in 1993, local government revenue was 78 percent of total government revenue, it decreased to 43 percent in 1994 and remained stable since then. Also the extrabudgetary revenue of local governments decreased to RMB 11.6 billion in 1997 (compared with RMB 14 billion in 1994). Due to decreasing extrabudgetary revenues and increasing financial responsibilities, local governments have had incentives to promote economic growth and local revenue by facilitating market-oriented economic activities.[488]

Figure 10: Revenue ratio of central and local governments, 1978-2006.

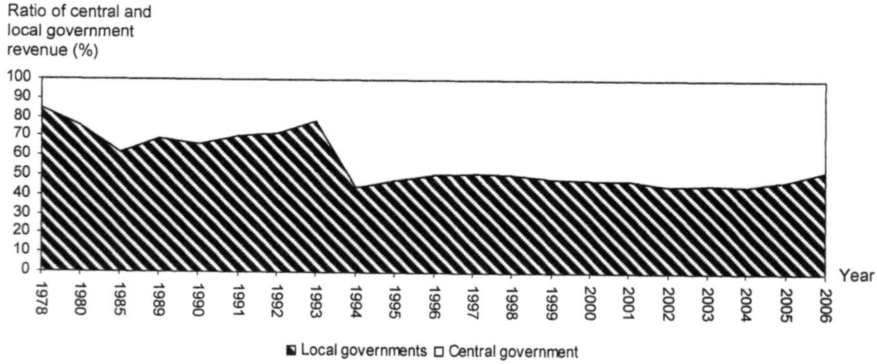

Source: China Statistical Yearbook (2007).

---

[485] With the tax and fiscal reforms, the central government aimed to establish a system that was more aligned to international best practices. Refer to Qian (2003), p. 40.

[486] Previously, China did not have a national tax bureau, and there was no such a need because all taxes were collected by local governments and shared with the central government. Refer to Qian (2003), pp. 40-41.

[487] The 1980s model had starved the central government of revenues, which fell as a fraction of GDP from 30 percent in 1970, to 23 percent in 1985, to 12.6 percent in 1993, to 10 percent in 1995. Refer to Qian (2003), p. 41 and Keefer (2007), p. 233.

[488] Refer to Ahrens and Mengeringhaus (2006), p. 95, Nee and Opper (2007), p. 101 and Lin (2001), p. 4.

Altogether, fiscal federalism has constituted a key institutional innovation. Fiscal federalism has affected the pervasiveness of soft budget constraints. While Walder (1995) assumes that fiscal federalism has hardened local governments' budget constraints, Nee et al. (2007) contend that fiscal federalism creates incentives for interjurisdictional competition that will eventually bring about a hardening of budget constraints at the firm level.[489] Most of all, revenue-sharing arrangements stimulated enthusiasm on the part of local governments to support and pursue market-oriented economic development. Local governments' financial independence has stimulated revenue-generating reforms.[490] It is moreover important not to obscure the enduring influence of the central government over local policy. Provincial autonomy is at the bequest of the central government rather than a legal right as in a federal structure.[491]

3.3.2.2 Collective ownership

According to the assertors of New Institutional Economics, the main condition for an efficient market economy is not only *"getting prices right"*, but also *"getting property rights right"* and *"getting institutions right"*.[492] As North (1997) pointed out, political institutions can play an important role in reducing transaction costs by improving the security of property rights and the enforcement of contracts.[493] The transition economy is featured by weak market structures, poorly specified property rights,[494] and institutional uncertainty. In a partially reformed system, hybrid government forms savor a transaction cost advantage for collective firms, because (local) governments may assist collective enterprises to secure reliable access to factor resources they need, serve as intermediaries in critical negotiations with banks for access to credit, fix local prices on key commodities, and approve and coordinate the investment of extrabudgetary funds. A continuing shift from redistribution to markets and secure property rights, however, induces change in the comparative costs of governance.[495] Market institutions become more dominant in the transition economy, and the institutional foundation of a market economy is incrementally constructed. This results in a relative increase in the cost of hybrid governance structures, and a decrease of transaction cost advantages for collective firms. Private companies are the beneficiaries of transition to market structures.[496]

---

489 According to Nee et al., governments themselves have by definition soft budget constraints as there is always a bailout guarantee through higher level governments, extra-budgetary fees, tax increases and public debt. For further information refer to Nee et al. (2007), p. 41ff.

490 Refer to Nee and Opper (2007), p. 101 and Nee (1992), p. 5.

491 Refer to Thun (2006), p. 35.

492 For further information refer to Coase (1992), North (1997) and Williamson (1994).

493 Refer to North (1997), p. 150 and Coase (1992).

494 For further information refer to Demsetz (1967).

495 Refer to Nee (1992), p. 4.

496 Refer to North (1990) and Williamson (1991)

In the early reform period, the central government encouraged the foundation of rural township and village enterprises (TVEs), which are the successors of collectively-owned industrial enterprises in people's communes. TVEs are best characterized as community enterprises with a governance structure in which the community government has control. The central government envisioned that these collective enterprises would facilitate structural employment changes and absorb the rapidly increasing supply of workers.

TVEs rapidly developed into an efficient and indispensable part of the Chinese economy due to the following reasons.[497] First, the central government issued regulations that were less hostile to TVEs than to private enterprises. Already in 1978, the central government declared that commune brigade enterprises were to strive for greater development, and encouraged provincial, city and county governments to grant these particular enterprises tax breaks.[498] In comparison, the central government did not allow private enterprises to operate until 1981, and limited their hiring of employees to no more than eight per enterprise.[499]

Second, TVEs' success can be traced to the incentive structure they faced. The social-economic development of rural townships and villages depended heavily on the economic success of local industrial enterprises, as up to 95 percent of local revenues stemmed from TVEs. Increasing revenues accrued to the local governments directly. Bureaucrats' interest was no longer solely in pleasing a bureaucratic superior, but in enhancing the prosperous growth of TVEs. Local cadres hence had a strong motivation to follow economic principals.[500] The rise of TVEs was related closely to the underdevelopment of input markets. Local governments contributed critical inputs to the growth of TVEs such as land and credit where factor markets were underdeveloped and prices of inputs were tightly controlled.[501] Furthermore, as TVEs had less or no access to soft credits in comparison to SOEs, they worked relatively autonomously within a basically competitive environment and under hard budget constraints.[502] Through the introduction of payment schemes and management responsibility contracts, TVE managers were also presented with personal incentives to promote the growth of TVEs.

The incentive structures constituted coalitions between local bureaucrats and entrepreneurs which Oi (1992) calls *"local corporatism"*.[503] While bureaucrats contributed bureaucratic connections, enterprise managers provided business ideas and managerial skills. Thus, both parties had become indispensable for the success

497 Refer to Opper (2001), p. 207.

498 Refer to Che and Qian (1998), pp.10-11.

499 This restriction was removed in 1984. Refer to Che and Qian (1998), p. 11.

500 Refer to Opper (2001), p. 207.

501 Refer to Che (2002), pp. 800-803, Li (1998), p. 395 and Li et al. (2006), pp. 10-11.

502 For further information on why TVEs face harder budget constraints refer to Che and Qian (1998), p. 17 ff.

503 For further information refer to Oi (1992).

of new businesses in the half-reformed Chinese economy.[504] They were de facto shareholders rather than short-term bribe-takers. Bureaucrats became pro-reform in principle, having incentives to lobby higher-level agencies for reduced regulations on behalf of local entrepreneurs.[505]

The development of China's TVEs was yet not uniform across regions. Jin and Qian (1998) find empirical evidence that the development of TVEs is negatively correlated with the locality's market development.[506] In the early reform years, TVEs were hence successful in localities with weak market structures, poorly specified property rights and institutional uncertainty. Local corporatism may reduce transaction costs when the institutional arrangements underpinning markets are weak and redistributive institutions still subordinate to market forces. As marketization has proceeded in the reform period, localities with high growth rates have been the ones that have economized on transaction costs by reducing bureaucratic interference in economic decisions of the enterprise. In the absence of contractual law hardened by routine compliance and enforcement, marketized enterprises need political allies who provide the backing and resources needed by entrepreneurs to compete effectively.[507]

TVEs were being privatized throughout the 1990s, as recessionary conditions in the domestic economy drove many collective enterprises to orient production even more to the world economy.[508] In addition, in the late 1990s, private ownership of enterprises gained legitimacy. The Constitutional Amendment of 1999 regarded the private sector as *"an important component"* of the economy.[509] Consequently, the benefit of TVEs in terms of more secure property rights decreased, and local governments transformed more and more TVEs into individual shareholdings.[510] As

---

504 Although most studies have focused on those new businesses established by local governments, in fact, many central-government agencies have also established their own business ventures. Refer to Li (1998), p. 395.

505 One negative effect of having bureaucrats sponsor businesses is that it increases their appetite for bureaucratic power. In the Chinese context, the economic and bureaucratic competition among regions seems to have kept this tendency in check. Refer to Li (1998), p. 395.

506 For further information refer to Jin and Qian (1998).

507 Refer to Nee (1992), p. 4 and p. 23.

508 Refer to Qian (2003), p. 40 and Nee (1992), p. 15.

509 However, the term privatization is avoided by the Chinese leadership, and SOEs are still a major pillar of the Chinese economy. In 2005, the Ministry of Commerce promulgated that the Chinese economic reform is carried out *"from exclusively public ownership to the pattern with the public sector remaining dominant and diverse sectors of the economy developing side by side"*. Refer to National People's Congress, "Constitution of the People's Republic of China", Amendment Three, Approved on 15.03.1999 by the NPC at its 2nd Session and Ministry of Commerce (2005), "Chinese Government's Administrative Mode Transformation", Internet Edition, reviewed 23.03.2006. For further information refer to Chinese Government (2005), "Economic System", Internet Edition, reviewed 28.03.2006.

510 Refer to Qian (2003), p. 40 and Ahrens and Mengeringhaus (2006), pp. 90-91.

the economy became increasingly marketized and both product and labor market competition intensified in the 1990s, the profitability of many TVEs deteriorated, while private enterprises started to boom in the same location.[511] In this regard, while the share of collective firms in national industrial output had increased from 22 to 39 percent between 1978 and 1996, it decreased from 38 percent to 3 percent between 1997 and 2006. While other enterprises such as private enterprises, FFEs and JVs were non-existent at the beginning of reform, they accounted for almost 87 percent of gross industrial output value in 2006 (refer to Figure 11). However, particularly in inland regions, local governments still frequently oppose market reform, harass private businesses and practice protectionist measures which result in economic autarky.[512]

To sum up, while the East Asian developmental states were committed to private property, growth at the local level in China was driven by collectively owned TVEs in the early reform period. State officials at the township level became entrepreneurs promoting the growth of their localities' TVEs, and securing a sound business environment within their jurisdictions.

Figure 11: Share of gross industrial output value by type of firm ownership, 1978-2006.[513]

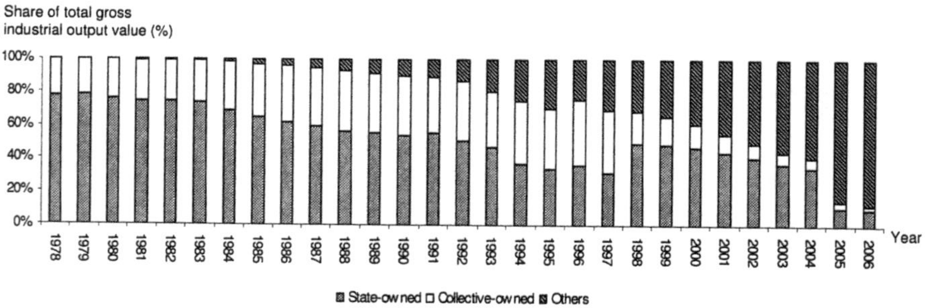

Source: China Compendium of Statistics 1949-2004 and China Statistical Yearbook (2006, 2007).

---

511 The potential social gains from privatization do not automatically lead to privatization unless the local governments have the incentives to do so. The significant benefits of TVE ownership to local governments are the tax revenues they extract from TVEs. After privatization, the township and village governments were able to keep all the privatization revenue. They were also able to continue to levy fees on local private firms, usually 1.5 percent of total sales. This "local tax" did not have to be shared with the higher level government. Township and village governments usually payed a fixed amount instead. Therefore, local governments supported, rather than opposed, privatization out of their own interests. Refer to Qian (2003), p. 40.

512 Refer to Nee (1992), p. 16.

513 The category "Others" includes Cooperative Enterprises, Joint Ownership Enterprises, Limited Liability Corporations, Share Holding Enterprises, Enterprises with Foreign Funds From Hong Kong, Macao and Taiwan, and FFEs.

3.3.2.3 Corruption

Klitgaard (1988) stated that three structural dimensions of a government institution are most critical in creating opportunities for corruption: the monopoly power of officials; the degree of discretion that officials are permitted to exercise; and the lack of accountability and the transparency in an institution.[514] China's decentralization process has triggered an increase in all three aspects. While the degree of discretion of local officials has increased to the extent of forming monopolized powers, accountability and transparency of exercising these powers have not been established.

Decentralization transferred power from the central government to the localities. Under economic and political pressures, officials at subnational levels no longer behave simply as state agents within the official budgetary boundaries, but assume the role of local economic principals. Local authorities enjoy extensive administrative and economic discretion in carrying out government policies. They control business licensing, resource distribution, administrative budgeting and local taxation, as well as trade and investment in their jurisdiction. In consequence, local officials have more opportunities to use and abuse their power. The surge of local bureaucrats' self-interests has transformed local officials from mere state agents into local economic principals with entrepreneurial and sometimes predatory behavior. Such a structure of governance provides enough room for local officials to render favorable treatment to special interests in exchange for personal gain.[515]

Based on statistics supplied by the CCP's Central Discipline and Inspection Commission, on average 130,000 - 190,000 party members have been punished and disciplined each year for various types of misdeeds and crimes since the early 1980s. The Central Discipline and Inspection Commission's data show that 16 percent of the CCP members disciplined and punished in 2006 engaged in economically corrupt activities. From October 1997 to September 2002, 28,996 cadres at the county and division levels as well as 2,422 officials at the department and bureau levels were prosecuted for corruption.[516] Land-related corruption is particularly widespread.[517] One case of a high-ranking official was Tian Fengshan, China's former minister of land and resources, who was sentenced on charges of job-related crimes to life imprisonment in late December 2005. His sentence makes it the mainland's highest level corruption conviction between 2001 and 2005. Tian was charged with accepting more than RMB 4.4 million in bribes between 1995 and 2003, when he served first as the governor of Heilongjiang province and then as a cabinet

[514] For further information refer to Klitgaard (1988).

[515] Refer to Gong (2006), p. 89.

[516] Refer to Pei (2007), p. 1.

[517] For a detailed elaboration on land-related corruption refer to Gong (2006), p. 89.

minister.[518] Altogether, Pei (2007) estimates that illicit activities such as bribery, kickbacks, theft, and misspending of public funds cost at least 3 percent of GDP.[519]

Overall, state capacity and autonomy which can be translated into coherent policy implementation has often been disrupted by the widespread corruption of civil servants at all levels. Corruption arises from the indistinct separation of rights and powers between the state, regulatory institutions and economic agents. By exploiting their political power of controlling licenses, franchises and cheap materials which had state-controlled prices, government officials favored their own companies, or took bribes from other entrepreneurs who were then granted privileges such as cheap resources.[520]

Even after almost 30 years of reform, the CCP remains severely imbued with corruption that critically impedes its efforts to implement a consistent and effective industrial policy. As long as the close connection between the state, regulatory institutions and economic agents benefits its members, regulators' incentives to detect corruption are scant and state-led anti-corruption campaigns will be a short-term priority of a rational government.[521]

3.3.2.4 Local protectionism

Not only were local officials' salaries affected by local growth, but also their individual career paths. As local officials' performance is assessed less by their compliance with the central government and more by local economic output, revenue growth and improvement in living standards, local governments have become eager to improve their jurisdiction's financial well-being.[522] Consequently, many localities have adopted protectionist measures such as trade barriers against one another. This resulted in the so-called *"dukedom economies"* phenomenon. Provinces, autonomous regions and municipalities (Beijing, Tianjin and Shanghai) were *"big dukedoms"*, prefectures and cities were *"middle dukedoms"* and counties were *"small dukedoms"*.[523] China's economy had become a *"ducal economy"* which intensified regional disparity.[524] Although Article 7 of the 1993 "Countering Unfair Competition Law of the People's Republic of China" prohibits local governments from utilizing administrative means to

518 Refer to People's Daily (2004), "Former land minister expelled from CPC Central Committee", Internet Edition, reviewed 02.01.2007.

519 Refer to Pei (2007), p. 2.

520 Refer to Xia (2000), p. 95.

521 Refer to Opper (2005a), p. 201 and p. 213.

522 Refer to Gong (2006), p. 93.

523 Refer to Montionola et al. (1995), p. 65 and Zheng (1995), p. 30.

524 Furthermore, Zheng describes the consequences of decentralization as "a centralized empire breaking up into many small kingdoms". Refer to Zheng (1997), p. 30 and p. 129.

erect trade barriers,[525] local governments use various measures to protect and support companies within their jurisdiction. Under the name of assistance to the local economy, local governments seek to cover trade barriers. Some regions set up barriers to limit the entry of similar commodities from outside through administrative economic and even legislative means, and thus protect local industry and stimulate market demand. These include approved import bans, discriminatory product and health certification standards, tariffs and dumping charges, the confiscations of profits earned from marketing foreign-provincial goods, as well as subsidies to local commercial units for buying locally produced products aimed at curtailing competition with home-province products and sustaining employment and the survival of uncompetitive local enterprises. Other regions fight "price wars" with other localities over similar products, and encourage local residents to buy local products only.[526] Protectionism has occurred most often in the markets of high profit-margin manufacturing goods (such as autos, tobacco products, and alcohol) and raw materials in short supply (such as cotton, silkworm cocoons[527], tobacco and aluminum).[528] In 2001, the World Bank reported that a bottle of Beijing's Yanjing beer that costs the equivalent of 18 cents in the capital, costs USD 1 in Sichuan province because of provincial fees and taxes.[529]

The imperfect policing of the common market allows local governments to insulate themselves from competition by erecting trade barriers. This has resulted in small production units with inefficient scales of production. Similar conclusions can be drawn regarding sectoral and geographic specialization and rationalization in the industrial sector. The consequence is that regions do not specialize according to their comparative advantages, but push strongly into similar industries and product groups. This results in a convergence of industrial production across different regions. A "repetitive and duplicative" economic structure has emerged. The local authorities' attempts to first capture and then protect these rents has led to the creation of further distortions.[530]

China thus appears as a collection of separate regional economies protected by barriers rather than a single market. Domestic trade protection pursues a dual objective of socio-economic stability preservation and fiscal revenue maximization. If economic reforms favor the reduction of internal barriers through the reduction of the public sector and the search for productivity gains, their disrupting effects put in movement destabilizing forces that impede domestic trade integration.[531] The

---

525 Refer to OECD (2003), "Objectives of the Competition Law of PRC and the Optimal Design of Competition Authorities", Internet Edition, reviewed 02.10.2006.

526 Refer to Steinfeld (2002), p. 18, Gong (2006), p. 93, Poncet (2005), p. 411 and Editorial Board of the Progress of China Industry Modernization (1999), p. 99.

527 For detailed information on the "silkworm cocoon war" refer to Young (2000), pp. 1092-1093.

528 Refer to Montinola et al. (1995), p. 65.

529 Refer to World Bank (2001), "China's Local Trade Barriers: A Hard Nut to Crack", Internet Edition, reviewed 25.10.2007.

530 Refer to Steinfeld (2002), p. 19 and Huang (2003), p. 261.

531 The disrupting effects may be layoffs, losses of inefficient SOEs, declining profits etc.

Chinese central government faces challenges to comply with WTO rules and promote domestic market integration. It has to strike a balance between economic reforms and inherent adjustment costs and to limit local governments' economic interventionism.[532]

In conclusion, while the incentive structure transformed local bureaucrats from mere state agents into local economic principals promoting market-driven growth, predatory behavior in the form of corruption and protectionism also increased.[533] Bureaucrats' rent-seeking activities bear internal tensions and weaknesses, and diminish the central government's overall coherence. Thus, the emergence of a strong, bureaucratic state could not be established. In this respect, the Chinese bureaucracy lacks the intense commitment to national development which its neighbors in East Asia had.[534] Containing rent-seeking is a key issue for the success of state and economic transformation in China.[535] To control rent-seeking behavior, a government needs to reduce its regulatory interventions to the minimum necessary to achieve important national goals. Where regulatory and tax interventions are necessary, discretionary authority on the part of government officials must be kept to a minimum. An activist industrial policy (including a variety of licenses, government control over critical imports, and government-directed loans at subsidized rates to enforce government industrial policy initiatives) is the antithesis of an effort to reduce rent-seeking behavior.[536] Altogether, although localism leads often to protectionism and "solos" of localities, local governments have actively enhanced the economic growth and transformation of their jurisdictions and thus of China.

3.3.3 Promotion of selected sectors, companies and projects

In the East Asian developmental states, only selected "upstream" industries and enterprises were targeted for preferential treatment such as protection, allocation of scarce production inputs and bureaucratic support. Similar to the East Asian developmental states, China has relied on different types of industrial policy tools to promote selected industries and enterprises during its reform: central government planning, empowering key industries with direct financing, preferential interest and tax rates, direct subsidies and a favorable supply of energy, raw materials, transportation facilities and funds for target industries, infant industry (trade) protection as well as pricing policies (state price controls over power and water supply) and administrative means (issuing direct orders to close down or merge

---

532 Refer to Poncet (2005), p. 426.

533 Refer to Gong (2006), p. 98.

534 Refer to Fewsmith (2001c), p. 107 ff and Nolan (2001), p. 93.

535 Refer to Zhu (2003), p. 158.

536 Refer to Perkins (2001), p. 8.

SOEs).[537] The relative importance of these instruments changed over the years as the whole economy moved towards a more open and market-oriented system. Some of the policy instruments had to be abandoned gradually. According to the terms of the GATT and WTO agreements, China decided to dismantle various protectionist mechanisms favoring domestic industries and products over foreign.[538] Even after China's WTO accession, however, central and local governments have applied most of the industrial policy tools the East Asian developmental states used to support domestic companies and enhance the country's economic transformation.[539] According to WTO law, member countries can continue to support R&D projects. Direct financial subsidies for R&D expenditure on specified science and technology (S&T) projects have thus become an essential instrument of industrial policy.

3.3.3.1 Industrial policy targeting S&T

As promulgated in the five-year plans, the central government attempts to establish and promote companies and technology-intensive products that are internationally competitive. The central government has directed its focus towards S&T since the 1980s, when it recognized the mutual interdependency of economic, scientific and technological development. Since then, it has reiterated that S&T is the centerpiece of China's economic modernization strategy.[540] The central government's "Report on the Outline of the Tenth Five-Year Plan for National Economic and Social Development (2001-2005)" focused on the expansion of technology and high-tech industries and the manufacturing of information technology products. Thus, China was to *"catch up with its neighbors"* and accelerate its development *"under the guidance of industrial policies"*.[541]

China's national technology policy comprises a set of mutually complementary S&T programs with the strategic aim of improving China's competitiveness in S&T.[542] Since 1987, S&T programs have received direct central government finance for R&D in priority sectors (such as space, laser and computing). They focus on applied

537 Refer to "Decision on Further Improving the Economic Environment, Straightening Out the Economic Order, and Deepening the Reforms (Excerpts) (Adopted at the Fifth Plenary Session of the 13th Central Committee of the Chinese Communist Party on 09.11.1989), p. VIII. For further information refer to Zhang and Long (1997), p. 266 and Lu (2000a), p. 345.

538 Refer to WTO Secretariat (2001), "Accession of the People's Republic of China - Decision of 10 November 2001", Internet Edition, reviewed 23.11.2006.

539 Refer to Weiss (2003), p. 245.

540 Refer to Miller (1996), p. 184.

541 Refer to NDRC (2006), "Strengthen the Integration of Science, Technology and Economy Enhance Independent Innovation Capability", Internet Edition, reviewed 18.12.2006.

542 Refer to Li (1989), "Resolutely Carry Out the Principles of Improvement, Rectification and Deepened Reform", p. XII. For a full overview of S&T programs refer to Ministry of Science and Technology of the People's Republic of China (2006), "National programs for science and technology", Internet Edition, reviewed 28.03.2006.

research and medium-term results. In the early reform period, central leaders realized that China's severe limits in R&D funding made it necessary to concentrate them on selected areas. Based on arguments of market failure and economies of scale, strengthened by a high level of uncertainty and the length of R&D cycles, central leaders assumed that this goal could be achieved better via planning than through market-means. They reaffirmed the necessity for state support of key programs which had to be provided at the central level, as local and provincial governments pushed too strongly for short-term profits.[543]

The individual programs follow a set of distinct core objectives and support close science-business interface to secure innovation activities with good prospects for productivity growth. Thus, the central government intends to maximize the commercialization of R&D output. The planning institutions gradually adjust national priorities and targeted research goals in response to the changing overall state development goals. The State Science and Technology Commission is the major institution in charge of formulating national S&T plans. In this regard, China's technology policy essentially relies on central planning and resource allocation, which is in line with its socialist planning tradition.[544]

The "Key Technologies Research and Development Program", the "863 (National High-tech Research and Development) Program" and the "973 Program" as well as the "Spark" and the "Torch" programs form the main body of state programs for S&T. First started in 1982, the "Key Technologies R&D Program" is a critical component of the five-year plans for the national economic and social development. Its strategic objectives are to promote the modernization of traditional industries and the optimization of industrial structures of national priority sectors. Its major aims are to carry out study and research on key S&T issues based on the principle of S&T pioneering.[545] In this regard, priority is on the research-business interface and the support of joint projects between universities, research institutes and enterprises. The core principle of the program is to concentrate efforts and the nation's resources in personnel, as well as establish the firm as the major venue of innovative activities. Therefore, in line with the program, the central government provides advanced applicable new technologies, materials, techniques and equipment in order to speed up the national modernization process in priority industries.[546]

Approved by the State Council in 1986, the "Spark Program" is the nation's first guided development program designed to develop the rural economy through S&T, and thus spur the development of TVEs.[547] One of its long-term development objectives is to move the rural economy in the direction of relying on scientific and

543 Refer to Gabriele (2002), p. 346 and Gabriele (2001), p. 20, Internet Edition, reviewed 01.05.2007.

544 Refer to Opper (2005b), p. 43 and Nee and Opper (2007), p. 104.

545 Refer to Chinese Government (2006), "National programs for science and technology", Internet Edition, reviewed 28.03.2006.

546 Refer to Opper (2005b), p. 44.

547 Refer to Chinese Government (2006), "National programs for science and technology", Internet Edition, reviewed 28.03.2006.

technological progress and on the improved labor performance of TVEs. Its priority is to develop regional pillar industries in rural areas. Projects listed in the program are entitled to favorable bank loans and preferential taxation policies.

The "863 Program" was created in 1987.[548] Its focus is on seven key R&D-intensive fields – automation, biotechnology, energy, information technology, lasers, new materials and space technology – and intends to accelerate development and maximize the results obtained from pooling together all national resources. The 863 Plan is a large and complex project which brings together specialists in many fields on cross-disciplinary projects such as computer integrated manufacturing systems in order to reduce the technology gap between China and foreign countries. The financial support required for the program comes mainly from special government appropriations. Although the program has been politically relevant, scientists have maintained most of the decision-making process governed by technical criteria and also make most financial decisions. Politicians granted them a large share of effective autonomy, "insulation" and real power, in a manner similar to that of planners in the developmental states of East Asia.[549]

The "Torch Program" grew out of a 1988 State Council Decision to accelerate the development of high tech manufacturing technology.[550] The Torch program directs the development of high and new technology industries, focusing mainly on the electronics sector.[551] The program promotes commercialization through venture investment by universities, the transfer of research results from universities and the Chinese Academy of Sciences, and the dual employment of professors and researchers. This has led to many ventures launched from universities.[552] The Torch program aims to create a beneficial innovation environment and promote the industrialization and commercialization of high and new technology products. The creation of High and Emerging Technology Industry Development Zones - with the aim of applying R&D to production and commercialization – also represents a major thrust of the Torch Program. New product projects listed in the program are entitled to priority in receiving bank loans and preferential taxation policies over a specified period of time. With the support of the Torch program, some of the former small firms have grown into large industrial groups, such as Lenovo Computers.[553] Since 1996, Lenovo has become the largest Chinese IT company and occupied first place in China's PC sales market. With its 2005 acquisition of IBM's PC business, Lenovo has become the world's third largest PC firm in terms of sales.

---

548 Ibidem.

549 Refer to Gabriele (2001), p. 21, Internet Edition, reviewed 01.05.2007.

550 Refer to Chinese Government (2006), "National programs for science and technology", Internet Edition, reviewed 28.03.2006.

551 Refer to Gabriele (2001), p. 20, Internet Edition, reviewed 01.05.2007.

552 Refer to Asian Development Bank Institute (2006), "The Internal Environment and Input Conditions", Internet Edition, reviewed 27.04.2007.

553 Before 2003, Lenovo was named Legend Computers. For further information refer to Yu (1999), p. 188 and Gabriele (2001), pp. 20-21, Internet Edition, reviewed 01.05.2007.

The Chinese central leaders were well aware of the risk of misallocation of state-guided R&D acquisitions due to the risk of selection and collusion.[554] In order to reduce misallocation, the central government promulgated the "Decision on the Reform of the Science and Technology Management System" in 1985.[555] The decision called for decentralization and a reduction of government competencies in the choice and selection of research proprieties. It encouraged breaking the close links between government and R&D facilities and emphasized the necessity of intensive competition in the field of R&D policy. The procedure of planned allocation of S&T funds was replaced by public competitions. Furthermore, the potential for the commercialization of S&T output emerged as a major criterion for funding decisions.[556] Overall, market mechanisms were to be substituted for administrative ones in the S&T system.

The 1995 "Decision on Accelerating S&T Development" accepted that the development of applied technologies should be left to the market; however, at the same time, called for the strengthening of government leadership in basic technology research. According to the decision, China has to rely on S&T to solve problems such as inefficient industrial structure, technological backwardness, and low labor productivity.[557] With the decision, the central government granted scientific research institutes full autonomy in choosing R&D projects, and encouraged them to form JVs with domestic and foreign partners. Moreover, the decision pointed out that the government would encourage non-state companies as it acknowledged their importance in the high-tech field.[558] The state's leadership role was undisputed throughout the reform period and reconfirmed in the 2006 "Report on the Work of the Government" which promulgated that the state *"will improve the mechanisms for encouraging independent innovation and adopt fiscal, tax, banking and government procurement policies that support enterprise innovation".*[559]

Altogether, during the reform period, the central government has emphasized increasingly the role of technology in promoting economic development, and shifted its goals and priorities in a more ambitious direction. The national S&T development programs are intended to guide the S&T sector by providing incentives for innovation and entrepreneurship.[560] The central leaders have focused on the establishment of the foundations of a national S&T system capable of realizing scientific and

554 The risk of resource misallocation may be even more pronounced in non-democratic regimes that are characterized to a larger extent by objectives of prestige with a strong signaling effect to the international community.

555 Refer to Opper (2005b), p. 44.

556 Ibidem.

557 Refer to US Embassy Beijing (1996), PRC State Council "Decision on Accelerating S&T Development", Internet Edition, reviewed 07.09.2006.

558 Refer to Naughton and Segal (2001), p. 11.

559 Refer to Wen (2006), "Report on the work of the government", Internet Edition, reviewed 09.05.2006.

560 Refer to Gabriele (2001), p. 22, Internet Edition, reviewed 01.05.2007 and Walsh (2003), p. 973.

technological breakthroughs in frontier, high-technology fields. The new strategy is founded on a more mature understanding of the S&T apparatus as a means to improve the overall national system of innovation. The central government emphasized the professionalization of research activities and the enhancement of the economic and social role of innovators. Resources are to be concentrated on a limited set of targets under the highest policy direction, and horizontal international research cooperation with public and private foreign partners is actively promoted.[561]

3.3.3.2 State effort to increase China's R&D capabilities

Along with S&T programs, the state has extended its expenditure on R&D and promoted science parks and R&D projects. These measures have increasingly become an instrument of industrial policy.

In the fields of top-level technology and research, China's S&T policy accords priority to centrally coordinated, state-sponsored, targeted R&D programs.[562] The 1995 "Decision on Accelerating S&T Development" set a quantitative target: gross expenditure on R&D was set to reach 1.5 percent of GDP by the year 2000.[563] This policy line was confirmed at the 15th Party Congress in 1997 and at the National People's Congress meetings in 1999. Although this goal could not be reached, between 1999 and 2006, annual R&D expenditures increased from 0.8 percent of GDP to 1.4 percent of GDP. Expenditure for Innovation Funds, as well as Science and Technology Promotion Funds more than doubled between 1999 (RMB 76.6 billion) and 2006 (RMB 174.5 billion) (refer to Table 5).[564] The majority of funding for S&T activities accrues in the business sector (as of 2006, funds raised by enterprises: 66 percent; government funds: 22 percent; loans from finance institutions: 12 percent).[565] In an international context, China ranked six after the USA, Japan, Germany, the UK and France with regard to total expenditure on R&D

---

561 Refer to Suttmeier and Cao (1999), "China faces the new industrial revolution", Internet Edition, reviewed 05.01.2007.

562 Despite the increase of enterprise-financed R&D along China's move towards a market economy (1999: 51 percent, 2006: 66 percent), in 2006, 22 percent of the funding for S&T activities was from the state. Calculation based on data from China Statistical Yearbook (2004, 2007).

563 Refer to US Embassy Beijing (1996), PRC State Council "Decision on Accelerating S&T Development", Internet Edition, reviewed 07.09.2006.

564 In 2006, government expenditure on Science and Technology Promotion Funds was though less than for supporting rural production (Science and Technology Promotion Funds: RMB 174.5 billion, expenditure for supporting rural production: RMB 216.1 billion). Refer to China Statistical Yearbook (2007).

565 Refer to China Statistical Yearbook (2007).

in 2005.[566] The proportion of scientist and engineers in national S&T population also increased between 1999 and 2006 from 55 percent to 68 percent (refer to Table 5).

Table 5: National S&T financing, personnel and output indicators, 1999-2006.

	1999	2000	2001	2002	2003	2004	2005	2006
Gross domestic expenditure on R&D (RMB billion)	67.9	89.6	104.3	128.8	154.0	196.6	245.0	300.3
Gross domestic expenditure on R&D as percentage of GDP	0.8	0.9	1.0	1.1	1.1	1.2	1.3	1.4
Innovation funds and science and technology promotion funds (RMB billion)	76.6	86.5	99.2	96.8	109.3	124.4	149.5	174.5
Personnel engaged in S&T activities (million persons)	2.9	3.2	3.1	3.2	3.3	3.5	3.8	4.1
Scientists and engineers (million persons)	1.6	2.0	2.1	2.2	2.3	2.3	2.6	2.8
Number of patent applications	134,239	170,682	203,573	252,631	308,487	353,807	476,264	573,178
Number of patent applications certified	100,156	105,345	114,251	132,399	182,226	190,238	214,003	268,002

Source: Data refer to the Ministry of Science and Technology (2007), "Output Indicators", Internet Edition, reviewed 09.11.2007; China Compendium of Statistics 1949 - 2004 and various years of China Statistical Yearbook.

In 2006, the NDRC stated to *"further strengthen guidance through programs and policy"* in order to support the independent innovation capability of domestic companies and enforce the S&T progress.[567] The central government grants incentives such as the provision of tax reductions in order to stimulate R&D activities of enterprises.[568] Already in 2004, the State Administration of Taxation promulgated that enterprises with foreign investment are granted tax reliefs for technology-intensive or knowledge-intensive projects that include products defined in the "Catalogue of High and New Technological Products" (promulgated in 2000). A condition of the tax relief is that the products must exceed 50 percent of the total income from yearly sales.[569]

National S&T output indicators show that between 1999 and 2006, the number of patent applications tripled and those actually certified doubled (in 1999, 100,156

566 Refer to IMD World Competitiveness Yearbook (2007), "Total Expenditure on R&D", Table 4.3.01, p. 429.

567 Refer to NDRC (2006), "Strengthen the Integration of Science, Technology and Economy Enhance Independent Innovation Capability", Internet Edition, reviewed 18.12.2006.

568 Refer to Jefferson (2004), p. 2.

569 Refer to State Administration of Taxation (2004), "Circular of the State Administration of Taxation concerning the Tax Preferential Policy Applicable to Enterprises with Foreign Investment with Regard to Technology-Intensive and Knowledge-Intensive Projects", Internet Edition, reviewed 23.03.2006.

patent applications were certified; the number increased to 268,002 certified patent applications until 2006) (refer to Table 5). Direct causal links between technology policies and innovation performance are hard to establish, however. It is not possible to infer from the numbers whether the increase of patent applications is the result of increased inputs or improved performance.

As Chinese planners have recognized the limits of targeted industrial policies, S&T reforms of the 1980s and 1990s aimed to introduce markets and promote entrepreneurialism.[570] With the aim of modernizing S&T, China combined science parks and national R&D projects to nurture the rise of high-tech firms. The Beijing municipal government established "China's Silicon Valley", the Haidian Science Park in 1988. The science park developed into a leading-edge R&D testing zone. It boasts more than 6,000 new high-tech enterprises with a combined staff of over 100,000. 70 enterprises whose sales exceed RMB 100 million and eight whose sales exceed RMB 1 billion are located in the Haidian Science Park. The number of R&D projects undertaken between 1992 and 1996 totaled 11,152.[571]

In the science parks, the government allocated resources to strategic sectors by adopting certain institutional devices. Targeted industries were granted low-cost loans from state banks with below-market interest rates and tax breaks. In order to promote national R&D projects, the State Planning Commission announced a policy to build approximately 100 national key laboratories and "S&T enterprises" in selected fields of basic science. These enterprises were spun off by national, provincial or city governments to commercialize the knowledge of public labs. Although S&T enterprises are nominally independent, the government obliged them to meet certain requirements in exchange for granting them a special legal status. These requirements were similar to reciprocal control mechanisms: they included a percentage of technology personnel, a percentage of sales contributed by new products, a percentage of products exported, the allocation of retained earnings, etc.[572] Thus, even in the high-tech phase of industrial development, the state retained its condition-based form of subsidy allocation, as in the East Asian developmental states.

Overall, the selective promotion of targeted industries has become a general feature of developmental states and one criterion of their success.[573] The central government has also supported selected industrial sectors, enterprises and projects. China's centralized, planned S&T strategy, carried out through administrative, albeit flexible instruments such as long-term programs and priority projects, resembles that of other Asian developmental states. Preferential policies have become an integral part of

570 Refer to Feigenbaum (1999), p. 123.

571 Refer to Haidian Science Park (n.d.), "Zhongguancun (Haidian) Science Park", Internet Edition, and Haidian Science Park (n.d.), "History", Internet Edition, both reviewed 02.10.2006.

572 Refer to Amsden and Hikino (2000), pp. 111-112.

573 Refer to Evans (1995), p. 58.

state intervention, and are designed to influence firms' business decisions. Selectivity of industrial policy focused on "upstream industries" (such as S&T projects) and on special geographical areas (special zones). The central government introduced particular S&T programs that indicate China's ambitions to catch-up with technologically and economically more advanced states. Central authorities granted high-tech projects special support such as tax incentives.[574] Hence, selective state intervention in China resembles the policies of the developmental states.

As the above measures and indicators demonstrate, China has made impressive gains in some key scientific and technological areas. Overall, the trend line is positive. Nevertheless, when compared to world standards, China's achievements and high-tech capabilities do not yet match those of industrialized nations, and it is likely to be some time before they do.[575]

3.3.4 Foreign participation

According to Dunning (1993), multinational firms generally have firm-specific advantages that might be related to their large endowments of intangible assets, such as superior technologies, patents, trade secrets, brand names, management techniques, and marketing strategies.[576] Once a multinational enterprise has set up a subsidiary, some of these advantages may not be totally internalized but spill over to domestic firms. FDI can therefore advance economic growth in the host economy through global technology transfers (including product, process, and distribution technology, as well as management and marketing skills). The means through which technology is transferred between MNCs and the host countries include explicit transfers, such as contracts, and implicit transfers, including "learning by doing" and the transmission of skills from foreign skilled labor to domestic employees working in the same factory.[577] FDI in the form of JVs functions particularly as a vehicle by which *"tacit knowledge"* is transferred from the foreign to the domestic partner.[578] FDI is hence thought to allow developing countries to "catch up" in the growth process by

574 Refer to Opper (2005b), p. 43 and Gabriele (2001), p. 13, Internet Edition, reviewed 01.05.2007 and Gabriele (2002), p. 344 ff and Nolan (1995b), p. 190.

575 Refer to Walsh (2003), p. 69.

576 For further information refer to Dunning (1993).

577 Saggi notes in the World Bank Research Observer that there are three potential channels of spillovers: demonstration effects (where firms adopt technologies through imitation or reverse engineering), labor migration (workers move to other firms and carry their knowledge with them), and vertical linkages (otherwise known as backward and forward linkages). The idea of vertical linkages rests on the concept that a foreign investment in one industry can indirectly produce benefits in other related industries. For example, suppliers of auto parts and components may benefit from having a new source of demand for their product if there is FDI into a manufacturer. This would be an example of a "backward" linkage. For further information refer to Saggi (2002), Blomström and Kokko (1998), p. 1 and Crespo and Fontoura (2007), p. 410. Also refer to Rodríguez-Clare (1996), Nelson and Winter (1982) and Knell and Radosevic (2000).

578 For further information refer to Polanyi (1967).

closing the technology gap through imitation and the adoption of established technologies. Along with the technology transfer, proponents expect that FDI will cause integration into the world economy, backward and forward linkages to related industries (spillovers), human capital-formation, and surges in domestic innovation. Furthermore, FDI is considered by many to be a strong contributor to economic growth and industrial development because it provides financing for worthy projects.[579] A World Bank study, however, notes that foreign investment does not necessarily stimulate new economic development. The absorption of outside technology is dependent upon the development of domestic technological capabilities and the government's "macroorganizational strategy".[580]

3.3.4.1 Substantial reliance on FDI

FDI is an important component of China's development strategy. The government hopes that FDI boosts economic growth and raises domestic investment.[581] From the beginning of the reform process, the central leaders, above all Deng Xiaoping, expressed the need to accelerate the pace of technology import as a key instrument of reform.[582] Deng was of the opinion that China's socialist economic base was big enough to absorb billions of foreign funds without *"shaking"* the *"socialist economic base"*.[583] In contrast to Maoist hostility to foreign capital,[584] the reform government assured foreign investors the good investment environment.[585] The main purpose of the central government in attracting foreign investment was not to supplement domestic savings, since the savings rate was high throughout the reform period.[586] The central government envisioned that FDI would accelerate productivity growth and the competitiveness of domestic industries through indirect spillover effects and

579 For further information refer to OECD (2002).

580 For further information refer to Saggi (2002), Gabriele (2001), Internet Edition, reviewed 01.05.2007 and Young and Lan (1997).

581 Also refer to Borensztein et. al. (1998) and Bosworth and Collins (1999).

582 Refer to Deng (1978), "Speech at the opening ceremony of the national conference on science", Internet Edition, reviewed 27.05.2006 and Deng (1979), "Some Comments on Economic Work", Internet Edition, reviewed 19.03.2006.

583 Refer to Deng (1984) "Building a Socialism with a Specifically Chinese Character", Internet Edition, reviewed 19.03.2006.

584 No foreign investment was permitted from 1949 to the late 1970s. Refer to Nolan (1995b), p. 184.

585 Refer to Deng (1979), "Some Comments on Economic Work", Internet Edition, reviewed 19.03.2006.

586 China's national savings increased from 30 percent of Gross National Product in 1980 to around 35 percent in 1991. China's savings ratio increased even further as it is expected to rise to 50.5 percent in 2005.

knowledge transfers.[587] It was furthermore an *"important content of China's fundamental principle of opening up to the outside world".*[588]

FDI in China has grown rapidly since 1978, especially in the 1990s. FDI inflow to China increased from USD 0.1 billion in 1980 to USD 69.5 billion in 2006.[589] In 2003, China overtook the USA as the biggest recipient of FDI. Moreover, China hosts the largest number of foreign affiliates, accounting for one third of all foreign affiliates of transnational corporations worldwide. In 2004, around 24 million workers (3 percent of total employment in China) were employed in foreign affiliates in China compared to less than 5 million in 1991.[590]

A useful measure to analyze China's dependency on foreign investment is FDI in relation to the economic size of the host country. The role FDI plays in the Chinese economy can be illustrated by benchmarking China against other economies. China's inward FDI stock as a percentage of GDP has exceeded that of Taiwan, Korea and Japan since the mid-1990s. In 2000, FDI accounted for 18 percent of GDP in China, 7 percent of GDP in Korea, 5 percent of GDP in Taiwan and 1 percent of GDP in Japan. The difference between China and Taiwan in particular has yet been shrinking since 2000. In 2006, the inward FDI stock as a percentage of GDP decelerated to 11 percent in China (compared with 14 percent in Taiwan) (refer to Figure 12).[591] Credit tightening measures initiated by the central government, slower profit growth (due to the central government's macro-regulation measures to cool down the economy) and modest growth in machinery and equipment imports have slowed FDI to a more sustainable pace.[592]

---

587 In particular, the transfer of management skills and technology were promulgated by Deng in 1992 during his Southern Tour. Refer to Deng (1992), "Excerpts From Talks Given in Wuchang, Shenzhen, Zhuhai and Shanghai", Internet Edition, reviewed 19.03.2006.

588 Refer to Ministry of Commerce (n.d.), "China's Absorption of Foreign Investment", Internet Edition, reviewed 17.04.2006. Deng stressed the benefit of foreign investments to China: *"The government [will] levy taxes on [FFEs], workers get wages from them, and we learn technology and managerial skills. In addition, we can get information from them that will help us open more markets."* Refer to Deng (1992), "Excerpts From Talks Given in Wuchang, Shenzhen, Zhuhai and Shanghai", Internet Edition, reviewed 19.03.2006.

589 Refer to UNCTAD (2007), p. 267.

590 In Japan, though, only 430,900 workers (0.8 percent of total employment in Japan) were employed in foreign affiliates in 2004. Ibidem, pp. 10-12.

591 However, the inward FDI stock as a percentage of GDP was "only" 8.0 percent in Korea and 2.5 percent in Japan in the same year.

592 Refer to World Bank (World Bank Office Beijing) (2005), "China Quarterly Update", Internet Edition, reviewed 17.07.2007 and People's Daily (2004), "Industrial profit growth starts to slow", Internet Edition, reviewed 15.08.2007.

Figure 12: Inward FDI stock as a percentage of GDP, by host region and economy, 1980 – 2006.

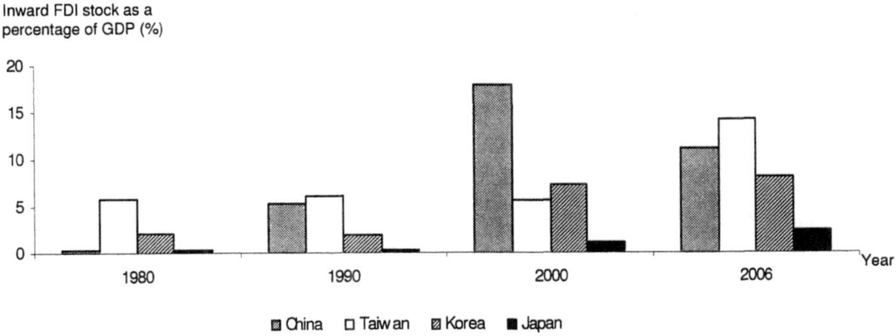

Source: UNCTAD (2006, 2007).

Further opposing the development approach of the East Asian developmental states, China's attraction of foreign investments included not only technical progress in the narrow sense of importing modern equipment for manufacturing plants. Instead, the Chinese central government envisioned raising the R&D capacity of domestic firms through technology transfer from FFEs to domestic enterprises. Among the FFEs are mainly three types of entry mode:

- *Equity Joint Ventures:* The "Law of the People's Republic of China on Sino-Foreign Equity Joint Ventures" was promulgated in July 1979.[593] An Equity JV is a limited liability firm incorporated and registered in China. Capital is contributed from both the foreign and local partners, who hold shared equities. It is treated as a distinct legal business entity subject in all aspects to Chinese laws and administrative procedures. Both partners are responsible for costs and divide profits in negotiated proportions.
- *Contractual Joint Ventures:* Contractual JVs are arrangements whereby Chinese and foreign partners cooperate in certain joint project activities according to the terms and conditions stipulated in a venture contract. Contractual JVs are used mostly for lower-value-added export-processing operations. The "Law of the People's Republic of China on Chinese-Foreign Contractual Joint Ventures" was promulgated in April 1988.[594] According to the

---

593 Refer to Ministry of Commerce (1979, revised 1990), "Law of the People's Republic of China on Chinese-Foreign Equity Joint Ventures", Internet Edition, reviewed 17.04.2006. The laws that were promulgated after 1979 specified the framework in which FFEs operate (such as taxes and foreign investors' rights). For further information refer to China Daily (2006), "Regulations of Qinghai Provincial People's Government on Encouragement of Foreign Investment", Internet Edition, reviewed 10.07.2007. For further information refer to Crespo and Fontoura (2007), p. 410.

594 Refer to China.org (1988, revised 2000), "Law of the People's Republic of China on Chinese-Foreign Contractual Joint Ventures", Internet Edition, reviewed 17.7.2007.

Contractual JV law, the Chinese and the foreign parties have to specify all issues covered in the cooperative enterprise contracts (the cooperation conditions, the distribution of the profits or products, the share of risks and losses, the method of management, the ownership of the properties of the enterprises when the cooperation ceases etc.).[595]

- *Wholly Foreign-Owned Enterprises:* In the early reform years, the Wholly Foreign-Owned Enterprise (WFOE) mode was not permitted except for policy experiments within the Special Economic Zones. Expansion of this mode to other areas occurred only in the late 1980s, when the "Law of the People's Republic of China on Wholly Foreign-Owned Enterprises" was promulgated in April 1986.[596] The WFOE law stipulated that China would allow foreign investors to establish foreign capital enterprises in the country. The law specifically prohibits the state from nationalizing or expropriating WFOEs. The law considers a WFOE as a limited liability company established in China with capital contributed exclusively by foreign investors. WFOEs paid higher taxes than JVs until the Unified Tax Law was passed in 1991, which treated all forms of FDI equally for tax purposes.[597]

The central government considers Equity JVs to be the preferred mode of FDI. The central government hopes that foreign management skills are transferred from the foreign to the Chinese partner. Almost all foreign investment enterprises are linked to a wide network of domestic suppliers, upon whom new standards of product quality, production methods and business concepts are imposed.[598] The Equity JV mode also has certain advantages from the investor's point of view, as foreign investors entering a country with different cultural, political, and economic systems from their own are likely to seek cooperative arrangements with local firms.[599] In transition economies, where requirements for adaptation and information are greater due to market imperfections, the appropriateness of Equity JVs is further reinforced.[600] The most commonly cited motives for selecting the Equity JV mode include the opportunity to gain rapid market entry, exploit economies of scale, obtain local know-how and vital raw materials, spread business risks, and meet host government demands.

---

595 For further information on the different forms of investment in China refer to Wang (1997).

596 Refer to Shanghai Foreign Investment Development Board (1986, revised 2000), "Law of People's Republic of China on Wholly-Foreign Owned Enterprises", Internet Edition, reviewed 17.07.2007.

597 Refer to Ministry of Commerce (1991), "Income Tax Law of the People's Republic of China on Enterprises with Foreign Investment and Foreign Enterprises", Internet Edition, reviewed 17.07.2007.

598 For further information on JVs in China refer to Pearson (1991).

599 For further information on international operations of MNCs refer to Dunning (1993).

600 For further information on Equity JVs refer to Beamish and Banks (1987).

As economic transition proceeds, China has increasingly become integrated into the global economy, and institutional uncertainties have receded gradually. MNCs have also gained business experience in the Chinese economy. Foreign entry modes therefore have evolved from an initial focus on risk-averse JVs to WFOEs, since those enjoy greater flexibility and independence in their business operations. Moreover, the foreign investors can more easily protect proprietary company information in a WFOE if the intellectual property rights system is not well established.[601] In 1994, 74 percent of FDIs were from JVs (49 percent of FDIs were from Equity JVs; 25 percent of FDIs were from Contractual JVs) and only 27 percent of FDIs were from WFOEs. By 2006, the proportion had reversed, as 78 percent of FDIs were from WFOEs and 21 percent of FDIs from JVs (17 percent of FDIs were from Equity JVs; 4 percent of FDIs were from Contractual JVs) (refer to Figure 13).

Figure 13: Share of contractual amount of FDI by type of firm ownership, 1994-2006.

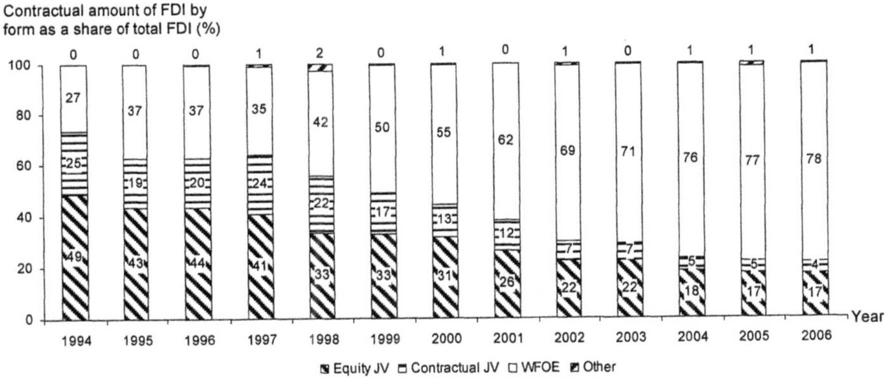

Source: China External Economic Statistical Yearbook (2005) and various years of China Statistical Yearbook. Note: The category "Other" includes foreign investments such as Cooperative Development.

The business activities of WFOEs are restricted and controlled by the state. WFOE investors need direct approval from the central government to make investments in public utilities, transportation, real estate, trusts, and leasing. As WFOEs are still prohibited from operating in such sectors as (life) insurance, media and telecommunications, foreign investors have no choice but to operate in JVs.[602]

601 For further information on FDIs during the reform era and the process of JV partner-selection in China refer to Fu (2000) and Luo (1998).

602 Refer to World Bank (2004), "China: A summary of Implementing GATS Commitments in Main Service Sectors", Internet Edition, reviewed 12.07.2007.

Altogether, China's FDI policy in the reform period contrasted with that pursued by the East Asian developmental states during comparable phases in their economic growth. The East Asian states severely limited FDIs during their reform years, while Chinese central and local level bureaucrats have actively attracted them.[603] Moreover, foreign investors have mainly operated in JVs as envisioned by central government policies on foreign investment.

3.3.4.2 State guidance of FDI

The central government's guidance of FDI has been twofold. It has issued different policies to inform state agents on the national FDI approach, and controlled inflowing investments through approval processes.

From the mid 1990s, government policies began to focus on linking FDI promotion to domestic industrial objectives.[604] At the beginning of 1993, China planned a series of measures to attract foreign investment in the areas of finance, communications, information technology, farm products processing, urban infrastructure and housing renovation.[605] After the central government had promulgated specific pillar industries in 1994, its policy toward FDI has become more specific. In 1995, the State Development and Planning Commission, the State Economics and Trade Commission and the Ministry of Foreign Trade and Economic Cooperation jointly promulgated the "Interim Provisions on Guiding the Orientation of Foreign Investment" and the attached "Catalogue for the Guidance of Foreign Investment Industries".[606] The two documents aimed to increase the clarity and precision of FDI policy. The Foreign Investment Catalogue generally lists specific industries and economic activities in which foreign investment is "encouraged", "restricted" or "prohibited". Projects not included in the Foreign Investment Catalogue are considered "permitted". Among the encouraged investments are new and high technology products and projects that strengthen the competing capability of products in international markets. Among the restricted foreign investments are projects that adopt *"out-of-date technologies".*[607] With this regulation, "sunrise industries" are promoted while "sunset industries" are restricted like in the East Asian developmental states. The central government ensured that foreign investment was compatible with government industrial policies, and that the Chinese state would

603 Refer to Nolan (1995b), p. 188.

604 Refer to Ministry of Commerce (2002), "Provisions on Guiding the Orientation of Foreign Investment", Internet Edition, reviewed 18.04.2006.

605 Refer to Lu (2000b), "Prospects of industrial policy regime after the WTO", Internet Edition, reviewed 17.11.2006.

606 Refer to Ministry of Commerce (2002), "Provisions on Guiding the Orientation of Foreign Investment", Internet Edition, reviewed 18.04.2006.

607 Refer to Ministry of Commerce (2003), "Policies and Preferences", Internet Edition, reviewed 10.07.2006.

retain control in the pillar industries. In the "restricted" categories, for instance, the equity stake of the foreign partner was limited and in the "prohibited" categories it was even barred completely.[608] Since then, the guidelines have been embodied in a large number of laws and regulations promulgated by the Ministry of Foreign Trade and Economic Cooperation (since 2003 by the Ministry of Commerce) and other government agencies. They are updated regularly reflecting the latest economic developments, policy re-orientations and priorities.[609]

In 1997, the Foreign Investment Catalogue was revised in accordance with the national industrial policy which aimed to adjust China's industrial structure and attract advanced technology. Accordingly, the scope of the encouraged projects broadened. The revised catalogue highlighted the policy to encourage FDI in the central and western regions and particularly aimed to promote export-oriented FDI projects.[610] The central government assumed that foreign investors would channel capital into industries that had the potential to compete internationally. The global linkages of MNCs would then facilitate their access to foreign markets and teach domestic companies about channels of distribution.[611] Projects that fell into the category of "permitted investments", but export all their products directly, were *"deemed as encouraged projects".*[612]

In 2002, the newly promulgated "Provisions on Guiding the Orientation of Foreign Investment" replaced the previous "Interim Provisions", and a new catalogue of industrial guidance for FDI was issued. While the number of "encouraged" categories increased from 186 to 262, the number of "restricted" categories decreased from 112 to 75. The central government permitted foreign entry to utility industries. This revision reflected the promises China had made for its WTO accession: the further opening up of service industries which includes financial services, tourism, telecommunications, transportation, accountancy, law services etc.[613]

---

608 Refer to Thun (2006), p. 59.

609 Since 2005, the central government has categorized industries no longer into four, but three types (encouraged, restricted and those to be eliminated) and thus reduced the complexity of FDI regulation. For further information refer to the "Decision of the State Council on Implementing the Interim Regulation on Promoting the Adjustment of Industrial Structure" and NDRC's "Guiding Catalogue for the Adjustment of Industrial Structure". Refer to NDRC (2005), "Major Measures to Promote the Adjustment of Industrial Structure", Internet Edition, reviewed 18.12.2006.

610 Refer to Liang (2004), p. 190.

611 Refer to Zhang and Song (2000), pp. 394-395.

612 Refer to Ministry of Commerce (2003), "Policies and Preferences", Internet Edition, reviewed 10.07.2006.

613 Refer to State Council (2002), "Provisions on Guiding the Orientation of Foreign Investment", Internet Edition, and State Development Planning Commission, the State Economy and Trade Commission, the Ministry of Foreign Trade and Economic Cooperation (2002), "Catalogue for the Guidance of Foreign Investment Industries", Internet Edition, both reviewed 18.04.2006. The guiding catalogue was updated again in 2004. Refer to NDRC and Ministry of Commerce (2004), "Catalogue of Priority Inudstries for Foreign Investment in the Central-Western Region", Internet Edition, and National Development and Reform Commission and Ministry of Commerce (2005), "Catalogue of Industries for Guiding Foreign Investment", Internet Edition, reviewed 22.04.2006.

The Ministry of Science and Technology and the Ministry of Commerce jointly promulgated the "Catalogue of Encouraged Hi-tech Products for Foreign Investment" in 2003.[614] Thus, they emphasized the central government's focus on developing the nation's high-tech capacities. The catalogue listed 917 high-technology products within 11 categories in accordance with technological domain, including information technology, software, aerospace, optical electronics, biological medicine and medical instruments, new materials, new energy, environment protection, geological instruments, nuclear and modern agriculture. The catalogue stipulated 721 items that should be developed imperatively in terms of technology and equipment, and identified 196 items which showed a big gap between China and abroad, as well as requirements of national security and environmental protection.[615] The central government hoped to attract advanced applicable technologies from abroad and strengthen the abilities of internal assimilation and independent innovation. The catalogue aimed to advise provinces, municipalities, autonomous regions and departments to encourage foreign investment in high-tech industry, to accelerate the pace in introducing advanced technologies from abroad, to strengthen the abilities of internal assimilation and independent innovation, and further improve the quality and level of foreign investment in the promulgated categories.

Overall, state guidance of foreign investments to preferred sectors reveals the strategic approach of using investment as a means of economic development. The analysis of the various policy documents regulating foreign investment shows that restrictions have been reduced gradually in line with proceeding economic reform, and government attention has been focused increasingly on high-tech FDIs.

In addition to the policies guiding inflowing investment, the central government has exerted strong influence on the landscape of foreign investment through its approval function of large-scale investment projects. In its 2004 "Interim Measures for the Administration of Examining and Approving Foreign Investment Projects", the NDRC promulgated the approval system of foreign investments in China. Depending on the investment sum, either the NDRC, the State Council or regional development and reform departments are responsible for the examination and approval of foreign investments (refer to Table 6):

- *Regional and county authorities* are authorized to approve "encouraged" projects with investment under USD 30 million and "permitted" projects under USD 10 million. They may authorize "encouraged" and "permitted" projects

614 Refer to Ministry of Science and Technology and Ministry of Commerce, "Catalogue of Encouraged Hi-Tech Products for Foreign Investment (2003)", Internet Edition, reviewed 17.04.2006.

615 Ibidem.

within municipal level development zones valued at USD 30 million or less.[616] The localities' autonomy has simplified the approval procedures.[617]

- *Provincial and municipal governments* can approve "encouraged" and "permitted" projects with investments under USD 100 million, and "restricted" projects with investments under 50 million.
- *The NDRC* has to approve "encouraged" and "permitted" investment projects exceeding an investment volume of USD 100 million.
- Approval from both *the NDRC and the State Council* is necessary for "encouraged" and "permitted" investment projects exceeding an investment volume of USD 500 million. *The NDRC and the State Council* have to approve FDI projects with an investment volume higher than USD 50 million for "restricted" projects.

Table 6: Approval of foreign investment projects, 2004.

Industry type	Size of project (including profit) (USD)	Type of approval required
Encouraged	up to 30 million	Regional and county level authorities
Permitted	up to 10 million	Regional and county level authorities
Encouraged/ Permitted	up to 100 million	Provincial level development and reform commission
	over 100 million	NDRC
	over 500 million	NDRC and State Council
Restricted	up to 50 million	Provincial level development and reform commission
	over 50 million	NDRC and State Council

Source: Own illustration according to NDRC (2004), "Interim Measures for the Administration of Examining and Approving Foreign Investment Projects", Article 3 and 4, Internet Edition, reviewed 24.04.2006 and Shanghai Government (2005), "Examination and Approval Jurisdiction", 22.10.2005, Internet Edition, reviewed 10.12.2006.

In conclusion, since opening up in 1978, China has extensively absorbed foreign investment. The experience of other East Asian states influenced Chinese decision-makers. The East Asian developmental states strictly controlled the amount of inflowing capital in order to keep a "healthy balance" and not become subservient to it.[618] Similar to its East Asian counterparts, the government in China has been controlling all inflowing capital. The central government's guidance of FDI can be

616 Refer to Shanghai Government (2005), "Examination and Approval Jurisdiction", Internet Edition, reviewed 10.12.2006.

617 Refer to Panagariya (2003), p. 5.

618 Refer to Johnson (1987), p. 163.

seen as one important industrial policy instrument that the developmental states also utilized. FDI-guidance was in line with the central leadership's economic and social development planning.

Unlike the East Asian developmental states that have not only controlled, but also systematically excluded FDI, China has attempted to attract FDI in order to quickly catch up technologically. So that foreign companies cannot dominate the domestic market, the Chinese foreign investment scheme forces foreign companies eager to set up businesses in certain sectors to form JVs with domestic companies. With the JV regulations, the central government aims to develop domestic companies through spillovers from foreign to domestic partners, and thus advance the nation's technological catch-up.

3.3.5 Export-oriented industrialization

China's development strategy at the central level has not focused exclusively on FDI-led growth, but also on export-led growth. Throughout the reform period, Chinese products have been exported, and companies such as Lenovo, TCL and Huawei have proved to be internationally competitive.

Krueger (1980) contends that growth performance has been more satisfactory under export promotion strategies (intended as a general bias toward exports, and not as a package of specific measures to encourage selective exports of particular items, themselves induced by a bias toward import substitution) than under import-substitution strategies.[619] Import substitution raises returns on the protected sector relative to the unprotected sectors, and thus creates rent in the economy and invites rent-seeking activities.[620] High import restrictions make the domestic production of importable products artificially more profitable relative to other products, typically those in the traditional sectors. Socialized credit risks and budgetary subsidies make financial resources cheaper to firms than otherwise would be the case. These rents attract new entrants to the industry.[621] The actual number of new entrants depends both on the size of the rents and the average size of the initial firms and their size of distribution. All else being equal, if an industry is populated with small firms, and if no firm enjoys a significant first-mover's advantage over others, the entries will be numerous.[622]

---

619 Refer to Krueger (1980), p. 288.

620 For further information refer to Krueger (1974).

621 Refer to Huang (2002a), p. 549.

622 In Thailand, the degree of import substitution policies was directly correlated with the number of auto plants. Between 1960 and 1978, the tariff rate on auto imports increased from 60 percent to 150 percent and the number of auto plants rose from 8 to 22 during the same period. Similar correlations can be found in Latin America. Refer to Kesavatana (1989) and Shapiro (1993).

3.3.5.1 Export promotion and import substitution

China was not a major trading nation before economic reform started in 1978. It mostly traded primary products with other developing nations.[623] In the years after 1978, China gradually started its re-integration into the global economy. The process of international economic integration marked a fundamental ideological shift. Similar to the export strategy of China's East Asian neighbors, in 1979, Deng called for exports even if they had to be subsidized at the beginning.[624]

China followed East Asia's example as a manufacturing export champion, moving the country towards a high level of participation in the world economy. Along China's reform path, virtually the entire eastern coast of China has exhibited an export-oriented economy.[625] While in 1980, the sum of total trade was USD 38.1 billion, in 2006, Chinese exports amounted to USD 969 billion and imports to USD 792 billion. In 2006, China's export proportion in GDP was 37 percent (compared with 6 percent in 1980) (refer to Figure 14).

Figure 14: Foreign trade, 1978-2006.

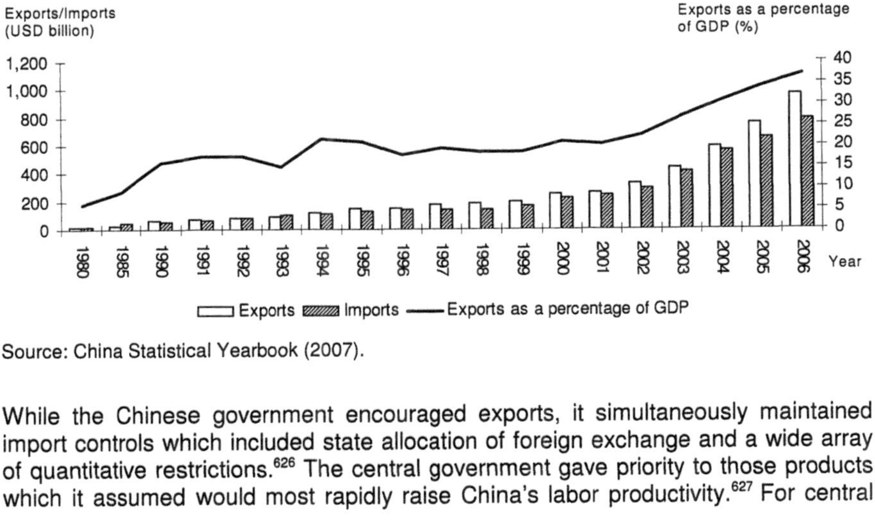

Source: China Statistical Yearbook (2007).

While the Chinese government encouraged exports, it simultaneously maintained import controls which included state allocation of foreign exchange and a wide array of quantitative restrictions.[626] The central government gave priority to those products which it assumed would most rapidly raise China's labor productivity.[627] For central

---

623 Refer to Breslin (1999), p. 1179.

624 Refer to Deng (1979), "Some Comments on Economic Work", Internet Edition, reviewed 19.03.2006.

625 Refer to Wang (1993), p. 199.

626 Refer to Vogel (1989).

627 For further information refer to Central Committee of the Communist Party of China (1985), p. 511-512, in: Central Committee of the Communist Party of China (1991).

level bureaucrats, it was apparent that a command economy which was economically and especially technically backward could not compete in open competition on world markets.[628] China's almost entire industrial sector was in the stage of an "infant industry", or specialized in the manufacturing of sunset products. It needed economic restructuring in order to become internationally competitive. Access to the Chinese market remained restricted throughout the reform period. Restrictions (such as import tariffs and quotas) were imposed on sectors where inefficient national producers in the state sector were vulnerable to international competition (e.g. the auto sector).[629]

3.3.5.2 Sectoral targeting of exports

The most important instruments of export targeting were production networks for exports (PNEs) and higher exchange retention rights to targeted sectors. The Seventh Five-Year Plan (1986-90) provided for the creation of PNEs. In the PNEs, the leading factories within the targeted sector were granted tax relieves, subsidies for technological upgrading, guaranteed supplies of raw materials and power, preferential access to transportation, and attractive purchase prices for their goods. The first industry group to benefit from this scheme was machinery and electronic goods. PNEs have also been created in light industrial products and textiles, as well as farm and sideline products.[630] Furthermore, the foreign exchange retention system (practiced since 1979) allowed selected exporting enterprises to retain a large share of foreign earnings.[631] Foreign exchange was needed to *"introduce technology from outside, import essential facilities and raw materials and repay the principal and interest of foreign loans".*[632] The capacity to earn foreign exchange mirrored the degree to which China had opened to the outside world. This in turn affected the scale and pace of domestic economic development.[633]

Particularly tax relief is a common practice adopted in international trade. The central government repaid a certain proportion of the consumption taxes and value-added tax to the enterprises, and thus reimbursed them for the taxes they had to pay on

628 At that time, China had not established a structure of modern firms, nor completed domestic price reform, nor entirely dismantled its material balance planning system, nor reformed its social security system. Refer to Nolan (1995b), p. 190.

629 Refer to Breslin (1999), p. 1188.

630 Refer to Panagariya (2003), p. 3.

631 By 1987, producers of electrical machinery and instruments were allowed to retain 100 percent of export earnings. Refer to Nolan (1995b), p. 189. For further information refer to Zhao (1987), p. 657, in: Central Committee of the Communist Party of China (1991).

632 Refer to Central Committee of the CCP and the State Council (1985): "Summary of the forum on the Changjian Delta, Zhujiang Delta and Xiamen-Zhangzhou-Quanzhou Triangle in Southern Fujian (Excerpts)", p. 444, in: Central Committee of the Communist Party of China (1991).

633 Refer to Zhao (1987), "Advance along the road of socialism with Chinese characteristics", p. 657, in: Central Committee of the Communist Party of China (1991).

exported goods.[634] Firms that were exporting were, moreover, granted a rebate on industrial and commercial taxes and preferential access to imported technology, and received credit at low interest rates for technical upgrading.[635]

In 1994, direct subsidies for exports were largely abolished due to escalating international pressure and China's ambitions to enter the WTO.[636] Under the transition review mechanism provided in China's Protocol of Accession, the European Community, Japan and the USA urged the country to cut its subsidies as required by the Subsidies Agreement.[637] The 2001 WTO Protocol finally required China to eliminate all export subsidies within the scope of the "Agreement on Subsidies and Countervailing Measures" (SCM Agreement) upon accession.[638] Under the SCM Agreement, developing country members have at least eight years, and transition economy members seven years, after WTO accession to phase out export subsidies. China's commitment to eliminate all export subsidies upon accession wiped out any transitional periods that were available to other accession countries under the SCM Agreement.[639] However, the central government still grants export subsidies for various product exports such as complete sets of equipment, high-tech products and mechanical and electronic products. Indirect subsidies for exports are low cost energy and inputs, preferential bank loans, and tax incentives:[640]

- The Export-Import Bank of China offers an "Export Seller's Credit". All the bank's capital comes from the government's fiscal allocation and is provided for the purpose of lending government support by observing the state industrial, foreign trade, financial and fiscal policies.[641] The loans that the bank provides to the exporter have usually a long maturity and preferential interest rates.[642]

---

634 Refer to People's Daily (2003), "Economist calls for abolishment of export tax rebate", Internet Edition, reviewed 07.08.2006.

635 Refer to State Council (1994), "Outline of State Industrial Policies for the 1990s", Chapter V, Internet Edition, reviewed 31.03.2006.

636 Refer to WTO (1994), "General Agreement on Tariffs and Trade 1994", Internet Edition, reviewed 27.11.2006. Moreover, the average tariff rate was reduced from 43 percent to about 17 percent and further reductions were promised. Refer to Zhu (2003), p. 155.

637 Refer to WTO (2004), "Transition period extended for export subsidies of developing countries", Internet Edition, reviewed 07.08.2006.

638 Refer to WTO (1994), "Agreement on Subsidies and Countervailing Measures", Internet Edition, reviewed 17.12.2006 and WTO (2001), "Report of the Working Party on the Accession of China", Internet Edition, reviewed 10.09.2006, p. 33.

639 China became member of the WTO on 11.12.2001. Under the SCM Agreement, the 8-year transitional period for developing country members ended on 31.12.2002, and the 7-year transitional period for transition economies ended on 31.12.2001.

640 Refer to Wade (2003b), p. xxi and Zhu (2003), p. 155.

641 Refer to Export-Import Bank of China (2006), "Export Seller's Credit", Internet Edition, reviewed 06.07.2007.

642 Ibidem.

- In pursuit of a central government goal to increase semiconductor output from USD 2 billion in 2000 to USD 24 billion by 2010, China applied discriminatory rates for value-added taxes on circuit chips. While China subjected all semiconductors to a value-added tax, domestic producers - whether wholly Chinese-owned or foreign-invested - received a value-added tax rebate for circuit chips designed and fabricated in the country, which made the effective value-added tax rate only 3 percent. The full 17 percent rate was only imposed on imported semiconductors.[643]

Altogether, even after WTO accession, central and local governments use industrial policy measures to promote exports or hinder imports in order to favor domestic over foreign industries. For these, Wade (2003) uses the expression *"below-the-radar"* industrial policy measures.[644]

3.3.5.3 The central government's devaluation policy to promote exports

The Chinese actively emulated Taiwan's and Korea's devaluation policy to encourage the growth of exports in the interests of development.[645] Like the East Asian developmental states, the Chinese government devalued the RMB during 1981-1994 as an attempt to cut imports and stimulate exports. After a prolonged phase of gradual nominal depreciations starting in 1980,[646] the RMB was devalued in January 1994 from 5.81 to 8.70 to the USD (refer to Figure 15). This improved price competition of domestically produced products. In the same year, the export growth rate was 31 percent.[647] Relative to the cost of exports from other states in Southeast Asia following export-led growth strategies, this move increased the relative competitiveness of Chinese exports. China adopted current account convertibility in 1996, and the RMB traded in a narrow band of RMB 8.19 to the USD until late 2005.[648] Being fixed against the USD for a decade in July 2005, central authorities dropped the peg to the USD in favor of a managed float against an unspecified basket of currencies.[649] The RMB's base exchange rate against the USD rose from

---

643 Refer to US Government Information (2005), "China's Industrial Policies Conflict with WTO Rules", Internet Edition, reviewed 11.07.2007.

644 Refer to Wade (2003b), p. xxi and Zhu (2003), p. 155.

645 Refer to Wang (1993), p. 90.

646 Major devaluations were: 14 percent in 1986, 21 percent in 1989 and 9.6 percent in 1990.

647 In comparison, the export growth rate was 8 percent in 1993. Calcuation based on data from the China Statistical Yearbook (2007).

648 Refer to Breslin (1999), p. 1183 and Holweg et al. (2005), p. 55.

649 The main components of the reference currency basket consisted of the currencies of China's major trading partners, including the US dollar, the euro, the yen and the Korean won. The Singapore dollar, the British pound, the Malaysian ringgit, the Russian rouble, the Australian dollar, the Thai baht and the Canadian dollar are also in the basket. However, the government has not announced the weights of the currency basket index.

RMB 8.28 to RMB 8.11, an appreciation of 2.1 percent. The authorities kept the existing trading bands of 0.3 percent on either side of a central rate against the USD (with the closing rate of the previous day becoming the central rate of the next day). The RMB is still assumed to be undervalued by more than 20 percent. American critics accuse Beijing of keeping the value of the RMB at an artificially low level.[650] In order to prevent the economy from overheating, in March 2007, China's central bank raised the prime rate to its highest level for eight years. The export boom is hence expected to slow down.[651]

Figure 15: Development of exchange rate RMB/USD, 1985-2006.

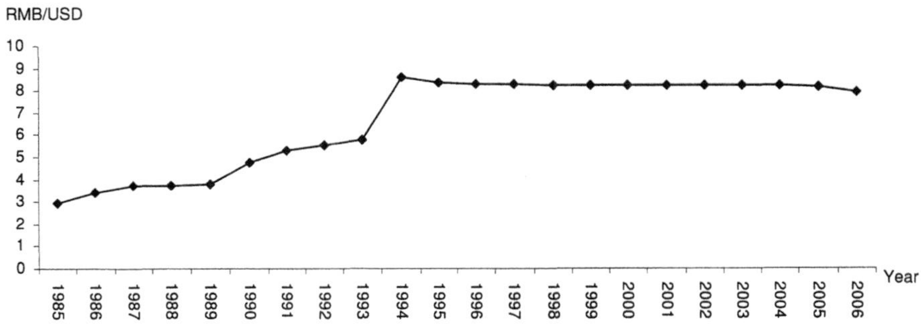

Source: China External Economic Statistical Yearbook (2005) and China Statistical Yearbook (2007).

Altogether, China's instrumental attitude towards international trade, and the pace of growth of Chinese exports, have a lot in common with that of the East Asian developmental states. The government introduced several export incentive programs for selected industrial sectors with the aim of enhancing competition and receiving foreign exchange earnings as well as management and technology know-how. Simultaneously, imports were tightly controlled by a wide variety of quantitative controls. Import substitution has protected specific infant industrial sectors from international competition. This makes an emulation of the developmental states' policy approach obvious. Due to the complexity of the economic system during the transition, and the characteristics of international integration, China had to choose different policy tools from those previously adopted by Japan, Korea and Taiwan.[652] Overall, the pattern of exports and imports is determined more by administrative decisions than by incentives at the level of the individual enterprise.

[650] Refer to Economist Intelligence Unit (2007), "China Economy: Critical issues - The Renminbi", Internet Edition, reviewed 10.07.2007.

[651] Refer to China Daily (2007), "Central bank raises interest rates, reserve requirements", Internet Edition, reviewed 23.10.2007. Also refer to Belke and Spies (2007), pp. 463-464.

[652] Refer to Zhang and Long (1997), p. 266.

3.3.5.4 Export-FDI nexus in Special Economic Zones

Already in 1979, the Central Committee established four Special Economic Zones as a particular type of export-processing zones. The first Special Economic Zones were opened in Guangdong and Fujian (Shenzhen, Xiamen, Zhuhai and Shantou) in 1979 and 1980.[653] The establishment of Special Economic Zones was designed to attract FDI into specifically designated export-oriented areas. These areas gained more authority over economic development.[654] In this way, they could experiment with the norms of a market economy. According to the gradual development strategy, most of China's economic reform measures were not applied simultaneously throughout the entire country. Experiments with a variety of innovations were conducted within selected, limited geographic areas and left a great deal of leeway to localities.[655] Not before the experiment proved to be successful, the reform was introduced to the rest of the nation. Gradualism in China was not so much the result of a particular theory of reform as of political deadlock and compromises within the CCP.[656]

As a means to attract FDIs and upgrade the international competitiveness of domestic firms, the central government offered foreign companies preferential tax rates according to the 1986 "Provisions of the State Council on the Encouragement of Foreign Investment".[657] Tax reductions available to FFEs are higher in the economic zones than those available under the national tax legislation. Table 7 shows that in the Special Economic Zones and National Development Zones, productive foreign enterprises are granted a reduced income tax rate of 15 percent instead of the normal 30 percent. Technology-intensive projects of non-productive enterprises, as well as energy and transportation projects, are rewarded with an income tax rate of 15 percent in all Special Economic Zones and National Development Zones.[658] Especially export enterprises have to pay a reduced income tax rate of 10 percent within Special Economic Zones and National Development Zones (compared with 15 percent outside these zones). Tax holidays of up to five years are available for companies in the special zones, depending on the amount of investment, the nature of the technology, and the duration of the project. Imported inputs used in exports or sold within the Special Economic Zones are free of indirect taxes such as import duty. Further measures to stimulate FDI are advantages in

---

653 Refer to Editorial Board of the Progress of China Industry Modernization (1999), p. 42.

654 The Ninth Five-Year Plan contends: *"All special economic zones and open coastal cities and areas should actively engage in international economic cooperation and serve as an example and a driving force for economic development in surrounding areas and the rest of the country".* Li (1996), "Report on the Outline of the Ninth Five-Year Plan for National Economic and Social Development and the Long-Range Objectives to the Year 2010", p. X. For further information refer to Yueh (2006), p. 5 and Montinola et al. (1995), pp. 62-63.

655 Refer to Deng (1985), "Special Economic Zones should shift their economy from a domestic orientation to an external orientation", Internet Edition, reviewed 19.03.2006.

656 Refer to Woo (1999), p. 123.

657 Refer to State Council (1986), "Provisions of the State Council on the Encouragement of Foreign Investment", Internet Edition, reviewed 23.04.2006.

658 The tax rate for energy and transportation projects is 15 percent outside the development zones.

manufacturing location, such as reduced land-use fees, priority in obtaining utilities, transport and communication facilities.[659] Accordingly, the main reasons for companies to locate in the special zones are particular policies and preferential treatment as well as flexible measures in carrying out foreign economic activities.

Table 7: Income tax rates concerning foreign enterprises in development zones, 2006.

Enterprises income tax rate	State Regulations	Special Economic Zones	National Development Zones
1. Productive enterprises	30%	15%	15%
2. Non-productive enterprises	30%	15%	30%
Knowledge-intensive and technology-intensive projects and technology development centers; projects with a long investment rewarding period	30%	15%	15%
Projects concerning energy, transportation, port or projections engorged by the governments	15%	15%	15%
Export-oriented enterprises if the export value of the year equals or exceeds 70 percent of the output value of the same year after the exemption-reduction period is over	15%	10%	10%

Source: Ministry of Commerce (2006), "Tax Policies Concerning Foreign Enterprises in China's Development Zones", Internet Edition, reviewed 23.03.2006. Note: Among the National Development Zones are Economic and Technological Development Zones, Free Trade Zones, High-Technology Industrial Development Zones, Border and Economic Cooperation Zones, and Export Processing Zones. Special regulations for Border Economic Cooperative Areas are not considered here.[660]

Meanwhile, each province has established Special Economic Zones and National Development Zones in which enterprises can profit from low tax rates, particularly for high-tech and export-oriented enterprises. With the central and local governments' policy approach of attracting foreign investment to special zones, China has attracted about 400 of the World Top 500 transnational corporations to Economic and Technological Development Zones.[661] Investment from foreign companies resulted in

659 Refer to State Council (1986), "Provisions of the State Council on the Encouragement of Foreign Investment", Article 5, Internet Edition, reviewed 23.04.2006.

660 For further information on types of zones and tax policies within the zones refer to United Nations Economic and Social Commission for Asia and the Pacific (2005), "Free Trade Zone and Port Hinterland Development", p. 50 ff, Ministry of Commerce (2006), "Tax Policies Concerning Foreign Enterprises in China's Development Zones", Internet Edition, and China Development Zones (2003), "The Tax Policies Concerning Foreign-Funded Enterprises and Foreign Enterprises in China's Development Zones", Internet Edition, reviewed 23.03.2006.

661 Refer to China Development Zones (2002), "World Top 500 in ETDZs", Internet Edition, reviewed 25.10.2006 and People's Daily (2005), "China: Share Wealth With the World", Internet Edition and People's Daily (2005), "Full text of Hu Jintao's speech at 2005 Fortune Global Forum", Internet Edition, both reviewed 10.07.2007.

a heated competition between provinces and localities. Localities have often ignored instructions from the central government, and strived to offer incentives to gain new investments or lure existing investments away from other parts of China.[662]

Various tax incentives for foreign enterprises have been widely criticized for lack of harmony as well as the resulting discrimination against domestic enterprises. In consequence, China has started to transform its tax system. The two parallel income tax laws for domestic and foreign enterprises[663] (irrespective of whether the company is located in a development zone or not) are abolished. Under the tax law, the actual income tax rate for a foreign invested company can be as low as 15 percent (as opposed to 33 percent for domestic enterprises).[664] In January 2007, the Chinese State Administration of Taxation announced to adopt uniform corporate income tax rates (25 percent) for both domestic and foreign companies effective as of January 2008. The new law creates a level playing field for domestic and foreign enterprises.[665] Apart from increased income tax, foreign companies will no longer enjoy some other tax incentives, including pre-tax reduction and tax rebate for re-investment. With the new tax law, Beijing replies to WTO demands of equal tax treatment and confirms its aim to particularly attract high-tech investments. From 2008 onwards, a preferential tax rate of 15 percent will only be granted to companies operating in specific industry sectors, such as high-tech, as well as energy efficiency, and environmental protection. Some MNCs have already adapted their business plans to the policy change. General Electric China has announced it will invest USD 50 million in its Shanghai-based technology center for products serving environmental protection, including more efficient airplane engines and wind power generators, seawater desalination technology, and energy-saving bulbs.[666]

---

662 Refer to The Economist (2005), "The insidious charms of foreign investment", Internet Edition, reviewed 12.12.2006.

663 The Interim Regulations on Enterprise Income Tax, effective 01.01.1994 which is applicable to domestic enterprises, and the Income Tax Law for Foreign Invested Enterprises and Foreign Enterprises, effective 01.07.1991, which is applicable to foreign invested enterprises and foreign enterprises.

664 Moreover, a foreign investor may be entitled to a tax reduction or exemption for dividend distributions. Another distinct advantage for foreign invested companies is that a foreign invested company can make a full deduction of salary and benefit expenses, while a domestic company may only deduct a specific portion of salary payments.

665 The new tax rate is lower than the average tax rates of neighboring countries in an effort to increase the competitiveness of enterprises and to boost China's attraction for foreign investors. The average enterprise income tax rate is 28.6 percent in 159 countries and regions around the world in which an enterprise income tax is applied, while that in China's 18 neighboring countries and regions is 26.7 percent. Refer to Ministry of Commerce (2007), "China's taxation authorities promise to well advance corporate income tax reform", Internet Edition, reviewed 21.02.2007, Xinhuanet (2007), "NPC to speed up legislation on social issues in 2007", Internet Edition, reviewed 21.10.2007 and People's Daily Online (2007), "China's parliament adopts enterprise income tax law", Internet Edition, reviewed 21.10.2007.

666 Refer to People's Daily Online (2007), "China's parliament adopts enterprise income tax law", Internet Edition, reviewed 21.10.2007.

Nevertheless, from the close link between FDI and export promotion since the 1980s, the question arises as to whether Chinese exports are driven by domestic or foreign companies? The breakdown of China's exports according to type of producing firm puts China's economic rise in perspective. Statistics indicate that from 1990 until 2006, exports from FFEs in China rose more quickly than did national gross exports (refer to Figure 16). The central government's incentives as well as China's competitive advantage of cheap labor have stimulated FFEs' export activities. While FFEs accounted for only 20 percent of Taiwan's manufactured exports in the mid-1970s, and only 25 percent of Korea's manufactured exports between 1974 and 1978, FFEs accounted for 58 percent of China's exports in 2006.[667] Exports from these businesses boost China's overall exports.[668]

Figure 16: Exports of FFEs, 1980-2006.

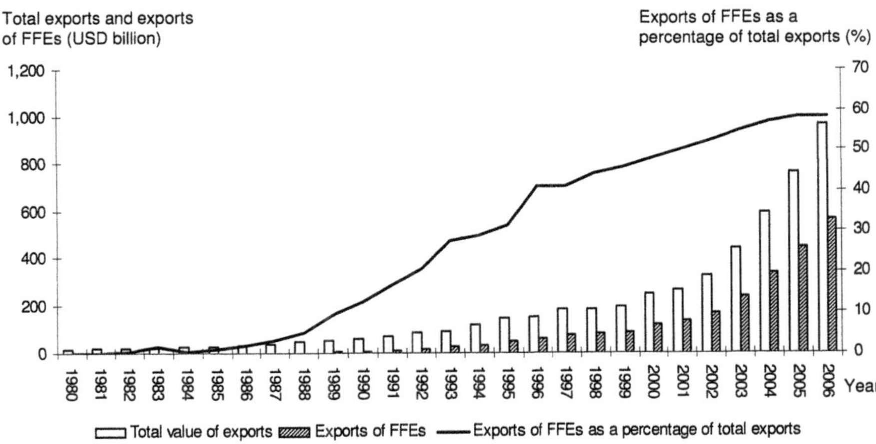

Source: China External Economic Statistical Yearbook (2005) and China Statistical Yearbook (2007).

FFEs have furthermore catalyzed the boom in exports of particularly (high) tech-oriented goods.[669] Establishing export bases for new and high-tech products in selected high-tech industrial development zones is an important part of the government's plan for developing trade through S&T. The Pearl River Delta, Yangtze River Delta and the Beijing-Tianjin region have the greatest concentration of such export bases. Consequently, export volumes of new and high-tech products from

667 Refer to Gilboy (Foreign Affairs) (2004), "The Myth Behind China's Miracle", Internet Edition, reviewed 16.10.2006.

668 Refer to People's Daily (2003), "FDI fueling China's economic boom", Internet Edition, reviewed 18.10.2006.

669 Refer to Abele (bfai) (2006), p. 12.

these areas account for over 80 percent of the national total.[670] The share of national exports of high-tech products increased from 4.0 percent in 1991 to 28.6 percent in 2005. The CAGR of high-tech product exports was 15.1 percent between 1991 and 2005.[671] Also, the share of high-tech products in manufactured imports was 30.0 percent in 2005. In the same year, the share of high-tech exports in industrial manufacturered exports was 30.6 percent (the share of high-tech imports in industrial manufactured imports was 38.5 percent) (refer to Table 8). 81 percent of high-tech exports were information technology and telecommunication products and 11 percent of high-tech exports were electronic products in that year.[672]

Table 8: National imports and exports of high-tech products, 1991-2005.

	1991	1993	1995	1997	1999	2001	2003	2005
Exports of high-tech products (USD billion)	2.9	4.7	10.1	9.7	24.7	46.5	110.3	218.3
Share in total exports (%)	4.0	5.1	6.8	5.3	12.7	17.5	25.2	28.6
Share in industrial manufactured exports (%)	5.2	6.2	7.9	6.1	14.1	19.4	27.3	30.6
Imports of high-tech products (USD billion)	9.4	15.9	21.8	19.8	37.6	64.1	119.3	197.7
Share in total imports (%)	14.8	15.3	16.5	13.9	22.7	26.3	28.9	30.0
Share in industrial manufactured imports (%)	17.4	17.7	20.3	17.4	27.1	32.4	35.1	38.5

Source: Refer to Ministry of Science and Technology, various years of S&T Statistics Data Books, Internet Edition, reviewed 10.11.2007.

The main reason for the rapid increase of high-tech exports is that the final production stage has been transferred to China from industrialized economies, while the actual Chinese value added is still estimated to be relatively low. As a result, the subsidiaries of MNCs still account for the bulk – nearly 90 percent – of total Chinese high-tech exports.[673] The European Central Bank expects, however, that over the medium term, China will climb the technology ladder rather quickly, aided partly by the dissemination of technology and management skills due to FDI. The enhanced technological capability of Chinese products can be seen from the angle of the product composition of the euro area's imports from China. More sophisticated goods from China, such as office machinery and telecommunications equipment, have experienced a large increase in euro area's imports over the past five years, even

670 Refer to Chinese Government (2005), "New and high-tech development zones", Internet Edition, reviewed 17.11.2006.

671 Calculation based on data from the Ministry of Science and Technology, various years of S&T Statistics Data Books, Internet Edition, reviewed 10.11.2007 and from China Monthly Exports and Imports data reprinted in Abele (2006), p. 12.

672 Calculation based on China Monthly Exports and Imports data reprinted in Abele (2006), p. 12.

673 Refer to European Central Bank (2005), "The next dimension for EU-China relations", Internet Edition, reviewed 26.02.2007.

though traditional and more labor-intensive goods – such as handbags, clothing and footwear products – remain the main import items.[674]

Overall, China has encouraged multinational affiliates to enter China through FDI. Tax incentives have encouraged foreign investors to export a large share of sales. The analysis showed that about 60 percent of China's manufactured exports are generated by foreign-owned firms. Tax reductions of FFEs have, however, put domestic enterprises at a disadvantage. The new income tax law indicates China's ambitions to slow the pace of foreign investment inflow, and establish a level playing-field for foreign and domestic companies in China. At the same time, the new income tax law stipulates that central bureaucrats increasingly focus on the country's high-tech development. While the central government's focus was the inflow of a broad spectrum of FDI in the early reform period, FDI attraction has become more selective and targeted to high-tech investments since the 1990s. This parallels the nation's industrial policy approach via its five year plans.

3.4 Financial system

In the East Asian developmental states, the financial system was a key instrument of industrial policy-making. The advocates of a bank- and credit-based financial system bring forward three arguments. First, in a bank-based system, enterprises depend heavily on banks for finance, and less on a broad public of shareholders. Hence, the long-term growth preferences of government officials and bank executives have more weight, and investment decisions are more insulated from the public's preferences. The economy's investment decisions, therefore, should be guided by long-term growth expectations. In a capital market-based system, alternatively, the public usually allocates potential savings to more short-term productive investment, financial speculation or consumption.[675] Second, a bank-based financial system gives the government a powerful mechanism for encouraging firms to enter specific sectors.[676] The state has many tools at its disposal, in order to direct investment decisions. In the developmental states, governments often provided guarantees for loans and consequently influenced the availability and cost of bank loans and the relaxation of antitrust bans.[677] The state was hence in a position to *"maximize induced decision-making"*.[678] Third, the state's control over the financial system, and thus over the allocation of credit to highly leveraged firms, can be used to make

[674] Ibidem.

[675] Refer to Wade (1990), pp. 364-365.

[676] Ibidem, p. 365 and Okimoto (1989), p. 142 ff.

[677] The Korean government is paramount in this respect as it acted as a guarantor for foreign credit which has financed its long-term investments. Refer to Amsden (1989), p. 945.

[678] Refer to Johnson (1982), p. 236.

business leaders support the government's objectives and the implementation of the industrial strategy.[679]

In the East Asian developmental states, under the direction of an industrial bureaucracy that was to a certain extent isolated from societal pressures, the government-controlled financial system channeled investment capital to alleged strategic sectors. Individuals, with no choice but to make their deposits in the closed financial system, ended up subsidizing large firms that received preferential credit.[680]

China also made use of the financial system as an industrial policy instrument. Deng stated in 1979: *"Some [...] projects can bring us quick profits, therefore, the finance departments and banks should support them".*[681] The pursuit of a socialist market economy has increased the need for reliance on the banking sector as the central government's major tool for macroeconomic control, following the decline of the state sector.[682]

3.4.1 Government influence over the financial system

The financial sector consists of two regulatory institutions (the People's Bank of China, which is the central bank, and the China Banking Regulatory Commission) as well as banking and non-bank financial institutions (refer to Figure 17). Although the role of other segments of the financial system like stock and bond markets has been growing in importance since the 1990s, the domestic banking system is still the main channel of financial intermediation. In comparison with other countries, China still depends on bank financing. In 2004, bank credit (of deposit-taking commercial banks) to the private sector accounted for 141 percent of GDP in China, compared with 46 percent of GDP in the USA. In the same year, stock market capitalization in China accounted for 27 percent of GDP compared with 138 percent of GDP in the USA.[683]

---

679 Obviously, this practice might easily be abused, if it becomes common to allocate credit for "loyalty" rather than for economic performance. Only sparing but well-publicized use may obtain the political gains without the legitimacy costs. Refer to Wade (1990), pp. 365-366.

680 Refer to Thun (2006), p. 56.

681 Refer to Deng (1979), "Some Comments on Economic Work", Internet Edition, reviewed 19.03.2006.

682 Enterprization of state commercial banks was therefore viewed as a constrained policy move and an entrenched version of the shareholding reform of SOEs. Refer to Leung and Mok (2000), p. 52.

683 Refer to Belaisch and Zanello (2006), p. 19.

Figure 17: Structure of the Chinese financial system.

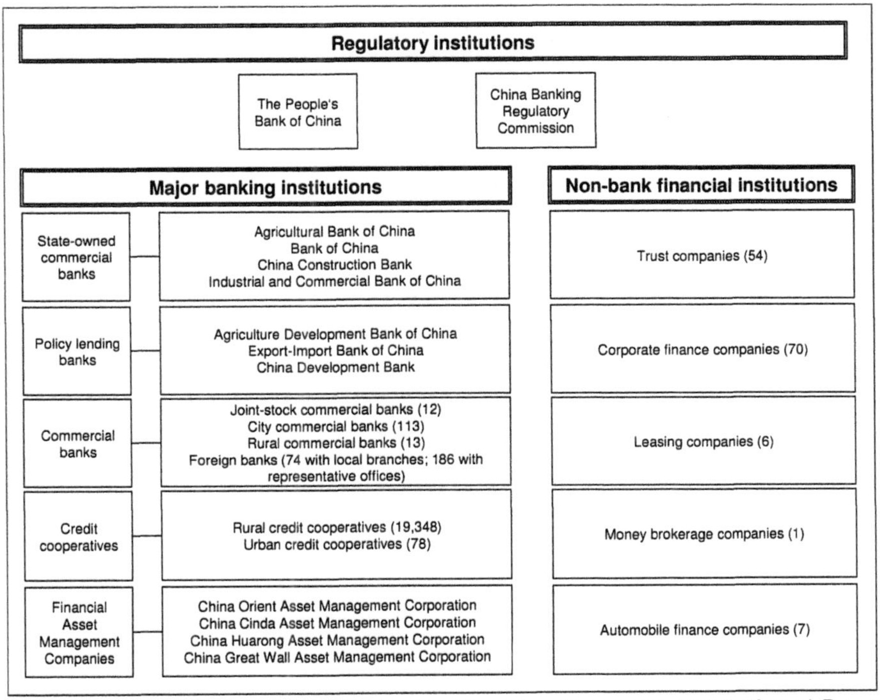

Source: Own illustration based on China Banking Regulatory Commission (2007), "Annual Report 2006", p. 30 and p. 130 ff, Internet Edition, reviewed 09.11.2007. Note: Figure only illustrates major finance institutions. Number of institutions in brackets.

Commercial banks, comprising four state-owned commercial banks, joint-stock commercial banks, city and rural commercial banks and foreign banks, dominate the financial sector. The top three types of banking institutions in terms of assets share were large state-owned commercial banks, joint-stock commercial banks and rural cooperative financial institutions. These institutions, respectively had assets accounting for 55 percent, 12 percent and 10 percent of the total assets of the banking sector in 2006. The assets share of the state-owned commercial banks has been declining over the years, with a decrease of 2.9 percentage points from 2003 and 0.9 percentage points from 2005. Meanwhile, assets share for the joint-stock commercial banks has been rising, with an increase of 1.7 and 0.5 percentage points from 2003 and 2005, respectively.[684] Institutional investors, notably insurance

684 Refer to China Banking Regulatory Commission (2007), "Annual Report 2006", p. 30, Internet Edition, reviewed 09.11.2007.

companies, securities investment funds and, particularly, pension funds, are in an early stage of development although they are growing rapidly. Financial instruments for long-term savings and for managing liquidity and risk are quite limited compared with more advanced economies.[685] China is hence heavily reliant on its banking system for financial intermediation, like its counterparts in East Asia.

The bank-dominated financial system has been under tight government control during the reform period. The People's Bank of China, in particular, has served the central government's policy interests. In 1983, the State Council announced the transformation of the People's Bank of China into a central bank, in order to complete the two-tier banking system by removing commercial lending activities from the People's Bank of China, and transferring them to the four state-owned commercial banks.[686] To achieve the government's annual money supply target, the People's Bank of China carried out national credit planning, and imposed an overall credit ceiling on all banks and financial institutions.[687] The People's Bank of China, however, is no independent central bank as known in industrialized countries. As it is ultimately overseen by the State Council, it operates under direct state supervision, and incorporates the state's policy goals in its monetary policy. This was manifested in December 2003, when the Standing Committee of the People's Congress adopted the "Law of the People's Republic of China on the People's Bank of China". Article 2 promulgates that the People's Bank of China has to perform functions assigned by the State Council.[688] Moreover, the State Council appoints or removes the bank's governor and deputy governors. The governor and the deputy governors of the People's Bank of China are nominated by the Premier of the State Council. The National People's Congress decides on their nomination.[689] Accordingly, the institutional design of the People's Bank of China, either its position under the State Council in the organization chart or the selection of its governors, is clearly linked to

685 Refer to OECD (2006b), p. 68.

686 The introduction of a two-tier banking system in 1979 was the first milestone in the modernization of the Chinese financial system. The government removed the monopolistic position of the People's Bank of China by establishing the Agricultural Bank of China, Bank of China and the China Construction Bank. The Agricultural Bank of China's objective was to foster rural banking business. It also took the supervisory authority of a network of rural credit cooperatives that provided small-scale rural banking. The Bank of China was responsible for foreign currency transactions, while the China Construction Bank focused on the construction sector. Refer to García-Herrero and Santabárbara (2004), pp. 12-13, Internet Edition, reviewed 13.05.2006.

687 The national credit plan matched annual fund usage (loans) with fund sources (deposits) and decided the volume of new currency issued to balance the gap between loans and deposits. The central allocation of credit quotas was supplemented by the People's Bank of China's mandatory control of the deposit and lending interest rates to ensure the fulfillment of credit plan goals. Refer to Lu (2006), p. 6.

688 *"The People's Bank of China shall, under the leadership of the State Council, formulate and implement monetary policy, prevent and mitigate financial risks, and maintain financial stability."* The People's Bank of China (2003), "Law of the People's Republic of China on the People's Bank of China", Article 2, Internet Edition, reviewed 01.06.2006.

689 Ibidm, Article 10.

the state and its industrial policy goals. In order to achieve a clear distinction between monetary policy and bank supervision objectives, in late 2003, China amended the "Law of the People's Republic of China on Banking Regulation and Supervision" to establish the China Banking Regulatory Commission to supervise the banking industry.[690] The China Banking Regulatory Commission should take over the supervisory and regulatory responsibilities for banks from the People's Bank of China. This would allow the People's Bank of China to focus on monetary policy, including an increased reliance on market-oriented instruments. The China Banking Regulatory Commission is also, however, no independent institution. It is overseen by the State Council as is the People's Bank of China.

In the first two decades of the reform era, the big four Chinese state-owned commercial banks (Agricultural Bank of China, Bank of China, China Construction Bank, Industrial and Commercial Bank of China) were also state-owned and largely insulated from market forces. They were used as a vehicle for macroeconomic control, and hence subject to strict interest rate control and credit quotas.[691] The four state-owned banks were required to support government objectives ranging from the expansion of priority sectors to underwriting loss-making SOEs rather than lending according to commercial bank decisions.[692] These administratively allocated funds are referred to as "policy loans", and can be regarded as directed credit programs. Policy loans accounted for about 35 percent of total loans made by state banks in the first half of the 1990s. Policy loans are well known for their poor returns and high risks, compared with commercial loans.[693]

With the introduction of a socialist market economic system in 1992, reforms accelerated in the banking and financial sector. The Chinese authorities created three so-called policy banks (Agricultural Development Bank of China, China Development Bank and Export-Import Bank of China) in 1994.[694] The policy banks are *"banks whose sole function is to make low-interest loans for state projects".*[695] The policy banks took over the state-owned banks' state-directed lending role and

---

690 Refer to People's Bank of China (2003), "Law of the People's Republic of China on the People's Bank of China", Internet Edition, and People's Bank of China (2003), "Law of the People's Republic of China on Banking Regulation and Supervision", Internet Edition, both reviewed 03.10.2006.

691 Refer to Leung and Mok (2000), p. 45.

692 Refer to Lardy (1998), p. 83.

693 Refer to Lu (2006), p. 8.

694 The overhaul of the banking system had at least three major aims: first, commercialize the four state-owned banks by separating commercial from policy lending; second, nourish a more diverse and competitive banking sector by allowing more commercial banks to enter the market; third, develop the People's Bank of China into an independent modern central bank with tasks such as regulating the national financial market and maintaining macroeconomic stability. Refer to Kwong and Lee (2005), p. 11 and Chinese Government (2006), "Reform of Financial System", Internet Edition, reviewed 28.03.2006.

695 Refer to Li (1993), "Report on the Work of the Government", p. X.

freed the big four from policy lending. They were to grant policy loans in accordance with state industrial policy and national plans. The capital sources of the policy banks were mainly government budgetary funds, social insurance, and postal and investment funds from a shrinking public sector.[696]

The Commercial Bank Law, promulgated in 1995, reconfirmed that the state-owned commercial banks should function as independent commercial banks, and that their credit policy should be independent of state involvement.[697] At the same time, however, the Commercial Bank Law stated that *"A commercial bank should issue loans [...] under the guidance of the industrial policies of the state".*[698] In addition, according to the 1995 Law, the supervisory boards of the state-owned commercial banks should consist of representatives of the People's Bank of China and relevant government departments.[699] These regulations contravened the official claim of the independent lending authority of state-owned commercial banks.

Altogether, Chinese banks have played a crucial role in the country's economic growth. Throughout the reform period, the state's influence over the banking system has been extensive. The institutional design of the financial system, as well as administrative and legal regulations, emphasize the financial sector's role as an industrial policy instrument. As in the East Asian developmental states, the organization of the financial system has enabled government-directed bank lending.

3.4.2 Sectoral and firm-level allocation of credit

After 1998, in the wake of the East Asian financial crisis, the People's Bank of China abolished loan quota control over the four state-owned commercial banks, and increased flexibility in the use of interest rates as a tool to allocate bank credit.[700] However, the state's control over the financial sector was not loosened, as the commercial banks are still not independent in their loan decisions.[701] Despite legal

---

696 Refer to Asia Times Online (2002), "China: Banking on bank reform", Internet Edition, reviewed 10.09.2006.

697 Refer to Nee et al. (2007), p. 39.

698 Refer to Standing Committee of the National People's Congress (1995), "Law of the People's Republic of China on Commerical Banks", Chapter IV, Article 34 A, Internet Edition, reviewed 18.10.2005.

699 Ibidem, Chapter II, Article 18. Since the establishment of the China Banking Regulatory Commission, the supervisory board of the state-owned commercial banks has been under the direction of the China Banking Regulatory Commission which is furthermore under the State Council.

700 Banks were allowed to offer loans according to risk premiums at rates of up to 20 percent above, or not less than 10 percent below, the official lending rates. Refer to Leung and Mok (2000), p. 51.

701 Evidence is provided by Leung and Mok (2000) that analyzed the commercialization of banks in China and Zhu (1999) that contends that *"China's financial sector has always been under the strong grip of the state".* Refer to Zhu (1999), p. 537.

reform of the banking sector to promote banks' formal autonomy in lending decisions, political intervention is prevalent.[702]

The empirical analysis of Nee and Opper (2007) highlights the sectoral distribution of government assistance in loan applications. Their results show that political ties are used as instruments to allocate scarce capital into preferred industrial sectors. Government assistance in loan applications is particularly common in high-tech sectors such as biotechnology and electronics which are in focus of the current industrial policy and technology programs (refer to Figure 18).[703]

Figure 18: Sectoral distribution of government assistance in loan applications, 2003.

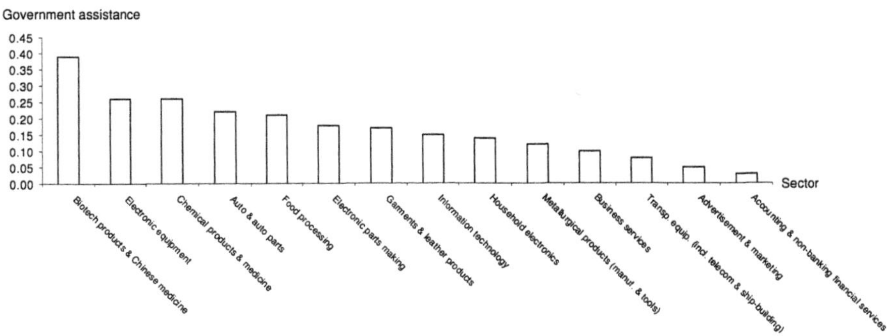

Source: Nee and Opper (2007), p. 26. Note: Nee and Opper's results are based on an empirical analysis of data from the 2003 World Bank Investment Climate Survey.

Unlike the East Asian developmental states, state-owned commercial banks provided SOEs with lending priority over non-state enterprises even after 1998, when mandatory policy lending was abolished.[704] In 2006, private firms and individuals only received 3.1 percent of the short-term loans of China's state commercial banks. National banks allocated 7.1 percent of total short-term loans to state-owned township enterprises. Banks only allocated 2.1 percent of total short term loans to enterprises with foreign funds (refer to Table 9).

702 Refer to Nee and Opper (2007), p. 110 ff.

703 Ibidem, p. 26.

704 While the four state-owned commercial banks are particularly heavily concentrated in lending to SOEs, joint stock and city commercial banks are more oriented toward non-state enterprises. The capital markets are even more the preserve of SOEs: nearly all of the currently listed companies were state controlled at the time of their initial public offering; and non-state enterprises are also virtually absent from the corporate bond market. Refer to OECD (2006b), p. 68.

The empirical tests of Park and Sehrt (2001) indicate that there is an inverse relationship between the rate of financial intermediation and the level of economic development among Chinese provinces. In less developed regions, political factors rather than economic fundamentals play an important role in lending decisions. Accordingly, provinces with higher intermediation rates have tended to be those with greater SOE output relative to GDP, and with less profitable SOEs. Fast growing, rich coastal provinces such as Zhejiang, Jiangsu, Fujian, and Shandong, had the lowest state bank intermediation rates from 1991 to 1997.[705]

Table 9: Credit funds balance sheet of financial institutions (funds usage), 2006.[706]

Item	2006	Percentage of total short-term loans
Funds Usage (RMB billion)	**36,523**	
Total Loans	22,535	
Short-term Loans	9,853	
Loans to Industrial Sector	2,865	32.8
Loans to Commercial Sector	1,667	19.1
Loans to Construction Sector	361	4.1
Loans to Agricultural Sector	1,321	15.1
Loans to Township Enterprises	622	7.1
Loans to Private Enterprises and Individuals	267	3.1
Loans to Enterprises with Foreign Funds	183	2.1
Other Short-term Loans	2,566	29.3
Medium-term & Long-term Loans	10,655	
Credit Loans	252	
Other Loans	1,774	

Source: China Statistical Yearbook (2007).

3.4.3 Fragility of the Chinese financial system

During the reform period, SOEs have operated in a soft budget system in which they were entitled to receive credits from state-owned banks.[707] State-owned banks mainly allocated credits to SOEs according to the state's targets, irrespective of their ability to repay them. The government has continuously poured subsidies into unprofitable SOEs in order to prevent them from bankruptcy and secure employment and overall political stability. In 2006, RMB 18 billion of subsidies were allocated to loss-making enterprises.[708] Hard budget constraints like commercial credit discipline

705 Refer to Park and Sehrt (2001), p. 626.

706 Due to rounding errors, percentage numbers add up to 113 percent.

707 For further information on soft budget constraints in state- or collectively-owned companies refer to Kornai (1992a,b).

708 The amount of subsidies to loss-making industrial enterprises declined during the 1990s. While subsidies to loss-making enterprises amounted to more than RMB 50 billion in 1985, banks allocated "only" RMB 29 billion to unprofitable enterprises in 1999. Refer to China Statistical Yearbook (2007).

from the financial sector or the implementation of bankruptcy proceedings on SOEs have progressed, but are not systematically applied to all SOEs.[709]

Subsidies in the form of state-directed lending to SOEs (rather than to profitable quasi-private or local private enterprises) either due to upper-level instructed policy loans or due to personal connections, have led to an accumulation of non-performing loans (NPLs).[710] Banks did not sufficiently verify enterprises' profitability, and the pricing of risk remained undifferentiated when making lending decisions. Therefore, except for some of the bigger banks, the financial quality of most Chinese banks remained poor, with low earnings, inadequate capital, and high levels of NPLs.[711]

In 1999, the central government created four asset management companies – Xinda, Huarong, Great Wall, and Orient – to buy and manage bad loans from the big four banks and China Development Bank. Each of the four asset management companies paired up with one of the big four state-owned commercial banks.[712] NPL purchases by the asset management companies were intended to help recapitalize the state banks and accelerate SOE reform. By the end of 2000, the four companies finished isolating and acquiring bad debts of state-owned commercial banks successively with a total amount of RMB 1,394 billion. Also, state capital injections into the capital base of state-owned commercial banks together with sales of NPLs to asset management companies (financed in part by the central bank) should restore the financial solvency of these banks.

Even after the transfer of NPLs to the asset management companies, the big four banks have bad loans on their books, as progress made by the asset management companies has been slow.[713] At the end of 2006, the share of outstanding loans in total loans (NPL ratio) was 7.1 percent compared with 17.8 percent in 2003 (refer to

709 The "Law of the People's Republic of China on Enterprise Bankruptcy" was adopted in 1986. In 2003, the "Law on Enterprise Bankruptcy" was reviewed. Refer to Ministry of Commerce (2003), "Law on Enterprise Bankruptcy", Internet Edition, reviewed 17.07.2006. In June 2007, a new bankruptcy law for all sorts of enterprises became effective. The law has taken a great leap forward in bringing the bankruptcy regime in China in line with international practice. It introduces the concept of an independent administrator, e.g. a professional organization (such as an accounting firm) or individual charged with managing the subject enterprise's affairs and overseeing the administration. This is very different from current practice in China where the bankruptcy process is under the control of a liquidation committee comprising mainly government officials and related parties. Refer to China.org (2006), "Law of the People's Republic of China on Enterprise Bankruptcy", Internet Edition, reviewed 25.10.2007.

710 For a detailed, yet older analysis on China's NPLs, refer to Lardy (1998), pp. 115-124.

711 Refer to OECD (2006b), p. 67.

712 Refer to China Daily (2001), "Tenth Five Year Plan of Banking Industry and its Development" (Yearbook of China Financial Market), Internet Edition, reviewed 28.03.2006.

713 From 1994 to 2002, RMB 199.54 billion were allocated to write-off NPLs of more than 3,000 bankrupt SOEs. In 1998, the government issued a special treasury bond of RMB 280 billion to boost the capital adequacy ratio of the four state banks. In fact, capital injection has been used in Japan and Korea, paid in cash or with bonds and stocks. Refer to Li (2003), "Continuously adjusting the layout and structure of China's state economy, propelling Chinese SOEs to participate in international competition and cooperation", Internet Edition, reviewed 10.09.2006. Also refer to Qin (2004), p. 879 and Chen (2003), p. 323.

Figure 19).[714] In fact, the substantial decrease of the NPL ratio after 2004 can almost entirely be explained by the transfers of NPLs to asset management companies as part of their restructuring and the infusion of USD 45 billion by the People's Bank of China.[715]

Figure 19: Total NPLs and NPL ratio of major state-owned and joint-stock commercial banks, 2003-2006.

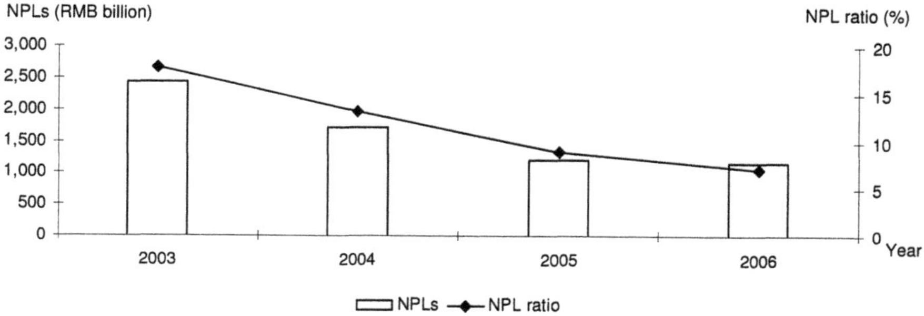

Source: China Banking Regulatory Commission (2003-2005), "Loan conditions of major banking institutions", Internet Edition, reviewed 05.04.2006 and China Banking Regulatory Commission (2007), "Annual Report 2006", p. 30 and p. 130 ff, Internet Edition, reviewed 09.11.2007.

In conclusion, the Chinese financial system is bank- and credit based like that of the East Asian developmental states. Most financing is regulated by banks' credits. Like the East Asian developmental states, the central government has actively directed and controlled the allocation of credit, and used the financial system as an industrial policy instrument to support selected key industries. In this sense, it has successfully supported loan applications for biotechnology projects.

At the same time, however, China failed to instruct hard budget constraints on SOEs, and the banking system allocates credit to value-destroying SOEs, not to the private sector, as was the case in the East Asian developmental states. While in the industrial sector non-state enterprises have been the driving force of growth, the financial sector has always been under the close supervision of the state (State Council, Ministry of Finance). The privatization trend observed in most of the real economy has been virtually absent in the financial sector.[716] The management of the banks has remained subject to close state control. Thus, state-owned commercial banks cannot make lending decisions in full autonomy from government interest.

714 In 2006, the pilot banks had only few NPLs left on their balance sheets (Bank of China: 4.0 percent, China Construction Bank: 3.3 percent and Industrial and Commercial Bank of China: 3.8 percent). However, the Agricultural Bank of China had still 23 percent of NPLs. Refer to respective banks 2006 annual reports, Internet Edition, reviewed 22.08.2007.

715 Refer to Yusuf and Nabeshima (2006b), p. 18.

716 Refer to OECD (2006b), pp. 67-68.

They are often forced to bail out loss-making SOEs because credits not only fulfil industrial, but also social policy goals (credits hinder state companies from insolvency and thus safeguard employment). State banks lack the power to force payment in the case of default or delinquency. In return, profitability cannot be used as a performance indicator, as in the East Asian developmental states.

The rethinking of the East Asian financial crisis, and the recognition of the cumulating problems in its own financial system, led China to pursue economic and financial reforms. Key areas of progress are improvements in the supervisory regime, including the establishment of the China Banking Regulatory Commission, the ongoing opening of the market to foreign financial institutions, expanded flexibility in setting lending interest rates, and the measures aimed at strengthening and modernizing state-owned commercial banks.[717]

3.5 Government-business relations

The East Asian developmental states relied on an institutionalized state-business partnership. Extensive cooperation and information-sharing between government and business enabled the developmental states to pick priority sectors in anticipation of future profit. In China, information is shared formally, as well as informally, between the state and the business sector. The frameworks typically used to describe the interaction between government and society (pluralism, societal corporatism, state corporatism, clientelism and monism) fail to fully grasp important aspects of government-business relations in China.[718]

Organizational policy has aimed to determine the shape of the party-state's institutions, and define their relationships with the business sector. Since 1989, chambers of commerce and trade associations have been built in every part of the country and in every sector of the economy.[719] The move to a market regulatory regime has led firms to have an interest in policy influence (and give government a reason to listen). Business associations then try to influence the formulation of public policy in terms of their member firms.[720]

Usually, before the central government adopts new policies, government and business (business associations or individual companies) exchange information on a regular base. Kennedy (2005) contends from interviews with officials in the people's congresses, the State Council, industrial ministries and local governments, that it is common practice to obtain the opinions of industry as part of their attempts to

717 Refer to Barnett (2004), p. 50.

718 In his analysis on business lobbying in China, Kennedy (2005) elaborates on these different frameworks.

719 Associations' functions have gained importance after China's accession to the WTO as Chinese companies need to better coordinate their activities to respond to more intense global competition.

720 Refer to Kennedy (2005), p. 28.

regulate the economy. Such exchanges of opinions are initiated by both sides. They occur during the consideration of specific laws and regulations, and as part of the process of regulatory oversight, which then might prompt a new policy initiative. One way for information exchange between the government and the business sector is the organization of formal hearings, where ministries at the national and regional levels obtain industry's opinions.[721] Consultations regarding commercial work, legislative regulations and other political questions of regularization, are held frequently. Participants are not only the leading CCP members, but also invited representatives from affected state organs, economic and social sectors and officially registered associations. In March 2006, the Ministry of Commerce held a symposium with 18 industry associations. The Ministry of Commerce especially heard suggestions of the associations in the process of applying trade remedy measures, maintaining security of domestic industries, responding to trade frictions and launching multi-lateral negotiations.[722]

Besides formalized information exchange at hearings and through business associations, there are indirect routes of contact between the Chinese state and businesses operating in China. The most prominent alternative to associations is direct interaction between the government officials and firms.

Nee (1989) and Bian and Logan (1996) contend that the importance of (political) connections for business success is negatively correlated with the degree of economic liberalization and marketization.[723] Although during the 1990s, guidance plans were replaced by indicative plans and the importance of planning dropped, the Mao era had left a legacy that stressed direct interaction between government and business. The legitimacy of direct interaction between SOEs and government has extended to domestic and foreign private firms. Entrepreneurs often articulate their interests privately, and thus informally, to policy-makers with whom they have *guanxi*.[724] The government-business relationship in China, however, goes far beyond informal information sharing. Due to strong state intervention in business activities, government and businesses are closely intertwined. This nexus is founded on bilateral alliances between local governments on the provincial, city or county level, and local business. In heavily state-regulated industrial sectors and regions, local government organizations are still in a position to control the access of local firms to important inputs and licenses, as long as strong macro-economic institutions that protect a market system based on fair competition are absent.[725] Entrepreneurs thus cultivate personal connections with powerful government bureaucrats to gain access

---

[721] Ibidem, pp. 48-49.

[722] Refer to Ministry of Commerce (2006), "MOFCOM Holding a Symposium with Industry Associations", Internet Edition, 15.03.2006, reviewed 30.03.2006.

[723] Refer to Nee and Opper (2007), p. 107. For further information refer to Nee (1989) and Bian and Logan (1996).

[724] Refer to Heilmann (2004), p. 61.

[725] Refer to Taube (2005), p. 5.

to resources and protect their firms from predatory interventions.[726] As cadres are evaluated by central government and party organizations according to their ability to promote economic development, create new jobs, etc. in their localities, they also rely on strong business partners. As a consequence, there exists a strong interdependency between local government and businesses.[727] Moreover, as market-oriented reforms represent a challenge to bureaucrats' ability to directly determine economic outcomes, government officials have run government-created associations so that associations will not usurp the bureaucracy's original powers. In this way, bureaucrats aim to continue the planning-era practice of direct interaction with businesses.[728] Especially if entrepreneurs depend on government contracts for their business, strong political ties with government officials is often the decisive factor in business success. The firm's economic performance then becomes dependent on its relations with state representatives, and the extent and quality of government involvement within the firm.[729]

Taube (2005) conceives that politics and the business sector in several cases even form an *"integrated organization".*[730] Local governments have developed organizational characteristics in many ways like those of industrial firms.[731] Many provinces and municipalities experienced government-led economic growth based on *"local state corporatism"*, where officials acted as the equivalent of a board of directors, or sometimes more directly as chief executive officers, in a corporation.[732]

Also the central government and its agencies frequently function like "China Inc.".[733] Even without detailed plan directives, the central government is involved in the pro-active design of industry structure and the opening of development paths for its "national champions". The case of CNOOC's bid for the American oil corporation Unocal, which was aborted due to strong political resistance in the USA in August 2005, provides an example of the merger between political interests and individual business strategies. Political interests may even dominate the latter. CNOOC would never have been able to raise the USD 18.5 billion it was bidding for the US company. As the deal would have fitted in the government's policy to improve the nation's access to natural resources, it offered to provide CNOOC the necessary financing by means of loans guaranteed by the state.[734]

---

726 Refer to Nee and Opper (2007), pp. 107-108. For further information refer to Wank (1996), Xin and Pearce (1996) and Peng and Luo (2000).

727 Refer to Taube (2005), p. 5.

728 Refer to Kennedy (2005), p. 47.

729 Refer to Nee and Opper (2007), pp. 106 -108. For further information refer to Findlay (1999).

730 Refer to Taube (2005), p. 4.

731 For further information refer to Walder (1995).

732 For further information refer to Oi (1992).

733 Refer to Taube (2005), pp. 4-5.

734 Refer to China Daily (2005), "US lawmakers meddle in CNOOC's Unocal bid", Internet Edition, reviewed 17.11.2006. For further information on how China uses its economic potential in order to reach strategic targets refer to Belke (2007), "Wirtschaftliche Macht als Instrument der Außenpolitik am Beispiel Chinas", Internet Edition, reviewed 10.11.2007.

State and business, mostly at the local level, and sometimes even at the central level, are closely entangled, and a clear separation between bureaucracy and firms can often not be found. The local party cadre is at the same time responsible for the provision of investment for a risky business plan, and the management of the established enterprise, in one jurisdiction. Institutionalized information-sharing in business associations is thus not necessary.

Altogether, relations between the government and private businesses are different from the East Asian developmental states. Regardless of China's great advances in its technical capabilities and successful industrial policy, the Chinese bureaucracy never succeeded in truly separating from the operations of the leading enterprises. Accordingly, active information sharing of (private) businesses with the state was only in particular cases institutionalized, as in the developmental states. Resulting from the legitimacy of direct interaction between SOEs and government bureaucrats, informal lobbying through *guanxi* networks between government officials and businessmen (of SOEs, private and foreign companies) have been prevalent throughout the reform period. Whether the government has thus only received information on "sunrise" industries and business needs as in the developmental states, or has also been captured by business interests due to its close involvement in business activities, remains debatable.

3.6 Conclusion

During the reform, China gradually abandoned central planning and import substitution and moved from state dominance toward a Chinese model of state-guidance (refer to Figure 20). China has chosen a modified path of the developmental state approach. It has not only adopted and emulated previous strategies of the East Asian developmental states, but also adapted its path to its special characteristics.[735]

Unlike the East Asian developmental states, China's industrial policy focused not only on exports, but also on FDI (export-FDI nexus). Furthermore, the rethinking of the East Asian financial crisis and thus the recognition of the cumulating problems in its own financial system led China to pursue further economic and financial reforms to build up market-supporting institutions largely based upon market-centered capitalism. In addition, particularly the local states in China resemble the East Asian developmental states. They are responsible for local prosperity, because they are empowered to carry out development, realigning revenue distribution between the central authorities and localities. These aspects demonstrate a revision of the previously most influential Japanese and Korean model.

735 In this context, *adoption* implies emulation of the criteria of the East Asian developmental state; *adaptation* means variation of the criteria of the East Asian developmental states, and adjustment to China's special characteristics. An adjustment of the East Asian Model has been assumed previously when analyzing the special characteristics of China.

Figure 20: The Chinese model of state-guidance.

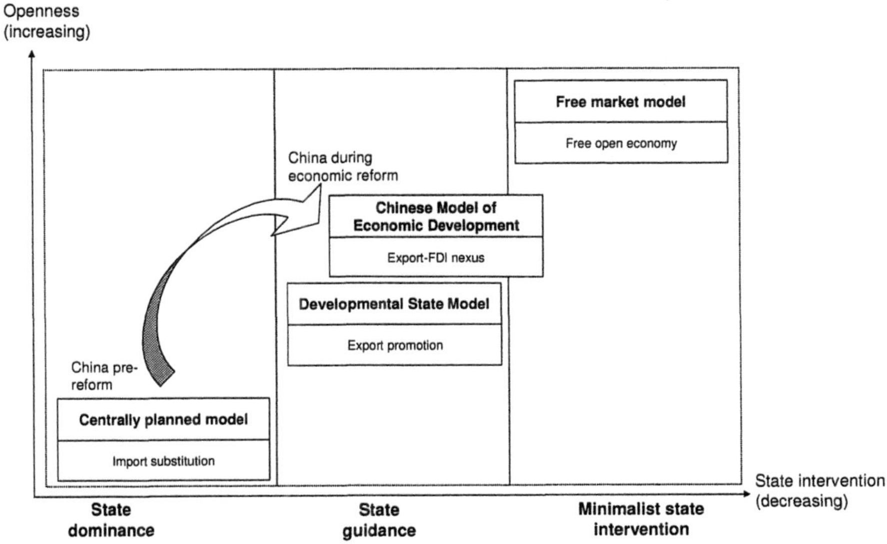

Source: Own illustration.

4 The auto industry in the light of the Chinese development approach

Chapter 3 analyzed China's economic development approach by concentrating on each criterion of the East Asian Developmental State Model. The analysis showed that – as in the East Asian developmental states - institutional reform and industrial policy have guided China's development process since 1978 and have had direct impact on changes in the real economy. At the same time, the analysis provides evidence that decisive differences between the development strategies of China and its East Asian neighbors exist.

In order to gain further insight into the Chinese model of economic development, Chapter 4 uses an empirical analysis of the auto industry. The global auto industry has entered a new phase. A combination of massive production overcapacity, together with structural-geographical shifts in market demand, continuing technological transformation, tightening environmental regulation, and changing relationships between auto assemblers and their component suppliers, have produced a crisis for most of the major auto manufacturers. At the same time, however, many developing countries have set up domestic auto production. They still see the auto industry as an important driver of industrial development and technological capability - not only because of its impact on the balance of trade, but also because of its potential for upgrading the various industries which feed into it. The auto sector is hence the object of continuing government intervention – particularly in China.[736] This sector's analysis consequently provides useful information on the outcome of state-led growth in China.

After elaboration of the research design, the chapter explores whether the criteria of the East Asian Developmental State Model can be found in China's approach to modernizing its domestic auto industry. The analysis centers on the following determinants of state-guidance in the auto sector:

- Bureaucratic framework of the auto industry (organization and quality of state agents involved in the sector's development).
- National industrial policy for the auto sector (foreign investment, trade, localism).
- Financial system as an industrial policy instrument to regulate the sector's growth.
- Government-business cooperation and information-sharing in the auto industry.
- Outcome of two decades of distinctive government support for the sector.

[736] Humphrey rightly poses the question as to how worthwhile an auto-centered development strategy might be under these circumstances. However, only few states reject building up a strong auto industry. In consequence of all these factors, interstate (and intrastate) competition has intensified. For further information on the impact of globalization and national development on the auto industry refer to Humphrey (2000) and Liu and Dicken (2006).

Overall, the chapter analyzes the industrial policy for the auto sector, and the measures implemented to transform domestic auto manufacturers into global players. The analysis concentrates on the unique measures of the Chinese development strategy, and explores whether state-guidance in the auto sector has succeeded in building up internationally competitive auto companies and overall rapid economic development. The findings allow inferences on the effectiveness of the Chinese model of state-led development.

4.1 Design of research

Traditional economic approaches largely overlook the dynamic process of industrial development as well as the role of changing government policies and institutional settings. In order to overcome these problems, the empirical analysis of the Chinese auto industry uses a mixed methods research approach. The accuracy of judgments can be improved by collecting different kinds of data bearing on the same phenomenon.[737] The research incorporates secondary statistics as well as qualitative and quantitative information in order to underpin theoretical arguments by empirical evidence. Triangulation is the superior method for identifying causal mechanisms and for process tracing.[738] It combines investigative depth with the coverage of various facets of the chosen research object and enables the researcher to incorporate exploration and explanation in the study.[739] As the secondary analysis approach and its sources have been discussed in Chapter 1.3, the following sections only highlight the qualitative and quantitative analysis used in Chapter 4.

The primary focus of research is one industry in a single country. The research methodology, however, also incorporates aspects of comparative analysis in order to examine whether any differences in the implementation of the national auto policies exist at the local level. Thus, variation at the sub-national level can be highlighted while the macroeconomic environment and the policy framework are set. The two municipalities that rank highest in auto production - Beijing, which is a "newly" industrializing area and Shanghai, which has been a traditional center of industrialization - are in the focus of analysis.[740] In 2006, output of motor vehicles was 683,700 units in Beijing followed by Shanghai with 682,200 units (refer to Figure 21).

737 Refer to Jick (1979), p. 602.

738 Refer to Bennett (1999), Yin and Moore (1987), Yin (1993; 1994) and Hamel et al. (1993).

739 Refer to Creswell (2003), p. 208.

740 Beijing is the capital, and thus the political center, of China where the CCP's Central Committee, the State Council, ministries and commissions are located. Shanghai, unlike Beijing, has thrived as a city of commerce and a window to the outside world. Due to its geographic position, situated on the banks of the Yangtze River Delta in East China, and its large harbor, the city was an ideal location for trade. It evolved into China's economic center with a strong industrial base. The analysis of Beijing and Shanghai does not claim to be representative of all localities in China.

Figure 21: Output of motor vehicles in provinces and municipalities, 2006.[741]

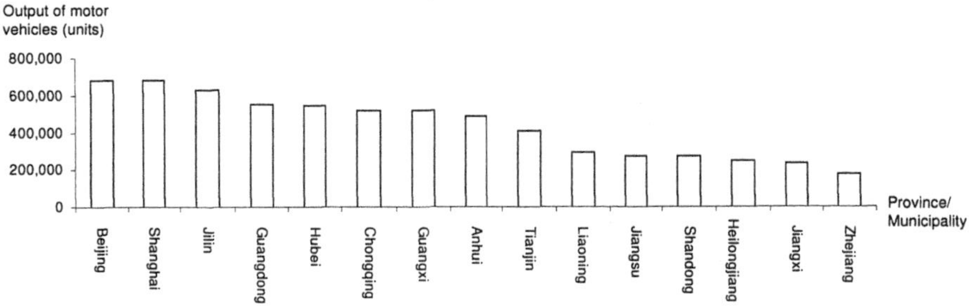

Source: China Statistical Yearbook (2007).

The analysis draws upon Thun's (2004a, 2004b, 2006) findings of Beijing as a *"Laissez-faire Local State"* and Shanghai as a *"Local Developmental State"*.[742] Accordingly, qualitative and quantitative research in this study focus not only on central state-guidance in the auto sector, but also on different approaches to local development in Beijing and Shanghai. It can thus be explored whether the municipal governments have been able to create internationally competitive domestic auto companies within the policy framework set by the central state.

4.1.1 Qualitative analysis

Qualitative research means *"any kind of research that produces findings not arrived at by means of statistical procedures or other means of quantification"*.[743] It is largely an investigative process where the researcher gradually makes sense of a social phenomenon by contrasting, comparing, replicating, cataloguing and classifying the object of study.[744] Qualitative research focuses on the process that is occurring, as well as the product or outcome.[745] This may be changing policy approaches as well as the shifting of leader's decision-making or state-business relations. Qualitative analysis creates an understanding of relationships or complex interactions, participants' perceptions and experiences.[746] In this line, qualitative research

741 Only the 15 provinces and municipalities with the highest output volume of motor vehicles are listed.

742 Refer to Thun (2004a,b) for further information on his analysis of the auto and supplier industry at the local state and, in particular, Thun (2006) for an illustration of "Alternative Patterns of Development" in Shanghai, Beijing and Guangzhou as well as Changchun and Wuhan. Refer to Thun (2006), p. 29 ff.

743 Refer to Strauss and Corbin (1990), p. 17.

744 For further information refer to Miles and Huberman (1994).

745 Creswell (2003), pp. 198-199.

746 Refer to Ellram (1996), p. 97, Yin (1994), pp. 3-4 and Creswell (2003), pp. 198-199.

approaches are used when the research objective is to identify mechanisms behind phenomena which cannot be tested quantitatively.[747] Qualitative research thus complements statistical analysis.[748]

4.1.1.1 Expert interviews as a method of qualitative research

The interview is an important source of information, and a frequently-used and highly-developed instrument of qualitative, empirical data collection.[749] Thus, it was chosen as an instrument for research in this study.

An interview is about communication between different persons in which different stimuli intend to cause reaction. It is a conversation that has a structure and a purpose. It uses a careful questioning and listening approach with the purpose of obtaining thoroughly-tested knowledge.[750] No objective, universal results can be conducted, however, because each reaction is a result of the subject's personal experiences. The instrument is most suitable, if experiences, and the opinions and assessments based on them, are to be covered, and when depth rather than breadth of understanding is necessary.

A specific form of applying interviews is the expert interview.[751] The interviewee is an expert when he or she has a complex knowledge regarding a specific topic or aspect.[752] The interviewer is responsible for initiating and directing the interview with regard to the question of research. The interviewer accordingly acts passively, while the interviewee has an active role, and is left with much leeway for the direction and the content of the interview. In this regard, the interviewee is of less interest than his or her capacity of being an expert in a certain field of activity. He or she is integrated into the study, not as an individual, but as representing a group (of specific experts). The interpretation of expert interviews mainly aims at analyzing and comparing the content of the expert knowledge.[753]

As the aim of this study is to collect information on the effectiveness of the Chinese development path, opinions and experiences of experts in China are appropriate to gain information on processes in the auto sector, as well as interactions between the state and private entrepreneurs. The expert interview in this respect is the best method of primary research.

---

747 Refer to Edin (2000), pp. 8-9.

748 Refer to Yin (1993) and de Vaus (2001), pp. 221 ff and Bitsch (2000), p. 229.

749 Refer to Yin (1994), p. 84.

750 Refer to Atteslander (2000), p. 114 and Kvale (1996), p. 6.

751 Refer to Meuser and Nagel (1991), pp. 441-468 and Flick (2002), p. 89.

752 Refer to Flick (1995), p. 100. For further information also refer to Flick et al. (1991).

753 Refer to Schnell et al. (1989), p. 295 and Flick (2002), pp. 89-90.

4.1.1.2 Interview partners and questionnaires

Information on the effectiveness of the Chinese auto industrial policy and its implementation was derived from interviews with experts in Beijing and Shanghai who are familiar with the development of the auto industry in China. The individuals for the proposed study were selected purposefully. Interviewees were identified who would best help the researcher to answer the question of research.

Eleven of the nineteen interviewed experts are managers of leading MNCs headquartered in Germany. Thus, cultural differences among companies can be excluded. The phenomenon of technology transfer is only likely to appear in MNCs where important parts of the value chain are present in China. All MNCs included in the qualitative analysis have at least one manufacturing site in China. Among the MNCs are the two original equipment manufacturers (OEMs) DaimlerChrysler[754] and Volkswagen (VW) as well as the two parts suppliers Bosch and ZF Friedrichshafen. DaimlerChrysler and VW both established production sites in Beijing and Shanghai, respectively, in the early 1980s, and have since then continuously expanded their China activities. Bosch and ZF Friedrichshafen also entered the market decades ago, and both now run more than 20 production sites in China. Their experience provides important information, as MNCs generally incorporate the Chinese government's trade, investment and industrial policies into their location and production decisions.[755]

Eight experts come from different institutional organizations located in Beijing or Shanghai. Among those are three experts from the Delegations of German Industry and Commerce (GIC) in Beijing, and one expert from the GIC in Shanghai, one expert from the Association des Constructeurs Européens d'Automobiles (ACEA) in Beijing, one expert from the China Association of Automobile Manufacturers (CAAM) in Beijing, and two experts from the State Information Center in Beijing. All institutions conduct research on the Chinese auto market, and provide strategic consulting to their clients who may be businessmen or governments. For a complete list of interviewees' names and affiliation, refer to Appendix I and Appendix II.

Those who agreed to participate in the interview were sent a letter including an overview of the research to prepare them for the session, and also a subject index, so they knew what topics to expect (refer to Appendix III).[756] The interviews involved on-site visits, and were conducted in face-to-face settings in the location of the

754 In August 2007, DaimlerChrysler completed the closing for the transfer of a majority interest in the Chrysler Group and for the related financial services business in NAFTA to a subsidiary of Cerberus Capital Management, L.P. The German automaker, which was renamed Daimler AG in October 2007, retained a 19.9 percent interest in Chrysler. The company's reorganization, however, does not have any impact on the insights gained from the interviews conducted in Beijing.

755 Refer to Wang (2001), p. 1.

756 Refer to Ellram (1996), p. 105.

interviewee's workplace in China.[757] Face-to-face interviews with top executives ensure that the source of information is indeed the intended addressee. The problem with mail survey is that employees not directly in touch with the studied issue might reply instead. All interviewees agreed that the session was digitally recorded. The duration of the interviews ranged from 45 – 90 minutes. Interviews with the State Information Center and the CAAM were attended by a Chinese-English translator.

Different questionnaires were prepared: one for the experts from foreign auto companies, one for the Chinese, and one for the foreign institutes, according to their different backgrounds (refer to Appendix IV).[758] With five pages, the questionnaires were complex. However, all questions were needed to fulfill the tasks of the research. The questionnaires used were semi-structured. The interview design allowed for movement in the formulation of questions, follow-up strategies and sequencing, and for posing subsequent questions that were not foreseen in the interview script.[759]

The questionnaires consisted of two types of questions: first, open-ended questions, which allow the respondents to answer in their own frames of reference, entirely uninfluenced by any specific alternatives suggested by the interviewer, and second, semi-structured questions which provide the interviewee with different choices for an answer.[760] These types of questions help to gather information, establish rapport and increase understanding. With regard to the open-ended nature of interviews, the respondent may assist as an "informant" rather than a respondent. Such persons not only provide the investigator with insights into a matter, but can also suggest sources of corroboratory evidence – and initiate the access to such sources.[761] The researcher, however, has to bear in mind that the statements of the interviewees mirror only their personal opinions and might be influenced by an emotional context rather than a solely rational one.[762] Moreover, the statements of the expatriates might differ from those of the Chinese experts working for governmental institutions, who do not want to or cannot speak as openly. Altogether, a potential poor fit between the research questions, the operationalized concepts and a respondent's understanding could be avoided by conducting expert interviews with open-ended questions at on-site visits.[763]

---

[757] One expert working for a German auto supplier company located in Shanghai was interviewed in Feuerbach, Germany.

[758] The interviewees could choose between English or German questionnaires. Appendix IV contains only the English questionnaire for company representatives. The questionnaires were not handed over to the interviewees, but functioned as a guideline to the interviewer.

[759] Pennings et al. (1999), p. 79.

[760] Refer to Sheatsley (1983), p. 204, Schnell et al. (1989), p. 302 ff and Atteslander (2000), p. 150 ff.

[761] Refer to Yin (1994), p. 84.

[762] Refer to Hewstone and Fincham (1996), pp. 177-218.

[763] This approach ensures construct validity.

4.1.1.3 Research design quality

It is generally hard to objectively evaluate qualitative information. Ensuring the suitability of qualitative research is central for the legitimacy of implications.[764] Three criteria are used to judge the soundness of research:[765]

- *External validity:* Qualitative research is concerned with testing the analytical soundness of a proposed conceptual framework and generalizing the results to a broader theory. External validity establishes the domain to which a study's findings can be generalized, and thus ensures the integrity of this process. It reflects how accurately the results represent the phenomenon studied, establishing generalizability of results. It can be achieved by including multiple interview partners with different backgrounds in the research design, as done in this study. This enables the researcher to apply replication logic.
- *Reliability:* Reliability is concerned with the repeatability of results. Will replication achieve the same results and conclusions? The objective of reliability is to minimize errors and biases in a study. Documentation of the procedures, methods and documents in each interview report is instrumental to reach that objective.[766]
- *Construct Validity:* Construct validity ensures the adequacy of the operational measures for the concepts researched. In order to increase construct validity, the researcher combines multiple sources of evidence (expert interviews as well as documents from the interviewee's workplace that was not restricted to internal use). During data collection, the researcher focuses on analytical insights, however, rather than on ensuring construct validity.

The expert interviews were conducted according to the framework of Yin (1994) (refer to Figure 22). Although reports were written after each interview, conclusions are drawn across individual interview results. The virtue of analysis across single interviews is that it permits the aggregation of data and information respectively.[767] The qualitative research design of this study guarantees external validity, reliability and construct validity.

---

[764] Internal validity is no further commented upon. It is necessary for experimental and quasi-experimental research (explanatory or causal research to establish causal relationships) and not for exploratory (descriptive) studies. Refer to Yin (1994), pp. 33-35.

[765] Refer to Yin (1994), p. 33 ff, Ellram (1996), p. 104 ff and Bonoma (1985), p. 201 ff.

[766] Furthermore, triangulation or multiple methods of data collection and analysis strengthens reliability as well as internal validity. Triangulation is less a strategy for validating results and procedures than an alternative to validation which increases scope, depth and consistency in methodological proceedings. Refer to Creswell (2003), p. 204 and Flick (2002), p. 227.

[767] Refer to Yin (1994), pp. 144-152.

Figure 22: Qualitative research design.

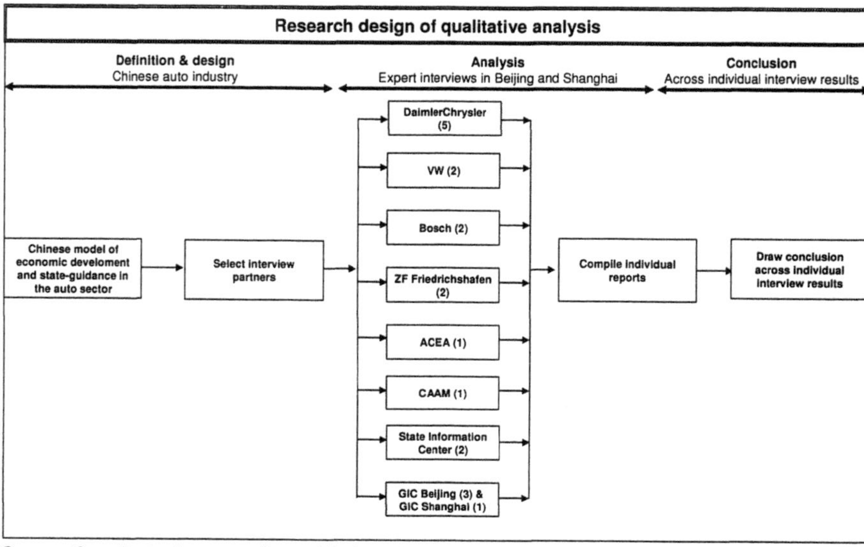

Source: Own illustration according to Yin (1994), p. 49. Note: Number of interviewees in brackets.

4.1.2 Quantitative analysis

In addition to analyzing data from various issues of the China Statistical Yearbook, the China Automotive Industry Yearbook (2006) and other sources of statistical data, the World Bank survey "Competitiveness, Technology and Firm Linkages in Manufacturing Sectors" (2001) is evaluated statistically.

4.1.2.1 The data sample

The World Bank conducted the survey "Competitiveness, Technology and Firm Linkages in Manufacturing Sectors" in 2001.[768] The survey comprises 1,500 firms, 300 firms each from five large cities: Beijing, Chengdu, Guangzhou, Shanghai and Tianjin. Firms in the sample belong to five manufacturing sectors (apparel and leather goods, consumer goods, electronic components, electronic equipment, and vehicles and vehicle parts) and five service sectors (accounting and related services, advertising and marketing, business logistics, communication services, and information-technology services). The sample covers 216 companies (14.4 percent of

[768] Most accounting data cover the period 1998-2000, while interview data are only for the year 2000.

total firms covered) in the auto ("vehicles and vehicle parts") sector. The statistical analysis of the survey data concentrates on three groups.

"Group auto sector – residual sectors":

Does the development of the auto industry differ significantly from that of the residual sectors covered in the sample?[769] Did the government actively and effectively promote the auto industry in comparison with the residual sectors? To answer these questions, the first group built is "Group auto sector – residual sectors". 14.4 percent of the interviewees (n=216) are active in the auto sector; 85.6 percent of the interviewees are in the residual sector (n=1284).

"Group auto sector – electronics sector":

As China declared the auto and the electronics industry as pillar industries in 1994, the analysis explores whether there are any significant differences between the two sectors. The second group is hence "Group auto sector – electronics sector". While the World Bank sample covers the electronic components sector and the electronic equipment sector separately, in the following analysis, both are merged in the category electronics sector. 395 respondents of the World Bank survey come from the electronics sector (26.3 percent).

"Group auto sector Beijing - auto sector Shanghai":

What similarities and differences can be observed between the auto industry in Beijing and that in Shanghai? If there are significant differences, this might be traced to the local municipalities' engagement in promoting the local auto industry. The third group is thus "Group auto sector Beijing and auto sector Shanghai". The World Bank sample includes 44 (2.9 percent) interviewed managers of the auto sector in Beijing and 40 (2.7 percent) respondents of the auto sector in Shanghai.

4.1.2.2 Methodology of the statistical evaluation

The World Bank data is analyzed by using the Statistical Package for Social Sciences (SPSS) (Version 12.0.1). Some string (alphanumeric) variables such as city and sector are converted into numeric variables. This guarantees the operationalization of the variables.

---

769 The auto sector includes vehicles and vehicle parts manufacturing. The residual sector comprises the following sub-sectors: apparel and leather goods, consumer goods, electronic components, electronic equipment, accounting and related services, advertising and marketing, business logistics, communication services, and information technology services.

The traditional classification of levels of measurement into different scales was developed by Stevens (1946).[770] This remains the basic typology and is the one used throughout this analysis. The variables of the World Bank sample can be categorized in three types of scales: nominal scale, ordinal scale and metric (ratio) scale.

For each variable, dependent on the scale, measures of central tendency, the mode, median or arithmetic mean, are calculated.[771] The mode, median and mean are used to describe the location of a distribution.[772] Furthermore, the standard deviation is calculated.[773]

Crosstabulation tables (contingency tables) display the relationship between two or more categorical (nominal or ordinal) variables. The size of the table is determined by the number of distinct values for each variable, with each cell in the table representing a unique combination of values.

In order to measure statistic differences between central tendencies of two groups, different tests are used. Tests for statistical significance are made against a null hypothesis that asserts that there is *no* systematic relationship between the variables.[774] When performing a significance test, the null hypothesis and alternative hypothesis are compared. In this analysis, p (probability) describes the level of significance. All p values of less than 0.05 are considered to be significant.

A quite general test for the comparison of two nominal variables is the Pearson Chi-Square Test for cross tables.[775] It is useful to see whether there is a statistically significant relationship between two samples from a nominal population distribution.[776] When the cross table is reduced to a 2x2 table, the test may also be used to check whether there is an association between two dichotomous variables, and whether two proportions are different from each other.[777] The Chi-Square Test assumes that the expected value for each cell is five or higher. The Fisher's Exact Test or the Likelihood Ratio Test is used if one or more of the cells have an expected frequency of five or less.[778] Additionally, the Fisher's Exact Test can be only performed on a 2x2

770 For further information refer to Stevens (1946), pp. 677-680.

771 The central tendency of a variable is the value on that variable that "attracts" most of the cases. Refer to Benninghaus (2005), p. 22 ff and p. 36 ff and Heiler and Michels (1994), p. 86 ff.

772 The mode is the most frequently occurring value (or values). It indicates the central tendency of nominal variables. The median is the value above and below which one half of the observations fall. For ordinal data the median is usually a good measure of central tendency since it uses the ranking information. The mean, also called the arithmetic average, is the sum of the values of all observations divided by the number of observations. Refer to Norusis/SPSS Inc. (1988), p. 39, Pennings et al. (1999), p. 117 and Benninghaus (2002), pp. 38-50.

773 It is the result of summing the squared deviations of the ratios about the mean, dividing the result by the total number of ratios minus one, and taking the positive square root.

774 Refer to Bortz (2005), p. 108 ff.

775 The Pearson Chi-Square Test is calculated by summing over all cells the squared residuals divided by the expected frequencies. Refer to Norusis/SPSS Inc. (1988), p. 54.

776 Refer to Pennings et al. (1999), p. 159.

777 Refer to Benninghaus (2002), pp. 77 ff and Pennings et al. (1999), p. 159.

778 Refer to Norusis/SPSS Inc. (1988), p. 55 and Bortz (2005), p. 491 ff.

cross table. The Pearson Chi-Square Test and Fisher's Exact Test are only appropriate when the data in the table are independent. A one-sided and two-sided version of Fisher's Exact Test can be calculated. In this analysis, the two-sided version is generally used, as there is no prior alternative to independence.[779]

The Mann-Whitney U Test is the most popular of the two-independent-samples tests.[780] An ordinal scale is sufficient.[781] The Mann-Whitney Test, also known as the Wilcoxon Test, does not require assumptions about the shape of the underlying distributions. It tests the hypothesis that two independent samples come from populations having the same distribution.[782] If the number of cases is smaller than 30, SPSS calculates the exact significance p value.[783]

An Independent-Samples T-Test is used when comparing the means of a normally distributed interval dependent variable for two independent groups.[784] The two-sample T-Test is fairly resistant to departures from normality. In this respect, even when samples are taken from a nonnormal population, the distribution of the sample means is approximately normal for sufficiently large samples. As the size of the sample increases, the sampling distribution of the mean approaches normality.[785] This assumes a number of cases larger than 30. By default, a 95 percent confidence interval for the difference in means is displayed. The column labeled Sig. (2-tailed) gives the smallest probability (largest confidence level) for which the null hypothesis can be rejected. One of the assumptions underlying the use of T-Test is the equality of variance. In SPSS homogeneity of variances is tested by "Levene's Test for Equality of Variances", with F value and corresponding significance. These are part of SPSS output for Two Independent Sample T-Tests. It tests the hypothesis that the variances of the two groups are equal. Provided the F value is not significant ($p>0.05$), the variances can be assumed to be homogeneous and the Equal Variance line values for the T-Test be used. If $p<0.05$, then the equality of variance assumption has been violated and the T-Test based on the separate variance estimates (unequal variances) should be used. The T-Test for unequal variances is an alternative way of computing the T-Test that accounts for heterogeneous variances and provides an

779 When both table variables are quantitative, Chi-Square yields the Linear-by-linear Association Test (Mantel-Haenszel-Test). Mantel-Haenszel Chi-Square, unlike ordinary and Likelihood Ratio Chi-Square, is an ordinal measure of significance. As the Mantel-Haenzel Chi-Square is not appropriate for nominal variables, it is left aside in this analysis. Refer to SPSS, Version 12.

780 It is equivalent to the Wilcoxon rank sum test and the Kruskal-Wallis test for two groups.

781 The Mann-Whitney Test checks whether two sampled populations are equivalent in location. The observations from both groups are combined and ranked, with the average rank assigned in the case of ties. The number of ties should be small relative to the total number of observations. If the populations are identical in location, the ranks should be randomly mixed between the two samples. The number of times a score from group 1 precedes a score from group 2 and the number of times a score from group 2 precedes a score from group 1 are calculated. The Mann-Whitney U statistic is the smaller of these two numbers.

782 Refer to Norusis/SPSS Inc. (1988), p. 137.

783 Refer to Bühl and Zöfel (2000), p. 259 ff.

784 Refer to Bortz (2005), p. 475 ff.

785 Refer to Norusis/SPSS Inc. (1988), pp. 79-80.

accurate result even when the homogeneity assumption has been violated (as indicated by the Levene Test).[786] The output for both formats shows the degrees of freedom (df) and probability (2-tailed significance).[787] If the number of cases is less than 30, before conducting a T-Test, the Kolmogorov-Smirnov Test has to be applied to test for a normal distribution.

The normal distribution of a variable is given if $p>0.05$.[788] In the analysis, the procedure remains virtually the same for tests of most hypotheses:

1. A hypothesis of no difference (called null hypothesis) and its alternative are formulated.
2. A test statistic is chosen to evaluate the null hypothesis.
3. For the sample, the test statistic is calculated.
4. The probability, if the null hypothesis is true, of obtaining a test value at least as extreme as the one observed is determined.
5. If the observed significance level is judged small enough, the null hypothesis is rejected.[789]

4.1.3 Shortcomings of the research approach

When conducting the empirical analysis of state-guidance in the auto sector, the following aspects have to be considered:

- Generalization of the results to a wider context should be undertaken with caution, as the analysis covers one industry setting in one emerging market. China's auto industry has experienced a remarkable development in the last two decades, and its institutional environment is very different from a developed economy. Nevertheless, the research findings are generalizable to theoretical propositions rather than populations or universe. In this sense, the empirical analysis of the auto industry does not represent a "sample", and the investigator's goal is to expand and generalize theories (analytic generalization) and not to enumerate frequencies (statistical generalization).[790] Therefore, in the trade-off between validity and generality[791], validity is of higher priority at the expense of generality. Triangulation is a rigorous

---

786 Ibidem, p. 80.

787 As in all statistical tests, the basic criterion for statistical significance is a "2-tailed significance" less than 0.05.

788 Refer to Bühl and Zöfel (2000), p. 259 ff and p. 295.

789 Refer to Norusis/SPSS Inc. (1988), p. 85.

790 Refer to Yin (1994), pp. 9-13.

791 Refer to Collier and Mahoney (1996), p. 69.

approach which, based on a carefully chosen sector, the auto industry, yields a generally applicable explanation.[792]

- The conducted expert interviews, as well as the World Bank survey, rely on voluntary information, and are thus subject to many sources of error: people deliberately distort the truth, inadvertently fail to recall events correctly, or refuse to participate. Refusals influence survey results by failing to provide information about a particular type of person – one who refuses to answer surveys at all, or avoids certain types of questions.[793]
- Although the World Bank sample is the most recent one of the auto industry at the local level, the data covers only the period 1998 – 2000. Due to China's rapid development, data from this time might be already outdated. Moreover, the sample's variables are analyzed with respect to specific groups, and not all of the interviewees in one group responded to all interview questions. In consequence, despite the large population (1,200 companies) of the sample, the counted answers may be small. If conclusions have to be drawn from small counts they may not be representative for the whole group. The sample is, however, valuable as it allows a statistical evaluation, and thus a quantitative basis of the research analysis.

These shortcomings are taken into account when analyzing the development of the auto industry. As insights are gained from secondary statistics, the statistical evaluation of the World Bank sample and up-to-date expert interviews, informed conclusions can be drawn, incorporating and abstracting the results from the various sources.

4.2 Bureaucratic framework of the auto industry

Although the central government's power over the auto industry diminished gradually in the reform era, a legacy of central planning has remained. Various central-level government agencies maintain strict control over the sector. In order to gain information on the effectiveness of policy-making and implementation in the auto sector, different indicators of bureaucratic competence are evaluated and international and regional comparisons drawn.

[792] Refer to Hamel (1993), p. 51.

[793] The totality of all cases about which conclusions are desired is called the *population*, while the observations actually included in the study are the *sample*. Refer to Norusis/SPSS Inc. (1988), p. 35 and p. 78.

4.2.1 Bureaucratic institutions shaping the auto sector's development

The State Council, and the NDRC in particular, shape the development of the auto sector. The State Council sets the general goal of China's industrial development by issuing five-year plans and approves (auto) JV or WFOE projects above USD 500 million investment volume.[794] The NDRC controls the establishment of vehicle factories and is responsible for the examination and approval of auto projects exceeding an investment volume of USD 100 million.[795] Sino-foreign auto projects usually exceed the threshold for State Council and NDRC approval; in consequence, both agencies have to approve each new auto project in China. The State Council and the NDRC subsequently wield extensive control over the sector. Foreign investors negotiate with the NDRC concerning their business plan, approval conditions, project timeline etc. The NDRC furthermore coordinates and implements national economic and social development plans, including auto industrial policies which guide the development of the sector. It issues public announcements with regard to legal regulations and standards for the auto sector.[796]

Other agencies participate in auto policy-making through their respective functions such as the Ministry of Commerce, which issues regulations on FFEs and is responsible for auto distribution; the Ministry of Science and Technology, which makes strategic planning for auto technologies; the China Banking Regulatory Commission, which has control over auto financing companies; the Ministry of Public Security, which is responsible for vehicle registration and traffic regulation; the State Environmental Protection Administration, which issues model-specific fuel consumption standards and regulates emission compliance; and the State Administration of Taxation, which exercises taxes on auto manufacturers and consumers (auto consumption tax). In addition, the General Administration of Quality Supervision, Inspection and Quarantine is in charge of homologation, standards and certification in the auto sector.[797] The General Administration of Customs regulates tariffs on imported components and completely knocked down (CKD)[798] kits; and the State Administration for Industry and Commerce is accountable for auto manufacturer and dealer registration. Altogether, at least eleven agencies have power over the auto sector.

---

794 In the early years of reform, the State Council was also responsible for certifying import quotas for motor vehicles and disassembled vehicle kits. This duty was assigned to the Machinery and Electronics Import Inspection Office in 1990. Refer to Harwit (1995), p. 46.

795 Refer to NDRC (2004), "Interim Measures for the Administration of Examining and Approving Foreign Investment Projects", Article 3 and 4, Internet Edition, reviewed 24.04.2006.

796 Refer to NDRC (2007), "Main Functions of the NDRC", Internet Edition, reviewed 16.01.2007.

797 Information based on official documents of respective agencies.

798 CKDs are sets of auto parts that are packaged in one country, then exported to another for assembly. It is a common practice among automakers to sell knocked down kits to their foreign affiliates in order to avoid high import taxes and/or receive tax preferences for providing local employment. An incomplete kit is known as semi knocked down (SKD).

In the organizational chart that shows the key bureaucratic institutions responsible for auto policy-making, the State Council is at the top (it has the highest bureaucratic rank), followed by the commissions, the ministries and the administrative organizations that are directly under the State Council. Commissions have a higher bureaucratic rank than the ministries, and unlike the heads of the commissions and the ministries, the leaders of the administrations do not belong to the State Council (refer to Figure 23).[799]

Beside these agencies, the Certification and Accreditation Administration of China (authorized by the State Department and responsible for issuing the China Compulsory Certificate, CCC)[800] and the Standardization Administration of the People's Republic of China (under the General Administration of Quality Supervision, Inspection and Quarantine) also establish the policy process for the auto sector.[801] The Standardization Administration carries out centralized administration for compulsory standardization in China. The China Auto Technology and Research Center also exerts influence on the sector. It was established in 1985 upon the approval of the China National Science and Technology Commission, and since 2003, it has been affiliated to SASAC of the State Council. It is accountable for standardization and technical regulations, product certification and testing research, quality system certification, information service and soft-science research, engineering management and design, enterprise management science research, auto high-tech development and application.[802]

799 The State Council is composed of a premier, vice-premiers, state councillors, ministers in charge of ministries and commissions, the auditor-general and the secretary-general. Refer to Lieberthal (1997), p. 3 and China.org (2007), "Political system and state structure", Internet Edition, reviewed 09.09.2007.

800 The CCC system was implemented in China on 01.05.2002 and became fully effective on 01.08.2003 as mandatory certification and marking. The aim of the certification system is to establish a uniform standard in China for selected products (19 product groups, 132 product categories). CCC has replaced the former "China Commission for Conformity of Electric Equipment" symbol for domestic products and the "China Commodity Inspection Bureau" symbol for imported products. This change ensures that domestic and international companies and their goods are treated equally in accordance with WTO rules. Both Chinese and foreign manufacturers are affected, therefore. The Chinese customs have been using CCC as the valid guidelines for the import into China of goods subject to certification. Refer to NDRC (2004), "Automobile Industry Development Policy No. 8 decree of the State Development and Reform Commission", Chapter 5, Article 20, Internet Edition, reviewed 11.04.2006.

801 Both rank lower than the agencies at ministry-level. Interview conducted with an expert of a Chinese auto government institution in Beijing on 16.06.2006.

802 Information based on official documents of respective agencies.

Figure 23: Key institutions engaged in auto industry regulation and oversight.

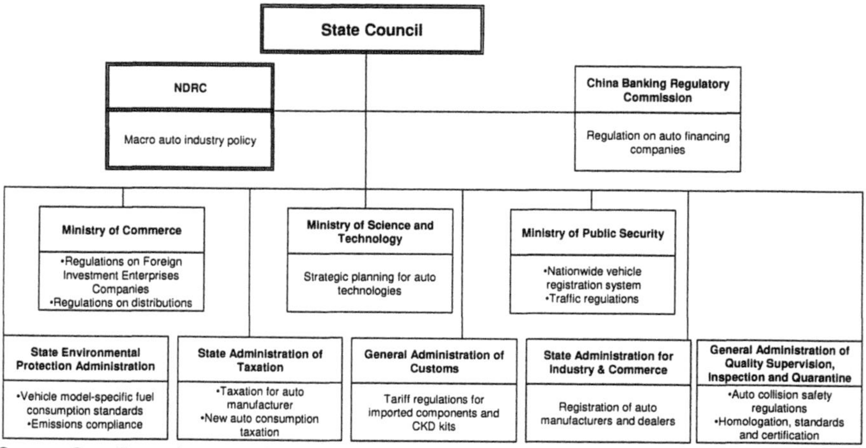

Source: Own illustration according to interviews with managers of OEMs and suppliers in Beijing and Shanghai, interviews with experts of a European and a Chinese auto association in Beijing between 08.06.2006 and 13.07.2006 as well as official documents of respective agencies.

SASAC has become the main body responsible for structural reform of the economy and for industrial policy. With the creation of SASAC, SOEs under the State Council (196 in 2003, when the commission was founded) became assets to be run by managers under market conditions rather than ministries.[803] SASAC sees its mission not only in improving governance, transparency and ultimately performance of SOEs, but also in increasing the value of public assets. As the government agency charged with exercising the authority of ownership, but without a privatization mandate, SASAC understandably interprets "reform" in a way that is consistent with its own bureaucratic interests, which include maintaining a large state sector.[804] As in 2003, 21.4 percent of SOEs were active in the auto industry; SASAC had subsequently obtained wide influence over the sector.[805]

In addition to central level state agents, different local actors have influenced the development of the auto sector throughout the reform period. A local planning commission formulates long-term development schemes, and an economic

803 Refer to Noble et al. (2005), pp. 11-12.

804 Refer to Naughton (2006), p. 2. Libecap contends that self-interested bureaucrats are likely to be influenced by the size of the budget made available to their bureaucracy. Cost or waste maximization is the assumption that self-interested bureaucrats maximize their budgets, which leads to quite different results in the polity compared with the results in private-market institutions. For further information refer to Libecap (1989).

805 Refer to Lee (2006), p. 26.

commission carries out these plans by regulating energy allocation, overseeing industrial laws etc. Foreign Economic Relation and Trade Commissions (such as the Shanghai Foreign Economic Relation and Trade Commission)[806] are responsible for JVs and other foreign investment projects at the local level. However, they play a minor role in implementing projects.[807]

In most cities, local leaders are actively involved in identifying and supporting JVs. Within the municipalities, the mayor generally has the most power to direct the development of the capital-intensive auto industry. Usually, one or two vice mayors also are instructed to work on the development of the sector. In 1990, "Auto Leading Small Groups" existed in municipalities such as Beijing, Shanghai, and Guangzhou. The small groups were composed of at least one vice mayor and representatives from the cities' economic, planning and international trade committees as well as representatives from the leading auto industrial corporations. The small groups offered a platform for information exchange between bureaucrats and businessmen. In the auto small groups, representatives of the state and the business sector acted officially as two separate groups, but were often merged. In Guangzhou, the board chairman of Guangzhou Peugeot, Xie Gancheng, was at the same time the vice chairman of the Machinery and Electronics Department under the Economic Committee.[808] In Shanghai, the auto leading small group complemented the role of the municipal government. Municipal leaders increasingly used their expertise and knowledge of the bureaucratic bodies governing Chinese industry to serve as advocates for their local industry. A prime example is the protection of the capital collected by means of the Shanghai component localization tax from 1988 to 1994. In 1990, the State Planning Commission demanded from Shanghai to turn half of the proceeds from the component tax over to Beijing in the interest of "balanced growth". Mayor Zhu Rongji played the pivotal role in protecting the localization fund. He told the State Planning Commission officials that the primary problem of the auto industry was that investment was too dispersed, and if the localization fund did not remain in Shanghai, the municipality would fail to develop a strong supply base. In the end, Shanghai sent a nominal portion of the localization fund to the central government, but the vast majority remained in Shanghai. Overall, the auto leading small groups charted a general course for the local industry, and provided a forum for coordination among the disparate government bodies. The strength of the small groups in promoting the local industry was dependent on its officials chosen as leaders.[809]

[806] Refer to Shanghai Foreign Economic Relation and Trade Commission (2006), Internet Edition, reviewed 17.01.2006.

[807] Refer to Harwit (1995), pp. 55-56 and p. 163.

[808] Ibidem.

[809] Refer to Thun (2006), pp. 110-133.

4.2.2 Policy-making and implementation

Policy-makers and academics agree that good governance matters in economic development. Governance consists of the traditions and institutions by which authority in a country is exercised. This includes the process by which governments are selected, monitored and replaced; the capacity of the government to effectively formulate and implement sound policies; and the respect of citizens and the state for the institutions that govern economic and social interactions among them.[810] Scholars have discovered that high-quality institutions have the power, over the long run, to raise per capita incomes and promote growth in all parts of the world.[811] An economy is expected to work much better when bureaucrats follow precise responsibilities and are more interested in enforcing efficient rules rather than in maximizing bureaucratic budgets.[812]

In China, multiple state agencies conduct policy-making for the auto industry, either on the central or the local government level. The following analysis explores whether the institutional organization has been conducive to effective governance in China and to efficient state-guidance in the auto sector. Information on governance and the effectiveness of policy-making and implementation is gathered from the expert interviews conducted in Beijing and Shanghai. Moreover, the IMD World Competitiveness Yearbook and the latest governance indicators from the 2006 World Bank report "China Governance, Investment Climate, and Harmonious Society" are used to analyze government effectiveness in China.[813] From the various sources, certain indicators provide valuable information on the effectiveness of government policy-making (coordination across institutions, adaptability of government policy to changes in the economy, policy transparency) and governance (regulatory quality, rule of law, and control of corruption).

The IMD ranking and the World Bank governance indicators are not sector specific, however. As overall government competence differs across regions,[814] not sectors, the rankings and indicators can nevertheless be applied to gain information on bureaucratic efficiency in the auto sector. Overall, the combination of auto-specific information from expert interviews together with information from the IMD ranking and the World Bank indicators on national and regional government efficiency provide satisfactory insight into governance in China. From the general bureaucratic

---

810 Refer to World Bank (2007), "Governance Matters 2007", Internet Edition, reviewed 20.10.2007.

811 Refer to International Bank of Reconstruction/The World Bank (2006), "A Decade of Measuring the Quality of Governance", Internet Edition, reviewed 10.10.2007.

812 For further information on the "grabbing hand" and the "helping hand" of the state refer to Shleifer and Vishny (1999).

813 The governance indicators are based on a longstanding research program of the World Bank Institute and the Research Department of the World Bank, initiated in the late 1990s.

814 Different indicators of government efficiency (taxes and fees, informal payments and bureaucratic interaction) are analyzed on a regional basis.

efficiency one can judge the bureaucratic competence as well as policy-making and implementation effectiveness in the auto sector.

As the previous analysis indicated, the Chinese government's ability to enforce industrial policy is weakened by China's bureaucratic organization.[815] Various ministries claim planning and management roles and aim to direct the sector's development. If more than two contracting parties can affect the income flow from a set of property rights, delineating each party's respective property rights becomes difficult. Vested interests and imperfect information on existing political, social, and economic positions of contracting parties lead to high transaction costs and markets operating below the (Pareto) efficient levels.[816] In addition, overlapping responsibilities result in inter-ministerial rivalries, and complicate industrial policy implementation.

Interviewees gave two examples of central-level coordination failure and revealed that *"the division of work between the various agencies involved in auto policy-making is complicated"*.[817] First, the NDRC and the Ministry of Commerce both have to approve JVs.[818] Although the two agencies cooperate closely, and their policy approaches seem to be consistent, there are internal quarrels, as both pursue different policy goals. While the Ministry of Commerce embarks on the strategy of liberalization and is pro WTO, the NDRC is the planning agency which issues strict regulations that sometimes do not conform to WTO law (e.g. local content regulations). Accordingly, as explored by the interviewees, foreign investors might obtain different information from NDRC and Ministry of Commerce bureaucrats on the requirements they have to fulfil in order to receive approval of planned auto projects.[819] Second, three government bodies oversee certification and accreditation in China: the Certification and Accreditation Administration of China, the General Administration of Quality Supervision, Inspection and Quarantine and the China National Certification and Accreditation Commission. Foreign interviewees reported that the three agencies have overlapping responsibilities. They complained that in order to receive the CCC, foreign companies have to make certain tests for the central government twice. One test for the Public Announcement Administration under the NDRC in order to get project approval, and another test for the Certification

---

815 Refer to Huang (2002a), p. 558 and Wang (2001), pp. 17-18.

816 Refer to Poulson (1994), p. 81. Fur further information refer to Libecap (1989) and Alston et al. (1999).

817 Interview conducted with an expert of a Chinese auto government institution in Beijing on 16.06. 2006.

818 After approval from NDRC and State Council, contract and regulations compliance documentation must be submitted to the Ministry of Commerce for approval, after which the Ministry of Commerce will issue an authorization certificate. The auto manufacturer then receives the certificate of approval from the Ministry of Commerce.

819 Interviews conducted with managers of a German OEM in Beijing between 08.06.2006 and 16.06. 2006.

and Accreditation Administration of China, which monitors auto imports and domestic production with respect to Chinese standards.[820]

As each ministry tries to increase its influence and follows its own interests, coordination between the different agencies is complicated and time-consuming.[821] Given the manner in which many governmental structures in China are fragmented vertically along functional lines, bureaucratic authorities of equal rank bargain continually and intensely – any resource that is scarce will be subject to bargaining.[822] According to a study of AT Kearney (2005), ten agencies are accountable for the content of industrial policies for the auto industry; five different agencies are responsible for fuel consumption standards and auto dealership franchising, and four different agencies are in charge of vehicle recycling requirements, emissions compliance, used car appraisal processes, tariff regulations for imported parts and auto side collision safety regulations (refer to Table 10).[823] Overall, unlike the far-reaching competence of a single pilot agency in the developmental states, state agencies' coordination effort negatively affects government efficiency in the auto sector.

At the same time, though, certain aspects of government policy-making and thus state competence are more pronounced in China than in the East Asian developmental states. The IMD World Competitiveness Yearbook (2007) indicates that China ranks ahead of Japan, Taiwan and Korea with regards to adaptability of government policy to changes in the economy and policy transparency. In detail, out of 55 countries, China ranks four with regard to the adaptability of government policy to changes in the economy, before Japan (rank 30), Taiwan (rank 33) and Korea (rank 34). Moreover, China ranks 19 regarding satisfaction of policy transparency compared with Japan (rank 32), Taiwan (rank 39) and Korea (rank 34) (refer to Table 11).

820 One foreign expert elaborated that the overlap of responsibility between different central level agencies is not limited to the auto sector. When it comes to decisions on the railway system, the Ministry of Construction is responsible for the metro railway system within one city. The Ministry of Railways is yet responsible for the metro railway system inbetween two cities. Interviews conducted with managers of a German supplier company in Shanghai on 19.06.2006.

821 Interview conducted with an expert of a European auto association in Beijing on 16.06.2006.

822 Refer to Thun (2006), p. 110.

823 A German manager of a supplier company in Shanghai referred to the study of AT Kearny during the interview on 13.07.2006.

Table 10: Coordination and agreement across policy-making organizations.

	NDRC	Ministry of Commerce	State Administration of Taxation	Ministry of Communication	China Customs	State Environmental Protection Administration	Ministry of Science and Technology	State Administration of Industry and Commerce	State Bureau of Quality and Technical Supervision and Quarantine	Ministry of Public Security
China Auto Industry Policy	x	x	x	x	x	x	x	x	x	x
Vehicle fuel consumption standards	x	x				x	x		x	
Vehicle recycling requirements	x					x		x	x	
Emissions compliance	x					x	x			x
Auto dealership franchising	x	x	x					x		x
Common process for used car appraisal	x					x			x	x
Nationwide vehicle registration system	x		x							x
Tariff regulations for imported parts	x	x	x		x					
Auto side collision safety regulations	x						x		x	x

Source: AT Kearney (together with the European Union Chamber of Commerce and the Auto Components Working Group) (2005).

Table 11: Government policy-making, 2007.[824]

"Out of 55 countries, China/Japan/Taiwan/ Korea rank..."	**China**	**Japan**	**Taiwan**	**Korea**
"Adaptability of government policy to changes in the economy is high"	4	30	33	34
"Transparency of government policy is satisfactory"	19	32	39	34

Source: IMD World Competitiveness Yearbook (2007), p. 328 ff.

In China, a counteractive set of laws is often necessary, as the auto industry has developed rapidly since 1978.[825] While in 2000, the passenger car parc in China was less than 5,000 units, it reached 17 million units in 2006.[826] Due to rapidly increasing passenger car sales, the central government regularly implements a raft of new legislative measures such as frontal and side crash tests to increase safety as well as emission standards (Euro norms) to combat rising pollution.[827] China adopted

824 The smaller the rank, the better government policy-making with regards to each indicator.

825 Interviews conducted with experts from a German public corporation in Beijing on 08.06.2006 and with experts from a Chinese state organization in Beijing on 13.06.2006.

826 Refer to Global Insight (2007), Asian Automotive Industry Forecast Report, September 2007, p. 4.

827 Interview conducted with an expert of a Chinese auto government institution in Beijing on 16.06.2006.

Euro II emission standards for all new cars in 2003.[828] Euro III standards were adopted nationwide in July 2007. Euro IV emission standards are scheduled for nationwide adoption by 2010.[829] The example shows that the standards and regulations domestic and foreign investors have to fulfil are transparent. Moreover, central level bureaucrats clearly target national regulations for the sector. They enact corrective regulations to adapt the development of the industry to changing macroeconomic, environmental or social conditions.[830]

While policy-making demonstrates to be adaptable to macro-economic changes, and government policy is transparent to economic subjects, governance lacks quality. The World Bank's governance indicators confirm that the regulatory burden (measuring the incidence of market-unfriendly policies) is larger in China ("Regulatory Quality": 46.3 percentile rank) than in Japan (87.3 percentile rank).[831] Further governance indicators such as "Rule of Law" (measuring the quality of contract enforcement, the police, and the courts, as well as the likelihood of crime and violence) and "Control of Corruption" (measuring the exercise of public power for private gain, including both petty and large-scale corruption and state capture) demonstrate that governance is far less pronounced in China ("Rule of Law": 45.2 percentile rank; "Control of Corruption": 37.9 percentile rank) than in Japan ("Rule of Law": 90.0 percentile rank; "Control of Corruption": 90.3 percentile rank) (refer to Table 12). The scale of corruption resulting from local governments' extensive economic regulatory rights[832] is larger than that of the East Asian developmental states.[833]

---

828 Euro I emission standards were adopted nationwide in China in 2000.

829 Refer to Global Insight (2007), Asian Automotive Industry Forecast Report, April 2007, p. 45.

830 Interview conducted with an expert of a European auto association in Beijing on 16.06.2006 and with managers of a German OEM in Beijing between 08.06.2006 and 16.06.2006.

831 The indicators are based on several hundred individual variables measuring perceptions of governance, drawn from 37 separate data sources constructed by 31 different organizations. The authors assign these individual measures of governance to categories capturing key dimensions of governance, and use an unobserved components model to construct six aggregate governance indicators in each period. The authors present the point estimates of the dimensions of governance as well as the margins of errors for each country and period.

832 Refer to Perkins (2001), p. 8.

833 With regard to bribery and corruption, the IMD World Competitiveness Yearbook also ranks China 44 among 55 countries and regions worldwide compared with Japan (rank 22), Taiwan (rank 27) and Korea (rank 29). Refer to IMD World Competitiveness Yearbook (2007), Survey question 2.3.15 (*"Does bribing and corruption exist/do not exist in your economy?"*), p. 348.

Table 12: Governance indicators, 2006.[834]

Governance Indicator	Country	Percentile Rank (0-100)	Governance Score (-2.5 to + 2.5)	Standard Error
Regulatory Quality	**China**	**46.3**	**-0.19**	**0.18**
	Japan	87.3	+1.27	0.20
Rule of Law	**China**	**45.2**	**-0.40**	**0.13**
	Japan	90.0	+1.40	0.14
Control of Corruption	**China**	**37.9**	**-0.53**	**0.14**
	Japan	90.3	+1.31	0.14

Source: Kaufmann et al. (2007), "Governance Matters VI: Governance Indicators for 1996-2006", Internet Edition, reviewed 01.10.2007.

Government efficiency varies widely across China. The World Bank (2006) report "China Governance, Investment Climate, and Harmonious Society" reveals that government efficiency (measured by informal payments in the form of travel and entertainment expenditures as a percentage of sales, days of bureaucratic interaction by managers and taxes and fees as a percentage of sales) is foremost in China's Southeast cities (Jiangsu, Shanghai, Zhejiang, Fujian, and Guangdong); followed by the Bohai cities (Shandong, Beijing, Tianjin, and Hebei); with Northeast (Heilongjiang, Jilin, Liaoning) and Central cities (Anhui, Henan, Hubei, Hunan, and Jiangxi) typically somewhere in the middle; and with Southwest (Yunnan, Guizhou, Guangxi, Sichuan, Chongqing, and Hainan) and Northwest cities (Shanxi, Shaanxi, Neimenggu, Ningxia, Qinghai, Gansu, and Xinjiang) lagging (refer to Table 13).[835]
Taxes and fees as a proportion of sales revenue appear to be lowest in the Southeast (4.1 percent) and Bohai (4.5 percent) cities and highest in the Northwest (5.8 percent) and Southwest (6.3 percent) cities.[836] Travel and entertainment relative to sales is highest in Northeast (1.4 percent) and lowest in Bohai (0.9 percent) cities. While laws and regulations tend to be consistent nationwide, enforcement is not. The amount of time enterprise staff must spend interacting with government bureaucracies (tax administration, public security, environmental protection, and labor and social security) varies widely. On a regional basis, firm interactions with major bureaucracies are highest in Northwest cities, followed by Bohai, Southwest and Northeast cities. Days of bureaucratic interaction are lowest in Central cities

834 The governance indicators aggregate the views on the quality of governance provided by a large number of enterprise, citizen and expert survey respondents in industrial and developing countries. These data are gathered from a number of survey institutes, think tanks, non-governmental organizations, and international organizations. The aggregate indicators do not reflect the official views of the World Bank, its Executive Directors, or the countries they represent. Countries' relative positions on these indicators are subject to indicated margins of error that should be taken into consideration when making comparisons across countries and over time.

835 Numbers are based on a survey of 120 cities (and 12,400 firms). Refer to World Bank (2006), "China Governance, Investment Climate, and Harmonious Society: Competitiveness Enhancements for 120 Cities in China", Internet Edition, reviewed 07.09.2007.

836 Ibidem.

(51.7 days) and Southeast cities (51.6 days) (refer to Table 13). The low "time tax" for Southeast cities is in line with their pro-business reputation. The similarly low figure for the less developed Central cities is somewhat surprising. It is also noteworthy that the average for Northeast cities falls below that for Bohai cities, despite the Northeast's legacy of greater government intervention in the economy. This may reflect Bohai cities' greater interaction with tax administration which administers various tax preferences.

Table 13: Taxes and fees, informal payments and bureaucratic interaction, 2006.

	Taxes and fees/sales (%)	Travel and entertainment/sales (%)	Days of bureaucratic interactions
Southeast (Jiangsu, Shanghai, Zhejiang, Fujian, and Guangdong)	4.1	1.0	51.6
Bohai (Shandong, Beijing, Tianjin, and Hebei)	4.5	0.9	71.9
Northeast (Heilongjiang, Jilin, Liaoning)	5.4	1.4	63.1
Central (Anhui, Henan, Hubei, Hunan, and Jiangxi)	5.0	1.2	51.7
Southwest (Yunnan, Guizhou, Guangxi, Sichuan, Chongqing, and Hainan)	6.3	1.2	65.9
Northwest (Shanxi, Shaanxi, Neimenggu, Ningxia, Qinghai, Gansu, and Xinjiang)	5.8	1.3	78.3

Source: World Bank (2006), "China Governance, Investment Climate, and Harmonious Society: Competitiveness Enhancements for 120 Cities in China", Internet Edition, reviewed 07.09.2007.

The data indicate that entertainment and travel expenditures (measured as a ratio of sales), which can be a vehicle for corruption, tend to be higher where local governments provide poorer service or where the tax burden is higher. This also confirms a study of Cai et al. (2005) which finds that higher entertainment/travel expenditures tend to be associated with poorer firm performance, and that the "quality" of entertainment/travel expenditures is correlated with corporate governance. According to their study, firms make large payments to government officials to offset bureaucratic burdens and the threat of opportunistic behavior by governments.[837] The results of Nee and Opper (2007) also show evidence that the power of government bureaucrats and party authorities over firm decisions is associated negatively with firm return on assets and equity. They analyzed a survey of 72 firms listed on the Shanghai Stock Exchange, asking about involvement either by government agencies or officials of the CCP in 63 different firm decisions, ranging from finance and investment to personnel and external relationships. On average, firms reported some involvement in all of these decisions.[838] The foreign interviewees likewise showed concerns about bureaucrats with their political rather than business

[837] For further information refer to Cai et al. (2005).

[838] For further information refer to Nee et al. (2007).

background deciding on the feasibility of auto business projects.[839] Political intervention is hence a concern for firm managers, and it affects business decisions.

Overall, unlike in the East Asian developmental states, various central level agencies are responsible for auto policy-making in China. This involves an extensive coordination effort between them, and increases transaction costs. The state agencies' policy goals and long-term direction of industrial policy are transparent and regulations are constantly adapted to the changed economic environment of China's fast economic development. In consequence, China ranks in an international comparison before its East Asian counterparts with regard to the adaptability of government policy to changes in the economy, and policy transparency. The central government's industrial policy is directed towards clear-cut, long-term development goals. At the same time, however, Chinese bureaucrats lack enforcement competence. The World Bank indicators show evidence of the hindrance of business activity by state bureaucrats, although varying across regions, and thus confirm the expert interviews' assessments. The incidence of market-unfriendly policies, disregard for the rule of law, and corruption, are factors that reinforce the conclusion that growth has proceeded despite a merely average governance environment.[840]

4.3 National auto industrial policy

Since the 1980s, China has attempted to re-structure its auto industry through an industrial policy approach closely modelled on that of Japan and Korea. Korea's success in restructuring its auto industry, in the 1970s and 1980s can be attributed to strong government support granted to the industry and the government's ability to distribute rent, selectively and strategically, to a few key firms. This enabled the selected manufacturers to acquire economies of scale more quickly than firms outside the government's focus.[841] The developmental states used variants of entry-restrictive policies, including industrial consortia, joint R&D programs, arranged mergers as well as licensing and granted direct and indirect support to business conglomerates.

Chinese state agents have actively regulated and directed the development of the auto sector throughout the reform period. Since the change to reform and openness

---

839 The conducted expert interviews in Beijing and Shanghai moreover indicate that senior managers have to spend more time for contingency plans than in other countries in case planned projects do not receive NDRC and State Council approval. One interviewee estimated that the management team of his company furthermore has to spend about 30-40 percent of its time for contingency plans (Hong Kong and Singapore: 2 percent and Malaysia 10 percent). Interview conducted with a manager of a German OEM in Beijing on 14.06.2006 and an expert of a Chinese auto government institution in Beijing on 16.06.2006.

840 Refer to Keefer (2007), p. 213.

841 For a descriptive account refer to Rodrik (1996).

at the end of the 1970s, the sector has been of strategic importance to China's development process for the following reasons:

- *Prestige:* Not only for China, but also for many other developing countries, the auto industry is a visual symbol of a modern economy. *"It represents China's fast industrialization and the country's economic and political strength."*[842]
- *Spillover effects to other sectors:* As extensive linkages create the potential for substantial positive spillover effects, state promotion of the auto sector aims to develop basic manufacturing capabilities in a wide variety of industries. The auto industry is related to many other industries such as metallurgy, petroleum, chemical, coal, light industry, electronics, and textiles. Auto production would consequently have positive spillover effects on other sectors. Moreover, as it is connected to different industries, it creates indirect jobs in services, aftersales etc. Thus, development of the auto sector is decisive for national economic growth.
- *Specialization and coordination among different companies and sectors:* The central leaders hoped that the development of the auto industry would encourage domestic manufacturers in many sectors to specialize and better co-ordinate their efforts. A complex network of relationships between firms, markets and governments would be set-up that would increase the country's overall economic competitiveness.[843]

Due to the auto sector's far-reaching economic influence on the country's overall development, state-guidance in the auto sector has been framed by industrial policy directives. Three policy documents have mainly shaped the sector's restructuring since the mid-1980s:

- In 1986, the central government officially promulgated the auto industry to be a strategic sector of development in its Seventh Five-Year Plan (1986-1990). The first auto industrial policy was introduced before similar efforts in other industries.[844] The Chinese government was determined to strengthen the presence of state-owned enterprises in the industry after the surge in auto demand and the establishment of initial JVs.
- In 1994, inspired by soaring motor vehicle sales by Japan and Korea (Japan sold more than 6.5 million vehicles worldwide in that year)[845], and in anticipation of eventual entry into the WTO, the State Council promulgated the "Industrial Policy for the Automobile Industry".[846] It was the first stand-alone

842 Interview conducted with an expert of a European auto association in Beijing on 16.06.2006.

843 Refer to Holweg et al. (2005), pp. 13-14 and Thun (2004b), pp. 233-234.

844 Refer to Iwagaki (1986), p. 11, Takayama (1991), p. 17, Zhang and Taylor (2001), p. 267, Noble et al. (2005), p. 6, Ravenhill (2005), p. 17 and Thun (2006), p. 55.

845 Data refer to Japan Automobile Manufacturers Association, "Japan's Motor Vehicle Statistics", Internet Edition, reviewed 22.06.2007.

846 Refer to State Council (1994), "Industrial Policy of China's Automobile Industry", Preamble.

policy document that was sector-specific and not integrated in the national five-year plan.[847] The main effect of the policy was a competitive rush by foreign auto assemblers and parts firms to enter the Chinese market, and to establish a favorable position before China entered the WTO.

- In May 2004, the NDRC released the "Automobile Industry Development Policy" which replaced existing guidelines implemented in 1994.[848] The 2004 auto policy confirmed the central government's goal of *"making the auto industry a pillar industry in the national economy by the year 2010"* and updated its guidance from a decade before according to the rules of the WTO.[849] At the same time, it raised barriers to entry to the market for auto assembly.

China has gradually shifted from overall central planning to market mechanisms in the auto industry during the reform period. The 2004 industrial policy confirms the government's intent to reinforce its management of industrial development until 2010 and supposedly also beyond.[850] The industrial policies for the auto sector concentrate on the transformation of state-owned auto manufacturers into exporting national champions with the help of foreign investors. The following analysis thus concentrates on the national policy approach towards FDI and trade in order to develop the domestic auto sector.

4.3.1 FDIs in the auto sector

The most important source of leverage for the state in the auto sector is its ability to regulate and control foreign investment. China has imported technology and established JVs between its key state-owned auto enterprises and well-established foreign partners since the early 1980s. The central government has attempted to use its regulatory control over FDI to promote the development of centrally sanctioned domestic firms. It was one of the few means by which state bureaucrats could give a tangible positive benefit to a particular firm. The three domestic auto groups that are at the core of the state's focus have each at least two major foreign assembly partners: Dongfeng has Citroën and Nissan, First Auto Works (FAW) has VW and Toyota, and Shanghai Automotive Industry Corporation (SAIC) has VW and General Motors (GM). Reliance on foreign investment to buildup the domestic auto industry is in many respects the defining feature of China's development approach for the sector.

---

847 Refer to Noble et al. (2005), p. 7.

848 NDRC (2004), "Automobile Industry Development Policy No. 8 decree of the State Development and Reform Commission", Internet Edition, reviewed 11.04. 2006.

849 Ibidem, Preamble.

850 This is reflected in the content of the 2004 industrial policy for the auto industry. The policy stipulates that by 2010 the auto industry will have been nurtured as a national pillar industry.

4.3.1.1 Designation of nine auto groups

In 1981, Premier Zhao Ziyang announced that in order to achieve production at world standards, *"large-scale development"* was necessary. The sector should

> *"switch from self-reliance and the all-under-one-roof mentality of small-scale development, to a cooperative industrial complex system, centered around large-scale factories based on modern technology, which allows for specialization in order to mass produce high-quality autos".*[851]

The desire for large business groups was a response to genuine weaknesses in the Chinese economy - fragmented production (in 1978, China had 56 auto assembly plants), uncoordinated technology transfer and thus redundant investment, low R&D capability, weak brands, and poor overall quality.[852] Large firms were thought to be a key element in the economic "miracles" of neighboring Korea and Japan. In Japan, industrial *keiretsu* were at the center of the development process, particularly in the sectors that were capital and/or technology intensive (primary products, construction, machinery, transportation, and electronics). Auto companies such as Toyota, Nissan, and Mitsubishi are Japanese *keiretsu*-groups.[853] Central leaders envisioned domestic business groups becoming internationally competitive and representing the country in the global economy.[854] Harwit (1995) and Thun (2006) report that in a series of meetings sponsored by the Ministry of Machinery Industry in 1986, Japan, Korea and Taiwan were cited as examples in which governments had successfully promoted industrial development through the establishment of large-scale indigenous firms that could compete on global markets, and thus should be imitated.[855]

The 1986 policy confirmed the state's effort to build large auto business groups and consolidate the existing production facilities under more centralized managerial structures.[856] In the mid-1980s, the central government had thus created six auto enterprise groups that aimed at forging backward and forward integration with the help of foreign JV partners. The government's preference, especially in passenger cars, has been to encourage SOEs to tie-up with foreign investors in JVs as a way to acquire technology, quality control, and managerial experience.[857]

---

851 Refer to Zhao Ziyang in Iwagaki (1986), p. 11.

852 Refer to Thun (2004a), p. 454 ff.

853 Also in Korea, massive *chaebols* such as Hyundai were the agents of economic expansion.

854 Refer to Thun (2006), p. 7.

855 Additionally, the policy bureau of the central State Science and Technology Commission carried out a major study of the passenger car industry in 1987. Refer to Harwit (1995), p. 36 and Thun (2006), p. 55 and Thun (2004a), p. 457.

856 Refer to Huang (2002a), pp. 542-546.

857 Refer to Noble (2006), "Overcapacity, Contract Design and the Emergence of Independent Auto Firms in China", Internet Edition, reviewed 01.08.2007.

In May 1983, Beijing Jeep Corporation, a JV between Beijing Auto Industry Corporation (BAIC) and American Motor Corporation (AMC)[858], was established as the first JV for manufacturing utility vehicles.[859] For the Beijing Jeep JV, Jeep Cherokee CKD kits were packaged in the USA by AMC, sold to Beijing Jeep, and then exported to China for assembly by the Beijing Jeep Corporation Chinese workers. One year later, Shanghai-Volkswagen (SVW) - a JV between SAIC and VW - was founded in Shanghai, followed by FAW-VW, Second Auto Works (SAW, later renamed Dongfeng)-Citroën, Guangzhou Peugeot[860] and Tianjin Daihatsu.[861] The designated domestic auto companies were to participate in global passenger car production networks through their JV partners. Central leaders hoped that technology in product development and production would be transferred from foreign to domestic state-owned producers.[862] This was necessary, as Chinese automakers were of low proficiency, and were not able to meet the international technology standards of passenger cars. The sanctioned six major car assemblers became known as the "Big Three plus Small Three", the former referring to the three Sino-foreign JVs of SVW, FAW-VW and SAW-Citroën, while the latter were the two JVs of Beijing Jeep Corporation and Guangzhou Peugeot plus Tianjin Daihatsu.

In 1987, the government designated FAW, SAW and SAIC as China's passenger car production bases. FAW and SAIC were to handle mid-size autos, with smaller cars coming from SAW, which had previously mainly produced trucks.[863] The three players were to become powerful business groups through mergers and alliances with existing small and medium-sized auto factories. Through the formation of business groups, the central government furthermore aimed to convert large single-vehicle firms into multi-vehicle conglomerates that explore economies of scope and amortize the price for R&D between their products.[864] One reason why concentration ratios in Korea and Japan were much higher than in China is the multi-product nature of their large auto firms.[865]

The policy approach did not result in the envisioned development of the Chinese auto industry, however. Local governments protected and bailed-out unprofitable auto SOEs within their jurisdiction in order to prevent them from bankruptcy or "hostile"

858 Chrysler bought AMC in 1987 and merged with Daimler-Benz to become DaimlerChrysler in 1998.

859 Beijing Jeep Corporation was the first major manufacturing JV of any kind that was established between a Chinese company and a foreign firm after the Cultural Revolution. For a detailed analysis of the establishment of Beijing Jeep Corporation refer to Mann (1989).

860 Guangzhou Peugeot was closed in 1997 and Honda took over Peugeot's position in Guangzhou.

861 Refer to Chinese Academy of Engineering and National Research Council (2003), p. 38.

862 Refer to Liang (2004), p. 228 and Lee (2003), p. 290.

863 Refer to Ravenhill (2005), p. 17.

864 For further information on the economic theory of the multiproduct firm refer to Teece (1982).

865 The big Korean and Japanese auto makers are large producers of passenger cars as well as trucks and buses. Toyota accounted for 26 percent of Japan's truck production and 34 percent of buses in 1975. Hyundai accounted for 34 percent of Korean truck production in 1987 and 31 percent of bus output. Refer to Sit and Liu (2000), pp. 661-662.

takeovers.[866] In addition, the state did not maintain its promulgated restriction to six large groups. After the 1987 designation, the government revised its policy, and in the early 1990s, issued permission to establish two new firms of the defense-industry for minicar production (Chang'an Manufacturing Company and Guizhou Aircraft Auto Company) due to pressure from the Central Military Commission. The two companies were enterprises under the central Military Commission and their profit was subject to the military. Their parent companies were the China Ordnance Industry Corporation and the Guizhou Aviation Industry Corporation which both had strong bargaining power and close relationships with top government leaders, as the former Vice Premier Zou Jiahua had been a minister responsible for the defense industry. The central government thus extended its policy approach to "Three Large, Three Small and Two Mini".[867]

As the reform and opening policy propelled growth, more and more localities and military-related units established JVs with foreign assembly and parts firms. In consequence, although China intended to stimulate consolidation of the industry and passenger car sales growth through the domestic production of state of the art models with foreign partners, it had 125 auto factories, more than 600 auto refitting factories and about 2,300 auto parts factories in the early 1990s.[868] All of these combined produced annually less than one month's production of any one of the American "Big Three" (Ford, GM, Chrysler) auto companies.[869] Although the six auto firms (plus Chang'an Manufacturing Company and Guizhou Aircraft Auto Company) accounted for 66 percent of vehicle production in 1995, their individual scale was small by international comparison: their average output volume was only 27,466 vehicles.[870] This is far below a company's efficient level of production, which is estimated to be between 250,000 and 300,000 vehicles, irrespective of location or segment.[871]

4.3.1.2 Attraction of foreign investors

In 1994, the State Council promulgated the new "Industrial Policy for the Auto Industry".[872] The policy revised the approach of restriction to nine major auto projects and arranged to lift the ban on new JVs as well as new cars and light commercial

---

866 Refer to Ravenhill (2005), p. 17.

867 The classification of "big", "small" and "mini" mainly indicates the scale of production. All the passenger cars in these two categories equipped with engine over 1.3 liters. The "mini" represents the car of less than one liter engine. Refer to Sit and Liu (2000), pp. 661-662, Lo (1997), p. 182, Huang (2002a), p. 546 and Tsuji (2004), p. 6.

868 Refer to Tsuji (2004), p. 6 and Lo (1997), p. 182.

869 Refer to Xia (2000), p. 90.

870 Refer to Tsuji (2004), p. 6.

871 Refer to Bain (1968), pp. 284-287.

872 Refer to State Council (1994), "Industrial Policy of China's Automobile Industry".

vehicle projects by 1996. Central leaders aimed to construct a market structure that was characterized by competition among a small number of big firms.[873] Through the JVs, selected local partners were to gain access to technology, managerial skills, and capital.[874]

Construction plans of large scale and new investments from domestic sources needed the approval of the State Council which consulted with the State Development Planning Commission, the State Economics and Trade Commission and the Ministry of Machinery Industry.[875] In addition, operational practices of FDI approval involved a set of requirements to promote domestic auto companies, but prevent foreign automakers from dominating the Chinese market:[876]

- Foreign equity could not exceed 50 percent in assembly and engine JVs. Moreover, each foreign firm could only establish two international JVs for one product category.[877] These regulations prevent foreign auto firms from operating without a domestic partner in China, and restrict their business activities in defined fields (limitation of JVs within one product category). The equity JV regulation guarantees that the Chinese partner has access to all crucial operations of the JV. In addition, foreign companies could not directly provide financing for vehicle purchase, offer after-sales services or distribute cars.[878] The regulations hinder international OEMs from acquiring full control of their China operations.
- The JVs were required to produce products according to international technical standards, have product patents and trademarks, product development and manufacturing technology and establish an internal R&D department. In this way, the state encouraged foreign OEMs to produce their latest models in China.
- The JVs were obliged to have independent international sales organizations and were to export products.[879] Thus, the domestic partner would gain access to international markets and obtain foreign exchange. China's leaders hoped to build up a remunerative export-oriented industry and emulate their more prosperous neighbors Japan and Korea.[880]
- The minimum scales of production were 150,000 for passenger cars of engine capacity below 1,600 cc; 100,000 for light trucks; 50,000 for vans; 10,000 for

873 Refer to Lo (1997), p. 185.

874 Refer to Thun (2004a), pp. 455-456.

875 Refer to State Council (1994), "Industrial Policy of China's Automobile Industry", Articles 12.56 and 12.57.

876 Refer to Wang (2001), p. 1 and p. 3.

877 Refer to State Council (1994), "Industrial Policy of China's Automobile Industry", Article 6.29.

878 Refer to Harwit (2001), p. 659.

879 Refer to State Council (1994), "Industrial Policy of China's Automobile Industry", Article 6.31.

880 The state also actively manages the imports of motor vehicles, motorcycles and key components, as China's auto industry was still not internationally competitive. Refer to Harwit (1995), p. 3.

heavy-duty trucks and 200,000 for motorcycles of engine capacity below 150 cc.[881] Thus, the central leaders aimed to avoid diseconomies of scale and consolidate the fragmented auto market.

Despite China's ambitions to become a WTO member, the auto policy introduced local content requirements the foreign partner had to fulfill.[882] The local content regulation was to raise the contribution of local parts and processes in assembled vehicles.[883] Article 9.44 of the policy contends that preferential import tariff rates vary according to the localization rate of auto products.[884] Passenger car ventures had to satisfy government-imposed local content requirements to qualify for preferential tariff rates on imported components.[885] Import tariff rates were set according to the company's local content rate. The tariff on CKD kits (originally between 100-150 percent) was reduced if the local content rate was increased. Three levels of local content for passenger cars (40 percent, 60 percent and 80 percent) and three levels for commercial vehicles and motorcycles (50 percent, 70 percent and 90 percent) existed. For passenger cars with a local content rate of 60-80 percent, the tariff rate on imported parts was 32 percent. For a local content of 40-60 percent and below 40 percent, the tariff was 48 percent and 50 percent, respectively.[886]

With the local content regulation, the central government aimed to create technological linkages between Sino-foreign manufacturers and domestic suppliers, and to ensure the indigenous capabilities of the entire car sector instead of turning it into an industry that only assembles auto parts for the international market. The state hoped to thus safeguard the national auto industry. At the same time, it could actively allow the globalization of its production by encouraging FDI inflow and advance its international competitiveness.[887]

Indeed, the 1994 policy effectively forced manufacturers to use the expected percentage of Chinese-made parts and components. While in 1994 only 24 percent of the VW Jetta parts were made by Chinese companies, by 2000, 84 percent of its

---

881 Refer to State Council (1994), "Industrial Policy of China's Automobile Industry", Article 3.10.

882 The local content regulation is prohibited according to WTO regulations. The local content clause stipulates that a certain percentage of the final product has to be from domestic production. Refer to WTO (2001), "Accession Protocol", (D) Judical Review, Article 7-3, Internet Edition, reviewed 09.10.2006 and Krugman and Obstfeld (2004), p. 273.

883 The local content is also one of the prerequisites for permitting a firm to produce a second vehicle model. Refer to Wang (2001), p. 12 and Lo (1997), p. 189.

884 Refer to State Council (1994), "Industrial Policy of China's Automobile Industry", Article 9.44.

885 Refer to China Business Review (1998), "Shifting Gears", Internet Edition, reviewed 16.10.2006.

886 Refer to State Council (1994), "Industrial Policy of China's Automobile Industry", Article 9.44.

887 Refer to Wang (2001), p. 12 and Sit and Liu (2000), p. 664.

parts were produced domestically.[888] Thus, the strategy of developing the domestic market had positive results.

4.3.1.3 Revised policy approach after WTO accession

One major policy development for the domestic auto industry was China's entry into the WTO in 2001. WTO regulations forced China to revise its 1994 industrial policy - the 2004 auto policy was the answer.

Following WTO accession, China eliminated some of the performance requirements imposed on foreign investors in 1994. In conformity with the WTO agreements on Trade-Related Investment Measures (TRIMs) and Trade-Related Intellectual Property Rights (TRIPs),[889] China agreed to abandon the local content regulation by 2004. In addition, the regulation that stipulated that foreign equity in auto engine ventures could not exceed 50 percent was dropped. Foreign investors could even avoid cooperation with domestic companies, and build wholly foreign-owned auto engine companies after 2004. Moreover, foreign investors were allowed to establish non-banking financing (captive auto financing) and engage in sales and distribution (sales and distribution had to be Chinese-owned pre-WTO) after 2004 (refer to Table 14). Furthermore, China's Accession Protocol provides that *"all measures applicable to motor vehicle producers restricting the categories, types or models of vehicle permitted for production, would gradually be lifted"* and completely removed two years after accession. After that phase, motor vehicle producers would be free to choose the categories, types and models they produced.[890]

WTO accession stimulated investment in the auto sector. Foreign and domestic investment in the auto industry was RMB 19.4 billion on a yearly average during the Ninth Five-Year Plan (1996-2000).[891] The accumulated investment in the auto industry during the Tenth Five-Year Plan (CAGR 2001-2005: 39.4 percent) was RMB 235.1 billion – 2.4 times more than during the years of the Ninth Five-Year Plan before WTO accession (refer to Figure 24).

888 For further information refer to Shanghai Government (2005), "Volkswagen Leading New Way In China—Tribute to the 20th Anniversary of Shanghai Volkswagen", Internet Edition, reviewed 21.07.2007.

889 Refer to WTO (2001), "Accession Protocol", (D) Judical Review, Article 7-3, Internet Edition, reviewed 09.10.2006.

890 Ibidem, Article 8-(b).

891 Total investment in the auto industry increased from RMB 2 billion during the Fifth Five-Year Plan (1976-1980) to RMB 4 billion during the Sixth Five-Year Plan (1981-1985), RMB 17 billion during the Seventh Five-Year Plan (1986-1990) and RMB 76 billion during the Eighth Five-Year Plan (1991-1995).

Table 14: China's WTO entry – implications for the auto industry.

Category	Pre-WTO (2001)	Post-WTO (2004)	Post-WTO (2006)
Local content	40% in first year of production, increasing to 60% and 80% in second and third years	No local content requirements	
Foreign participation in sales and distribution	Limited to wholesaling through JVs	Limited to wholesaling through JVs	Will be allowed to own vehicle wholesale, retail organizations; integrated sales organizations permitted by 2006
Auto engine	Foreign companies can invest up to a 49% stake	Up to 100% stake	
Auto financing	Foreign non-bank financial institutions prohibited from providing financing	Four foreign financing institutions are expected to begin operations in 2004	Gradual roll-out of operations from selected cities to nationwide

Source: Ministry of Commerce (2002), "The Commitments to the WTO and the International Practices of the Auto Industry", Internet Edition, reviewed 23.03.2006.

Figure 24: Total investment in the auto industry (including parts and components), 1976-2005.

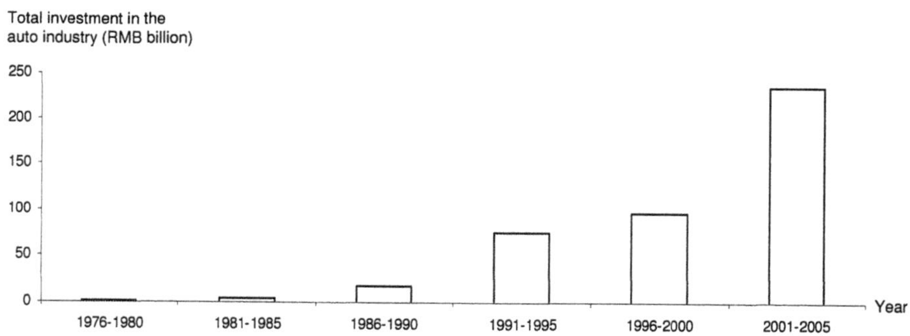

Source: China Automotive Industry Yearbook (2006).[892]

China's WTO accession made a modification of China's auto industry policy necessary. The auto industry faced the challenge of how to keep its independence in the aftermath of WTO accession and the liberalization of business activities of foreign investors. According to the goal of avoiding foreign investors' domination in the market, China increased investment barriers with the promulgation of the 2004 auto policy.[893] Although administrative screening had been simplified over the years, a series of criteria for investment projects of auto vehicle production were kept or newly introduced:

892 All data from the China Automotive Industry Yearbook (2006) were translated by DaimlerChrysler.

893 Refer to NDRC (2004), "Automobile Industry Development Policy No. 8 decree of the State Development and Reform Commission", Chapter 1, Articles 1-4.

- Foreign investors are still granted 50 percent equity participation in JVs at maximum.
- The threshold investment level of new auto projects was raised to RMB 2 billion, and a R&D center with investment of over RMB 500 million has to be built.[894] These conditions impose restriction on projects below the expected investment level. The central government also hopes that this regulation will encourage the industry's consolidation and act as a disincentive for smaller private firms to enter the market. The R&D requirement forces foreign investors to transfer technology know-how to China.
- The new industrial policy forbids the transfer of production licenses, and thus blocks the entry of mostly private firms through mergers of small incumbents.
- The policy stipulates the encouragement of auto enterprises' R&D and technical innovation capability. It supports enterprises that develop products with China's own intellectual property right (IPR), and promotes Chinese proprietary (newly created and established) brands.[895] *"The threshold for future auto projects will thus be whether foreign investors are willing to produce cars in China and sell them with their own brand."* [896]

The key of the auto industry policy was to rationalize the industry in order to maintain its independence after the phasing out of protectionist tariffs related to its WTO accession, and support major state-owned corporations.[897] The revised approach, however, left the state with many policy tools. As stipulated by the 2004 auto policy, investors have to fulfil requirements on scale, local R&D and restrictions on kit imports and JV formation. Among the policy measures are also controls on tax breaks, preferential financing, as well as discretionary authority over a range of regulatory issues from distribution to pollution control, and compulsory labelling of domestic parts.[898] Particularly, JVs approval of, and thus discretion over, domestic-foreign project formation is an important policy tool. The World Bank sample "Competitiveness, Technology and Firm Linkages in Manufacturing Sectors" (2001) confirms that the government is not only involved in project approval, but also participates in the setting-up of Sino-foreign auto projects by assisting auto companies in identifying foreign investors. A significant difference exists between the auto sector and the residual sectors (Pearson Chi-Square Test: $p=0.036$, 2-sided) in view of government assistance in identifying foreign investors in the year 2000. While 11.2 percent ($n=24$) of the managers in the auto sector answered that they received this form of official assistance, only 8.1 percent ($n=104$) of the interviewees in the residual sectors confirmed that they were granted state assistance in identifying

894 Ibidem, Chapter 10, Article 47-5.

895 Ibidem, Chapter 1, Article 3.

896 Interview conducted with experts from a Chinese government institution in Beijing on 13.06.2006.

897 Refer to Taylor Wessing China Desk (2004), "New Automobile Policy", p. 1.

898 Refer to Noble et al. (2005), p. 10-14.

foreign investors (refer to Table 15, Table 16). The government, moreover, assisted the auto sector significantly more (Pearson Chi-Square Test: p=0.006, 2-sided) than the residual sectors, in locating foreign technology to license (refer to Appendix V, Table A49, Table A50) and identifying potential foreign clients (Pearson Chi-Square Test: p=0.029, 2-sided) (refer to Appendix V, Table A51, Table A52).

Table 15: Descriptive Statistics: Government agency's or official's assistance in identifying foreign investors in the auto sector and in the residual sectors, 2000.

			Government agency's or official's assistance in identifying foreign investors			Total
			Yes	No	N.A.	
Group_autosec_ressec	Auto sec	Count	24	162	29	215
		% within Group_autosec_ressec	11,2%	75,3%	13,5%	100,0%
	Residual sec	Count	104	921	259	1284
		% within Group_autosec_ressec	8,1%	71,7%	20,2%	100,0%
Total		Count	128	1083	288	1499
		% within Group_autosec_ressec	8,5%	72,2%	19,2%	100,0%

Source: Data compiled from World Bank survey "Competitiveness, Technology and Firm Linkages in Manufacturing Sectors" (2001).

Table 16: Chi-Square Test: Government agency's or official's assistance in identifying foreign investors in the auto sector and in the residual sectors,

	Value	df	Asymp. Sig. (2-sided)
Pearson Chi-Square	6,639[a]	2	,036
Likelihood Ratio	6,906	2	,032
Linear-by-Linear Association	6,569	1	,010
N of Valid Cases	1499		

a. 0 cells (,0%) have expected count less than 5. The minimum expected count is 18,36.

2000.

Source: Data compiled from World Bank survey "Competitiveness, Technology and Firm Linkages in Manufacturing Sectors" (2001).

Even after China's WTO accession, state bureaucrats use industrial policy instruments to guide economic development. China's WTO entry did thus not destroy industrial policy for the auto industry, but constrained and disciplined it. With its assistance in identifying foreign investors and locating foreign technology to license, the government helped domestic auto companies to cooperate with foreign firms. The World Bank sample "Competitiveness, Technology and Firm Linkages in Manufacturing Sectors" (2001) provides indication that licensing technology from foreign firms differs significantly between the auto sector and the residual sectors

(Pearson Chi-Square Test: p=0.000, 2-sided) (refer to Table 17, Table 18) and between the auto sector and the electronics sector in particular (Pearson Chi-Square Test: p=0.046, 2-sided) (refer to Appendix V, Table A53, Table A54). While in the auto sector 30.1 percent (n=40) of the managers confirmed that their company licensed technology from a foreign company, in the residual sector only 15.6 percent (n=91) of the managers stated the same (refer to Table 17, Table 18). Companies in the auto sector, moreover, licensed processes from a foreign firm significantly more often than companies in the residual sectors (Pearson Chi-Square Test: p=0.001, 2-sided), and in the electronics sector in particular (Pearson Chi-Square Test: p=0.035, 2-sided) (refer to Appendix V, Table A55, Table A56, Table A57, Table A58).

Table 17: Descriptive Statistics: Introduction of new products into the plant by licensing technology from a foreign firm in the auto sector and in the residual sectors since 1998.

			Licensed technology from foreign firm		
			Yes	No	Total
Group_autosec_ressec	Auto sec	Count	40	93	133
		% within Group_autosec_ressec	30,1%	69,9%	100,0%
	Residual sec	Count	91	492	583
		% within Group_autosec_ressec	15,6%	84,4%	100,0%
Total		Count	131	585	716
		% within Group_autosec_ressec	18,3%	81,7%	100,0%

Source: Data compiled from World Bank survey "Competitiveness, Technology and Firm Linkages in Manufacturing Sectors" (2001).

Table 18: Chi-Square Test: Introduction of new products into the plant by licensing technology from a foreign firm in the auto sector and in the residual sectors since 1998.

	Value	df	Asymp. Sig. (2-sided)	Exact Sig. (2-sided)	Exact Sig. (1-sided)
Pearson Chi-Square	15,161[b]	1	,000		
Continuity Correction[a]	14,208	1	,000		
Likelihood Ratio	13,737	1	,000		
Fisher's Exact Test				,000	,000
Linear-by-Linear Association	15,140	1	,000		
N of Valid Cases	716				

a. Computed only for a 2x2 table

b. 0 cells (,0%) have expected count less than 5. The minimum expected count is 24,33.

Source: Data compiled from World Bank survey "Competitiveness, Technology and Firm Linkages in Manufacturing Sectors" (2001).

Overall, the FDI strategy has been coherently oriented towards the long-term goal of establishing internationally competitive Chinese auto companies. The regulatory framework for the auto industry focuses on technology transfer from foreign investors to domestic auto companies. Therefore, the state encourages domestic auto companies to license foreign technology and establish JVs with foreign OEMs for technology transfer. The interviewees confirmed that China has been raising the threshold for approval of investment projects step by step, and only selectively approves FDI projects in order to *"avoid China becoming a mere production base for MNCs".*[899] The design of the industrial policies for the auto industry demands that foreign auto investors fulfil strict requirements for project approval. Since 1994, central and local governments selected MNCs for cooperation according to their alleged willingness to engage in technology transfer.[900] The difficulty for policy-makers is drawing the distinction between legitimate competition and the crowding out of domestic carmakers by foreign competitors.

4.3.2 Trade policy for the auto sector

The East Asian developmental states have been successful examples of a dualistic trade policy. Korea has used entry quotas to protect its infant auto industry. The main constraint on allocating rent among domestic firms through administrative means is that their enforcement costs are high.[901] If governments fail to coordinate their activities and restrict entry, financial resources and market opportunities might become dispersed among many firms leading to scale diseconomies, at least in the short run.[902]

In addition to import substitution, export promotion was a central component in the development of Korea's auto industry. In the late 1980s, almost 50 percent of its total domestic auto production was destined for export markets. This success had been achieved by Korean companies exporting for the most part under their own brand names. The Hyundai Excel became the best-selling import model in the US market in 1987.[903] The Korean government had followed the Japanese example of promoting

899 Quotation comes from an interview conducted with an expert of a European auto association in Beijing on 16.06.2006. Moreover, interviews conducted with experts from a Chinese government institution in Beijing on 13.06.2006, with an expert of a Chinese auto government institution in Beijing on 16.06.2006 and with managers of a German OEM in Beijing between 08.06.2006 and 16.06.2006 confirm the central government's policy approach.

900 Refer to Lo (1997), p. 189.

901 Refer to Huang (2002a), pp. 549-550.

902 Excessive entry is costly in two ways in industries characterized by increasing returns. One is a static effect: excessive entry causes many plants to operate under minimum efficient scale and higher unit costs than otherwise, because financing or markets are dispersed among numerous producers. The other is a dynamic effect. When adjustment to competition is not instantaneous, protection delays the maturity of the infant firms, and increases the protected industry's dependency on market-distorting policies, making temporary protection a long-lasting proposition.

903 Refer to Ravenhill (2001), p. 2.

auto exports in order to position its firms better in the international market.[904] Export promotion was necessary to accelerate economies of scale. The size of the Korean domestic market for autos was small in the 1970s and 1980s, despite its rapid economic growth. Focusing solely on the domestic market would have limited auto firms' growth potentials and resulted in sub-optimal scales.[905] Exporting forced Korean firms to compete overseas and prompted them to improve their products' quality by meeting international safety, fuel efficiency and emission standards. Auto firms export performance thus served as an objective criterion to assess firms' performance, and ensured economic rather than political allocation criteria.[906]

4.3.2.1 Import substitution

With his theory of "national economics", List (1841) argued that a country entering the early stages of industrialization was at a disadvantage in relation to those nations that were already industrialized. The new, industrializing firms could not successfully compete against the established foreign industrial enterprises which had already incurred all the required start-up costs and which could sell their products at prices that reflected all the cost-efficiencies of mass production and an already existing highly-skilled labor force. The government of an industrializing nation had to erect protectionist barriers to keep the prices of foreign manufactured goods as high as the costs of production of the new industrializing domestic enterprises. Only in this way would those domestic firms have a chance to survive in the market and establish themselves firmly enough to finally face the older foreign industrial enterprises on an open field of free trade at some point in the future.[907]

---

[904] In 1953, Japan revised its Anti-Monopoly Law to pave the way for the formation of more cartels and the protection of its export sector. For further information refer to Yamamura (1967). In 1980, 56 percent of the cars produced in Japan were exported. Data refer to Japan Automobile Manufacturers Association, "Japan's Motor Vehicle Statistics (Production and Exports)", Internet Edition, reviewed 07.09.2007.

[905] The need to export in order to achieve economies of scale in Korea is illustrated by comparing Korea and Japan. In part because of a smaller domestic market, Korea pushed for export promotion harder than Japan. It took Korea only about five years after beginning auto production to export 15 percent of the output, whereas it took Japan more than ten years. For further information refer to Amsden and Kim (1989).

[906] Refer to Huang (2002a), p. 557.

[907] Refer to List (1841). For further elaboration on import substitution policies refer to Alexander (1987), Little et al. (1970) and Pazos (1987). For information on trade policy as an input to development refer to Krueger (1980).

4.3.2.1.1 Infant-industry protection of the auto sector through tariff barriers until 2001

With the 1986 auto policy, China chose an import substitution policy approach to promote the domestic auto industry.[908] Entry barriers placed on foreign counterparts were to prevent nascent ("infant") domestic auto firms from being crowded out by MNCs and becoming foreign-part assembly plants. The 1986 policy expected to substitute for foreign cars by implementing trade barriers and thus protect domestic automakers.[909] The central government set the tariff rate on autos at 200-220 percent in 1986, and introduced quotas that restricted the import of foreign vehicles to 30,000 units per year.[910] Moreover, foreign auto companies were not allowed to act as vehicle importers or conduct marketing in the domestic market.[911]

Tariffs remained above 200 percent until the early 1990s. Only in anticipation of eventual entry into the WTO, were tariffs on cars gradually lowered after the promulgation of the 1994 auto policy. Sectoral comparison, however, shows that tariff reductions for the auto sector were low - China maintained protection for the auto sector. While the average weighted tariff across all industries was 21 percent in 1995,[912] in 1997, tariffs on autos were only lowered to 80 percent for vehicles with an engine size smaller than 3,000 cubic capacity and 100 percent for vehicles with an engine size bigger than 3,000 cubic capacity.[913] In addition to high tariff rates, central leaders kept restrictive import licensing to a number of product categories including motor vehicles, key parts for vehicles, crane lorries, vehicle tyres, motorcycles, and key parts for motorcycles.[914] Altogether, 89 items of auto products were subject to quotas, which represented 60 percent of Chinese machinery and electronic products. Besides, only Dalian, Tianjin, Shanghai and Huangpu ports were permitted to import complete vehicles. They were centrally controlled in order to keep imports within the state's planned quota, and functioned as an administrative barrier to foreign imports. Imports of used vehicles were prohibited.[915]

Although the 1994 industrial policy emphasized the importance of passenger car production for industrial development,[916] it neglected the demand side of the

908 Refer to Iwagaki (1986), p. 11, Takayama (1991), p. 17, Zhang and Taylor (2001), p. 267, Noble et al. (2005), p. 6, Ravenhill (2005), p. 17 and Thun (2006), p. 55.

909 Refer to Wang (2001), pp. 2-3 and Huang (2002a), pp. 542-546.

910 Refer to He and Yang (1999), p. 14.

911 Refer to Ministry of Commerce (2002), "The Commitments to the WTO and the International Practices of the Auto Industry", Internet Edition, reviewed 23.03.2006.

912 Refer to Chinese Academy of Engineering and National Research Council (2003), p. 27.

913 Refer to He and Yang (1999), p. 15.

914 Refer to Wang (2001), p. 7.

915 Refer to He and Yang (1999), p. 15.

916 Refer to State Council (1994), "Industrial Policy of China's Automobile Industry".

market.[917] Given tariff protection and administrative barriers, the auto sector produced higher profits than other manufacturing industries.[918] Rents created by the protection measures ballooned car prices as enterprises of both domestic and foreign investors reaped short-term profits through high prices. In the case of SVW, the domestic sales price in 1993 was around RMB 200,000 per car (and the production cost around RMB 85,000), which at the official exchange rate was double the world price.[919]

As a result of high prices and profit expectations, 22 out of 30 provinces had declared their auto industry as the pillar sector of their economies for the 1996-2010 period as of January 1997. The 122 final assembly plants had a combined output volume of 11,888 units of motor vehicles in 1997.[920] Small-scale projects (mostly assembly plants that relied heavily on CKD kits) became lucrative, and thus economies of scale were no more a necessary condition for profitability. In consequence, the protectionist regime caused the proliferation of inferior car producers in China.[921] Besides, due to high prices resulting from the protected market, demand for passenger cars was low. China's production capacity for passenger cars (1.37 million units) was much higher than domestic demand (600,000 units) in 1997.[922] Overcapacity was a consequence of redundant investment in the auto sector, and the high profit anticipation caused by persistent excess profits.[923]

4.3.2.1.2 Reduction of tariff barriers and introduction of non-tariff barriers since 2001

The accession terms China had to agree upon to join the WTO were among the stiffest ever required and constituted massive challenges to existing practices.[924] The accession commitments relevant to motor vehicles banned many of the most important industrial policy tools China had used to protect its domestic market (refer to Table 19):

- *Tariff cuts on vehicles:* At accession, tariffs on passenger cars were 70 percent (80 percent for cars with engines over 3.0 liters); by 2005 they fell to

[917] Not before 1984, the state had officially permitted private ownership of autos to help create a market for auto companies in China. Refer to Gallagher (2006), p. 38.

[918] Refer to Nee (2002), p. 5.

[919] Refer to Lo (1997), p. 190, He and Yang (1999), p. 16 and Wang (2001), p. 8.

[920] Refer to Huang (2002a), pp. 558-559.

[921] Refer to Wang (2001), p. 8.

[922] Refer to Global Insight (2002), Asian Automotive Industry Forecast Report - China, March 2002, p. 140 and FOURIN (2005b), p. 1.

[923] Refer to Huang (2002a), pp. 558-559.

[924] For the accession documents and related materials, refer to WTO (2001), "Accession documents", Internet Edition, for a concise summary of commitments regarding the motor vehicle sector, refer to US Department of Commerce - International Trade Administration (2001), "Autos and Auto Parts", Internet Edition, both reviewed 09.10.2006.

38-43 percent (depending on the engine size). Since July 2006, tariffs on passenger cars have been 25 percent.

- *Tariff cuts on auto components:* Auto parts tariffs, which averaged 17.4 percent on accession, dropped to 10 percent in July 2006.[925]
- *Gradual elimination of quotas and licenses:* Aggregate import quotas covering motor vehicles and parts were gradually loosened (20 percent per year after 2004).[926] All import licenses and quotas were phased out in January 2006.[927]

Table 19: Impact of WTO entry on the Chinese auto industry.

Category	Pre-WTO (2001)	Post-WTO (2004)	Post-WTO (2006)
Import tariffs on vehicles	70-80%	38% -43%, depending on size of engine	25% for all vehicles
Import tariffs on auto components	15-50%	10-40%	10%
Import licenses and quotas	Annual quota of 30,000 vehicles per year from foreign OEMs	Quota decreased by roughly 20% per year	Quota to be phased out

Source: Ministry of Commerce (2002), "The Commitments to the WTO and the International Practices of the Auto Industry", Internet Edition, reviewed 23.03.2006.

Low passenger car imports as a share of domestic demand have been possible even after WTO accession and involved tariff reductions, because China still pursues a development approach to the auto industry that is dominated by import substitution. In line with the reduction of tariff rates, the price of an imported Mercedes Benz S600 fell by RMB 1.1 million in 2002. Other luxury cars were about 15-20 percent cheaper in 2003 than those sold before WTO accession.[928] Indeed, auto imports increased after WTO accession: China imported 58,000 vehicles in 2000, and 166,000 vehicles in 2006. From the total numbers, however, one cannot infer that auto imports gained importance to meet increasing demand. While total passenger car imports accounted for 7.8 percent of demand in 2002; total passenger car imports as a percentage of demand have been decreasing since then. In 2006, only 3.4 percent of passenger car demand came from imports, because of high import tariff rates (refer to Figure 25). Even in 2007, import tariffs on cars are still substantially higher in China than in many other countries. Import tariffs on passenger cars are 25 percent in China,

---

925 Refer to WTO (2001), "Accession Protocol", (D) Judical Review, Article 7-3, Internet Edition, reviewed 09.10.2006.

926 Refer to MOFCOM (2004), "Announcement of the Ministry of Commerce on the Issues of Replacing and Issuing Automatic Import Permit of Automobile Import Quota", Internet Edition, reviewed 09.10.2006.

927 Refer to Ministry of Commerce (2002), "The Commitments to the WTO and the International Practices of the Auto Industry", Internet Edition, reviewed 23.03.2006.

928 Refer to Xinhuanet (2006), "A Review of China's Car Industry in Past 5 Years", Internet Edition, reviewed 26.07.2007.

compared with 10 percent in the European Union (EU), 8 percent in Korea and 2.5 percent in the USA.[929]

Figure 25: Imports of passenger cars after WTO accession.

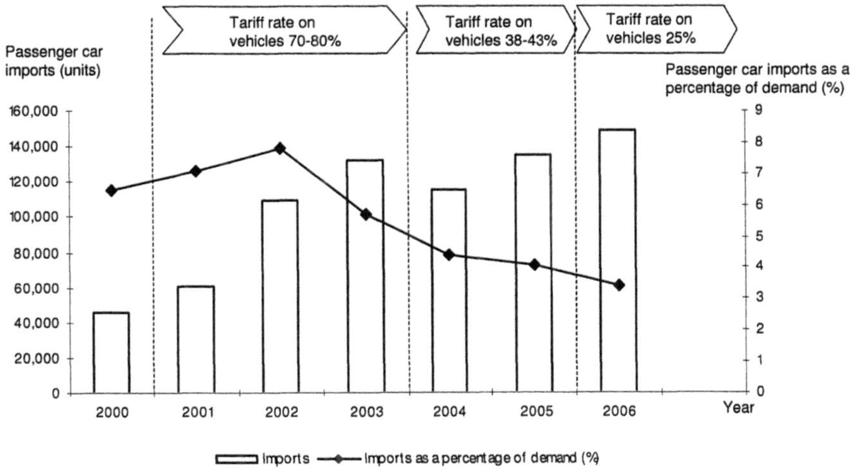

Source: Own illustration based on data from Global Insight (2007), Asian Automotive Industry Forecast Report, April 2007, p. 4.

In addition to the 25 percent tariff rate on imported passenger cars, the central government has stipulated regulations that aim to diminish imports and favor domestic production since its WTO accession. The government has established nontariff barriers such as certification, licensing, and testing requirements on products and production materials in a number of areas which force foreign manufacturers to produce locally, rather than import vehicles.

In most cases, the requirements on imports involve government approval of all products and materials covered before they are allowed to enter the market. Due to the lack of capacity to administer the requirements, they often function as barriers to those products' and materials' access to the Chinese market. Particularly, mandatory certification (CCC) as well as local content regulations function as nontariff barriers in the auto sector:

1. China Compulsory Certification: Standard certification and testing are in effect barriers to imports. In spite of the WTO Agreement on Technical Barriers to Trade, additional tests in Chinese laboratories are required for vehicles and parts, although

929 Refer to European Commission, Market Access Database, Internet Edition, reviewed 11.07.2007.

test results supported by foreign certificates are made available. China does not recognize any international certification standards, and importers must have their products retested in China. The European Commission (2007) contends that *"additional testing and certification requirements are disproportionate as they would not seem to provide additional safety, health, or environment benefits".*[930] The certification process in China can be prohibitively expensive as CCC is typically subject to a number of (unpredictable) tests which usually have to be repeated every year. There is no way of predicting or influencing whether and when a commission will hand out the certificates. If a manufacturer has several manufacturing facilities, these must all be certified.[931] The main difference between the certification system in China and those in other countries is that no foreign test agencies have the required accreditation. Type approval has to be carried out in Chinese laboratories only.[932]

The system tends to be *"overbuilt",* requiring that all products or materials covered, regardless of the presence of any indicators of non-compliance with Chinese law, undergo lengthy reviews. This procedure aims to encourage foreign companies to move production to China and avoid imports, as it is *"time-intensive, costly and an administrative burden".*[933] In addition, China's designated testing bodies are not independent of the government. In many cases, testing facilities are closely connected with research institutes that engage in R&D activities related to foreign products. This raises IPR concerns among foreign companies.[934]

2. Local content regulation: The localization regulation is another measure that aims at import substitution. Through the localization regulation, the national government discourages kit assembly using imported parts and subsystems. In this way, it tries to foster the development of the industry, as foreign companies have to invest domestically in core technology and vehicle subsystems. Officially, as part of its commitment to the WTO, China abandoned the 40 percent localization rate. The central government, however, issued new regulations for importing vehicles, auto systems and components. In this regard, the Customs General Administration, the NDRC, the Ministry of Commerce and the Ministry of Finance jointly issued the "Measures for the Administration of Import of Automobile Components and Parts

930 This applies to Standards, Sanitary and Other Technical Requirements. Refer to European Commission, Market Access Database, Internet Edition, reviewed 11.07.2007.

931 At the time the interviews were taken, the certification process took between three and seven months. Interview conducted with an expert of a Chinese auto association in Beijing on 16.06.2006.

932 China, however, also has to implement the regulatory framework necessary to allow foreign-invested testing and certification organizations to conduct conformity assessment services for the domestic market. Majority-owned ventures were to be allowed in this area by no later than 11.12.2003. Refer to China Business Review (2003), "Navigating China's Standards Regime", Internet Edition, reviewed 20.07.2007 and China Business Review (2004), "WTO: China enters year three", Internet Edition, reviewed 03.10.2006.

933 Interview conducted with an expert of a European auto association in Beijing on 16.06.2006.

934 Refer to Businessweek (2003), "Navigating China's Standards Regime", Internet Edition, reviewed 19.07.2007.

Featuring Complete Vehicles" in 2005.[935] Under the legislation, eight key parts (engine, vehicle body, transmission, driving axle, non-driving axle, frame, braking system, steering system) as well as CKD and SKD kits were taxed as completely built up (CBU)[936] imports from April 1, 2005:

- If both vehicle body and engine are imported, the vehicle will be regarded as a CBU import.
- If either vehicle body or engine is imported, plus any three or more of a combination of transmission, driving and driven axles, chassis, steering and braking, the vehicle will be regarded as a CBU import.
- Alternatively, if any five or more of a combination of transmission, driving and driven axles, chassis, steering and braking are imported, the vehicle will be regarded as a CBU import.
- As of July 1st, 2008, if the total cost of imported components accounts for 60 percent or more of a complete vehicle retail price, the vehicle will be regarded as a CBU import.[937]

China's leaders claimed that the above policy aimed at curbing tariff evasion by importers who tried to avoid paying the 25 percent tariff. However, according to the foreign respondents, the Administrative Measures regulation was de facto a substitute for the pre-WTO local content regulation.[938] The resulting additional charge penalizes imported components, and forces auto companies to source components locally rather than to import them. The stipulation of the regulation was to reach 40 percent local content after one year, and 60 percent local content after three years.[939] Overall, the new law demanded production of the whole car in China, because imports of key components would have become too expensive to be profitable in China. The policy-makers' key intention was to further improve the quality of FDI in the auto sector. They aimed to transform the sector into a *"global auto manufacturing*

---

935 Refer to the General Administration of Customs, NDRC, Ministry of Commerce and Ministry of Finance (2005), "Measures for the Administration of Import of Automobile Components and Parts Featuring Complete Vehicles", Internet Edition, reviewed 09.10.2006.

936 Vehicles are CBU if they are almost completely assembled in the country of origin, but partly disassembled before export. To gain some extra tax preferences, the manufacturer needs to further localize the car, i.e. increase the share of parts produced by local manufacturers, such as tires, wheels, seats, headlights, windscreens and glass, batteries, interior plastics, etc. down to the engine and transmission.

937 Refer to the General Administration of Customs, NDRC, Ministry of Commerce and Ministry of Finance (2005), "Measures for the Administration of Import of Automobile Components and Parts Featuring Complete Vehicles", Internet Edition, reviewed 09.10.2006.

938 Interviews conducted with managers of a German OEM in Beijing on 14.06.2006.

939 Refer to Global Insight (2006), Asian Automotive Industry Forecast Report, August 2006, China, p. 50.

base rather than assembly center" and propel the development and reorganization of the local auto parts industry.[940]

Trade lobby groups from different countries presented their objections to the WTO, as WTO law promulgates that members have to offer the same trade policies to all WTO members (most-favored-nation status).[941] The European Commission considers that China has failed to comply with its obligations under the GATT 1994, the Agreement on Trade-Related Investment Measures, the Agreement of Subsidies and Countervailing Measures and the Protocol on the Accession of the Peoples Republic of China. The issue was referred to a WTO Panel by the Dispute Settlement Body in October 2006 at the request of the European Commission, Canada and the USA.[942]

In July 2006 (one month after the interviews were conducted in China), following the complaints of the trade lobby groups, the Chinese government announced a postponement of the implementation of the Administrative Measures until July 1st, 2008. The import duty on CBU imports is therefore 25 percent, while the import tariff on parts and components is 10 percent. After the postponement, it is still not entirely clear whether CKD and SKD kits will be subject to duty of 25 percent or 10 percent but the back-tracking implies that these will be subject to the lower rate. Large and luxury models typically have lower levels of local content. Consequently, production is particularly vulnerable to this regulation.[943] While the Administrative Measures have been postponed, China has still not abandoned its 40 percent local content regulation for the auto sector. In November 2006, the US-China Economic and Security Review Commission stated in its report to the Congress, that *"Chinese regulations still require automakers to exceed a 40 percent domestic content requirement or face higher tariffs on the imported auto parts".*[944] These discriminatory tariffs pressure continuously China-based auto assembly companies to use parts manufactured in China.

Data of the World Bank survey "Competitiveness, Technology and Firm Linkages in Manufacturing Sectors" (2001) also indicate that the auto sector faces constraints on imports. There is a significant difference (Levene's Test: p=0.000, T-Test: p=0.034 equal variances not assumed) between the auto sector and the residual sectors with respect to how many days consignments of a major imported raw material took on average to clear local customs. While it took 11.8 days in the auto sector (n=77), it took 7.0 days in the residual sectors (n=357) (refer to Table 20, Table 21) and 6.7

940 Interviews conducted with managers of a German OEM in Beijing on 14.06.2006.

941 Refer to WTO Secretariat (1999), "Guide to the Uruguay Round Agreements".

942 Refer to European Commission, Market Access Database, Internet Edition, reviewed 11.07.2007. For further information refer to European Commission, "WT/DS339 - Measures affecting imports of automobile parts", Internet Edition, reviewed 25.07.2007.

943 Refer to Global Insight (2007), Asian Automotive Industry Forecast Report, April 2007, p. 62.

944 Refer to US-China Economic and Security Review Commission (2006), "2006 Report to Congress," Internet Edition, reviewed 29.07.2007, p. 12 and p. 167 ff.

days in the electronics sector (n=194). The difference between the auto sector and the electronics sector is also significant (Levene's Test: p=0.000, T-Test: p=0.025 equal variances not assumed) (refer to Appendix V, Table A59, Table A60).

The challenge for the Chinese government is consequently to come up with a strategy to encourage localization while keeping within the spirit of its WTO agreement. The interviewed experts explained that China's cost structure and expanding scale are already encouraging greater localization (and thus competition) and the outsourcing of global operations.[945] However, interviewees from auto companies added that their companies' profitability considerations should decide about the products and the amount of localization in China. The Chinese government should therefore not rely on protection by a local content policy but on market forces.[946]

Table 20: Descriptive Statistics: Days for consignments of a major input experienced before clearing local customs in the auto sector and the residual sectors, 2000.

	Group_autosec_ressec	N	Mean	Std. Deviation	Std. Error Mean
Days for consignments of a major imported raw material to clear local customs	Auto sec	77	11,8312	19,08871	2,17536
	Residual sec	357	7,0420	8,36297	,44262

Source: Data compiled from World Bank survey "Competitiveness, Technology and Firm Linkages in Manufacturing Sectors" (2001).

Table 21: Independent Samples T-Test: Days for consignments of a major input experienced before clearing local customs in the auto sector and the residual sectors, 2000.

		Levene's Test for Equality of Variances		t-test for Equality of Means						
									95% Confidence Interval of the Difference	
		F	Sig.	t	df	Sig. (2-tailed)	Mean Difference	Std. Error Difference	Lower	Upper
Days for consignments of a major imported raw material to clear local customs	Equal variances assumed	30,567	,000	3,454	432	,001	4,78915	1,38637	2,06428	7,51403
	Equal variances not assumed			2,157	82,393	,034	4,78915	2,21993	,37331	9,20499

Source: Data compiled from World Bank survey "Competitiveness, Technology and Firm Linkages in Manufacturing Sectors" (2001).

Moreover, due to the continuous protection of the auto market, profits of auto manufacturers remain high. Profit expectations as well as the incentives for high-volume production have resulted in overcapacity in the auto market. While the actual

---

945 Interviews conducted with experts from a German public corporation in Shanghai on 19.06.2006.

946 Interview conducted with an expert of a European auto association in Beijing on 16.06.2006 and with a manager of an OEM in Beijing on 09.06.2006.

sales volume was 3.3 million passenger vehicles in 2005, capacity was more than 6 million (refer to Figure 26).[947] The growth of auto production has been slowing since 2004 (growth of auto assembly was 72 percent in 2004 and 14 percent in 2005)[948], and thus the operation rate has also been decreasing. In order to combat rising overcapacity in the auto industry, the NDRC issued another circulation on the restructuring of the auto industry in 2006. The focus of the document is on newly founded car projects. The circulation stipulates that if an existing auto maker applies to establish a new plant at any other place, its vehicle sales in the previous year should be 80 percent over its approved or filed production capacity.[949] With this regulation, the state further increased the threshold for foreign projects. Altogether, the protective regime of the auto industry (imposing high tariffs on finished-vehicle imports together with licenses and quotas) persists despite extensive trade and economic liberalization in most other sectors in the late 1990s.

Figure 26: Overcapacity in the Chinese passenger car market, 1998 – 2005.

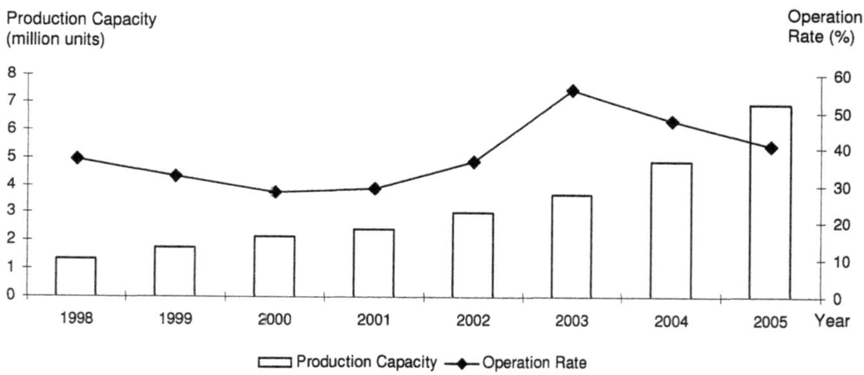

Source: FOURIN (2005b), p. 1.

4.3.2.2 Export promotion

At the beginning of China's reform path, central bureaucrats only needed to look at their prosperous neighbors Japan and Korea to see the stimulating effect a vibrant export-oriented auto sector could have on a nation's economy.[950] The 1994 auto industrial policy intended to encourage auto companies' export activities. According to Article 3.12, exporting auto enterprises would enjoy preferential treatment, such as

947 Refer to Global Insight (2007), Asian Automotive Industry Forecast Report, April 2007, p. 4.

948 Ibidem.

949 Refer to China Auto (2007), p. 8.

950 Refer to Harwit (1992), p. 141.

tax exemptions, from the regulatory tax for fixed asset investments and special permissions in utilizing foreign capital starting from 1996.[951] The policy also clarified that the state would provide preferential loans for exporting companies in order to establish internationally competitive domestic auto manufacturers.[952] Article 8.39 promulgated that

> *"The state encourages auto industry enterprises to make efforts to expand and take part in international competition, which should be regarded as the development objective of auto enterprises".*[953]

Despite preferential treatment for exporting enterprises, export volumes remained low in the mid-1990s. In 1995, only 1.4 percent of passenger cars produced in China were exported. In comparison, Korea exported almost 50 percent of its domestic passenger car production in the same year.[954] Until 2003, exports of passenger cars as a percentage of domestic car production had not increased (1.3 percent of domestic car production).[955] High car prices due to import tariffs on parts, as well as low quality, hindered domestic manufacturers from exporting.

Since the 2004 Auto Industrial Policy, the state has been aiming to increase exports of cars and auto components 20 times by 2010, to USD 100 billion (2003: USD 4.7 billion).[956] This policy encourages investment in export-oriented JVs, and uses the following measures to increase auto companies' export activities.[957] The government issues special export loans via the Export-Import Bank of China, which is a fully government-owned policy bank under the State Council.[958] In 2005, the Export-Import Bank of China loaned RMB 5 billion to domestic auto maker Chery for its overseas business expansion. The loan was to aid Chery in its foreign investment and overseas contracts for its cars, and other mechanical, electrical and high-tech

---

951 Refer to State Council (1994), "Industrial Policy of China's Automobile Industry", Article 3.12.

952 Ibidem, Article 8.39.

953 Ibidem, Article 8.40.

954 Chinese companies' products were not yet internationally competitive. Besides, with their investments in China, foreign companies aimed to produce locally for the Chinese market instead of using China as an export hub as most MNCs had production facilities in other markets from where they exported worldwide. Refer to Global Insight (2002), Asian Automotive Industry Forecast Report - China, March 2002, p. 140 and Global Insight (2002), Asian Automotive Industry Forecast Report – South Korea, March 2002, p. 104.

955 Refer to Global Insight (2006), Asian Automotive Industry Forecast Report, December 2006, p. 4.

956 Refer to World Markets Analysis (2004).

957 Refer to NDRC (2004), "Automobile Industry Development Policy No. 8 decree of the State Development and Reform Commission", Chapter 1, Article 2, Internet Edition, reviewed 11.04. 2006.

958 Refer to China Export-Import Bank (n.d.), "The Export-Import Bank of China", Internet Edition, reviewed 27.08.2007.

products.[959] In addition, central and local governments encourage exports by tax refund. FFEs established in Beijing can enjoy preferential policies formulated by the central government and Beijing Municipality. As provided in Articles 80 and 81 of the "Enforcement Regulations for the Law of the People's Republic of China on Income Tax of Enterprises with Foreign Investment and Foreign Enterprises", a foreign investor receives full refund of the charged income tax if he reinvests *"directly earned profits in enterprises with advanced technology and export orientation within a period of not less than 5 years".*[960] Moreover, as provided in the Preferential Policies Provided by Beijing Economic and Technological Development Zone for Investors, export-oriented foreign enterprises enjoy a reduced corporate income tax rate of 10 percent even after the expiry of the corporate income tax exemption and reduction period *"if the output value of export products in the current year has reached above 70 percent of the product output value of the enterprise in the same year".*[961] These regulations function as incentives for foreign auto companies to use China as an export hub, and at the same time discipline companies through strict requirements on the amount and period of exports.

MNCs are still limited to 50 percent ownership of domestic JVs, but, they can hold majority stakes in auto and motorcycle JVs if their operations are geared solely towards exports.[962] The new guidelines followed the precedent when the NDRC allowed Honda to take a majority stake in its export-oriented JV with Guangzhou Auto in 2003.[963] The regulation aims to encourage foreign manufacturers to expand their export activities and set up export-oriented plants.

To sum up, the analysis of China's national auto industrial policies showed that, unlike from policies in the East Asian developmental states, industrial policy for the auto sector and its signals aimed at foreign investors have been inconsistent in China during the reform period:[964]

- After the opening to the world in the 1970s, industrial policy encouraged state-owned auto manufacturers to update the old 1960s Soviet technology by acquiring more advanced technology from MNCs. The government-owned

[959] Refer to People's Daily (2005), "China aids domestic auto maker for overseas expansion", Internet Edition, reviewed 19.07.2007.

[960] Refer to Beijing Municipal Bureau of Industrial Development (n.d.), "Auto Manufacturing Industry - Development Advantages", Internet Edition, reviewed 21.07.2007.

[961] Ibidem.

[962] Refer to NDRC (2004), "Automobile Industry Development Policy No. 8 decree of the State Development and Reform Commission", Chapter 10, Article 48 and 49, Internet Edition, reviewed 11.04. 2006.

[963] Honda, in its export JV, has a 65 percent stake, while Dongfeng Motor and Guangzhou Auto hold 25 and 10 percent, respectively. Refer to People's Daily (2003), "China's Automobiles to Tap for Overseas Markets", Internet Edition, reviewed 21.07.2007. Chapter 4.3.3.1 discusses on how the Guangzhou Development District lobbied for the Honda export JV.

[964] For further information refer to Amsden (2001), p. 151 ff.

auto firms both licensed technology from the Japanese and negotiated JVs with US and European auto companies during that time.

- After several major Sino-foreign JVs had been established, the government reconsidered this strategy in its 1994 auto policy. Chinese auto firms had become mere assemblers of foreign CKD kits of their foreign JV partners. The central government wanted to cultivate indigenous technological capabilities so that domestic companies could become internationally competitive. With the auto policy of 1994, China erected even higher trade barriers for its infant industry and introduced strict demands on foreign investors with respect to technology transfer. In this regard, the 1994 auto policy was a landmark policy that imposed far-reaching technology-transfer requirements on foreign investors.
- After China's WTO entry in 2001, the state had to abandon most of the requirements placed on foreign investors, and dismantle trade protections introduced in 1994. This indicates another turnaround in Chinese policy for the auto industry.

4.3.3 Localism in the auto industry

Local governments are increasingly the agents of industrial development at the level of the firm. The developmental role attributed to local governments is a direct result of economic decentralization, the dominant characteristic of China's transition from central planning to a market economy. Local governments in China actively promote their localities' growth and thus contribute to the nation's industrial development. Local states are not nation-states, however. The central government sets the framework of rules within which local governments operate (such as taxation policy, environmental policy, corporate law etc.) and the form of interaction with the global economy (tariff policy, participation in international organizations etc.). During the reform period, local governments have experimented with new policy approaches within their jurisdiction, which have not always complied with national policy directives.[965] The auto sector provides examples of both the positive and negative results of local developmentalism.

4.3.3.1 Incentives to boost the development of the auto sector

Local bureaucrats are responsible for the economic management of the auto sector. Except for the China National Heavy-Duty Truck Corporation, Dongfeng and FAW, which are under the direct authority of the central government, Chinese car manufacturers are under the direct control of a ministry or a provincial or municipal government. BAIC, SAIC, and Tianjin Auto Industry Group Corporation (TAIC) are under the jurisdictions of the respective municipalities of Beijing, Shanghai and

[965] Refer to Thun (2004a), pp. 460-461 and Thun (2006), p. 80.

Tianjin. The Guangzhou city government oversees Guangzhou-Peugeot. Chang'an and Guizhou are, respectively, under the control of the ministerial-level entities China North Industries Corporation and China National Aviation Industry Corporation.[966]

Provincial and municipal governments take a deep interest in the promotion of auto firms to enhance local industrialization. In competition with other provinces for foreign auto companies, local bureaucrats strive to attract foreign auto companies into their jurisdiction that should form JVs with local auto companies.[967] In the mid-1980s, there were 17 Chinese parties negotiating simultaneously with Honda, and 22 others with Ford, to attract the respective firms to their local development zones.[968] *"Local level governments even have their staffs that are travelling around the world to attract foreign investors to local development zones."* [969] Managers of industrial development zones give speeches at conferences and fairs, and praise the investment climate of their locality.[970]

Local administrative authorities use several policy instruments to support local firms.[971] They provide preferential help for domestic and international investors in their jurisdictions, including favorable leasing fees for land, low rents for production halls, and administrative support in the form of fast approvals. Speedy approval of investments in facilities, marketing and financial products provide competitive advantages for cooperative companies. The approval process of Chang'an Ford Mazda Engine Company to build a plant near Nanjing took about one month. In contrast, Toyota had to wait several years for approval to assemble cars in Tianjin and in Guangzhou. Furthermore, local governments provide financing, infrastructure and free trade zones.[972] The most important incentive is preferential tax treatment in the local development zones. Tax reliefs, however, are not solely directed towards the encouragement of auto companies, but are applicable to all encouraged investments. The China-Singapore Suzhou Industrial Park grants technologically advanced manufacturing enterprises a local income tax reduction (in addition to the

966 Refer to China Business Review (1998), "Shifting Gears", Internet Edition, reviewed 14.10.2006.

967 Refer to People's Daily (2003), "China sets to put breaks on auto industry", Internet Edition, reviewed 16.10.2006 and interview conducted with an expert of a Chinese auto government institution in Beijing on 16.06.2006.

968 Refer to Lo (1997), p. 177.

969 Interview conducted with a German manager of a supplier company in Shanghai on 13.07.2006.

970 At the 2006 Global Business Forum in Hannover, representatives of the Suzhou High-Tech-Park, the Kunshan Development Zone and the Zhang Jiagang Development Zone explored the advantages of their parks and development zones for foreign investors (they held speeches and had standings at the fair). Refer to Global Business Forum (2006), "Sourcing Asia", Internet Edition, reviewed 06.06.2007.

971 Refer to Hebei Provincial Department of Commerce (2002), "The Provisions of Hebei Province Concerning Further Optimizing of the Investment Environment and the Encouragement of Foreign Investment", Chapter II, Article 4 (Examination, Approval and Registration), Chapter III (Investment Environment and Service) and Chapter IV, Article 22 (Key Sectors to Attract Foreign Investment and Preferential Policies), Internet Edition, reviewed 27.08.2007.

972 Refer to Noble et al. (2005), pp. 14-15.

already reduced tax rates in development zones) of 3 percent for two years and a reduced tax rate of 7.5 percent (instead of 15 percent) for the following three years. Thereafter, enterprises pay a rate of 10 percent for the next 3 years.[973]

The World Bank sample "Competitiveness, Technology and Firm Linkages in Manufacturing Sectors, 1998 – 2000" (2001) also indicates that the primary reason for the location[974] of a plant is *"fewer regulatory requirements and taxes based on government's assignments"* (refer to Table 22). There is no significant difference between the three groups in this respect (refer to Appendix V, Table A45, Table A46, Table A47, Table A48).[975]

Table 22: Descriptive Statistics: Reasons for location of plant for companies in the auto sector, 2000.

		Reasons the plant was located here when plant was established				Advantages for locating plant here now			
		Local market size	Proximity to other firms in the same line of business	Low rents or cost of buying property	Fewer regulatory requirements and taxes based on government's assignments	Local market size	Proximity to other firms in the same line of business	Low rents or cost of buying property	Fewer regulatory requirements and taxes based on government's assignments
N	Valid	57	53	84	87	63	52	69	50
	Missing	159	163	132	129	153	164	147	166
Median		2	2	2	1	2	2	2	1

Source: Data compiled from World Bank survey "Competitiveness, Technology and Firm Linkages in Manufacturing Sectors" (2001).

The foreign auto managers interviewed explained that local governments support foreign auto companies in order to benefit domestic manufacturers, create jobs, and promote the overall economic environment of the locality.[976] Foreign auto managers agreed that the subsidies and preferential conditions that local governments offer foreign companies, are a matter of negotiation between foreign investors and local bureaucrats. Incentives vary not only between localities but also between foreign companies in the same locality. Due to the aim of foreign companies to enter the growing Chinese auto market, local governments are in a good position to negotiate with foreign investors. Accordingly, the negotiations with domestic partners and the local governments of different provinces can make the negotiation process lengthy

973 For a detailed listing of tax incentives refer to China-Singapore Suzhou Industrial Park Development Co., Ltd (2007), "Preferential Policies", Internet Edition, reviewed 17.01.2007.

974 The question was twofold, asking for "reasons the plant was located here when it was established" and for "advantages for locating plant here now".

975 The only significant difference (Mann-Whitney U-Test: $p = 0.027$) is between the auto sector and the electronics sector with regard to the proximity to other firms in the same line of business as an advantage for locating a plant in the same region now. While managers in the auto sector ranked this advantage two, managers of the electronics sector ranked it three. This difference is, however, obvious, as especially the vehicle parts manufacturers are heavily dependent on their customers, the vehicle manufacturers and locate their plants close to them. Refer to Appendix V, Table A45, Table A46, Table A47, Table A48.

976 Interviews conducted with experts from a German public corporation in Beijing on 08.06.2006.

for foreign investors.[977] Moreover, regional inconsistencies in regulation and enforcement, coupled with sometimes weak communication between government ministries, complicate investment and the business planning decisions of foreign investors. With regard to the auto industry, regional inconsistencies exist in connection with emission standards. While Euro III standards were adopted nationwide in July 2007; Beijing and Shanghai had already adopted Euro III standards at the beginning of 2006. Euro IV emissions standards are scheduled for adoption in Beijing by 2008, in Shanghai by 2009.[978] Whilst other emerging markets also show regional inconsistencies in regulations and enforcement, the sheer size of China and its economic growth, exacerbates the situation and presents major obstacles to foreign auto companies active in China.[979]

As the economic performance of large auto groups is linked to the locality's growth – SVW contributed 8 percent of Shanghai's GDP in 2002[980] - local bureaucrats try to adjust central-government regulations to their companies' needs. Until 2004, the legislation regulating investment in the auto industry permitted a foreign manufacturer to have no more than 50 percent of ownership in a JV with a Chinese partner. In 2003, central bureaucrats approved the JV of Honda with Guangzhou Auto, in which the foreign partner would have a majority with 65 percent ownership, only because the local authorities of Guangzhou Development District appealed to central level agencies on the auto maker's behalf.[981] The export plant was designed to manufacture 50,000 "JAZZ" cars annually, which would be exported particularly to European markets. The export JV would not only increase the locality's tax revenue and provide new jobs, but would also enable its domestic producer Guangzhou Auto to gain experience with international market structures, regulations and sales networks. The application approval took only six months. Moreover, the municipal government granted the export JV preference and support on land price, electric and administrative charges etc.[982] The reason the central authorities made an exception was that the Honda production facility in Guangzhou Development District was established to produce exports. Export performance is the most persuasive evidence of technical upgrading; it is a standard "control" mechanism for governments that seek to assess the relative performance of domestic firms.[983] In the 2004 auto

[977] Interviews conducted with German managers of two different supplier companies in Shanghai on 13.07.2006 and 19.07.2006.

[978] Refer to Global Insight (2007), Asian Automotive Industry Forecast Report, April 2007, p. 45.

[979] Refer to the Business and Industry Advisory Committee to the OECD (BIAC) (2007), "BIAC Priorities for Regulatory Reform in China", Internet Edition, reviewed 28.07.2007.

[980] Refer to People's Daily (2003), "China sets to put breaks on auto industry", Internet Edition, reviewed 16.10.2006.

[981] Refer to Bureau of Foreign Trade and Economic Cooperation of Guangzhou Municipality (2005), "Guangzhou Honda Automobile Export Base project", Internet Edition, reviewed 07.09.2007.

[982] Refer to Bureau of Foreign Trade and Economic Cooperation of Guangzhou Municipality (2005), "Guangzhou - An Automotive Industry Base with the Strongest Competitiveness in the World", Internet Edition, reviewed 07.09.2007.

[983] Refer to Amsden (2001), p. 8.

industrial policy, the new legislation came into force permitting foreign companies in the auto industry to have up to 70 percent of shares if their production was solely destined for export.[984]

This example shows that local governments actively lobbied for their local auto manufacturers if this benefited their jurisdiction. The case also demonstrates that national directives are not perceived as direct orders at the local level. The authorities in Special Economic Zones make adjustments, negotiate with the central government on behalf of their investors, and generally approach the directives with pragmatic flexibility.[985]

4.3.3.2 Protectionist measures to safeguard local auto companies

For industries that enjoy increasing returns to scale, there is a natural tendency to have production clustered in a few places. The scale-economies theory of international trade calls attention to the theory of regional specialization. In an industry where there is a significant fixed cost of production or a decreasing average variable cost of production, a firm would enjoy a low average cost of production by producing a large volume of goods and services, which in turn enhances the firm's competitiveness and increases the demand for its products. The positive feedback eventually leads to a high (geographic) concentration of production.[986] The empirical findings of Bai et al. (2004) show that regional specialization in China is low for industries that yield high profit and tax, and for industries with large shares of state ownership – both arguments apply to the auto industry in China.[987]

The long-term goal of transforming domestic auto companies into global players is impaired by conflicts between the central government and local governments. While central bureaucrats pursue balanced growth of the national auto industry, local state agents promote fast economic industrialization irrespective of national inconsistencies.[988] Due to the high degree of financial autonomy and local leaders' peculiar incentive systems under the policy of fiscal federalism, local governments (especially those with small tax bases) safeguard and expand their licensing authority. Even after the central government's attempt to rein in local investment after the tax reforms in 1994, creative local officials use different sources of capital for favored projects: foreign investment, extra-budgetary funds, control over local banks, even local curb markets.[989] The incentives local governments grant foreign auto

---

984 NDRC (2004), "Automobile Industry Development Policy No. 8 decree of the State Development and Reform Commission", Internet Edition, reviewed 11.04. 2006.

985 Refer to Asia Times (2006), "China's extra-special zones", Internet Edition, reviewed 17.01.2007.

986 For further information refer to Marshall (1920) and Krugman (1991).

987 Refer to Bai et al. (2004), p. 399 ff.

988 Interview conducted with experts from a Chinese government institution in Beijing on 13.06.2006.

989 For further information on the consequences of fiscal federalism refer to Tsai (2004).

companies thus do not always correspond to national regulations. Accordingly, there is no industrial policy in the sense of the selective and coordinated allocation of resources. Central agencies have no policy instrument for the control of resource allocation by provincial governments. It has been very difficult for the central government to identify one or several specific locations or provinces to promote specific industries. In this respect, the Eleventh Five-Year Plan criticizes local governments for attracting foreign investment, contrary to industrial policy regulations.[990] Although NDRC approves the setting-up of new auto companies, local governments find ways to circumvent central approval procedures:

- Chery originated from the auto project of the local government of Wuhu City in Anhui province. As it did not get any central license approval to start a new auto company, the local government of Wuhu set up an auto parts company, Anhui Auto Part Industrial, in March 1997.[991] Wuhu's mayor, Zhan Xialai, became the company's president. Although they had no license to produce cars, they never stopped the car production plan initialized in 1995. In 1998, the factory for entire car production began construction and in December 1999, the first "Qi Rui (Chery)" sedan rolled of its assembly line. The local government offered incentives in the form of tax reliefs to the cab companies in Wuhu city to purchase the first batch of Chery cars as taxis.[992]
- In order to circumvent national directives, local companies buy licenses from other local players who are no longer active in the auto business, but have kept their license. Another option to get round from central establishment approval is, as the interviewed experts confirmed, to split the investment volume into different phases so that the promulgated investment volume is lower than the one which is necessary for NDRC approval.[993] Between 1981 and 1995, more than 80 percent of the FDI projects that came from the USA, Japan or Hong Kong were approved at the provincial level with investment capitalization of less than USD 30 million.[994] This contrasts with the national auto policy approach, which emphasized economies of scale. The threshold of

[990] Refer to People's Daily Online (2006), "China's new policy stresses quality of foreign investment", Internet Edition, reviewed 15.11.2006.

[991] Chery did not receive central government approval to manufacture cars before 2001.

[992] Refer to Luo (2005), "The Growth of Independent Chinese Automotive Companies", Internet Edition, reviewed 02.08.2007. Similarly, when FAW Group Corporation posted a net loss of RMB 570 million for the first quarter of 2005, the local government of Jilin province guaranteed FAW supply of energy and special treatment on land use and encouraged the purchase of FAW cars within the province by tax incentives. Refer to China Business Infocenter (2005), "FAW posts big loss, government tries to help", Internet Edition, reviewed 27.08.2007.

[993] Interviews conducted with managers of a German OEM in Beijing between 08.06.2006 and 16.06.2006.

[994] Refer to Wang (2001), p. 9. For further information on the threshold of USD 30 million refer to Shanghai Government (2005), "Examination and Approval Jurisdiction", 22.10.2005, Internet Edition, reviewed 10.12.2006.

USD 30 million has hence reinforced the miniaturization of FDI projects (not solely auto projects) and provincial officials' rent-seeking behavior.[995]

In order to reach high economic growth, local governments introduce protectionist measures to safeguard local auto companies from interregional competition and defend their tax base. Local governments *"patronize local companies and protect their pet projects".*[996] Intraregional trade barriers have caused the fragmentation of markets and diseconomies of scale. A local government could protect the local market for autos simply by directing enterprises under its control to purchase from a particular manufacturer, or by attaching higher registration and licensing fees to cars manufactured in other localities (as the Wuhu city government did to promote Chery). Central agencies could prevent local manufacturers from expanding beyond their home jurisdiction - it used the security bureau to deny licenses to cars that were not manufactured by an approved plant - if a firm was content to stay within the home locality, however, the local government could provide it with all necessary approvals.[997] Thus, local governments could raise the barriers of market entry for outside entrepreneurs, or impose a ban on the import of certain types of products to protect local business interests. In Hubei province, in late 1999, the Wuhan bureaucracy offered special tax relief to the purchasers of Citroën-Fukang cars which were produced within the province. Those who "imported" non-Fukang cars to the province had to pay a special fee of up to RMB 70,000.[998] Similarly, a bus company in a city of Anhui province had already received approval from the city government before it purchased new buses. As soon as the city government discovered that the new buses were not manufactured in Anhui province, it banned the buses from being used within its jurisdiction.[999]

Local trade barriers, indeed, affect the domestic market strongly: interprovincial trade fell from 37 percent of national retail trade in 1985 to about 25 percent in 2000.[1000] As the central agencies have not been powerful enough to enforce central-government policies that prohibit interregional trade barriers, some local governments have used their political freedom to maintain substantial trade barriers to protect local auto manufacturers from other provinces' competitive products.[1001] Particularly when the auto industry faced weak demand in the 1990s, some cities introduced local policies to restrict imports of compact cars from other provinces.[1002] Cross-provincial

995 Refer to Wang (2001), pp. 9-10.

996 Interview conducted with an expert of a European auto association in Beijing on 16.06.2006. Also refer to Bai et al. (2004), p. 398.

997 Refer to Thun (2004a), p. 462.

998 Refer to Harwit (2001), pp. 668-669.

999 Refer to Chou (2006), p. 10.

1000 Refer to Tenev et al. (2002), p. 21.

1001 Refer to Montinola et al. (1995), p. 14.

1002 Refer to People's Daily (2001), "Auto Industry Faces Challenges", Internet Edition, and China Business Review (1998), "Shifting Gears", Internet Edition, both reviewed 14.10.2006.

protectionism was appreciated by the MNCs and local governments alike, as both possessed controls over the share of auto JVs.[1003]

Although the central government favored big assemblers, and discriminated against small operations in an attempt to achieve economies of scale, the auto market continues to be fragmented. The rivalry among provinces for generating high rates of growth has encouraged bureaucrats of many provinces and cities to establish the industrial policy for the auto industry according to their jurisdiction's conditions. Local states' ambitions to participate in the sector's growth spurred the establishment of auto assembly plants in almost every province.[1004] The protected local markets resulted in the survival of spatially dispersed small and inefficient indigenous assemblers.[1005] The state had insufficient capacity to regulate these defections from a unified common market.[1006] Local governments' independent FDI screening process (below the threshold of USD 30 million), and the increased inter-jurisdictional competition for FDI, have contributed to the fragmented auto market. In addition, as confirmed by the experts interviewed, local governments have often financially pepped up small-scale, unprofitable companies in their jurisdiction, because the bankruptcy of local companies would endanger social stability, local economic growth and the bureaucrats' political career.[1007]

Due to local protectionism and national local content regulations, joint-venture auto producers had to use locally-made parts in their vehicles and began to cultivate their own auto parts suppliers. Despite having the same foreign partner, SVW and FAW-VW established their own independent network of suppliers, promoting domestic suppliers within their locality. Foreign investors in JVs would also bring their own auto parts suppliers to China and establish JVs producing auto parts. As a result, China's auto parts industry became fragmented, like the industry of auto manufacturers. Most manufacturers were small or medium-sized, and economies of scale were almost impossible to achieve.[1008]

1003 Refer to Wang (2002), p. 9.

1004 Refer to Zhu (2004), pp. 427-428.

1005 Chapter 4.3.2.1.1 elaborated that protection resulted in high prices and thus profitability of small-scale auto manufacturers.

1006 Refer to Thun (2004a), pp. 461-462.

1007 Interviews conducted with an expert of a European auto association in Beijing on 16.06.2006 with experts from a German public corporation in Beijing on 08.06.2006. According to an interviewed Chinese expert, even the central government (NDRC) has been reluctant to issue proofs of insolvency, because stakeholders and employees would ask NDRC for aid, social payments, reimbursement and compensation. NDRC is seen to be responsible as it gave project approval. Interview conducted with an expert of a Chinese auto government institution in Beijing on 06.06.2006.

1008 Refer to People's Daily (2004), "Problems linger in auto parts sector", Internet Edition, 07.07.2004, reviewed 06.10.2006.

Overall, the development of the Chinese auto industry in the reform era has largely been influenced by local authorities and enterprises.[1009] Decentralization may lead to positive economic outcomes when local governments are forced by the central government to adhere to hard budget constraints. However, if central state agents do not have the ability to impose such budget constraints, local governments have little incentive to constrain spending (they continue to support and/or subsidize inefficient and unproductive enterprises), and economic results are likely to be worse.[1010] In China during the early to mid-1990s, this latter situation was more the norm. Decentralization was, in many respects, a result of central government weakness, and this made it difficult to impose discipline on local governments. Although the interests of local governments did overlap with national objectives to a certain extent, they were not identical. *"Chinese-style federalism"* and local governments' opposition and malfeasance undermined the central state's capacity to implement market reform. Fiscal arrangements create incentives for local governments to promote auto companies within their jurisdiction. As a result, they put local interests above national ones. Japanese firms were protected from international competition during their high-growth stage, but at least in some industries, glaring inefficiencies were kept in check by fierce competition within the domestic marketplace. Local governments in China attempt to benefit from the artificially high profits that result from a domestic auto market protected from international competition. This has in turn spurred distorted incentives and suboptimal outcomes in the auto industry.[1011] Local protectionism has impeded regional specialization and the progress of mass auto assembly. Domestic competition has been hampered by a weak central authority, which could not enforce market integration regulations effectively.[1012] The key problem of the central government's ability to direct auto sector development was hence its inability to properly constrain local governments.

4.3.3.3 Different development approaches for the auto sector - Beijing and Shanghai

There have been differences between local development approaches, as the structures of the auto sector in Beijing and Shanghai show. While Shanghai, together with Jiangsu, has successfully established the development of the auto industry with a broad supplier network, Beijing has been struggling. The development of the auto industry in Beijing and Shanghai has to be seen in the light of the state-directed development of the auto industry. Not only the national policy approach to guide the growth of the auto industry, however, but also local governments' ambitions to accelerate auto production within their jurisdiction, influenced the sector's development.

1009 Refer to Lo (1997), p. 179.

1010 For further information on decentralization and the challenge of hard budget constraints refer to Rodden (2001).

1011 Refer to Thun (2004b), p. 242, Thun (2006), p. 258 ff and Wang (2002), p. 17.

1012 Refer to Bai et al. (2004), p. 398 and Huang (2002a), p. 540 and p. 551.

After 1978, central bureaucrats decided on auto production in different municipalities/provinces, and determined that JVs would be established. The earliest JV to assemble motor vehicles was Beijing Jeep Corporation (BAIC together with AMC) in 1983. In fact, it was the very first Chinese manufacturing JV signed with any foreign company after China reopened to the West in the late 1970s.[1013] BAIC is 100 percent owned by the municipal government of Beijing. The central government envisioned Beijing Jeep Corporation manufacturing light commercial vehicles and *"Beijing developing a cluster for this segment"*.[1014] There was a strong motivation for the JV in the late 1970s. While the Americans wished to establish a base in Asia that would enable them to manufacture cars at low cost, and compete in the growing region, the Chinese hoped for technology. After the JV started in 1984, the two sides disagreed over the product to be produced. The Americans wanted the new product to be similar to AMC's existing line of Jeeps, but Chinese bureaucrats wanted a newly-developed military Jeep for the army. Neither the government nor AMC, however, had the money to develop a new vehicle. The conflicting goals of the two partners restricted the development of the auto industry in Beijing. In addition, after the JV deal was signed, the Americans learned that the "real" negotiations had just begun. Chinese business people were much more accustomed to doing business based on personal relationships and the charisma of business leaders and tended to view concluded contracts as a base for negotiation. The Americans, on the other hand, viewed contracts as binding, and put much less emphasis on the aspects of personality in business.[1015] After long-winded discussions between the two partners and few sales, Beijing Jeep Corporation went bankrupt, and had to shut down its plant in early 1986.

Only after intervention by Premier Zhao Ziyang, did the central government provide large loans to cover the fact that the high-profile Beijing Jeep project was unable to expand or develop new models.[1016] Beijing Jeep was also given preferential import tariffs, and special permission to convert AMC's share of dividends (RMB 6.9 million) into US dollars at the official government exchange rate.[1017] Moreover, the Public Security Bureau purchased the JV's Jeeps to renew its fleet.[1018]

In 1987, AMC was acquired by Chrysler. Although Chrysler showed willingness to invest more in China, it did not obtain official permission to produce passenger cars in addition to utility vehicles. Besides, its main products failed to develop a mass market appeal, and sales peaked at only 26,000 vehicles in 1996. Gallagher (2006)

1013 Refer to Gallagher (2006), p. 47.

1014 Interviews conducted with managers of a German OEM in Beijing between 08.06.2006 and 16.06.2006.

1015 For further information on Beijing Jeep and Western business activities in China refer to Mann (1989).

1016 The State Bureau of Supplies delivered RMB 16.8 million. Refer to Harwit (1995), p. 75 and Noble (2006), "Overcapacity, Contract Design and the Emergence of Independent Auto Firms in China", Internet Edition, reviewed 01.08.2007.

1017 Refer to Young and Tan (2001), p. 5 and Harwit (1995), p. 74.

1018 Refer to Harwit (1995), p. 76.

contends that the JV was *"strangled by its conservative state ownership"*, but *"kept alive by Beijing's reluctance to let it fail"*.[1019] During the years after the merger of Chrysler with Daimler-Benz in 1998, DaimlerChrysler was beset with merger challenges and did not focus much attention on Beijing Jeep Corporation, which played a small role in its corporate structure. Indeed, in 1998, Beijing Jeep's total revenues were approximately equivalent to USD 399 million, of which DaimlerChrysler's share was about USD 169 million. This represented 0.1 percent of DaimlerChrysler's total sales (USD 131.8 billion) in that year.[1020]

In 1984, the central government planned the establishment of China's second auto JV, SVW, in Shanghai. With the VW – SAIC venture, the state intended to build an *"auto cluster for passenger cars in Shanghai"*.[1021] SAIC's primary purpose in establishing a JV was to increase its capabilities by catching up with the advanced world's level. *"The interests of SAIC and the Shanghai municipal government were identical"*, because SAIC was 100 percent owned by the municipal government.[1022]

SVW, like BAIC, started its operations, manufacturing CKD kits. Soon after SVW's foundation, it became market leader in China with a rise in sales volume from 7,000 vehicles in 1985 to over 200,000 cars since 2000. Due to an increase of passenger car demand during the late 1980s and early 1990s, and national import tariff barriers, the JV was able to dominate the Chinese auto market until the mid-1990s. In the early 1990s, SVW captured 70 percent of the Chinese market for passenger cars.[1023] The Shanghai municipal government had spurred growth of SVW by buying much of the company's output of its Santana model for taxis and municipal vehicles.[1024] Due to sustained tariff levels, prices remained high, and the JV was able to realize anticipated profit margins. In 1996, the Shanghai municipal government banned from municipal streets cars that had an engine capacity of below 1.6 liters in order to exclude cars from rival auto manufacturers in Tianjin.[1025]

The growth of SVW, and the financial support of the municipal government suppliers (in the mid-1990s, about RMB 5 billion extrabudgetary funds were in the localization fund) cultivated a strong supply base in Shanghai. As SAIC owns the vast majority of supply firms in Shanghai, it has had strong bargaining power with foreign suppliers that aimed to follow VW. *"VW's foreign suppliers had to venture with SAIC's*

[1019] Gallagher (2006), p. 49.

[1020] Refer to Young and Tan (2001), p. 4 ff.

[1021] Interviews conducted with managers of a German OEM in Beijing between 08.06.2006 and 16.06.2006.

[1022] Interviews conducted with managers of a German OEM in Beijing on 14.06.2006.

[1023] Refer to Ministry of Commerce/International Property Protection (2006), "Chinese auto joint ventures go their own way", Internet Edition, reviewed 29.08.2007.

[1024] Still in 2004, the Santana 2000 cars dominated the cab fleet with market share of around 54 percent. Refer to Shanghai Government (2005): "City seeks better, more spacious cabs", Internet Edition, reviewed 28.07.2007.

[1025] Refer to Thun (2004a), p. 461 ff and Thun (2006), p. 259.

suppliers, otherwise SAIC would have delegated the order to a competitor".[1026] *"SAIC even negotiated the percentage of products that have to be exported by the supplier JVs."* [1027] SAIC, furthermore, controls the finances and personnel of supply firms within its group. Besides, once one firm of SAIC's conglomerate introduces a new technology, the group ensures that the technology will also be introduced in the other companies of the SAIC conglomerate.[1028]

As a result of the municipal bureaucrats' approach to developing its auto and supply industry, Shanghai is the only municipality that has been able to rely heavily on the local supplier sector. Within the domestic market, which continues to be the primary focus of most Chinese auto firms, the overall strength of the Shanghai supply sector has proven to be durable, as competition has increased. Not only was the value of Shanghai's auto parts output three times greater than any other locality in 2003, but it has also helped to transform the neighboring provinces of Zhejiang and Jiangsu into major bases of component production. Compared with Shanghai, Beijing had about ten times less output of auto parts in 2003 (refer to Figure 27). The superiority of Shanghai (and its neighboring provinces) over Beijing with regard to auto parts production, is also indicated by the number of suppliers located in the two municipalities. In 2004, 64 auto suppliers were located in Shanghai and only 23 in Beijing. In consequence, 90 percent of the components for the SVW Santana, and well over 60 percent of the components for the Shanghai-GM Buick, are manufactured within the municipal borders of Shanghai. No other municipality has reached even 25 percent. In 2002, Beijing Jeep sourced 50 percent of its components (by value) from Shanghai.[1029]

Figure 27: Output of auto parts by region, 2003.

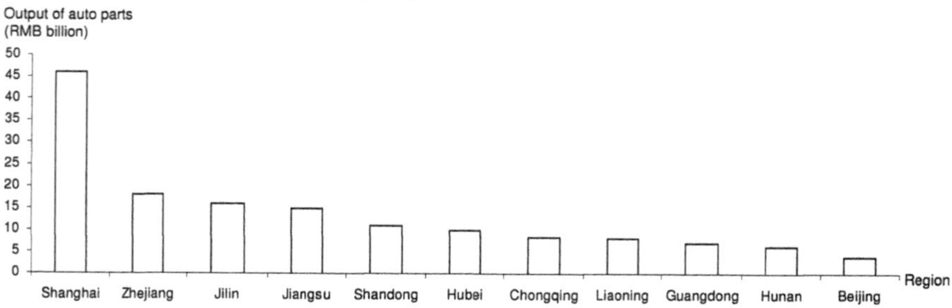

Source: FOURIN (2005a), p. 11.

[1026] Interviews conducted with managers of a German supplier company in Shanghai on 19.06.2006.

[1027] Interview conducted with a German manager of a supplier company in Shanghai on 13.07.2006.

[1028] Refer to Segal and Thun (2001), p. 570 ff and Thun (2004a), p. 470 ff.

[1029] Refer to Thun (2006), pp. 71-72.

The statistical analysis of the World Bank survey "Competitiveness, Technology and Firm Linkages in Manufacturing Sectors" (2001) also provides indication that the municipal government in Shanghai has more actively assisted its local auto manufacturers to develop. The government's assistance in identifying potential foreign suppliers is 4.5 percent (n=2) in the auto industry in Beijing and 7.5 percent (n=3) in Shanghai. The difference between the auto sector in Beijing and the one in Shanghai is significant (Likelihood Ratio Test: p=0.016, 2-sided) (refer to Table 23, Table 24).

Table 23: Descriptive Statistics: Government agency's or official's assistance in identifying potential foreign suppliers in the auto sector in Beijing and Shanghai, 2000.

			Government agency's or official's assistance in identifying potential foreign suppliers			
			Yes	No	N.A.	Total
Group_autosec_ Beijing_Shanghai	Auto sec Beijing	Count	2	41	1	44
		% within Group_ autosec_Beijing_ Shanghai	4,5%	93,2%	2,3%	100,0%
	Auto sec Shanghai	Count	3	29	8	40
		% within Group_ autosec_Beijing_ Shanghai	7,5%	72,5%	20,0%	100,0%
Total		Count	5	70	9	84
		% within Group_ autosec_Beijing_ Shanghai	6,0%	83,3%	10,7%	100,0%

Source: Data compiled from World Bank survey "Competitiveness, Technology and Firm Linkages in Manufacturing Sectors" (2001).

Table 24: Chi-Square Test: Government agency's or official's assistance in identifying potential foreign suppliers in the auto sector in Beijing and Shanghai, 2000.

	Value	df	Asymp. Sig. (2-sided)
Pearson Chi-Square	7,528[a]	2	,023
Likelihood Ratio	8,276	2	,016
Linear-by-Linear Association	2,748	1	,097
N of Valid Cases	84		

a. 4 cells (66,7%) have expected count less than 5. The minimum expected count is 2,38.

Source: Data compiled from World Bank survey "Competitiveness, Technology and Firm Linkages in Manufacturing Sectors" (2001).

Both municipalities are characterized by extensive foreign participation through FDIs; however, Shanghai has been more open towards foreign investment than Beijing. In 2005, Shanghai used USD 6.2 billion foreign investments, while Beijing only used

USD 3.5 billion. In addition, while in Shanghai 23.1 percent of foreign capital were JV enterprises in 2005, only 19.7 percent of foreign capital were JVs in Beijing. With more than 70 percent, WFOEs absorbed the largest share of foreign capital in both municipalities (refer to Table 25). Markedly different between the two municipalities, however, is the share of gross output value of the auto industry. In Shanghai, the largest share of gross output value of industry (63 percent, USD 146.2 billion in 2006)[1030] was generated by FFEs, which play a key role in industrial development. In Beijing, the largest share of gross output value of industry (56 percent, RMB 47.1 billion in 2005) came from domestic enterprises.[1031]

Table 25: Amount of foreign capital actually used grouped by investment manner in Beijing and Shanghai, 2005.

	Beijing	Shanghai
Total amount of foreign capital actually used (in USD million)	**3,525**	**6,174**
Joint Ventures (as a percentage of total foreign capital used)	19.7	23.1
Cooperative Ventures (as a percentage of total foreign capital used)	6.7	2.6
Wholly foreign owned enterprises (as a percentage of total foreign capital used)	73.6	74.3

Source: Beijing Statistical Yearbook (2006) and Shanghai Statistical Yearbook (2007).

The Shanghai municipal government especially used its position to attract foreign investors. Municipal bureaucrats even made the investing MNCs compete with each other in providing capital and technology. The key contest took place in 1997, when GM obtained the license to establish a second JV (after VW) with SAIC, which Ford and Toyota had also envisioned. GM had already proven its commitment to China's auto market by establishing parts plants in China, many of them oriented to exports. GM agreed to make a USD 1.6 billion investment in a high-tech facility to produce modern models (Buick Regal and Century), and to help SAIC build an R&D center. In return, the Shanghai municipal government helped GM to complete construction in less than two years (by issuing construction approvals fast, and providing land), and gave GM much greater freedom to choose suppliers and handle labor than VW had enjoyed. Stimulated by GM's entry, SVW also invested in the development of new models, and hoped for similar treatment from the municipal government.[1032]

The World Bank sample also shows that the municipal government of Shanghai has more actively assisted local auto companies in attracting foreign technology into their jurisdiction than the Beijing municipal government. 10.0 percent (n=4) of the managers in the auto sector in Shanghai stated that they received government assistance in locating foreign technology to license, while only 6.8 percent (n=3) of

[1030] The number includes enterprises from Hong Kong, Macao and Taiwan.
[1031] Refer to Beijing Statistical Yearbook (2006) and Shanghai Statistical Yearbook (2007).
[1032] Refer to Lee (2003), p. 285 and p. 291.

the managers of the auto sector in Beijing answered the same. The difference is significant (refer to Table 26, Table 27).[1033]

Table 26: Descriptive Statistics: Government agency's or official's assistance in locating foreign technology to license in the auto sector in Beijing and Shanghai, 2000.

			Government agency's or official's assistance in locating foreign technology to license			
			Yes	No	N.A.	Total
Group_auto_Beijing_Shanghai	Auto sec Beijing	Count	3	40	1	44
		% within Group_auto_Beijing_Shanghai	6,8%	90,9%	2,3%	100,0%
	Auto sec Shanghai	Count	4	27	9	40
		% within Group_auto_Beijing_Shanghai	10,0%	67,5%	22,5%	100,0%
Total		Count	7	67	10	84
		% within Group_auto_Beijing_Shanghai	8,3%	79,8%	11,9%	100,0%

Source: Data compiled from World Bank survey "Competitiveness, Technology and Firm Linkages in Manufacturing Sectors" (2001).

Table 27: Chi-Square Test: Government agency's or official's assistance in locating foreign technology to license in the auto sector in Beijing and Shanghai, 2000.

	Value	df	Asymp. Sig. (2-sided)
Pearson Chi-Square	8,895[a]	2	,012
Likelihood Ratio	9,853	2	,007
Linear-by-Linear Association	2,991	1	,084
N of Valid Cases	84		

a. 3 cells (50,0%) have expected count less than 5. The minimum expected count is 3,33.

Source: Data compiled from World Bank survey "Competitiveness, Technology and Firm Linkages in Manufacturing Sectors" (2001).

In order to improve local auto companies' innovation capabilities, the Shanghai municipal government encouraged the cooperation of domestic and foreign companies with local universities. In June 2000, VW donated RMB 5 million to jointly set up an auto research center with Tongji University.[1034] Four years later, VW und Tongji University signed a memorandum of their joint R&D efforts on fuel cell

[1033] Footnote a of the Chi-Square Test indicates that three cells have expected count less than five, therefore, the Likelihood Ratio Chi-Square Test is used (instead of the Pearson Chi-Square Test). The differences are significant (Likelihood Ratio Test: p=0.007, 2-sided).

[1034] Refer to People's Daily (2001), "Volkswagenwerk AG President Lectures in Shanghai", Internet Edition, reviewed 26.08.2007.

technology.[1035] Among the leaders of fuel cell-related research is the Pan Asia Technical Automotive Center in Shanghai, a JV with GM and SAIC.[1036]

The 2001 World Bank survey also indicates the close cooperation between auto companies and universities located in Shanghai. According to the World Bank data, 13.6 percent (n=6) of the managers of the auto industry in Beijing confirmed that the local university performed R&D for their plants in the year 2000. In the auto industry in Shanghai, in 2000, 37.5 percent (n=15) of the companies instructed the local university to perform R&D for them. The difference between the auto industry in Beijing and Shanghai is significant (Pearson Chi-Square Test: p=0.012, 2-sided) (refer to Table 28, Table 29).

Although the municipality of Beijing, similar to that of Shanghai, has promoted the development of the local auto industry, its development approach seems to be less targeted towards auto manufacturers and suppliers, as the statistics of the World Bank sample show. In addition, Beijing's disadvantage was the central leaders' decision to establish a production hub for light duty trucks in Beijing. The Beijing Jeep venture never found a mass market for its utility vehicles, and the company struggled to produce more than 15,000 – 20,000 vehicles in the 1990s. After 1995, light commercial vehicle production in Beijing decreased, while passenger car production in Shanghai increased. Light duty trucks did not correspond to customers' demands to the extent passenger cars did. Accordingly, from the mid-1990s until 2004, the production of motor vehicles in Shanghai grew faster than the production of motor vehicles in Beijing (refer to Figure 28).

Table 28: Descriptive Statistics: Contractual or long-standing relationship with the local university to perform R&D for the plant in the auto sector in Beijing and Shanghai, 2000.

			Local university		
			Yes	No	Total
Group_autosec_ Beijing_Shanghai	Auto sec Beijing	Count	6	38	44
		% within Group_ autosec_Beijing_ Shanghai	13,6%	86,4%	100,0%
	Auto sec Shanghai	Count	15	25	40
		% within Group_ autosec_Beijing_ Shanghai	37,5%	62,5%	100,0%
Total		Count	21	63	84
		% within Group_ autosec_Beijing_ Shanghai	25,0%	75,0%	100,0%

Source: Data compiled from World Bank survey "Competitiveness, Technology and Firm Linkages in Manufacturing Sectors" (2001).

1035 Refer to Volkswagen (2004), "Volkswagen and Tongji sign a Memorandum Joining Hands to Develop Fuel Cell Vehicles for the Future", Internet Edition, reviewed 26.08.2007.

1036 Refer to US Department of Energy (2006), "Major Government-Supported Fuel Cell Vehicle Projects", Internet Edition, reviewed 26.08.2007.

Table 29: Chi-Square Test: Contractual or long-standing relationship with the local university to perform R&D for the plant in the auto sector in Beijing and Shanghai, 2000.

	Value	df	Asymp. Sig. (2-sided)	Exact Sig. (2-sided)	Exact Sig. (1-sided)
Pearson Chi-Square	6,364[b]	1	,012		
Continuity Correction [a]	5,155	1	,023		
Likelihood Ratio	6,496	1	,011		
Fisher's Exact Test				,022	,011
Linear-by-Linear Association	6,288	1	,012		
N of Valid Cases	84				

a. Computed only for a 2x2 table

b. 0 cells (,0%) have expected count less than 5. The minimum expected count is 10,00.

Source: Data compiled from World Bank survey "Competitiveness, Technology and Firm Linkages in Manufacturing Sectors" (2001).

As a consequence of passenger car growth in China, the municipality in Beijing also *"aimed to develop a passenger car cluster in its jurisdiction and supported local passenger car manufacturers".*[1037] The municipal government in Beijing has granted BAIC, formerly Beijing Jeep Corporation, and its JV company Beijing Benz-DaimlerChrysler Automotive Ltd. (BBDCA), special support in spurring development and passenger car production. However, the NDRC did not approve the production of Mercedes-Benz C- and E-class passenger cars by the JV partners DaimlerChrysler and BAIC before May 2004.[1038] According to a foreign interviewee, among the local subsidies the JV receives, is the provision of property at preferential rental fees in the Beijing Development Area.[1039] BBDCA is, however, only slowly advancing, and its production volume is still low (BBDCA has a production capacity of 100,000 vehicles and sold 30,000 units in 2006).[1040] It seems as if the central government imposed requirements on the foreign partner DaimlerChrysler in order to improve BBDCA's business performance before the NDCR would approve further projects of DaimlerChrysler's in China. Indeed, the NDRC did not issue approval of DaimlerChrysler cooperation with the Beijing-based Chinese commercial vehicle manufacturer Beiqi Foton before DaimlerChrysler sold the 50 percent stake of its Yaxing Benz bus JV in Yangzhou.[1041]

1037 Interview conducted with an expert of a Chinese auto government institution in Beijing on 16.06.2006.

1038 Refer to DaimlerChrysler (2004), "Fertigung von Mercedes-Limousinen in China durch Staatsrat genehmigt", Internet Edition, reviewed 22.05.2006.

1039 Interview conducted with a manager of a German OEM in Beijing on 08.06.2006.

1040 Refer to China Daily (2007), "Beijing Benz May Break Even in 2007", Internet Edition, reviewed 13.09.2007.

1041 For further information refer to Financial Times Deutschland (2007), "Daimler krempelt China-Strategie um", 22.05.2007, p. 7.

While the municipal government in Shanghai has concentrated its support on SAIC in particular, Beijing has not only ambitions to develop BBDCA, but also aggressively promotes Beijing Hyundai Motor Corporation, a JV between Korea's Hyundai Motor Company and municipal Beijing Automotive Industry Holding. Beijing Hyundai was established in 2002.[1042] *"The municipal government provides the JV cheap land for its production base and promotes the JV's Sonata as Beijing's official taxi model."*[1043]

Due to the municipality's effort to promote passenger car production in its jurisdiction, motor vehicle production in Beijing has increased since its slump in 1998, and has caught-up with Shanghai. Passenger car sales growth in Beijing was in line with the increase in passenger car (rather than light commercial vehicle) demand after WTO accession in 2001 (CAGR 2001-2006 of passenger cars: 38.3 percent, CAGR 2001-2006 of light commercial vehicles: 13.7). In 2005, auto production in Beijing amounted to 586,000 vehicles – representing 10.3 percent of China's total auto production (5.7 million vehicles). Shanghai's output of motor vehicles was 484,500 units in 2005. However, it increased to 652,800 units in 2006 (refer to Figure 28).[1044]

Overall, due to the competition for foreign MNCs, municipal governments invest in the construction of industrial parks, and offer bureaucratic services and fast approvals as well as a well-established infrastructure. With the settlement of foreign MNCs within their jurisdiction, and the setting-up of Sino-foreign JVs, local governments aim to promote local auto companies. Since the establishment of its first auto JV in the 1980s, the Shanghai government has more actively assisted the development of domestic auto companies than has the Beijing municipal government. Shanghai has been successful in establishing an auto cluster in its jurisdiction. Its JV SVW is manufacturing on a large scale. With pressure and support from the Shanghai municipal government, SVW fostered the development of a group of local suppliers that grew into the heartland of the Chinese auto industry.[1045] The Shanghai municipal government actively followed an integrated development path towards establishing an auto industrial base in its location, and building a tight network between OEMs and suppliers. As a result, the Shanghai, and Jiangsu area has developed into an auto cluster, integrating OEMs and suppliers. Almost half of the parts manufacturers in China are located in Shanghai and in nearby provinces such as Jiangsu and Zhejiang. Hardly any auto suppliers are located in the Beijing area yet. The municipal government in Shanghai has been able to use its power and resources to advance the auto sector within its jurisdiction. Beijing did not succeed in

[1042] Interview conducted with a manager of a German OEM in Beijing on 08.06.2006 and with an expert of a Chinese auto government institution in Beijing on 16.06.2006.

[1043] Interviews conducted with experts from a Chinese government institution in Beijing on 13.06.2006, with managers of a German OEM in Beijing on 14.06.2006 and with an expert of a Chinese auto government institution in Beijing on 16.06.2006.

[1044] Refer to Shanghai Statistical Yearbook (2006), Internet Edition, reviewed 05.01.2007 and Global Insight (2007), Asian Automotive Industry Forecast Report, April 2007, p. 4.

[1045] Refer to Noble (2006), "Overcapacity, Contract Design and the Emergence of Independent Auto Firms in China", Internet Edition, reviewed 01.08.2007.

its objective of promoting the auto sector as a core industry. The gross output value of the auto industry was RMB 68.8 billion in Beijing (in 2005) compared with RMB 146.2 billion in Shanghai (in 2006).[1046] The findings are in accordance with those of Segal and Thun (2001), which contend that Shanghai rather than Beijing was essentially a local developmental state.[1047] Most of all, however, Shanghai benefited from the national plan of establishing an auto cluster for passenger cars in Shanghai, and one for light duty trucks in Beijing, as passenger cars rather than light duty trucks experienced high growth rates during the reform period. Beijing has only "recently" focused on passenger car production within its municipality. However, neither the municipal bureaucrats in Beijing nor those in Shanghai have been able to create internationally competitive domestic passenger car producers. In this segment, both municipalities are dominated by Sino-foreign JVs (SVW in Shanghai, BBDCA and Beijing Hyundai in Beijing).

Figure 28: Production of motor vehicles in Beijing and Shanghai and national new light vehicle registrations, 1995-2006.

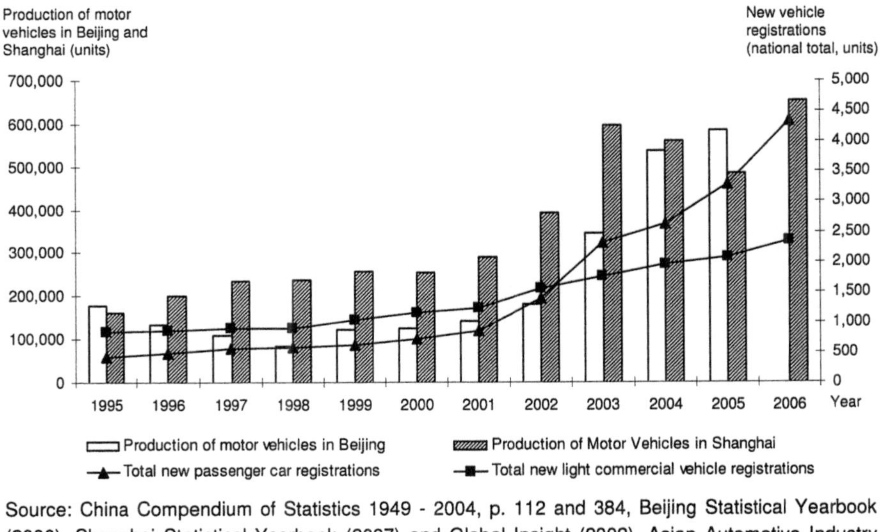

Source: China Compendium of Statistics 1949 - 2004, p. 112 and 384, Beijing Statistical Yearbook (2006), Shanghai Statistical Yearbook (2007) and Global Insight (2002), Asian Automotive Industry Forecast Report, March 2002, p.140 and Global Insight (2007), Asian Automotive Industry Forecast Report, April 2007, p. 4. Note: Data on production volume of motor vehicles in Beijing are not published for 2006 yet.

[1046] Refer to China Automotive Industry Yearbook (2006) and Shanghai Statistical Yearbook (2006).

[1047] Refer to Segal and Thun (2001), p. 562.

4.4 Financial system as an instrument to regulate the auto sector's growth

The Chinese state wields power over the financial system by specifying credit quotas for each sector. The experts interviewed confirmed that credit is allocated to key sectors in the government's focus for development.[1048] The larger the company's share of capital from bank loans, the more influence the state can exert on its business activities by regulating the credit volume. Among the companies in the World Bank sample "Competitiveness, Technology and Firm Linkages in Manufacturing Sectors" (2001), 27.1 percent (n=215) of the auto companies' capital share was from bank loans. This was significantly higher than in the residual sectors where bank loans only amounted to 17.5 percent (n=1271) of the companies' capital (Levene's Test: p=0.000, T-Test: p=0.000 equal variances not assumed) (refer to Table 30, Table 31).[1049] The same trend applies to the electronics sector that received significantly fewer bank loans than the auto sector (Levene's Test: p=0.003, T-Test: p=0.032 equal variances not assumed) (refer to Appendix V, Table A61, Table A62).

Table 30: Descriptive Statistics: Approximate shares of capital from different sources in the auto sector and the residual sectors (in percent), 2000.

	Group_autosec_ressec	N	Mean	Std. Deviation	Std. Error Mean
Retained earnings/internal funds	Auto sec	215	43,0372	37,48718	2,55660
	Residual sec	1271	52,8961	40,06173	1,12372
Bank loans	Auto sec	215	27,0884	31,95816	2,17953
	Residual sec	1271	17,5445	26,96722	,75642
Loan from a parent or partner company	Auto sec	215	5,2651	18,73149	1,27748
	Residual sec	1271	8,9119	25,46271	,71422

Source: Data compiled from World Bank survey "Competitiveness, Technology and Firm Linkages in Manufacturing Sectors" (2001).

1048 Interviews conducted with experts from a German public corporation in Beijing on 08.06.2006 and with managers of a German OEM in Beijing between 08.06.2006 and 16.06.2006.

1049 In all sectors, retained earnings and/or internal funds were the biggest share of companies' capital, this share was significantly higher in the residual sectors (52.9 percent, n=1271) than in the auto sector (43.0 percent, n=215) (Levene's Test: p=0.013, T-Test: p=0.000 equal variances not assumed). Loans from a parent or partner company were significantly higher in the residual sector (8.9 percent, n=1271, Levene's Test: p=0.000, T-Test: p=0.013 equal variances not assumed) than in the auto sector (5.3 percent, n=1271) (refer to Table 30, Table 31).

Table 31: Independent Samples T-Test: Approximate shares of capital from different sources in the auto sector and the residual sectors (in percent), 2000.

		Levene's Test for Equality of Variances		t-test for Equality of Means						
									95% Confidence Interval of the Difference	
		F	Sig.	t	df	Sig. (2-tailed)	Mean Difference	Std. Error Difference	Lower	Upper
Retained earnings/internal funds	Equal variances assumed	6,144	,013	-3,368	1484	,001	-9,85894	2,92763	-15,60167	-4,11620
	Equal variances not assumed			-3,530	302,769	,000	-9,85894	2,79266	-15,35442	-4,36345
Bank loans	Equal variances assumed	18,528	,000	4,665	1484	,000	9,54392	2,04579	5,53097	13,55687
	Equal variances not assumed			4,137	268,002	,000	9,54392	2,30706	5,00166	14,08618
Loan from a parent or partner company	Equal variances assumed	15,056	,000	-2,010	1484	,045	-3,64676	1,81450	-7,20602	-,08751
	Equal variances not assumed			-2,492	362,720	,013	-3,64676	1,46358	-6,52493	-,76860

Source: Data compiled from World Bank survey "Competitiveness, Technology and Firm Linkages in Manufacturing Sectors" (2001).

Since the late 1990s, banks have accepted indirect finance for car purchase and auto investments, because auto markets were developing quickly. Indirect finance means that businesses and individuals make use of normal bank lending to purchase vehicles, and use business assets or property as collateral. During the boom years of 2002 and 2003, the credit volume increased and much credit was risky, because the fluctuation and instability of personal incomes in some sectors and regions was severe. Due to the absence of a reliable credit screening system and personal credit history, banks often allocated credit to small-scale unprofitable local companies or customers that were not credit-worthy.[1050]

According to a national directive, credits have been reduced, to avoid financial institutions' dead debts, and to circumvent overcapacity and traffic collapse in the big cities since the beginning of 2004. Cars purchased on credit accounted for only 10 percent of total car purchases in China in 2006, representing a steep fall from 2003, when auto-financing arrangements accounted for 30 percent of total sales.[1051] Indeed, the government's credit tightening measures had a negative effect on car buying behavior, especially at the top end of the market. This resulted in decelerating car sales growth rates in 2004. While the growth in passenger car sales was 57 percent in 2002 and 77 percent in 2003, it was "only" 17 percent in 2004. Quarterly data in particular show the government's influence on the deceleration of passenger car sales growth in 2004. The growth in passenger car sales is usually the largest in the fourth quarter of each year (90 percent in the fourth quarter of 2002, and 101 percent in the fourth quarter of 2003). Passenger car sales growth was, however, -4

[1050] Refer to Global Insight (2007), Asian Automotive Industry Forecast Report, April 2007, p. 23.

[1051] In more developed markets, approximately 70 percent of car sales are financed through loans, suggesting that there is potential for a big increase in car sales if the government allows a further increase in lending to consumers. Refer to Global Insight (2007), Asian Automotive Industry Forecast Report, April 2007, p. 23.

percent in the fourth quarter of 2004 (refer to Figure 29).[1052] The state's credit policy has successfully spurred auto growth when the financial system set credit below market prices; it triggered a deceleration of growth when economic slowdown was targeted. The state uses the financial system as an industrial policy instrument to regulate the auto market, by either extending or restricting credit for auto companies and purchasers. In addition to specifying credit quotas, bureaucrats exert strong influence on the development of the auto market by restricting and controlling companies' vehicle financing activities.

Figure 29: Chinese quarterly passenger car sales, 2002-2005.

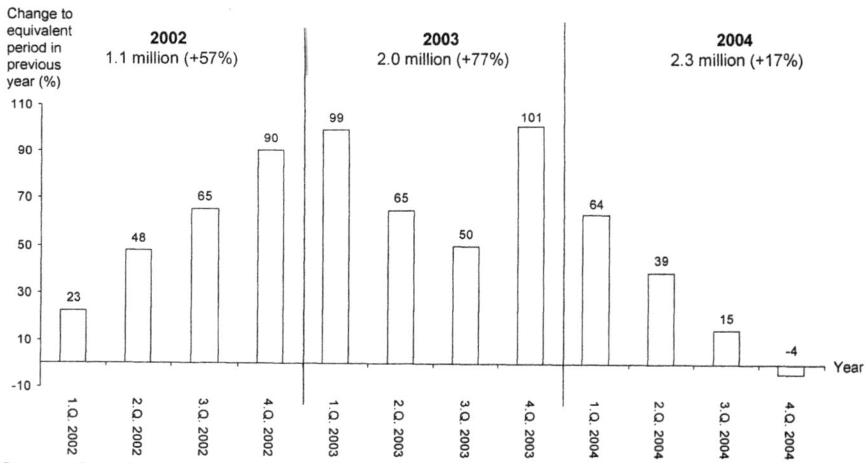

Source: Own illustration based on data from the German Association of Automobile Manufacturers (VDA) (2005).

According to a WTO regulation, China is "forced" to open the non-bank auto financing sector.[1053] The central government aims to gradually expand market mechanisms for the financial sector. Since 2004, the state has allowed foreign auto manufacturers to establish finance companies and provide car-financing deals. In August 2004, GM was the first foreign auto company to obtain government approval for establishing a JV car-financing company.[1054] Other foreign car companies,

---

1052 Quarterly growth rates refer to changes to the same quarter of the previous year.

1053 Refer to WTO (2001), "Accession Protocol", (D) Judical Review, Article 7-3, Internet Edition, reviewed 09.10.2006.

1054 Refer to People's Bank of China (2004), "Administrative Rules for Automotive Loans", Internet Edition, reviewed 27.08.2007 and People's Daily (2004), "GM obtains approval for auto finance", Internet Edition, reviewed 21.07.2007.

including VW, Ford, Toyota and DaimlerChrysler have followed suit since. Altogether, seven auto finance companies operate in China.[1055]

Membership of the WTO resulted in lower tariffs on imports, and consequently lower prices on many locally-made models. Finally, economic gains in China have produced a large and growing middle class that can afford a new car. While consumer finance has had a limited role in auto sales in recent years,[1056] the approval of captive auto finance operations in the country has opened the market to an even greater number of buyers. The surge in auto sales has positively contributed to national economic growth during the last decade; in the meantime, however, overcapacity and the fear of an overheating economy, as well as environmental and social costs (pollution, roadway-accident deaths) are forcing central and local leaders to shift their economic growth targets, and address the costs of expansion. In response to the growing Chinese urban middle class eager to purchase private vehicles, the Shanghai municipal government now "sells" license plates at auctions every month for about RMB 40,000 each (which is more than the RMB 39,800 price tag for Chery Automobile's 1.1 liter-engine QQ subcompact car) in order to regulate the growth rate of auto sales within the municipality.[1057]

Overall, the Chinese government uses the financial system as an industrial policy instrument and steers the growth of the auto sector by regulating the volume of auto loans. It fears the domination of foreign captive financing (and thus a loss in state power) as well as unbalanced growth in the sector. Hence, state agents have only gradually reduced the restrictions on foreign auto financing companies since WTO accession.

4.5 Government-business cooperation and information sharing in the auto sector

Information between government and business representatives of the auto sector is shared in a formalized way. First, NDRC holds hearings or seminars to inform auto companies on special topics, or to ask foreign OEMs for their assessment of the development of the Chinese auto market. NDRC also sends *"red head letter"* papers to companies.[1058] These letters provide formal notice on major national guidelines.

1055 Refer to China Banking Regulatory Commission (2007), "Annual Report 2006", Internet Edition, reviewed 09.11.2007.

1056 Between January and October 2006, 223,688 passenger cars were registered in Beijing, however, only 3.8 percent of these were financed by loans. Refer to China Auto (2007), p. 9.

1057 Refer to Shanghai Government (2006), "Shanghai: car license plate prices set record", Internet Edition, reviewed 14.07.2007 and Reuters (2007), "Shanghai license plate pricier than small car", Internet Edition, reviewed 06.09.2007.

1058 Interview conducted with an expert of a Chinese auto government institution in Beijing on 16.06.2006.

Moreover, NDRC organizes forums and expert panels, where information on relevant auto topics is announced, and drafts of laws and regulations are discussed with experts.[1059]

The state does not announce all information relevant to auto companies to the same extent, however.[1060] Thus, being a member of a business association is important for gaining market information. The World Bank survey "Competitiveness, Technology and Firm Linkages in Manufacturing Sectors" (2001) shows that membership in business associations differs significantly (Pearson Chi-Square Test: p=0.016, 2-sided) between companies in the auto sector and companies in the residual sectors. While 62.0 percent (n=134) of the auto managers interviewed confirmed that their company is a member of a business association, in the residual sectors only 53.2 percent (n=683) of the respondents confirmed this (refer to Table 32, Table 33).

Table 32: Descriptive Statistics: Firm's membership in a business association in the auto sector and in the residual sectors, 2000.

			Member of a business association		
			Yes	No	Total
Group_autosec_ressec	Auto sec	Count	134	82	216
		% within Group_autosec_ressec	62,0%	38,0%	100,0%
	Residual sec	Count	683	601	1284
		% within Group_autosec_ressec	53,2%	46,8%	100,0%
Total		Count	817	683	1500
		% within Group_autosec_ressec	54,5%	45,5%	100,0%

Source: Data compiled from World Bank survey "Competitiveness, Technology and Firm Linkages in Manufacturing Sectors" (2001).

1059 Interviews conducted with managers of a German OEM in Beijing on 08.06.2006.

1060 Ibidem.

Table 33: Chi-Square Test: Firm's membership in a business association in the auto sector and in the residual sectors, 2000.

	Value	df	Asymp. Sig. (2-sided)	Exact Sig. (2-sided)	Exact Sig. (1-sided)
Pearson Chi-Square	5,831[b]	1	,016		
Continuity Correction [a]	5,480	1	,019		
Likelihood Ratio	5,896	1	,015		
Fisher's Exact Test				,018	,009
Linear-by-Linear Association	5,827	1	,016		
N of Valid Cases	1500				

a. Computed only for a 2x2 table

b. 0 cells (,0%) have expected count less than 5. The minimum expected count is 98,35.

Source: Data compiled from World Bank survey "Competitiveness, Technology and Firm Linkages in Manufacturing Sectors" (2001).

Indeed, the World Bank sample shows that the most important reason to be a member of a business association is to gain market information. 90.3 percent (n=121) of the members whose business is in the auto sector confirm this. Significantly fewer members active in the residual sectors (79.4 percent, n=542) gave the same answer (Pearson Chi-Square Test: p=0.003, 2-sided) (refer to Table 34, Table 35). The World Bank sample furthermore shows that being a member of a business association is one way to gain information on the development of the auto market, and future laws and regulations.

Table 34: Descriptive Statistics: Helping members to get market information is one function the most important business associations perform on a regular basis for companies in the auto sector and in the residual sectors, 2000.

			Helps members get market information		
			Yes	No	Total
Group_autosec_ressec	Auto sec	Count	121	13	134
		% within Group_autosec_ressec	90,3%	9,7%	100,0%
	Residual sec	Count	542	141	683
		% within Group_autosec_ressec	79,4%	20,6%	100,0%
Total		Count	663	154	817
		% within Group_autosec_ressec	81,2%	18,8%	100,0%

Source: Data compiled from World Bank survey "Competitiveness, Technology and Firm Linkages in Manufacturing Sectors" (2001).

Table 35: Chi-Square Test: Helping members to get market information is one function the most important business associations perform on a regular basis for companies in the auto sector and in the residual sectors, 2000.

	Value	df	Asymp. Sig. (2-sided)	Exact Sig. (2-sided)	Exact Sig. (1-sided)
Pearson Chi-Square	8,769[b]	1	,003		
Continuity Correction [a]	8,068	1	,005		
Likelihood Ratio	9,985	1	,002		
Fisher's Exact Test				,002	,001
Linear-by-Linear Association	8,759	1	,003		
N of Valid Cases	817				

a. Computed only for a 2x2 table

b. 0 cells (,0%) have expected count less than 5. The minimum expected count is 25,26.

Source: Data compiled from World Bank survey "Competitiveness, Technology and Firm Linkages in Manufacturing Sectors" (2001).

Foreign auto companies can give feedback to the relevant central level agencies not only via business associations, but also via auto working groups, as one interviewee indicated. The Auto Working Group under the European Chamber of Commerce in China (of which the Chief Representative of ACEA in China is the Vice Chairman) compiles yearly position papers on the development of the Chinese auto business environment. The paper is in Chinese and English and is officially given to the Chinese government and the European Commission. Its content is a review of market development and prospects, and contains suggestions on regulatory reform. Its impact on China's policy decisions is, however, questionable.[1061]

An interviewee of a European auto association in Beijing stated that auto companies usually obtain timely information from central agencies on upcoming technical standards/norms. However, some laws *"fall from the sky"*, and are an *"unpleasant surprise"* for foreign investors. While the time-horizon for emission standard requirements is provided until 2010, the "Measures for the Administration of Import of Automobile Components and Parts Featuring Complete Vehicles" were implemented as a reaction to the official phase-out of local content regulations, with only short notice for foreign investors. The regulation was discussed only with Chinese companies in advance, to the disadvantage of foreign investors.[1062] Therefore, managers of auto companies rely on informal lobbying activities to acquire information on the state's latest regulations, or try to informally discuss specific regulations and their interpretation with government officials. There are no institutionalized regular meetings between government representatives and foreign business associations; they rather meet irregularly and ad hoc.[1063]

1061 Interview conducted with an expert of a European auto association in Beijing on 16.06.2006.

1062 Ibidem.

1063 Ibidem.

An interviewee from a Chinese government institution explained that, as the auto sector is still dominated by SOEs, central-level auto companies such as FAW and Dongfeng report their production data to SASAC; and local companies such as BAIC and SAIC give reports to their municipal governments.[1064] The central government also negotiates all subject terms of contracts FAW and Dongfeng sign. Some general managers of the large auto companies even sit on the CCP Central Committee.[1065] At the local level, the municipal governments of Beijing and Shanghai are involved in the businesses of BAIC and SAIC, respectively. A foreign interviewee explained that the chairman of the Supervisory Board of BAIC, which is owned by the municipal government, Lu Hao, is also the vice mayor of Beijing. Furthermore, Chairman An Qingheng who is the CEO of BAIC and of BBDCA, is at the same time a civil servant.[1066] Even private companies such as Chery are backed by high-ranking officials. The Congressional-Executive Commission on China reports that Chery Automobile received millions of US dollars in subsidies from the Ministry of Science and Technology in 2004.[1067] Accordingly, there is no purely private sector in the Chinese auto industry. In addition, high-ranking managers of Chinese state-owned auto companies are often at the same time local-level bureaucrats. As a result of this close interaction between the state and domestic auto companies, information flows directly from the (state-owned) auto companies to the responsible bureaucrats. In China, an institutionalized form of information exchange between the state and the business sector - as set up in the East Asian developmental states – is less important than informal information flow.

The central government does not envision insulation of the elite bureaucracy from business activities. Politics, bureaucracy and private businesses build a symbiosis. Most domestic auto companies have the support of central or local bureaucrats (in 2005, 33 percent of the assets of the total auto sector were state-owned) and are thus powerful in negotiations with foreign companies.[1068] This may have advantages or disadvantages for foreign investors, depending on the respective interests of the partners. The interviewees in the supplier sector agreed that, once the local bureaucracy no longer required operation in JVs, they chose to establish WFOEs.[1069] The interviewees of the OEMs asserted that their domestic partner was dominant

[1064] Interview conducted with experts from a Chinese government institution in Beijing on 13.06.2006.

[1065] Refer to Liu and Dicken (2006), p. 1235.

[1066] However, An Qingheng had no government post at the time the interview was conducted. Interview conducted with a manager of a German OEM in Beijing on 08.06.2006.

[1067] Refer to Congressional-Executive Commission on China (2005), "Annual Report, V. Development of Rule of Law and the Institutions of Democratic Governance", Internet Edition, reviewed 27.08.2007.

[1068] Refer to Ministry of Commerce (2005), "The Status Quo of Foreign Investment in the Automotive Industry", Internet Edition, reviewed 23.03.2006.

[1069] Only auto suppliers are allowed to build WFOE, OEMs have to establish joint-venture companies with a Chinese partner. Interviews conducted with supplier companies in Shanghai on 19.06.2006 and 20.06.2006.

because of advocates in the municipal government and the resulting selective state assistance. In this respect, one challenge to their investment in China is the cooperation with state-owned companies and the responsible state officials when doing business with a Chinese state-owned company.

For foreign auto companies, the most effective way to lobby for their interests is still to stay in close contact with the Ministry of Commerce and the NDRC. Both agencies grant especially big MNCs personal meetings and early information on upcoming regulations and laws, as large-scale auto OEMs are decisive for domestic growth. For smaller companies, it is very difficult to get an appointment. Central agencies' subsidiaries on the local level have not enough power although they are part of the central level agency. Therefore, all companies have representative offices or holdings in Beijing. A Chinese interviewee of a German auto company revealed that *"only direct contact to the central level government agencies enables companies to lobby for details of enacted laws".*[1070] The World Bank survey "Competitiveness, Technology and Firm Linkages in Manufacturing Sectors" (2001) also confirms that managers in the auto sector do not expect business associations to (formally) represent their members' concerns to the government. 39.8 percent (n=53) of the auto managers who are members of business associations specified that they are members of a business association because it represents its members' views and concerns to the government. In the residual sectors, 47.4 percent (n=324) of the members of business associations confirmed this and in the electronics sector, 48.7 percent (n=109) of the members of business associations confirmed this (refer to Table 36 and Appendix V, Table A63). There is no significant difference between any of the three groups.

Table 36: Descriptive Statistics: Representation of members' views to the government as one function the most important business association performs on a regular basis for companies in the auto sector and the residual sectors, 2000.

			Representation of members' view and concerns to the government		
			Yes	No	Total
Group_autosec_ressec	Auto sec	Count	53	80	133
		% within Group_autosec_ressec	39,8%	60,2%	100,0%
	Residual sec	Count	324	359	683
		% within Group_autosec_ressec	47,4%	52,6%	100,0%
Total		Count	377	439	816
		% within Group_autosec_ressec	46,2%	53,8%	100,0%

Source: Data compiled from World Bank survey "Competitiveness, Technology and Firm Linkages in Manufacturing Sectors" (2001).

[1070] Interview conducted with a Chinese manager of a German OEM in Beijing on 14.06.2006. The same was stated by experts from a German public corporation in Beijing on 08.06.2006.

The data confirm that, although formalized consultations and briefings on auto issues take place between state organs and private businesses, information exchange between foreign auto companies, and between foreign auto companies and state officials, take place rather informally. Personal contacts between company employees and bureaucrats in charge are most effective with regard to information exchange and company lobbying. In foreign auto enterprises, the position of company representative thus needs to be filled by Chinese managers who have a broad network with central-level agencies. This network often dates back to university (Qinghua University, Beijing University). Lobbying then functions via direct calls and meetings, instead of business associations or official seminars etc. *"Official seminars are rather used to network and keep contact to important persons"*, as one Chinese employee in a foreign auto company confirmed. *"Seminar breaks are more important than speeches and presentations."* [1071] In general, good government relations are a central determinant of doing business, and entrepreneurs make significant financial investments in maintaining political connections. Auto companies' performance is subsequently not solely dependent on their ability to respond to market signals, but also on the quality of relations with state representatives.

Overall, bureaucrats' far-reaching involvement in the business activities of (state-run) domestic auto firms has enabled them to gain detailed information on the sector's development and companies' needs. The institutionalization of information exchange, as in the East Asian developmental states, has been less important, however, than informal and ad-hoc consultations between foreign investors and state representatives. China's institutional design has, in consequence, facilitated favoritism (and thus opportunities for corruption) in auto enterprises with widespread *guanxi* networks, and informational asymmetry between domestic and foreign companies, putting foreign OEMs and suppliers at a disadvantage.

4.6 Two decades of state-promotion in the auto sector

The industrial policies for the auto sector indicate that there is a long tradition of government intervention in the Chinese auto industry. State guidance has had mixed results. In fact, when the objectives of the industrial policies for the auto sector – employment growth, concentration of production in key manufacturers, high local content and high production volumes of passenger cars – are compared with the current state of the industry, it can be seen that the central government has achieved its objectives in some respects. The ultimate goal of the policies for the auto industry has been to establish internationally competitive Chinese "proprietor" brands with the help of foreign JV partners. Proprietor brands include brand name, R&D facility, supplier base and production facility owned by Chinese OEMs. Policy success can

[1071] Interviews conducted with managers of two German OEMs in Beijing on 08.06.2006 and 14.06.2006.

be measured by the structure of the auto market, as well as technology know-how, market share and the export activities of domestic auto companies.

4.6.1 Achievements

During the 20 years of state-guidance in the auto sector, China has successfully climbed up the global ranking of the largest passenger car markets.[1072] While China ranked seven in 2001 (sales: 0.8 million units), it was the third largest market for passenger cars in 2006 (sales: 4.3 million units) – ranking before Germany where 3.5 million passenger cars were sold in the same year.[1073] At the same time, China has not relied on imports to meet its growing demand for passenger cars. Passenger car production rose from 0.4 million units in 1996 to 4.3 million units in 2006.[1074] In 2006, passenger car production accounted for 64 percent of total vehicle production in China (compared with 26 percent in 1996) and for 9.3 percent of passenger car production worldwide.[1075] Domestic auto production has created jobs for Chinese workers in the auto and supplier industry. Already in 2001, 1.5 million people were employed in the auto industry in China. The number increased to almost 1.7 million people by 2005.[1076]

In line with increased auto production volumes (and thus economies of scale) and cheaper imports, pre-tax profit in the auto industry has risen since the 1990s, and particularly after WTO accession (pre-tax profit in 1990: USD 0.9 billion, in 2003: USD 12.5 billion). Between 2000 and 2003, the CAGR of total pre-tax profit was 37.5 percent (refer to Figure 30).

In order not to lose control over the industry to foreign investors, bureaucrats have regulated inward investment in various ways: screening, foreign equity limits and local content requirements to narrow the technology gap etc.[1077] Due to the maximum-equity regulation, foreign auto manufacturers have been unable to dominate the Chinese auto market.[1078] While granting foreign firms access to the growing domestic auto market, the state has been able to aggregate support in key firms (in the form of JV partnerships) and concentrate domestic car production. Since

[1072] The CAGR of passenger car sales was 40 percent between 2001 and 2006. Calculation based on data from Global Insight (2007), World Car Sales Forecast Report, April 2007, p. 30.

[1073] Data from Global Insight (2004), Automotive World Car Sales Forecast Report, April 2004, p. 25 and Global Insight (2007), World Car Sales Forecast Report, April 2007, p. 30.

[1074] The gross output value of auto production as a share of total production rose from 2.1 percent in 1990 to 4.1 percent in 2005. Refer to China Automotive Industry Yearbook (2006).

[1075] Refer to Global Insight (2007), World Car Sales Forecast Report, April 2007, p. 30.

[1076] Refer to China Automotive Industry Yearbook (2006).

[1077] Refer to Wang (2001), p. 3.

[1078] Refer to Sit and Liu (2000), p. 671.

2004, thirteen auto manufacturers (nine of them foreign-invested JVs) have produced over 90 percent of the total output of passenger cars in China.[1079]

Moreover, the JV and the localization requirements on foreign investors have forced the FDIs of auto-producing MNCs to establish passenger car production locations in China (mostly in coastal provinces, refer to Figure 31). Due to an almost stagnating triad (Japan, USA, and Europe),[1080] foreign investors were eager to set up assembly plants in the Chinese auto market, and participate in the rapid sales growth of the domestic auto market. China's auto industry is thus becoming integrated into the global production networks of transnational corporations.[1081] In addition, MNCs have had to localize manufacturing in China in order to circumvent high tariffs on imports, and fulfil local content requirements. This investment has benefited auto parts suppliers because demand for local auto parts and components has increased. These "backward linkages" from Sino-foreign JVs, and the Chinese auto industry in general, are contributing to economic growth in China.[1082]

Figure 30: Total pre-tax profit in the auto industry (foreign and domestic invested, complete vehicles and components), 1990-2003.

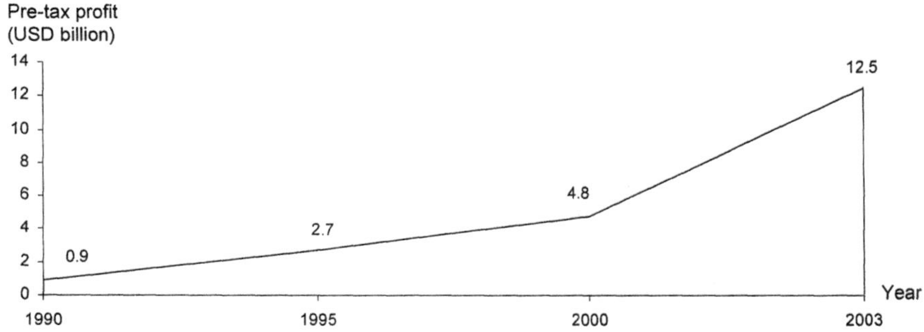

Source: Automotive Industry of China - China Auto Supplementary Issue (2004), pp. 34-35.
Note: Data in RMB were converted into USD using FERI exchange rates for each year.

1079 Refer to VDA (2005), "International Auto Statistics", p. 65.

1080 Global Insight expects that the CAGR of passenger cars sales in the period 2007 until 2017 will be 6.4 percent in China, compared with 0.2 percent in Japan, 0.4 percent in Western Europe and 1.3 percent in the United States. Refer to Global Insight (2007), World Car Sales Forecast Report, April 2007, p. 33.

1081 Refer to Liu and Dicken (2006), p. 1230.

1082 Refer to Gallagher (2006), p. 23.

Figure 31: Production locations of foreign OEMs in China.

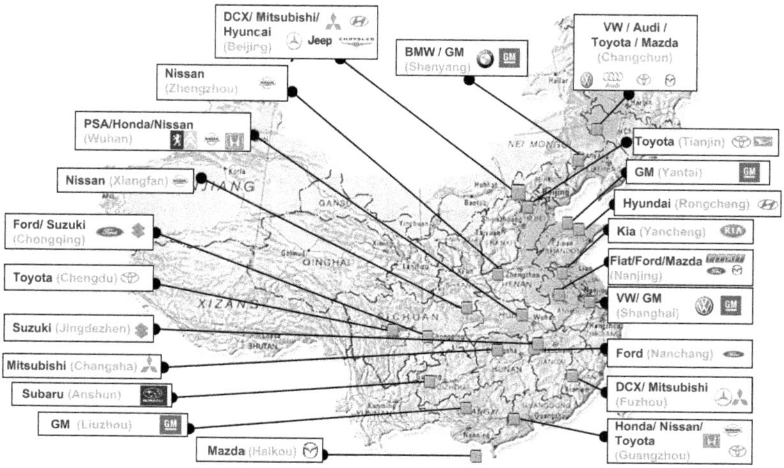

Source: Own illustration.

Today, as envisioned by the state, most manufacturers in China assemble domestically made vehicles rather than CKD kits, and have set up the whole value chain of vehicle assembly in China. Accumulated production figures in December 2006 show that only 4.6 percent of total vehicle production in China was CKD production (338,125 units). While the production of domestically made vehicles increased by 27 percent (sales of domestic made vehicles: +25.1 percent) in the period January-December 2006 compared with the same period in the previous year, CKD production decreased by 20.1 percent (CKD sales: -20.4 percent) (refer to Table 37). In this regard, the policy approach of combining FDI attraction (and guidance) and import substitution (high tariffs, local content requirements) has successfully forced foreign manufacturers to produce and source in China, and thus support the development of domestic OEMs and suppliers.

Table 37: Auto production and sales, 2006.

	Production		Sales	
	Accumulated (January - December 2006)	Change (%)*	Accumulated (January - December 2006)	Change (%)*
Total	**7,279,726**	**27.3**	**7,215,972**	**25.1**
Domestic made	6,941,601	31.1	6,877,991	28.8
CKD	338,125	-20.1	337,981	-20.4

Source: FOURIN (2007), p. 21. *Note: Change refers to equivalent period of the previous year.

The central government has gradually increased the threshold for foreign auto investments in China. State regulations have forced MNCs to introduce and produce their most recent car models in China (125 new models came on the market between 2000 and 2006).[1083] The latest regulations on foreign investment in the auto sector even force foreign auto manufacturers to develop new brands in China. In this regard, Guangzhou Honda and SVW announced in July 2007 that they would set up R&D facilities and develop self-branded vehicles in China.[1084] Furthermore, competition among foreign auto manufacturers and the reduction of import tariffs have lowered car prices. The average price for an entry-level compact car in China, which ranges from USD 8,000 to USD 16,000, fell by 28 percent between 2000 and 2005.[1085] In general, intense price competition and promotional activity by virtually all auto manufacturers, as well as production localization, are drivers of auto technology modernization and overall growth of auto sales in China.

Increasing competition and overcapacity have contributed to overseas expansion by Chinese OEMs since China further opened its market. While in 2001, the total export volume of passenger cars from China was 3,579 units, it was 123,245 units in 2006.[1086] In 2005, the total export volume of vehicles and parts even exceeded the corresponding imports for the first time.[1087] This achievement was not only a milestone for the domestic auto industry, but also confirmed China's ambition to become a leader in the global auto market. However, China's export volume represented only 2.4 percent of its output volume in 2006.[1088] While OEMs in Japan and Korea focused on exports, due to their small domestic markets, OEMs producing in China have concentrated on sales in the domestic market, with its large population and the high number of cities with strong purchasing power (especially in the coastal areas).[1089]

The FDI-led growth strategy for the auto sector has contributed to the economic success of the auto industry in China in a number of ways. The regulatory framework in combination with the race for market share in the growing auto market, has attracted investment from almost all top global OEMs, who are committed to

1083 Refer to Businessweek (2007), "The Quality Drag on China's Car Industry", Internet Edition, reviewed 18.07.2007.

1084 Refer to Hong Kong Trade Development Council (2007), "Honda to create brand for China auto market", Internet Edition, and China Economic Net (2007), "SVW to develop new model for Chinese and US markets", Internet Edition, both reviewed 11.08.2007.

1085 Refer to Businessweek (2006), "China's Booming Car Market Defies Pundits", Internet Edition, reviewed 18.07.2007.

1086 Refer to Global Insight (2007), Asian Automotive Industry Forecast Report, April 2007, p. 57.

1087 Refer to China Auto (2007), p. 4.

1088 Refer to Global Insight (2007), Asian Automotive Industry Forecast Report, April 2007, p. 4.

1089 As demand in major cities slows or begins to saturate, the large number of second-tier and third-tier cities will drive growth. Refer to Global Insight (2007), World Car Sales Forecast Report, April 2007, p. 14.

introducing their latest models onto the market. Through the JV regulation, Chinese auto firms could acquire manufacturing expertise from their foreign partners; and tariff protection and subsidized credit have helped domestic producers to increase economies of scale. Moreover, fierce competition among OEMs subsequently contributed to a sudden modernization of auto technology. Domestic auto companies have achieved greater product development capability and China has shifted from importing all manufacturing technology to developing some technology. New vehicle products have been developed jointly with foreign partners.[1090]

4.6.2 Shortcomings

While rapid industrialization was achieved with the help of foreign investments, the auto sector remains fragmented, as small-scale manufacturers are protected by local governments. Furthermore, China's original plan of developing its auto industry through trading market access for technology, has had limited results. State regulations could not provide domestic firms with technology know-how and independent design skills. In consequence, international competitiveness is still limited.

4.6.2.1 Fragmentation of the auto market

The policy framework for the sector aimed to develop the infant Chinese auto industry by protecting domestic auto producers through import barriers.[1091] In order for infant industry protection to work, it is important for governments to have reliable information about how large the protective tariffs should be, and over what period of time the tariff should be imposed. If governments set tariffs for too short a period, then firms may not learn enough to compete with the rest of the world once the tariffs are removed. If tariffs are imposed for too long a period to protect infant industries, then firms might not have incentives to improve efficiency. Protection may then dampen the competitive edge of domestic firms, either in terms of costs or pricing. It may also encourage new entry into the industry by domestic firms that aim to benefit from deterred competition and rents arising from high prices for locally produced vehicles.[1092] In consequence, the number of entrants expecting high returns on investments increases. Either of these developments could mean that the hoped-for improvements in competitiveness through learning and economies of scale do not materialize. Strong policy capacity and powerful institutions are necessary to implement countermeasures. While in a free market economy, effective competition encourages mergers and acquisitions, within the protected market, governments

[1090] Refer to Chinese Academy of Engineering and National Research Council (2003), pp. 12-13.

[1091] Refer to Zhang and Taylor (2001), p. 270 and Thun (2006), p. 291.

[1092] Berglas and Razin introduced the element of profits into the Stolper and Samuelson (1941) analysis of protection. They contend that in the short run, protection is likely to increase profits. For further information on protection and real profits refer to Berglas and Razin (1974).

have to encourage or directly organize mergers in an effort to concentrate rent in a few firms.[1093] As experience from other emerging economies such as Korea and Thailand shows, policies to protect the domestic market must be combined with strict control of new entrants in order to promote the rapid growth of key firms in the industry.[1094]

While the industrial policies for the auto sector have supported concentration of production in a few companies, consolidation of the sector has not proceeded, but more companies have entered the lucrative auto market. During the 1980s, local states assisted (state-run) firms to enter the auto business. They aimed to participate in the high profits of the auto market, resulting from high tariff barriers. While 56 OEMs existed in 1980, 114 OEMs had entered the auto business by 1985.[1095] Although the state reiterates in its industrial policies for the auto sector the importance of a consolidated auto market, the number of auto manufacturers has been relatively stable throughout the last two decades (the number of OEMs only decreased from its high point of 124 OEMs in 1992/3 to 117 OEMs in 2005) (refer to Figure 32). Out of the 117 OEMs in 2005, 104 OEMs produced fewer than 100,000 vehicles. 60 OEMs produced between 100 and 10,000 units and 22 OEMs even produced less than 100 vehicles (refer to Figure 33) which is far below the efficient level of production.

Figure 32: Number of OEMs in the auto industry, 1980-2005.

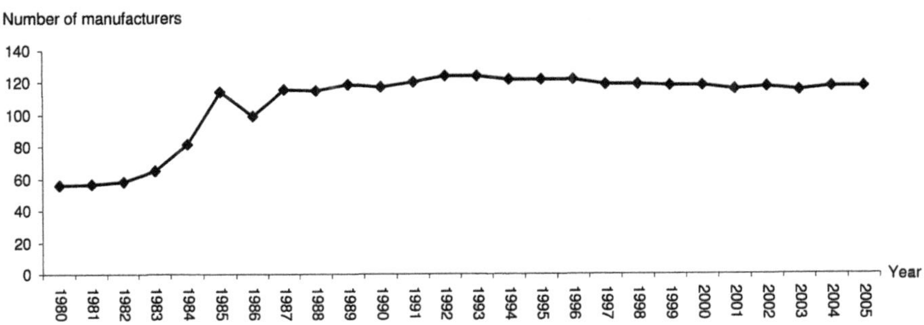

Source: China Automotive Industry Yearbook (2006).

1093 Refer to Huang (2002a), pp. 538-540.

1094 For further information refer to Auty (1996), Waitt (1993) and Chaudhuri (1989).

1095 In 1985, Japan only had 49 vehicle manufacturers. Refer to VDA (1990), "International Auto Statistics", p. 132.

Figure 33: Number of OEMs in the auto industry producing x units of vehicles, 2005.

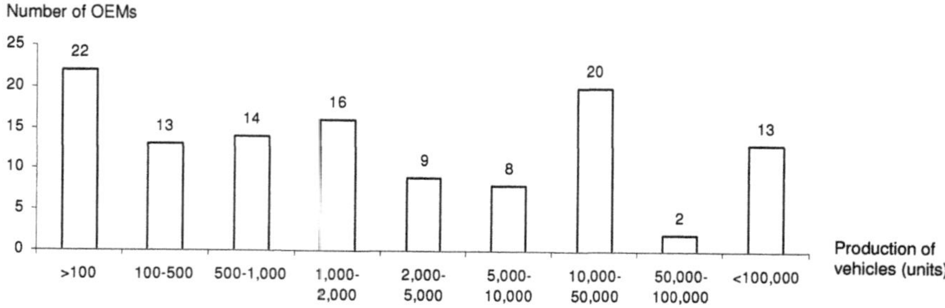

Source: China Automotive Industry Yearbook (2006).

China's protective import tariffs have fueled redundant investment in the auto sector. Moreover, central level agencies have been too weak to enforce competition within the protected domestic market and control of new entrants, due to its decentralized and fragmented administrative planning power.[1096] Provincial and local governments have tried to protect their indigenous auto sector, often bargaining successfully for special permission that circumvents national regulations.[1097] For the same reason, the central government has never ceased to reduce excess capacity, and never succeeded in eliminating it.[1098] Local protectionism also prevented mergers and acquisitions of domestic firms and resulted in the survival of spatially dispersed small indigenous assemblers. The numbers suggest that local governments protected even uncompetitive auto firms from insolvency and covered their operating losses with ongoing access to funds for unprofitable companies. Thus, employment and social stability could be ensured within the locality.

Even after China's WTO accession and the lowering of tariffs, nontariff barriers and local protectionism of small scale auto companies have hindered the auto sector's consolidation process. In an attempt to cut the number of domestic producers, the government raised the minimum investment for a manufacturing plant to RMB 2 billion in 2004. The threshold for auto investments was to be a disincentive for smaller private firms to enter the market. The introduction of new regulations to consolidate the market indicates that the state refuses to reduce intervention and

1096 Producers of vehicle parts are as fragmented as vehicle manufacturers. Many world-class auto parts suppliers followed the MNCs to China: Delphi Auto Systems, Bosch, Valeo, Siemens, Dana, Allied Signal, Lucas Varity, United Technologies, ITT, TRW, Rockwell, Tenneco, Cooper etc. Suppliers invested in upstream and (or) downstream industries in order to supply complementary services. Refer to People's Daily (2004), "Problems linger in auto parts sector", Internet Edition, reviewed 06.10.2006.

1097 Refer to Sit and Liu (2000), p. 663.

1098 Refer to Noble (2006), "Overcapacity, Contract Design and the Emergence of Independent Auto Firms in China", Internet Edition, reviewed 01.08.2007.

strengthen market mechanisms, because domestic auto companies are still in an infant stage of development. If market principles expanded, non-competitive domestic companies would be replaced by an increase in imports and the local presence of foreign companies. Moreover, being linked to a broad range of industries such as parts, machine tools, steel and chemistry, the auto industry has a large impact on the national economy. The auto industry not only influences the production, but also the technology levels of the entire country. As long as local governments are able to eliminate competition within their jurisdiction, and the central government does not ease protection of the whole sector (non-tariff barriers, local content and equity regulations), consolidation of the market will proceed slowly.

A fragmented industrial structure is costly. Auto plants are highly capital-intensive and the high fixed costs mean that, for any given output level, a production structure with a few producers is more capital-saving than one with numerous, independent producers.[1099] This is reflected by the amount of profit made by OEMs and suppliers in the auto industry.[1100] Out of 2,637 enterprises in the auto industry (OEMs and suppliers), the profit of 985 enterprises was less than RMB 0.1 million in 2005. Only 80 enterprises were able to make more than RMB 100 million profit in the same year (refer to Figure 34).

Figure 34: Number of OEMs and suppliers in the auto industry making x amount of profit, 2005.

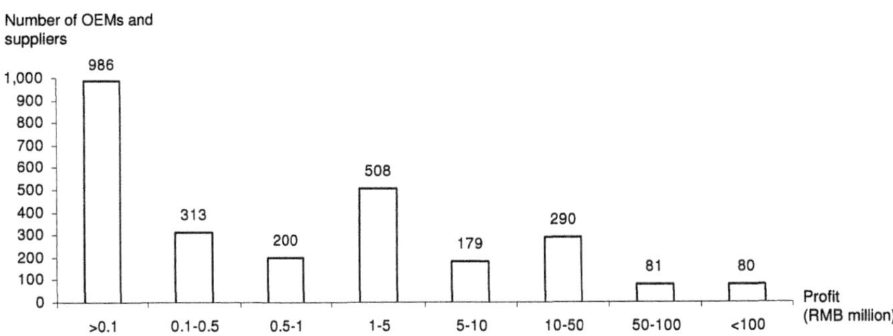

Source: China Automotive Industry Yearbook (2006).

Compared with the Japanese auto market, too, the performance of the Chinese auto industry (as indicated by total revenue and total revenue per employee ratio) has been low. Between 2001 and 2004, the total revenue of the auto industry increased

[1099] Refer to Huang (2002a), p. 545.

[1100] As data for OEMs only is not available, the aggregate of OEMs' and suppliers' profit is taken into account.

from USD 51.4 billion to USD 110.0 billion. The total revenue of the auto industry in Japan, however, was four times that of China in 2004 (USD 442.1 billion). Although in China the total revenue of the auto industry per employee also increased in the period 2001-2004 (2001: USD 34,100, 2004: USD 64,900), the total revenue of the auto industry per employee was "only" USD 64,900 in China in 2004 – compared with Japan where it was nine times higher (USD 586,100) in the same year (refer to Table 38).

Table 38: Total revenue and total revenue per employee in the Chinese and Japanese auto industry, 2001-2004.

Manufacture of motor vehicles and motor vehicle parts	Unit	2001	2002	2003	2004
China					
Total revenue	USD billion	51.4	71.8	98.4	110.0
Total revenue per employee	USD 1,000	34.1	45.7	61.3	64.9
Japan					
Total revenue	USD billion	332.7	344.8	388.7	442.1
Total revenue per employee	USD 1,000	462.3	475.0	521.3	586.1

Source: VDA International Auto Statistics, various issues. Note: Data on China in RMB and on Japan in Yen were converted into USD using FERI exchange rates for each year.

The sector is not competitive at an international level, as the comparison between China and Japan indicates. The Chinese auto sector is catching up quickly, however: between 2001 and 2004, the CAGR of total revenue per employee was 23.9 percent in China, and 8.2 percent in Japan.[1101]

Overall, protectionism in China's auto industry has been inspired by Japan's and Korea's development pattern. The East Asian developmental states pursued import substitution policies, using high tariff rates to protect local auto manufacturers. In Korea, institutional centralization was used effectively to force firms to compete abroad, thus mitigating the anti-competitive character of certain aspects of import substitution policies.[1102] In this regard, institutional centralization may facilitate entry restriction and promote economies of scale in the presence of high rents. Unlike the institutional centralization in the East Asian developmental states, in China, resources are allocated by divided bureaucratic institutions. Policies and regulations

1101 Calculation based on data from the VDA International Auto Statistics, various issues.

1102 Export contests, in which bureaucracy allocates rents based on the export orders firms received, ensure that rent is assigned on the basis of objective and monitorable criteria, and of criteria that cannot be easily manipulated by policy-makers. However, there is an institutional context to administration of the export contests: export contests are more easily set up under a system in which the monitoring functions, and where the rent controls and disbursement are all lodged in one agency, as in the case of the Korean government in the 1970s and 1980s. Refer to Huang (2002a), p. 551.

for the auto industry are dispersed among several government agencies at the central and local level, making policy implementation harder to enforce.[1103] Fragmentation, miniaturization and low revenue per employee are a consequence of protectionism combined with weak central level institutions, and of short-termism – the focus on short-term profits instead of, and often at the expense of, long-term development.

4.6.2.2 Limited market share and technology know-how

In China's Eleventh Five-Year Plan, which was published in November 2006, the government notes that monopolies of foreign businesses have emerged in certain industries because of inflowing foreign investments and that *"independent innovation"* of Chinese companies has to be strengthened.[1104] This is true for the domestic auto industry, which is dominated by foreign companies. Between 2000 and 2006, Chinese OEMs have only been able to increase their domestic market share by 3 percentage points, and reached 22 percent market share in 2006. Foreign JVs still account for the majority of the auto market (refer to Figure 35).

Figure 35: Market share of Chinese OEMs and foreign JVs, 2000 and 2006.

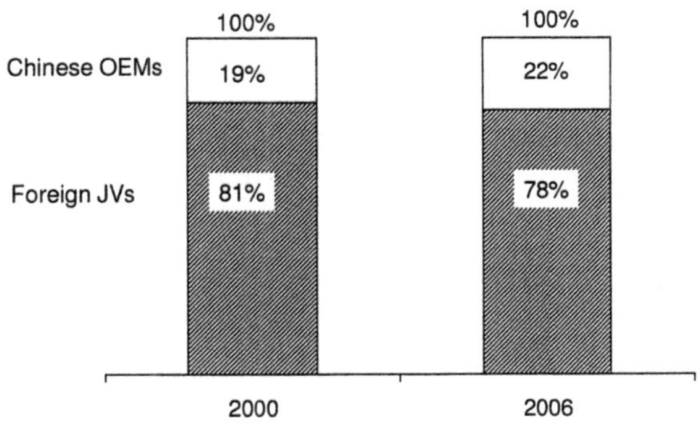

Source: Calculations based on data from Global Insight, Asian Automotive Industry Forecast Reports, December 2002 and April 2007.

1103 The Chinese Ministry of Machinery Industry oversees the manufacturing aspects of the auto industry, but has no authority over the trade sector. Domestic trade of final auto products is regulated by the Ministry of Internal Trade. Foreign trade in auto products is similarly outside the power of the Ministry of Machinery Industry, and is subject to regulatory power and administrative restrictions imposed by the Ministry of Foreign Trade and Economic Relations. Refer to Huang (2002a), p. 551.

1104 Refer to NDRC (2006), "Outline of the Eleventh Five-Year Plan for National Economic & Social Development of the People's Republic of China", Chapter 7 and 9, Internet Edition, reviewed 14.11.2006.

The passenger car market in particular is dominated by Sino-foreign JV companies. Of the eleven manufacturers that sold more than 200,000 passenger cars in 2006, eight were JVs (Shanghai-GM, SVW, FAW-VW, Beijing Hyundai, Guangzhou Honda, FAW-Toyota, Dongfeng-Nissan, Dongfeng Peugeot Citroën; total market share 53.4 percent) and three were independent manufacturers (FAW, Chery, Geely Automotive; total market share: 18.4 percent) (refer to Table 39).[1105]
The biggest state-owned automakers (SAIC, FAW and Dongfeng) all have foreign auto partners. SAIC together with its JV partners GM and VW, and FAW-VW sold more than 1.1 million passenger cars in 2006, and had 26 percent of total passenger car market share in the same year.[1106] SAIC, although successful with its JV partners, has not yet been able to introduce self-branded models. The manufacturer has invested USD 1.7 billion in its attempt to have own-brand cars as it hopes to penetrate developed markets. In 2007, SAIC started mass production of its first own luxury model, Roewe 750.[1107] SAIC has set a target to sell more than 200,000 passenger cars a year under its own brand by 2010.[1108] The model is based on the design of the Rover 75 sedan, which the company purchased from UK's now-defunct MG Rover Group Ltd.[1109] FAW is also producing on a large scale together with its JV partner VW.[1110] Independent manufacturer FAW sold more than 300,000 vehicles in total in 2006 (market share: 7.7 percent). Of the 343,000 cars produced, only 4,562 vehicles, however, were of its own car brand Red Flag, but 47,265 Mazda 6 and 164,792 Daihatsu Charade sedan cars.[1111]

Particularly noticeable is the dynamic development of independent local Chinese auto manufacturers. The biggest independent producers are Chery and Geely.[1112] Chery has little government ownership, and Geely is privately-owned. Chery and Geely have market shares of 6 percent and 5 percent respectively, and sales volumes of more than 200,000 passenger cars in 2006 (refer to Table 39). Neither has ever ventured with any foreign partner.[1113] They sell own-brand cars and have

---

[1105] Independent manufacturers are the ones that operate without a foreign partner.

[1106] Shanghai-GM sold about 450,000 passenger cars and SVW and FAW-VW sold almost 350,000 passenger cars each.

[1107] Global Insight expects that SAIC will produce about 11,000 cars of its own Roewe brand in 2007. Refer to Global Insight (2007), Asian Automotive Industry Forecast Report, April 2007, p. 145.

[1108] Refer to Global Insight (2007), Asian Automotive Industry Forecast Report, April 2007, p. 140 and J.D. Power (2007), Global Truck and Car Forecast, Second Quarter 2007, p. 297.

[1109] Other Roewe vehicles will follow: the next one being the W2, based on the smaller Rover 25.

[1110] FAW-VW sold 345,300 passenger cars in 2006 (market share: 7.9 percent). Refer to Table 39.

[1111] Refer to Global Insight (2007), Asian Automotive Industry Forecast Report, September 2007, p. 149.

[1112] China Brillance and Harbin Hafei only had sales volumes of 73,100 and 65,400 passenger cars in 2006, respectively.

[1113] Chery, based in Anhui province, transformed itself from an auto parts company into a car manufacturer. Geely, based in the south-eastern province of Zhejiang, was originally a motorcycle company. The expansion of the auto market provided various motorcycle companies with new business opportunities. Its experience of producing motorcycles was an advantage in making this transition.

major expansion plans.[1114] They produce small, cheap cars and have about 50 percent of this segment's market share. Independence does not necessarily mean isolation, however. Private companies are similarly integrated into *guanxi* networks, which incorporate companies, organizations and institutions. Moreover, they often enjoy the same support from local political authorities as state-run firms, because they are prime drivers of many local economies.[1115]

Table 39: Passenger car sales by manufacturer, 2006.[1116]

	Sales of passenger cars (1,000 units)	Market Share (%)
Shanghai-GM	446.9	10.3
SVW	349.1	8.0
FAW-VW	345.3	7.9
FAW	**333.8**	**7.7**
Beijing Hyundai	290.0	6.7
Chery	**260.9**	**6.0**
Guangzhou Honda	260.1	6.0
FAW-Toyota	219.2	5.0
Dongfeng-Nissan	211.3	4.9
Geely Automotive	**204.3**	**4.7**
Dongfeng Peugeot Citroën	201.3	4.6
Changan Ford	135.6	3.1
Dongfeng Yueda Kia	115.0	2.6
Changan Suzuki	112.1	2.6
China Brilliance	**73.1**	**1.7**
Harbin Hafei	**65.4**	**1.5**
Dongfeng Honda	63.4	1.5
Other	791.9	18.2
Total	4,349.9	

Source: Global Insight (2007), Asian Automotive Industry Forecast Report, April 2007, p. 32. Note: Passenger car sales now include all multi-purpose vehicles and all sports-utility vehicles. Others include CBU imports. Chery sales exclude exports. Due to rounding errors, percentage numbers add up to 103 percent.

While no satisfactory evidence can be provided, one can conclude from the market shares and sales of Chinese passenger car manufacturers, that without brands and independent product technologies, the Chinese partners of the JVs lost their independence. They have few self-developed products. Domestic manufacturers'

[1114] In 2006, Chery sold 132,326 cars of its QQ model. Geely announced that it hoped to increase output to 750,000 units annually by 2010, half of which would be exported. Refer to Global Insight (2007), Asian Automotive Industry Forecast Report, April 2007, p. 142 and Economist Intelligence Unit (2007), "China: Automotive Profile", Internet Edition, 14.01.2007, reviewed 15.07.2007.

[1115] Refer to Noble (2006), "Overcapacity, Contract Design and the Emergence of Independent Auto Firms in China", Internet Edition, reviewed 01.08.2007.

[1116] Domestic companies without foreign JV partner are marked bold.

prospects of producing their own-brand cars have been stifled by the dependence of their partners' technology and brand reputation.[1117]

Limiting the maximum equity stakes of the foreign partner in share holding companies does not achieve the objective of management control and technology enhancement set by the central authorities. These results are in line with Mansfield and Romeo (1980). They contend that parent firms transfer technology to wholly-owned subsidiaries in developing countries one third faster, on average, than to JVs or licensees.[1118] Technology transfer is thus relatively limited under the pattern of JV. Nearly all foreign investors have tremendous influence on the operation of JVs, even though they only have minority equity shares. The foreign JV partner usually controls important management activities such as sales, purchasing and finances, as well as technology transfer, production control, and quality control. The spill-over effect is so far limited to the achievement of mastering production techniques and imitating designs. Foreign firms have fought for the protection of their key technologies, and have mostly relocated the manufacturing of simple products.[1119]

Yet it is questionable, how successfully foreign manufacturers can protect their core technology. The past years have seen a sharp increase in IPR disputes in China's auto industry between domestic and foreign manufacturers. The following two examples illustrate some of the legal issues involved:

- *Toyota versus Geely for trademark infringement and unfair competition:* At the end of 2002, Toyota filed a lawsuit against Geely for trademark infringement and unfair competition. Geely used terms such as "Toyota's power" and "equipped with Toyota engines" for sales promotion, because Geely's engines are manufactured by a third party with Toyota's authorization. Geely was China's first domestic car manufacturer to be sued for IPR infringement. The court did not sustain the claims raised by Toyota. Through the lawsuit, however, Toyota succeeded in distinguishing its trademark from Geely's trademark through media coverage.
- *GM versus Chery for unfair competition:* In June 2003, GM's accusation was that Chery's QQ model was a copy of GM's Spark (known as Matiz in Korea), a model manufactured by GM's Korean subsidiary GM Daewoo. In 2004, the State Intellectual Property Office stated that, as GM Daewoo did not file for patents for its designs, these designs were not protected in China. In November 2005, the parties reached a settlement. GM Daewoo was not able to sue and win, because it did not have patents for its designs in China.[1120]

1117 This conclusion is in line with Gallagher's research results. For further information refer to Gallagher (n.d.), p. 2, Internet Edition, reviewed 25.04.2007.

1118 For further information refer to Mansfield and Romeo (1980).

1119 Refer to Wang (2001), p. 11 ff.

1120 Refer to Ministry of Commerce (2006), "IPR disputes in China's automobile industry", Internet Edition, reviewed 23.07.2007.

While China's effort to address IPR problems must be recognized, IPR infringements remain widespread. Recent news on cyber-spies in German, British and US government institutions suggest that hackers have also infiltrated thousands of company computers with Trojan horses to acquire technology know-how.[1121] The TRIPS Agreement requires China to implement effective enforcement procedures, and to provide civil and criminal remedies that have a deterrent effect. However, IPR enforcement is weak (particularly at the local level) due to lack of coordination between Chinese government ministries and agencies, local protectionism and corruption, high thresholds for criminal prosecution, and weak punishments.

In a reforming socialist economy like China, as in any other complex modern economy, the main progress of technical generation and innovation is the enterprise, in which in-firm or externally-generated new knowledge is applied to market-oriented production, and eventually commercialized.[1122] Indeed, Chinese auto manufacturers have started to set up their own R&D facilities. However, China's leading passenger car producer, SAIC, did not set up its first own R&D center before 2002, despite revenues of RMB 120 billion that year (and despite mass-producing with its JV partners since 1984).[1123]

The long-term development of the industry is particularly harmed by insufficient R&D investment by domestic auto companies.[1124] The expenditure of Chinese auto companies on R&D usually accounts for less than 1 percent of their sales volume, whereas the amount is between 3-5 percent for foreign auto companies.[1125] While GM invests USD 5-6 billion in R&D every year, the total development budget of the domestic auto industry is USD 0.27 billion.[1126] In addition, the industry has been suffering from a severe shortage of R&D personnel. The R&D staff of FAW accounts for 2.6 percent of the total staff number. This is small compared to Toyota, where 9.8 percent of the total staff are R&D.[1127] Out of ten independent Chinese passenger car manufacturers, with an investment of 6.8 percent of total sales revenues in R&D,

1121 Refer to Spiegel (2007), "Prinzip Sandkorn", p. 18 ff.

1122 Refer to Gabriele (2001), p. 23, Internet Edition, reviewed 01.05.2007.

1123 A SAIC spokesperson said that the establishment of the Automotive Engineering Academy of SAIC signified the beginning of China's efforts to develop auto technology independently. Refer to People's Daily (2002): "China's Leading Car Producer Sets up R&D Center", Internet Edition, reviewed 03.09.2007.

1124 Kokko and Blomström contend that the negative relationship between technology transfer requirements and technology inflows result from the deficiency of local content policy *and* accompanying protectionist measures. The combination of high domestic content requirements and the protected Chinese auto has reduced competition between domestic and foreign suppliers. In consequence, both domestic suppliers and carmakers might have less incentive to update their technology and continuously adjust their operations and technologies to changing market conditions. For further information refer to Kokko and Blomström (1995).

1125 Refer to Beijing Review (2006), "Growing Pains or Growing Gains?", Internet Edition, reviewed 16.07.2007.

1126 Refer to Beijing Review (2006), "Getting out of first gear", Internet Edition, reviewed 08.08.2006.

1127 Ibidem. Note: Calculation based on recent FERI exchange rates.

Chery invested the largest share of revenue to expand its R&D capabilities (Hafei Auto: 2.9 percent, Geely: 0.6 percent and Great Wall: 0.8 percent) (refer to Table 40).[1128]

Table 40: Key figures of independent passenger car manufacturers, 2004.

	Amount	Chery Auto	Geely Auto	Hafei Auto	Great Wall Motor
Net Sales	RMB million	5,110.7	3,425.4	6,101.6	3,408.2
Export Value	USD million	31.0	22.3	35.3	23.9
Number of employees	Persons	7,441	7,760	5,047	2,620
Number of R&D Engineers	Persons	728	180	217	326
R&D Expenses	RMB million	348.16	20	177.74	27.64
R&D Expenses/Net Sales Ratio	Percent	6.8	0.6	2.9	0.8

Source: FOURIN (2006), p. 9.

The World Bank sample indicates that joint research with government institutions is less pronounced in the auto sector than in the electronics sector. While 9.9 percent (n=39) of the companies in the electronics sector had a contractual or long-standing relationship with government institutions to perform R&D, only 5.2 percent (n=11) of the auto sector had such a relationship with a state institute in 2000. The difference is significant (Pearson Chi-Square: 0.041, 2-sided) (refer Table 41, Table 42). The R&D requirements on foreign investors have had a negative impact on the government's effort to provide financing for state-run R&D institutes.

Table 41: Descriptive Statistics: Contractual or long-standing relationship with a government research institution to perform R&D for the plant in the auto sector and in the electronics sector, 2000.

			Government research institution		
			Yes	No	Total
Group_autosec_ electronicssec	Auto sec	Count	11	202	213
		% within Group_autosec_ electronicssec	5,2%	94,8%	100,0%
	Electronics sec	Count	39	353	392
		% within Group_autosec_ electronicssec	9,9%	90,1%	100,0%
Total		Count	50	555	605
		% within Group_autosec_ electronicssec	8,3%	91,7%	100,0%

Source: Data compiled from World Bank survey "Competitiveness, Technology and Firm Linkages in Manufacturing Sectors" (2001).

[1128] Among the ten independent car manufacturers considered here are furthermore Tianjin FAW Xiali, Chang'an Auto, Brillance Jinbei, BYD Auto, Lifan Auto and Beiqi Foton.

Table 42: Chi-Square Test: Contractual or long-standing relationship with a government research institution to perform R&D for the plant in the auto sector and in the electronics sector, 2000.

	Value	df	Asymp. Sig. (2-sided)	Exact Sig. (2-sided)	Exact Sig. (1-sided)
Pearson Chi-Square	4,167[b]	1	,041		
Continuity Correction a	3,560	1	,059		
Likelihood Ratio	4,468	1	,035		
Fisher's Exact Test				,045	,027
Linear-by-Linear Association	4,160	1	,041		
N of Valid Cases	605				

a. Computed only for a 2x2 table

b. 0 cells (,0%) have expected count less than 5. The minimum expected count is 17,60.

Source: Data compiled from World Bank survey "Competitiveness, Technology and Firm Linkages in Manufacturing Sectors" (2001).

Industrial collaboration and horizontal networking are also uncommon in China. In the National Industrial Statistics of the 2000 R&D Census, Chinese industrial firms reported that they spent 93 percent of their USD 2.7 billion total R&D outlay in-house, but only less than 1 percent on projects with other domestic firms.[1129] The 2001 World Bank sample shows that 3.8 percent (n=8) of the auto companies and 5.3 percent of the companies of the residual sectors (n=67) had long-standing joint R&D programs with private companies (refer to Table 43). There is no significant difference between the auto sector and the residual sectors. The numbers suggest that few Chinese firms develop alliances with, or invest in, companies in other provinces due to strong political ties to their local state officials. In consequence, firms and localities are "isolated" from the rest of the economy.

Altogether, domestic auto companies are still depend on foreign OEMs' technology and brands. The foreign JV partners have granted SOEs only marginal insight into core technologies. It remains debatable how much help Chinese auto manufacturers will receive from their foreign partners in terms of developing their own brands, as this could turn partners into competitors. Accordingly, the domestic partners have made little progress in transferring technology and design know-how from their JV operations to (their wholly-owned) non-JV operations. The dynamic, autonomous development has rather come from independent local firms such as Chery and Geely.[1130] Realizing that JVs may not be the best way for Chinese auto makers to

[1129] China's research institutes are increasingly insular, too, especially since market reforms have forced them to commercialize their operations. In 2000, only 38 of China's 292 national industrial research institutes devoted more than one-third of total activities to collaborative projects, even though these institutes are specifically tasked with diffusing technology. Refer to Gilboy (2004), "The Myth Behind China's Miracle", Internet Edition, reviewed 16.10.2006.

[1130] Refer to Noble (2006), "Overcapacity, Contract Design and the Emergence of Independent Auto Firms in China", Internet Edition, reviewed 01.08.2007.

develop their product-development capability, the Chinese government is revisiting its policy, and calling for more self-developed products and self-owned technology. The government has urged the largest state-owned OEMs to establish internally-driven product development. However, it will certainly take time until domestic OEMs are able to fully develop their own products, rather than imitate the products of MNCs.

Table 43: Descriptive Statistics: Contractual or long-standing relationship with private companies to perform R&D in the auto sector and in the residual sectors, 2000.

			Private companies		Total
			Yes	No	
Group_autosec_ressec	Auto sec	Count	8	205	213
		% within Group_ autosec_ressec	3,8%	96,2%	100,0%
	Residual sec	Count	67	1208	1275
		% within Group_ autosec_ressec	5,3%	94,7%	100,0%
Total		Count	75	1413	1488
		% within Group_ autosec_ressec	5,0%	95,0%	100,0%

Source: Data compiled from World Bank survey "Competitiveness, Technology and Firm Linkages in Manufacturing Sectors" (2001).

4.6.2.3 International competitiveness

Neither foreign OEMs nor Chinese auto manufacturers export on a large scale. Given the size of the domestic market, foreign producers focus on domestic sales; and Chinese auto manufacturers cannot yet meet international production and design standards.

The managers of German auto companies interviewed explained that, despite government export promotion measures, such as tax reliefs or majority ownership, foreign car manufacturers in China largely engage in marginal export activity with their JV partners, but rather focus on sales in the growing domestic market.[1131] DaimlerChrysler, VW, Bosch and ZF Friedrichshafen produce domestically solely for the Chinese market. The low quality of parts available in China, and business risks such as the high cost structure due to tariffs and nontariff barriers, unfavorable regulatory framework, insecure IPRs etc. discourage foreign OEMs and suppliers from exporting. In consequence, foreign auto OEMs still focus on the domestic market rather than on export from China. According to the foreign interviewees, OEMs suffer from overcapacity in the Chinese market, which pressures foreign

[1131] Interviews conducted with managers of OEMs in Beijing between 08.06.2006 and 14.06.2006.

OEMs to export in the mid- to long-run.[1132] Exports will only increase when MNCs make China the global production hub for selected models. This is unlikely to happen in the current policy environment. Foreign OEMs and suppliers might export from China in the future, in order to improve their cost structures, and encounter increasing overcapacity in the Chinese market by using China as a low cost production base – not because of government export promotion incentives, such as loans from the Export-Import Bank, tax exemptions or majority ownership.[1133]

The Chinese SOEs that have a foreign JV partner are not equipped to become international global players, although they are the backbone of the auto industry policy and are promoted by the state. FAW exported 13,903 units in 2005.[1134] SAIC is still focussing on establishing itself in China, and consequently a major push in export markets is unlikely in the medium term. Most passenger car exporters are domestic manufacturers (refer to Figure 36), who produce small cars they sell for less than USD 10,000 (average price of exported cars from China in 2006: USD 7,400)[1135]. Among the top ten exporters are Chery, which exported 51,638 units, and Geely, which exported 9,171 units. Both manufacturers started their exports soon after their first product launch in order to meet the challenge of competition and overcapacity in the domestic market.[1136] Chery and Geely proactively follow the path towards international competitiveness, and are looking to expand in export markets.

Figure 36: Top ten exporting companies, 2006.

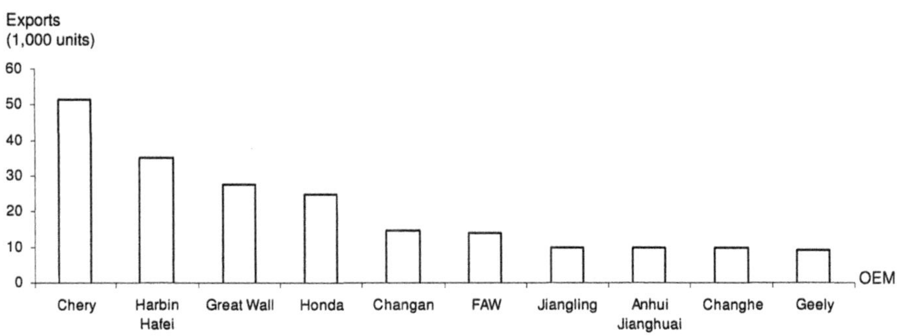

Source: Global Insight (2007), Asian Automotive Industry Forecast Report, April 2007, p. 57. Note: Data for FAW based on 2005 figure.

1132 Interview conducted with a manager of a German OEM in Beijing on 09.06.2006.

1133 In the near term, the main thrust of auto exports will be in the area of components, engines and transmissions. However, exports of built-up vehicles will grow more gradually.

1134 Refer to Global Insight (2007), Asian Automotive Industry Forecast Report, April 2007, pp. 57-59.

1135 Ibidem, p. 57.

1136 Chery exported its first vehicles to Syria in October 2001; Geely started exporting in November 2003.

Moreover, car export volumes are low, because domestic companies cannot meet international production costs yet. First, total production costs in China are not competitive, due to high import tariffs on auto parts. Mostly due to quality reasons, about 70 percent of passenger car manufacturing equipment in China is still imported.[1137] Second, as the state aimed to attract foreign companies to invest in China, it granted foreign OEMs tax exemptions which at the same time put domestic auto manufacturers at a disadvantage.[1138] High tax rates reduced domestic auto manufacturers' international price competitiveness. Unlike domestic enterprises, foreign-owned enterprises were exempted from urban construction tax, regional and additional education tax, property tax, land-use tax and water conservancy fund. Moreover, foreign-owned enterprises enjoyed a reduced income tax rate of 15-25 percent, while the income tax rate for a domestic enterprise such as Chery was 33 percent in 2005 (refer to Table 44). Income tax from domestic enterprises accounted for more than 17 percent of the total income tax collected in China in 2006 – compared with 4 percent from foreign invested enterprises. In order to establish a level playing field for foreign and domestic enterprises, the National People's Congress has passed a new Enterprise Income Tax Law which sets the income tax rate for domestic and foreign companies at 25 percent from January 2008 (refer to Chapter 3.3.5.4).[1139]

Table 44: Tax rates of Chery Automobile Co., Ltd. and foreign-owned companies, 2005.

Items	Chery Automobile Co., Ltd.	Foreign-owned companies
Urban construction tax	(value-added tax + consumption tax + business tax) x 7%	None
Additional education tax	(value-added tax + consumption tax + business tax) x 3%	None
Property tax	12%	None
Land-use tax	RMB 0.5 / square meter	None
Regional education tax	(value-added tax+ consumption tax + business tax) x 1%	None
Water conservancy fund	sales revenue x 0.0006	None or less
Income tax	33%	15-25%

Source: China Auto (2006), December 2006, p. 12.

Global Insight (2007) reports that in 2006, around 1,175 manufacturers exported vehicles from China. However, over 669 of these exported fewer than 10 units, and 204 companies exported just 1 unit.[1140] The exporting domestic auto manufacturers mainly sell their cars to developing countries, for the most part to the Middle East and Africa. Of the vehicles that FAW exported in 2005, 21 percent were passenger cars

1137 For example, over 80 percent of the robots used in auto production lines are imported. Refer to China Business Press, "China's dependence on imported manufacturing equipment up to 70%", reported in CAND (2007a), p. 5.

1138 Interviews conducted with experts of a Chinese government institution in Beijing on 13.06.2006.

1139 Refer to Asia Times Online (2007), "Taxing times for China's foreign firms", Internet Edition, reviewed 12.10.2007.

1140 Ibidem.

exported to Syria, and 10 percent were trucks exported to North Korea.[1141] Domestic auto companies cannot yet fulfil the international safety and emission standards of developed countries. According to the J.D. Power Initial Quality Study - which measures product quality, using a metric called "PP100"[1142] or problems per 100 vehicles - China's industry average PP100 rating stands at 231, or almost twice the US average of 124. With domestic Chinese brands, quality problems are almost twice as frequent as with locally-built international brands (an average of 368 PP100 for domestic brands, compared with 189 for international brands). These gaps are particularly significant in such critical components as powertrain, driving experience, and handling - areas that require heavy investment in R&D and production management systems. However, in 2000, when J.D. Power first started measuring initial quality in China, domestic brands reported more than 800 PP100, on average, and international or JV brands showed more than 400. In the past six years, the quality of cars has increased, resulting in a more than 50 percent reduction in quality defects for both domestic and international brands.[1143] Recent landmark examples have, however, reinforced consumer doubt about potential design and quality issues with Chinese cars. The Jiangling Motors Group envisioned exporting its Landwind model to Europe. However, it had to stop exporting when the German ADAC rated the Chinese-made sports-utility vehicle as *"not meeting European safety standards"* in September 2005.[1144] The Landwind crash test delivered the worst result ever in the history of ADAC crash testing. The Brilliance BS6 also failed the German crash test in June 2007. The BS6 sedan won only one out of five possible stars in the crash test carried out in accordance with European New Car Assessment regulations.[1145]

In order to accelerate international competitiveness and overseas expansion, Chinese OEMs have taken different approaches. Some Chinese OEMs have recruited functional experts from MNCs experienced in international markets:

- Chery employed a former DaimlerChrysler executive as its international business division head, and a former Ford Motor manager to lead its engineering institute. Moreover, the former director of the Production Optimization Technology Department of VW (China) Investment Co. has assumed the position of Vice General Manager at Chery.[1146]

[1141] Refer to Global Insight (2007), Asian Automotive Industry Forecast Report, April 2007, p. 59.

[1142] The smaller the rating of PP100 the better the quality of the car.

[1143] Refer to Businessweek (2007), "The Quality Drag on China's Car Industry", Internet Edition, reviewed 18.07.2007.

[1144] Refer to ADAC (2005), "Das erste chinesische Auto im ADAC-Crashtest", Internet Edition, reviewed 13.09.2006.

[1145] Most European-made cars win four or five stars in the crash test, so the result is not encouraging for the BS6, which aimed to compete against the likes of the VW Passat and Audi A6 when it was launched at the Geneva Motor Show in March 2007. Refer to Spiegel Online (2007), "Brilliance versagt im Crashtest", Internet Edition, reviewed 03.09.2007.

[1146] Refer to CAND (2007b), pp. 6-7.

- Geely hired a former Daewoo engineer to lead product development.[1147]
- SAIC hired more than 150 British engineers.
- Brilliance hired a former DaimlerChrysler executive to head its R&D center and focus on building its own indigenous car models.[1148]

Chinese OEMs have also used global mergers and acquisitions to enter foreign auto markets. SAIC acquired Ssangyong to gain access to the Korean auto market.[1149] Chinese auto manufacturers, moreover, enter into cooperation with foreign auto producers, to use their expertise and sales and distribution networks to enter global auto markets. Chery is to produce small-cars for Chrysler. These low-cost cars under Chrysler brand names (Dodge and Jeep) will be exported to the USA and Europe starting in 2009.[1150] Some of the Chinese OEMs are negotiating JVs with local partners to assemble pre-made CKD kits in developing markets such as Malaysia or Iran.[1151] Other manufacturers are hiring agents to establish networks for penetrating export markets. As more Chinese OEMs go international, management will become more experienced. This trend will be accelerated by the influx of returning talent from the sizable pool of Chinese working abroad.[1152]

Overall, the promotion of exports by internationally competitive local Chinese producers has not advanced in the way expected by central leaders. Overseas expansion by domestic and foreign OEMs is still quite limited. Although the Chinese government announced that it would promote exports of motor vehicles, its policy focus has been import substitution. However, in the coming years, autos "made in China" by Chinese and foreign manufacturers will increasingly be oriented towards exports due to rising overcapacities. While the government pushes for more exports and overseas expansion in the near term, most OEMs consider that exporting from China is more of a long-term objective.

1147 Refer to Sun (2006), p. 40.

1148 Refer to Businessweek (2006), "China's Drive for Local Car Brands", Internet Edition, reviewed 08.08.2007 and Businessweek (2006), "China Carmakers' Global Talent Hunt", Internet Edition, reviewed 08.08.2007.

1149 Refer to Sun (2006), p. 40.

1150 Refer to International Herald Tribune (2007), "Chrysler deal to help Chery enter US market", p. 14.

1151 Since 2005, Chery has produced its QQ in Iran and announced plans to assemble sedans and sports-utility vehicles in Kaliningrad, Russia. Geely also plans to start building its Free Cruiser in Malaysia, and is plans to set-up factories in Russia and Mexico to eventually supply cars to Western Europe and the USA. Refer to Businessweek (2006), "China's Drive for Local Car Brands", Internet Edition, reviewed 08.08.2007.

1152 Refer to Sun (2006), p. 40.

4.7 Conclusion

Modelled on Korea's and Japan's industrial development, central leaders want to build up China's auto industry. The state has played an important role in the development of the auto industry in the transition period from a planned to a socialist market economy. As in the East Asian developmental states, China's industrial policy documents for the auto industry have set concrete goals and strategies for stimulating the growth of the industry, and focused on developing internationally competitive domestic companies.

At the core of the East Asian developmental state concept was the idea that the state could help firms overcome the obstacles of late development. The question is whether China's development strategy for the auto sector has succeeded in building up strong Chinese firms. Chinese policy-makers have used various instruments of industrial policy to reach this target: regulation of trade, attraction and control of foreign investment, subsidies and credit quotas issued by the state-controlled financial system etc. The World Bank sample "Competitiveness, Technology and Firm Linkages in Manufacturing Sectors" (2001) indicates that the electronics sector has received less government attention than the auto sector although the central government declared both to be pillar industries in 1994. China has a strong comparative advantage in electronics assembly (high value parts manufactured at low labor costs) so that the government does not fear abandonment or marginalization. In this sense, as the empirical analysis revealed, auto companies received more bank loans and more government assistance in locating foreign technology and processes to license from foreign firms. This resembles the East Asian developmental state approach of granting preferential policies, particularly to industries and companies in need of state support.

Even after China's WTO accession, government intervention and regulation has been central to the development of the auto sector. The government's policy for the auto sector has managed to prevent domestic manufacturers from being crowded out by large MNCs, which have been competing for market share since the 1990s. The MNCs have been willing to venture with domestic manufacturers, produce in large scale, source locally, introduce their latest products to the market, invest in R&D facilities, and spur the development of the domestic auto industry. Chinese companies have gained production know-how from foreign JV partners, and began to gain expertise in R&D and design after the introduction of the latest regulations on foreign investors. The sector's growth has, moreover, provided new jobs and contributed to overall economic growth.

Despite the size of the auto market and intensive government support in developing domestic state-owned auto firms, the Chinese auto industry remains in the infancy stage of development.[1153] The domestic auto market is fragmented, and domestic manufacturers' technical skills are not yet fully developed - they are still dependent on their foreign partners for advanced technology. While evidence is limited, from the

---

[1153] For further information on five successive stages of development in the auto sector refer to Abrenica (1998), pp. 13-14.

analysis one can conclude that regulation of FDI for the benefit of state-owned auto manufacturers has reduced the incentive for indigenous Chinese technological innovation. Moreover, Chinese products face challenges in meeting international standards. In consequence, domestic auto manufacturers have failed to export on a large scale so far.

It is too early, however, to be pessimistic about the central government's policy to develop its domestic auto industry. The major players of the Chinese auto industry (FAW, SAIC and Dongfeng) have large-scale production volumes and are seeking for independent brands and export expansion.[1154] It took Japanese and Korean OEMs, such as Toyota and Hyundai, almost 30 years to build up and optimize their product-development process to the point of launching self-developed products onto the global market. Given their current status, it might similarly take Chinese OEMs another 10 to 15 years before they can fully master the product development skills required to compete in European, US or Japanese markets.[1155]

To sum up, the Chinese state has not been able to implement and enforce a consistent strategy for the acquisition of technological capabilities from foreign investors in the auto industry.[1156] Besides, local authorities have a strong position in local economic policy-making. They own most of the Chinese auto companies, and have successfully resisted central-government intervention and regulation.[1157] State ownership in the auto sector, and government interference in business activities, has enabled ruling elites to convert their political power into economic wealth and privilege at the expense of equity and efficiency.[1158]

1154 It is though also premature to believe that Chinese OEMs are strong enough to challenge the major global OEMs today.

1155 It might take "only" four to five years more for Chinese OEMs to increase their export volume from levels of thousands of units annually to hundred thousands of units that would justify a fully functioning global network. It might then take another five to seven years for those local OEMs to fully master the new product development know-how to launch new products into mainstream markets.

1156 With the 1994 auto industry policy, an attempt was made by the Chinese government to articulate such a strategy, but the government had to gradually reverse its policies in the aftermath of WTO accession. For further information on how the Korean auto industry progresses technologically, refer to Amsden (1989b) and Lee and Lim (2001).

1157 Refer to Gallagher (2006), p. 24.

1158 Refer to Pei (2006c), "The Dark Side of China's Rise", Internet Edition, reviewed 04.11.2007.

5 Evaluation and lessons from China's model of economic development

China's capability to leapfrog up the developmental hierarchy in its economic growth and industrial development since 1978 has been the central interest of this analysis. While previous studies analyzed different aspects of China's development approach with regard to the East Asian developmental state theory, this study "translated" the experiences of the three East Asian developmental states Japan, Taiwan and Korea into specific criteria (institutional setting *and* policy indicators) for successful economic transformation. An East Asian Developmental State Model was set up and used as a role model to systematically analyze China's development. The analysis, moreover, concentrated on the effectiveness of China's model of economic development, using the auto industry as a basis for empirical research. From the mixed-methods approach (analysis of secondary statistics, statistical evaluation of the World Bank sample and up-to-date expert interviews) new insights into state-guidance in one of China's key sectors could be gained. From the results one can infer that Chinese auto manufacturers have benefited from the government's policy for the sector. However, continuous policy and government intervention in business activities, e.g. by state-ownership, local protectionism and strict requirements on foreign investors, has restricted competition and the sector's full development potential.

5.1 China – the new developmental state

The analysis of China's economic development rests upon the political economy approach of the developmental state theory, which is one of the most persuasive attempts to explain East Asian success. The developmental state model is based on continuous but selective state interventions in markets and firms to shape the course of economic development. The authoritarian developmental states' industrial guidance has enabled these late-industrializing economies to mount and sustain high levels of economic growth. The analysis confirmed that during the post-Mao economic reforms, China has evolved into a transforming state similar in most of its core characteristics to the East Asian developmental states:

- Like the East Asian developmental states, China's central leaders undertook economic reforms prior to political reforms and have retained the authority to crush dissent. Bureaucratic reforms facilitated better educated leaders supportive of economic reforms.
- From the beginning of its reform, China has strived to achieve economic growth and industrial transformation by a strong involvement of the government.[1159] The Chinese developmental state has followed the East Asian government-led development model in which industrial policy plays a central role in directing economic development. The central government has issued national industrial policies in the form of five-year and annual plans based on a

[1159] Refer to Nee (1992), pp. 24-25.

comprehensive long-term strategy. The elite bureaucracy in China, like that in the East Asian developmental states, has actively intervened in the economy by guiding, disciplining and coordinating the market in order to achieve its economic development goals. Despite the WTO principle of "national treatment", no level playing field for all economic subjects exists in China. As a result, the allocation of resources and therefore the industrial structures created are to a considerable extent not the outcome of market processes but rather the central government's industrial design.[1160] The analysis showed that the Chinese developmental state has continuously modified its policies in a creative and innovative manner, in accordance with the prevailing development strategy as well as the changing domestic and international environment.[1161] In this way, one strength of the Chinese model is its constant adaptation.

- Like their East Asian counterparts, central leaders in China have used different industrial policy mechanisms (selected protection of, and preferential treatment for, specific "sunrise" industries, such as tax reliefs and credits at low interest rates) as well as trade policy (import substitution *and* export promotion) to develop the national economy. Policy support has consisted of the selective adoption of regulations in accordance with the appropriate pace and pattern of the transition towards a market economy.
- As in the East Asian developmental states, Chinese enterprises have been supported by the government's "national champions" policy. Enterprises such as Lenovo have already reached a developmental stage where they are competitive in the global markets.
- The Chinese state has constructed a positive economic and investment climate through the gradual liberalization of product and labor markets, increasing openness to foreign trade, infrastructure investments, property reforms and privatization. Its institutional reforms have provided economic agents with security for planning, investing and economic risk taking. The state has had the capacity to construct an institutional environment that provides positive incentives to entrepreneurs and managers at the firm level to invest in economic growth.[1162]

Therefore, China's economic performance since 1978 can be attributed to the adoption of the development strategies previously implemented by Japan, Korea and Taiwan. The analysis of China's economic development, using the East Asian Developmental State Model as a role model, confirms that China's path of development makes it the latest member of the group of successful developmental

---

[1160] Refer to Taube (2005), pp. 5-6.

[1161] This has been the case, in particular, in the run-up to, and in the aftermath of, its accession to the WTO. Refer to UNCTAD, "Key Issues in China's Economic Transformation", Internet Edition, reviewed 12.02.2007.

[1162] Refer to Nee et al. (2007), p. 43.

states. This assertion is in line with previous works on China such as Nee (1992), Nee et al. (2005), Wu (2000), and Stiglitz (2002).[1163] This study in consequence reinforces their results by using a different research approach. Although the analysis proved that the Chinese reform experiment shares core characteristics with the developmental states in East Asia, one should not conclude from this that China is following a coherent strategy of emulating the East Asian Developmental State Model.

5.2 Uniqueness of the Chinese development approach

The analysis of the Chinese developmental state's approach towards restructuring its domestic industry, specifically the auto industry, exemplifies the uniqueness of the Chinese developmental state. The nation's distinct path of development is characterized by an innovative form of state-led growth. China's economic achievements over the past two decades have made its development experiences special in many ways.

Unlike the East Asian Developmental State Model, the Chinese developmental state pursues an economic development path characterized by decentralization and foreign investment. China has successfully incorporated both criteria in its development strategy, in order to spur local entrepreneurship and advance to international technology standards. Both characteristics particularly shape the development of the auto industry that has been used for empirical analysis. The analysis also showed that state ownership of central and local auto companies, as well as far-reaching government intervention in business activities, have had negative economic consequences.

(1) Decentralization:

Crucial to China's economic success, decentralization has assigned local governments' considerable discretion over economic policy. In many areas, officials have used this authority to create markets and build up internationally active companies.[1164] With the introduction of fiscal federalism, the local officials' revenues became positively correlated with the prospering of local economic enterprises.[1165] The incentives applied have induced a change in bureaucrats' behavior. Local governments have provided an entrepreneurial business environment. The municipal government in Shanghai (rather than its counterpart in Beijing), together with local business groups, fostered ties between auto firms and local university research institutes. They also attracted foreign investments in the auto sector, and supported

---

[1163] Refer to Nee (1992), Nee et al. (2005), p. 5, Wu (2000), p. 151 and Stiglitz (2002).

[1164] Refer to Weingast (1995), p. 23.

[1165] Refer to Li (1998), p. 39-397.

the establishment of a local supplier community. This development approach resembles active state-guidance in Japan and Korea. At the same time, the central government's loss of control over local officials has directly limited its ability to intervene adversely. Without political liberalization, China transformed its bureaucratic system substantially during its reform process, and introduced market-based incentives at all levels of the bureaucracy.[1166] In this respect, China did not pursue top-down planning like the East Asian developmental states, but rather a bottom-up approach of local state-led economic growth.

However, it was shown that this "Chinese-style federalism", as an intermediate institutional arrangement, is not perfect. While representing the interests of the central government as state agents, local governments simultaneously act in accordance with local interests in competition with other jurisdictions, thus questioning official budgetary boundaries.[1167] Under economic and political pressures, they assume the role of local economic principals, manipulate national economic policies to pursue particular local goals and defend local interests.[1168] The central government tolerates, and even rewards, officials who use any means to produce local investment and employment knowing that local economic growth promotes social and political order. The pursuit of independent policies at various government levels has frequently impeded a coherent policy approach. In the auto sector, economic (fiscal) decentralization has created incentives for local governments to support the development of local auto firms and sometimes flout the interest of the central government and its long-term policy approach. National import substitution for the auto sector in combination with local protective high tariffs and market restrictions have led local governments to launch new independent auto assembly projects in anticipation of high profits.[1169] While the central government aims to guide the development of the sector, its policy approach is impeded by various local bureaucracies that established provincial auto bases in order to stimulate local economic growth. This has provoked duplicate construction and fragmentation and has hindered the consolidation of the auto industry.[1170] The Chinese economy is therefore characterized by politically monopolized and isolated local markets.

1166 Refer to Tenev (2006), p. 24.

1167 Refer to Gong (2006), p. 94.

1168 Refer to Gilboy (2004), "The Myth Behind China's Miracle", Internet Edition, reviewed 16.10.2006 and Gong (2006), p. 94

1169 The central government pursues import substitution for the auto industry rather than export promotion as in other sectors. In order to protect domestic firms and lessen foreign exchange outflows, the government imposed high tariff rates, quotas and import licenses on foreign-made motor vehicles. Protectionist measures and deterred international competition generated high prices and profits in the domestic market. The analysis showed that China has used local content and certification measures and imposed high tariff rates on vehicles and selected auto components even after the transition period of China's WTO accession.

1170 The same applies for the domestic auto supply industry which is fragmented and uncompetitive compared with international norms, with little economy of scale.

Altogether, a key determinant of China's development strategy is the uncertain and unclear relationship between central and local authorities. The central government has increasingly been unable to force provincial authorities to adhere to central government policy directives. Until and unless this relationship is stabilized, it will be extraordinarily difficult to develop a coherent and cohesive national strategy for development: in Johnson's words, to facilitate *"the national mobilization of a united people for economic goals".*[1171] China will need a strong, integrating central authority (like the pilot agency in the East Asian developmental states) to bring entrepreneurial initiatives into a rule-based national context.[1172]

(2) Foreign investment:

Maybe the most defining feature of China's economic reform is its approach towards FDI.[1173] In order to spur its national modernization drive, the Chinese developmental state has attracted foreign investment. China's FDI policies have been proactive, both at the central level and the provincial and municipal level.[1174] The Chinese developmental state is more open towards foreign participation than its East Asian counterparts were at a comparable stage of development. By welcoming foreign investment, China has linked its domestic industry to international markets which is increasingly important in times of globalization. FDIs that have entered China since the 1990s have clearly benefited China's modernization efforts and its global competitiveness. The analysis of the auto sector showed that the central government implemented a sector-specific policy, relying on foreign auto manufacturers to build JVs with selected local SOEs or cooperatives and collectives. In this way, domestic state-owned companies were to overcome their technology shortage and establish a modern car industry with the help of foreign OEMs. While in several post-socialist East and Central European countries, and in many other developing countries, the auto industry is dominated by MNCs, the central government has successfully prevented domination of auto production by foreign manufacturers with this regulation.[1175] Sino-foreign contract or venture agreements, as well as foreign high-tech R&D investments, have caused positive spillover effects (e.g. job creation, local production and sourcing, and modernization of the domestic auto industry).

Although foreign investment in the auto industry has contributed positively to the sector's modernization, in the segment of passenger cars, Chinese car manufacturing is not yet competitive in global markets. The strict regulation on FDI inputs has had negative effects by contributing to domestic auto manufacturers' dependence on foreign technology and know-how. While evidence is limited, the analysis provides indication that assistance from the state (and subsequently foreign

1171 Refer to Johnson (1987), p. 139.

1172 Refer to Taube (2005), p. 7.

1173 Refer to Pei (2006a), p. 3.

1174 Local governments even compete for foreign investments as their jurisdictions' financial well-being (through fiscal federalism) and their own political career depend on local development.

1175 For further information refer to Pavlinek and Smith (1998) and Swain (1998).

investors) has served as a substitute for domestic entrepreneurship, and weakened the competitiveness of Chinese auto firms. The most ambitious and innovative Chinese auto companies are private manufacturers, or manufacturers with little government participation, and outside the central government's center of attention such as Geely and Chery.

Many domestic auto manufacturers concentrate on short-term gains, rather than on increasing operational efficiency and commitment to developing new technologies. Although the central government provides incentives for domestic companies to invest in long-term technology development, Chinese firms often focus on developing privileged relations with officials in the CCP hierarchy, and rely on *guanxi,* to realize short-term profit. State and private auto firms in China (whether in Beijing, Shanghai or other jurisdictions) lag behind foreign OEMs, because they have failed to invest in the type of long-term technological capabilities that their Japanese and Korean predecessors built during the 1970s and 1980s. This poses an ongoing dilemma for Chinese policy-makers: Not only do Chinese officials fear being cut off from foreign technology; they also fear becoming too heavily dependent on it.[1176] This is a realistic concern, given China's still-limited indigenous high-tech capabilities in the auto industry, and foreign investors' engagement to gain market share in the domestic market. China's industry is left with inefficient but still-powerful Chinese SOEs, increasingly dominant foreign firms, and few profitable private auto firms.

The capability to export can simply be used to evaluate the international competitiveness of firms. Industrial policy in the East Asian developmental states aimed at cost and price competitiveness in world markets. Subjecting domestic firms to international competition is generally considered to be a crucial concern to promote the development of them – certainly when the economy is integrated in the world economy and abides the rules of the WTO. Chinese auto manufacturers, however, are not yet internationally competitive and thus exports, of mostly small domestic manufacturers, only increase slowly. As long as domestic auto manufacturers are not capable of producing and selling cars on global markets, the central government will not give up its "infant industry" policy of assistance through protection and limited equity stakes of foreign investors. China's industrial policy, as highlighted by the analysis of passenger car industry, is not able to ensure competitive conditions in markets due to a specific combination of restrictive and regulatory policy measures, mainly reflected by entry restrictions. In the mid- to long-run, protection must be gradually reduced and the domestic auto market must further open up to international competition in order to increase the competitiveness of its domestic auto producers.[1177] Chinese companies must expand their R&D capabilities, including new product design and advanced manufacturing techniques to become global players. Besides, they will have to invest heavily in manufacturing facilities in order to accommodate new vehicle designs.

[1176] Refer to Walsh (2003), p. 116

[1177] The restrictions on auto imports and on the operations of foreign firms in China have already been reduced since China's WTO entry.

(3) Government intervention in business activities and state ownership:

While the governments of Korea and Taiwan, following the Japanese path, were deeply committed to market mechanism and private ownership, the Chinese party-state remains in direct control of large parts of the economy through ownership of dominant enterprises in strategic sectors.[1178] In the auto sector, state bureaucrats and SOEs exploit their bargaining power to influence the formulation of industrial policy and pursue further rents. Particularly SOEs, as targets of strong government support, have the strongest influential power for the formulation of the industrial policy. The analysis of the auto sector showed that state ownership of key auto firms and Chinese bureaucrats' direct intervention in free market mechanisms have caused economic inefficiencies. The high level of prices and profits has been evidence of the lack of competition in the industry, resulting in welfare losses. The protectionist model of regulation in the name of industrial policy persists, because of the special consideration of the government given to the strategically important and politically sensitive large-sized SOEs which are a guarantor of employment. Moreover, state bureaucrats in China did not have the power to demand from the high-priority auto sector to meet performance goals as in the East Asian developmental states.

The withdrawal of government from business activities has happened only partially in China. Following the privatization of TVEs and small- and middle-sized SOEs in the early 2000s, local governments are less involved in influencing economic decisions within the firm as they attempt to improve the business environment to attract entrepreneurs and investments to their region.[1179] In the auto sector, however, state ownership and government interference in business activities is still widespread.[1180] The development of local governments' dual role as both state agents and local economic principals, has allowed local government officials to remain at the center of economic activities. Public power and private economic interests have become intimately connected.[1181] When enterprises are owned and controlled by the state, economic decisions necessarily become political decisions, and price competition is supplanted by forms of personal competition driven by the quest for political power and privilege. Bribery and corruption then become the rule rather than the exception. The resulting uncertainty surrounding economic transactions destabilizes economic development.[1182] Chinese authorities have so far refused to decontrol markets and prices in large segments of China's vast economic landscape.

The state's economic dominance preserves systemic economic inefficiency, as scarce resources are funneled to local elites and bureaucratic constituencies.

[1178] Refer to Nolan (1993b), p. 206.

[1179] Refer to Nee and Opper (2007), p. 123.

[1180] In the electronics sector, by contrast, "regulatory capture" is less pronounced due to a relatively weak position of large SOEs owned by the central government.

[1181] Refer to Gong (2006), p. 99.

[1182] Refer to Dorn (1989), p. 564.

Tensions rise between economic modernization and the many institutional flaws of authoritarian rule (e.g. lack of political accountability, weak rule of law, and corruption). To activate the full potential of China's distinct developmental model, and overcome structural imbalances in the industrial economy, further progress toward instituting a market economy is needed. As in the capitalist East Asian developmental states, private property rights need to be put on an equal basis with other forms of ownership, creating legal norms and regulations – and the means to enforce them – that protect private property rights.[1183] In particular, a constitutional framework, which insulates economic life from political opportunism, appears to be a necessary condition for social and economic stability. In the following years, governments at every level need to be gradually phased out of economic activities, and to return to social and political management.[1184]

Ultimately, economic and political reforms are inseparable. As long as the ruling elite prevents the full expansion of free market mechanisms, the quest for economic and social stability will fail to be realized. Fearing that a more comprehensive approach would threaten the supremacy of the CCP,[1185] the Chinese government has consistently resisted steps to further reduce the role of the state in the economy and increase judicial independence. In short, economic reform in this kind of political system will inevitably be piecemeal, and the transformation to a full market economy fail, as further reforms diminish the ruling regime's power and threaten its survival.[1186] In the long run, reformers might buildup a modern polity with open electoral politics that moves China beyond an antiquated CCP dictatorship. The question remains as to whether China can, like many of its East Asian neighbors, evolve along a neoauthoritarian development path, and move eventually toward a more open society.

To summarize, the analysis showed that China adapted the East Asian Developmental State Model to a particular Chinese type of developmental state, which is a hybrid form of strategies advocated by different streams of development thinking. The regulation mechanism of economic development in China is an

---

1183 Refer to Nee (1992), p. 24 and Nee (2000), p. 87.

1184 The CCP is aware of this situation. This becomes apparent when studying the latest policy document, the Eleventh Five-Year Plan. The plan focuses strongly on social balance within the country. Of the 22 goals, only two relate to economic growth - total GDP and per capita GDP - and four to changes in economic structure - share of services in the economy and in employment, spending on R&D, and the urbanization rate. The other 16 relate to population growth, use of resources, the environment, and standards of living. Refer to National Development and Reform Commission (2006), "Outline of the Eleventh Five-Year Plan for National Economic & Social Development of the People's Republic of China", Internet Edition, reviewed 14.11.2006.

1185 To come into line with international norms, China has undertaken economic legal reforms, although questions remain as to the judiciary's independence from the CCP.

1186 For further information refer to Pei (2006a), pp. 7-13 and p. 202. (22/76), Pei (2006b), "Has China Fallen into a Trapped Transition?", Internet Edition, reviewed 04.11.2007, Pei (2006c), "The Dark Side of China's Rise", Internet Edition, reviewed 04.11.2007 and Pei (2007), "Corruption Threatens China's Future", Internet Edition, reviewed 04.11.2007.

innovative combination of factors from the East Asian developmental states, the legacies of the past command economy as well as of the newly adopted market mechanism, including international capital flows. In implementing economic policy, China has adopted a gradual approach, with an emphasis on stability, reflecting the fact that it takes time to improve the infrastructure of the market-based system, including the legal and regulatory framework, banking system, accounting standards, professional expertise, and institutional capacity.[1187] Far-reaching government intervention in business activities, and the absolute rule of the CCP, however, hinder the full potential of the distinctiveness of the Chinese developmental state. China will approach a mature developmental state, though unique in its characteristics, once an independent legal system protects private economic agents from arbitrary state intervention.[1188]

5.3 Lessons from China's new model of economic development

China's experience highlights the principle that "institutions matter" in understanding the diverse economic performance of different countries. China is already becoming an exporter of economic know-how, providing lessons in growth-promotion to its neighbors. As Tenev (2006) states, India is examining China's experience with special trade and investment zones, and Vietnam is paying attention to China's experience with state-enterprise reform.[1189] Accordingly, the analysis intends to transform the results of the Chinese development strategy into specific criteria valuable for other transforming countries. These lessons, however, do not mean to provide a "blueprint" of economic transformation for developing countries. Different governments have different capacities to guide the market. Developmental objectives might not only differ from country to country, but require selective approaches for different sectors. While a highly interventionist policy might suit one sector best, it might be counterproductive in another, which needs a more laissez-faire approach.[1190]

China's model of economic development is intertwined with its unique political model. Moreover, China occupies an unrivaled niche in the world's political economy – its vast populace and large geographical size alone accords it global influence. Accordingly, no lessons can reliably be extrapolated from China's distinctive development path.[1191] From the analysis, it is possible to look at the Chinese experience and draw seven premises in the field of reform – which do not claim to be exhaustive - for transitional and late industrializing economies:

1187 Refer to Hu (2007), p. 37.

1188 Refer to Nee and Opper (2007), p. 123.

1189 Refer to Tenev (2006), p. 23.

1190 Refer to Wade (1988a), p. 130, Oi (1995), p. 1146 and Segal and Thun (2001), p. 582.

1191 Refer to Tenev (2006), p. 23.

- *State capacity and insulation from the political demands of society:* The analysis showed the importance of the government's role, as an economy makes the transition from a command to a market-based economy. The central government elaborated and formulated the long-term development goals of China's development path, and clearly articulated its policy reforms. The analysis of the East Asian developmental states showed that strong state capacity is necessary for the development process, so that the regime retains sufficient power to control the course of reform. This should exist at both the central and local levels. Unlike weak authoritarian states such as Africa and Latin America,[1192] the Chinese central government maintained its ability to guide economic activity during the reform period. The state bureaucracy has persistently used its power to decide on the content and speed of reform, and actively guided the industrial development process. In China, however, state capacity and coherence have been impeded by the "solos" of local governments. State capacity is particularly necessary to ensure an institutional environment conducive to private-sector investments and economic growth.
- *Decentralization and local incentives:* Reform and transition in geographically vast countries do not have to be directed solely by a centralized, national government. In a large economy, decentralization serves as a good mechanism for creating appropriate incentives for productive private activities that foster economic prosperity. Fiscal decentralization increases the autonomy of local governments, and gives them the incentive to promote economic growth. The central government, however, must ensure that local governments operate with hard budget constraints, in order to guarantee that local authorities are accountable for their decisions. Transfers between levels of government must be rule-based, expenditure responsibilities must be clearly allocated, and the ability of local governments to borrow funds must be limited. In addition, the national government must be able to circumvent local protectionism, which would impede domestic competition and preserve a common domestic market.[1193] Otherwise, effort and investment will continuously flow toward activities that are characterized by low productivi-ty.[1194] As long as private-sector institutions are not developed sufficiently to fill the void left by government withdrawal, the complete removal of government from coordination activities (and thus a total reliance on market coordi-nation) might not be feasible.[1195] Accordingly, different government levels should have adequate incentives to perform.[1196]
- *Openness to foreign trade:* The ability to graduate from import substitution to export promotion is a key factor in the successful pursuit of industrialization.

[1192] Also unlike the USSR, which undertook political reform before beginning the task of economic restructuring.

[1193] For further information refer to Burki et al. (1999).

[1194] Refer to Thun (2006), pp. 37-38 and p. 287.

[1195] Refer to Aoki et al. (1997), p. 13.

[1196] Refer to Oi (1995), p. 1147.

The key to developing countries' export success is the early rejection of import substitution policies in favor of outward-looking policies.[1197] Domestic companies' export expansion depends on the policy package which does not shelter the imports of competing industries, but gives priority to export oriented activities. Openness to foreign trade makes domestic companies measure their international competitiveness in foreign markets and prevents government officials from pursuing policy approaches that are no longer appropriate because it limits their ability to reduce the cost of mistake. Although import substitution is a necessary step to protect infant industries and to industrialize developing countries, there are serious problems associated with this strategy. The analysis of the Chinese auto industry shows that if protectionist measures such as tariffs are imposed for too long a period, protection may dampen the competitive edge of domestic firms. Protectionism may furthermore encourage new entry into the industry by domestic firms that aim to seek rents arising from high prices for locally produced vehicles.[1198] The exposure of Chinese companies to international competition serves as a counterbalance to enliven nonprofitable companies by institutional incentives in the medium- to long-run.[1199]

- *Attraction of foreign investments:* China's open-door policy has spurred FDI in the country, linking the Chinese economy with international markets and importing technology and management know-how. Thus, domestic companies can adapt to international standards and become internationally competitive. This is particularly important in times of globalization and economic integration. China's decentralized development model, in combination with its reliance on inward FDI, is an example of how regional development could occur in a continental-sized market economy. However, the danger that domestic companies might become subservient to FDI, particularly foreign technology, and weaken domestic entrepreneurship, needs to be eliminated by encouraging domestic investment in potentially dynamic private Chinese firms which compete with international companies.
- *Financial system:* The soundness and stability of the financial system is an essential ingredient of the appropriate macroeconomic framework for development.[1200] In this regard, while policy loans may help to develop specific industrial sectors during the initial stage of economic reform, hard budget constraints on credit lending, and an independent financial supervisory body, are essential for the banking system once it has matured. Otherwise, crony capitalism might be the result.

1197 Refer to Ng et al. (1992), pp. 225-226.

1198 Berglas and Razin introduced the element of profits into the Stolper and Samuelson (1941) analysis of protection. They came to the conclusion that in the short run, protection is likely to increase profits. For further information on protection and real profits, refer to Berglas and Razin (1974).

1199 Refer to Thun (2006), p. 287.

1200 Refer to Elson (International Monetary Fund) (2006), p. 40.

- *Legal system:* China's path towards economic prosperity requires a modest legal infrastructure at a supra-individual level beyond social relationships, which is centered on the protection of property and contract rights. It is necessary for China to step up the establishment of a legal system, conforming to national conditions for opposing monopoly and guaranteeing fair trade. Developing countries need to make the transition from "rule by law" to a version of "rule of law".[1201] The rule of law promises to move countries past the first phase of political and economic liberalization to a deeper level of reform.
- *Retreat of the state in the long run:* Direct state intervention in free market mechanisms is likely to yield negative economic effects. While at the early stage of transition to a market economy, the "helping hand" of the government may be helpful or even necessary,[1202] the government is expected to gradually withdraw from direct involvement in the economy for the transition to be complete. As the economy evolves toward increased reliance on market mechanism, and as private property forms are backed by law and the state, the higher transaction costs of intervention by government bureaucrats act increasingly as a drag on economic performance.[1203] Political interference in economic life should decline in industrial sectors and regions, to the extent that an emergent market economy replaces the centrally planned economy.[1204] The state's functions should then concentrate on building market institutions, e.g., property rights, legal system and market structures, and realize the rational allocation of resources.[1205]

The successes and failures of East Asia's and China's policy practices and their paths of technological progress indicate that as long as the economy is in a low state of development, the capabilities of firms are modest, and the efficiency of markets is hampered by poor integration and the underdevelopment of property-rights arrangements in the economy. Due to these unstable circumstances, the ability of the private sector to solve challenging coordination problems is suspect. During this time, government policy may successfully facilitate development. As the economy matures, however, the ability of the private sector improves, and the scope for policy becomes more limited.[1206] Overall, a state should create an environment that encourages market-oriented investment, ensure that the economy's dominant resource steering mechanisms are sensitive to economic efficiency, and "find" an engine of growth to generate dynamism and leadership. How these objectives are

---

1201 As Hayek puts it, rule of law *"means that a government in all its actions is bound by rules fixed and announced beforehand - rules which make it possible to foresee with fair certainty how the authority will use its coercive powers in given circumstances, and to plan one's individual affairs on the basis of this knowledge"*. Refer to Hayek (1976, reprinted in 1994), p. 80.

1202 For further information refer to Frye and Shleifer (1997).

1203 Refer to Nee (1992), p. 23.

1204 For further information refer to Nee (1989, 1992).

1205 Refer to Nee and Opper (2007), p. 95.

1206 Refer to Aoki et al. (1997), p. 22.

best achieved in a particular economy depends on its own history as well as its external environment.[1207] Economic development does not call for a particular policy recipe, but it does require a disciplined, balanced approach to policy-making in order to achieve fundamental goals. Further studies might examine industries in different developing countries, and with different degrees of industrial dynamics. In this regard, this study intends to stimulate academic and policy debate on this topic. An international comparative approach might be a sound strategy.

1207 World markets today will not tolerate large export subsidies as in the East Asian developmental states, and many of the technologies required to participate aggressively in world markets cannot be acquired anymore by copying or reverse engineering. This argues for more import and investment liberalization than was the case with the economies that based their development on export promotion in the 1960s.

Appendix

Appendix I: List of experts interviewed in China

Interviewee	Affiliation	Location	Institution	Contact Person	Department	Position	Date of Interview
1	DaimlerChrysler (China) Ltd.	Beijing	OEM	Dr. Jie Li	Corporate Affairs	Vice President	08.06.2006
2	DaimlerChrysler (China) Ltd.	Beijing	OEM	Matthias Wollenberg	Joint Venture Project FOTON China (Aftersales)	Head	12.06.2006
3	DaimlerChrysler (China) Ltd.	Beijing	OEM	Thomas Nothdurft	Sales CV	Senior Manager	16.06.2006
4	DaimlerChrysler (China) Ltd.	Beijing	OEM	Dr. Ulf Ausprung	Corporate Strategy Northeast Asia	Senior Manager	09.06.2006
5	DaimlerChrysler (China) Ltd.	Beijing	OEM	Yongqing Ye	Market Intelligence Dept.	Head	08.06.2006
6	Mercedes-Benz (China) Ltd.	Beijing	OEM	Peter Honegg		President & CEO	14.06.2006
7	Volkswagen (China) Investment Company Ltd.	Beijing	OEM	Gerald Schwarz	Business Planning	Director	14.06.2006
8	Volkswagen (China) Investment Company Ltd.	Beijing	OEM	Prof. Jiayou Zhao	Corporate Relations	Director	14.06.2006
9	Bosch (China) Investment Ltd.	Shangai	Supplier	Dr. Peter Kilgenstein	Original Equipment Sales	Executive Vice President	13.07.2006
10	Bosch (China) Investment Ltd.	Shangai	Supplier	Dr. Ingo Thomas	Business Development	Director	20.06.2006
11	ZF (China) Investment Co., Ltd.	Shangai	Supplier	Dr. Guohong Ye		President & CEO	19.06.2006
12	ZF (China) Investment Co., Ltd.	Shangai	Supplier	Dr. Rolf Gall	Engineering Center	Head	19.06.2006
13	ACEA	Beijing	Association	Dr. Dominik Declerq		Chief Representative	16.06.2006
14	State Information Center	Beijing	Government	Changming Xu	Business Counsulting Center	Director	13.06.2006
15	State Information Center	Beijing	Government	Luming Huang	Business Counsulting Center	Vice Director	13.06.2006
16	CAAM	Beijing	Government	Jie Yao		Deputy Secretary General	16.06.2006
17	Delegation of German Industry & Commerce Beijing	Beijing	Public corporation	Florian Kessler	Legal and Business Consultation Services	Head	08.06.2006
18	Delegation of German Industry & Commerce Beijing	Beijing	Public corporation	Chang Liu	Legal and Business Consultation Services	Manager	08.06.2006
19	Delegation of German Industry & Commerce Shanghai	Shangai	Public corporation	Bernd Reitmeier	Head of Division Investment Services, Trade Promotions, Company Pools, Procurement Services, Legal Services, IT Services	Deputy Managing Director	19.06.2006

Source: Own illustration.

Appendix II: Experts' affiliation

DaimlerChrysler AG:

DaimlerChrysler was formed in 1998 by the merger of the Daimler-Benz AG and the Chrysler Corporation. DaimlerChrysler is the fifth-largest auto producer in the world, with sales of 4.7 million units (behind GM, Toyota, Ford and VW) and 360,385 employees worldwide as of end-2006.[1208] DaimlerChrysler is divided into five divisions: the Mercedes Car Group, Chrysler Group, Truck Group, Financial Services as well as Van, Bus and Other Activities. The company produces cars and trucks under the brands Mercedes-Benz, Smart, Maybach, Chrysler, Dodge and Jeep, among others.

All of DaimlerChrysler's business units are represented in China. DaimlerChrysler has sought to achieve growth in Asia by establishing JVs with local Chinese players:

- DaimlerChrysler has had a long-standing JV with BAIC[1209] for production of sports-utility vehicles since 1983.[1210] Together with BAIC, a new JV called Beijing Benz-DaimlerChrysler Auto Ltd. (BBDCA) produces Mercedes-Benz E-class sedans (and plans to produce the 2007 generation of C-class sedans) in a new facility at the Beijing Development Area. The two parties are investing Euro 1 billion in the assembly plant.[1211] The first locally produced Mercedes-Benz rolled off the assembly line in the second half of 2006. Output will be gradually increased to around 25,000 units annually.
- In partnership with Fujian Motor Industry Group and Taiwan-based China Motor Corporation, DaimlerChrysler set up a new JV named Fujian Daimler Automotive Co Ltd. in 2007. Fujian Motor holds a 50 percent stake in the JV, with DaimlerChrysler and China Motor holding the remainder.[1212] In December 2006, the JV received government approval to produce up to 40,000 Mercedes-Benz Sprinter, Vito and Viano multipurpose vehicles annually in a new facility in Fuzhou.[1213]
- DaimlerChrysler now produces medium and heavy trucks with BAIC's Beiqi Foton following the project approval in January 2007. DaimlerChrysler is the second largest shareholder of Beiqi Foton with a 24 percent stake.

1208 Refer to DaimlerChrysler AG (2007), "Annual Report 2006", Internet Edition, reviewed 29.06.2007.0

1209 BAIC also has a JV with Hyundai.

1210 The Beijing Jeep JV was signed in January 1983 between state-owned BAIC and American Motors Corporation being the first auto JV to be established in order to produce light duty trucks. The American Motors Corporation was acquired by Chrysler in 1987 and merged with Daimler-Benz later in 1998.

1211 Plans also exist to relocate the current Jeep and Mitsubishi production to this new facility.

1212 The 50 percent share of DaimlerChrysler and China Motor Corp. Taiwan is composed of the following: DaimlerChrysler: 67.5 percent, China Motor Corp. Taiwan: 32.5 percent.

1213 Refer to CAND (2007b), p. 5.

- DaimlerChrysler Financial Services set up vehicle financing in China in September 2005.
- At the beginning of 2007, DaimlerChrysler signed a letter of intent with Chery Automobile to distribute Chery-made vehicles in the North American Free Trade Area (NAFTA) region, European region and possibly other global markets. This agreement provides the framework for how the two companies cooperate strategically and introduces a new business model that allows them to introduce all-new products more quickly, with less capital spending.[1214]

VW AG:

The German carmaker launched production of its first small car in 1945, and has established its reputation as a leading volume carmaker since then. The VW Group's activities center on two main businesses: auto and financial services. The auto division consists of the VW Group, the Audi Group, the commercial vehicles division and other companies. The VW Group consists of four major volume brands, namely Volkswagen, Audi, SEAT and Skoda, and a number of niche luxury brands, namely Bugatti, Bentley and Lamborghini. In addition, the German company produces a range of light commercial vehicles under the VW brand. In 2006, the VW Group sold a total of 5.7 million vehicles worldwide, making it the world's fifth largest carmaker.[1215]

The brand's second largest market is China where the VW Group has formed two JVs with two of the country's largest vehicle manufacturers:

- SVW is a JV with SAIC. Both partners (VW and SAIC) have 50 percent of the equity stakes.[1216] SVW operates two vehicle plants along with an engine plant. The company produces the market's leading Santana line of family cars, which includes 11 models as well as the VW GOL, Golf, Passat and Polo.[1217] Output reached 345,000 units in 2006.[1218] With many capital increases over time, the registered capital of SVW has reached RMB 10 billion.[1219] In 2005, the JV contract for SVW was extended for another 20 years.[1220]
- The VW Group has a 40 percent stake in a JV with FAW. Located in Jilin Province, FAW-VW produces the Audi A4 and A6 models, along with the Golf Bora, Golf and Jetta models. Total production amounted to 361,000 units in

1214 Refer to DaimlerChrysler AG (2005), "Facts – DaimlerChrysler in China", p. 3.

1215 Refer to Volkswagen AG (2007), "Annual Report 2006", Internet Edition, reviewed 29.06.2007.

1216 Refer to Shanghai Volkswagen (2005), Internet Edition, reviewed 29.06.2007.

1217 VW introduced its Passat model into SVW in 1998, the Polo in 2001, the Gol in 2002, and the Bora and Golf into FAW-VW in 2001 and 2003, respectively.

1218 Refer to Global Insight (2007), "Volkswagen Group Company Profile", Internet Edition, reviewed 29.06.2007.

1219 Refer to Shanghai Volkswagen (2005), Internet Edition, reviewed 29.06.2007.

1220 Ibidem.

2006.[1221] The VW Group has also established three JVs focusing on the production of engines and drive train components in China. The VW-FAW Platform Corporation in Changchun has produced running gear components including axles since 2006. At the VW-FAW engine JV, the German company is preparing for the production of an advanced low emission and low fuel consumption engine.

VW plans to double the existing annual production capacity in the next five years to 1.6 million vehicles. To reach this goal, VW intends to invest a further Euro 6.0 billion of its domestic operating profit in the country.[1222]

Robert Bosch GmbH:

The Bosch Group is the world's largest auto parts and components manufacturer and one of the largest private companies in the world. Bosch primarily manufactures and sells auto technology, industrial technology products, consumer goods and building technology. Bosch designs and produces precision auto components and systems sold to vehicle and powertrain manufacturers. Auto operations generated around 62 percent of Bosch's 2005 sales. The Group also has activities in a number of other areas, including power tools, household appliances, thermo-technology, automation technology, packaging machinery and communications technology. In 2006, Bosch employed around 258,000 people worldwide –149,000 of them in the auto sector. [1223] The group had total auto sales in 2006 of EUR 27.2 billion.[1224]

From 1909 to 2005, Bosch made a total investment of EUR 620 million and established 26 enterprises in China. Bosch's main operations in China are conducted by its auto components business.[1225] The auto components segment represents over half of Bosch's business in China. As of 2006, Bosch planned to invest a total of EUR 620 million in China until 2008 by expanding the company's ongoing activities. In 2006, sales in China exceeded EUR 1.3 billion, with 13,800 people employed in China.[1226]

In China, Bosch's auto production plants are located in Changsha, Shanghai, Suzhou and Wuxi. Between 2000 and 2005, the number of Bosch manufacturing facilities in China doubled, from 10 to 20.[1227] Bosch's first engineering center in China was built in Shanghai in 1997 and makes parts for gasoline engines. In 2004, Bosch opened

---

1221 Refer to Global Insight (2007), "Volkswagen Group Company Profile", Internet Edition, reviewed 29.06.2007.

1222 Refer to Weider (2004), p. 29.

1223 Refer to Global Insight (2007), "Volkswagen Group Company Profile", Internet Edition, reviewed 29.06.2007.

1224 Refer to Robert Bosch GmbH (2007), "Annual Report 2006", Internet Edition, reviewed 29.06.2007.

1225 Refer to Robert Bosch GmbH (2007), "Bosch in China", Internet Edition, reviewed 29.06.2007.

1226 Ibidem.

1227 Refer to Robert Bosch GmbH (2007), "Business/Economy", Internet Edition, reviewed 29.06.2007.

an engineering center for diesel systems in Wuxi, east of Shanghai and in May 2005, it opened another in Suzhou. The center in Suzhou validates materials and components sourced in China for use in Bosch operations worldwide and will be able to release products for global use from China, speeding up the sourcing process. In December 2004, Bosch set up an auto parts company in central Hunan Province, taking over some of the assets owned by a local auto parts producer, CNAIC Changdian Co., one of its long-term licensees based in Changsha, Hunan's capital. The key auto companies make safety products, diesel fuel-injection systems, spark plugs and electronic systems.

ZF Friedrichshafen AG:

ZF Friedrichshafen, based in Germany, is a leading independent manufacturer of chassis components, transmissions, steering systems, axles and other auto components, as well as complete modules. In 2005, the auto business accounted for around 87 percent of sales. ZF Friedrichshafen employed 55,050 people at 125 locations in 25 countries at the end of 2006. It is Germany's third-largest auto supplier and one of the top fifteen largest suppliers worldwide. In 2006, ZF Friedrichshafen's turnover amounted to Euro 11.659 million.[1228] ZF Friedrichshafen is a supplier to all major vehicle manufacturers, including Ford, GM, BMW, DaimlerChrysler and VW. Among ZF Friedrichshafen's customers are also the largest Chinese OEMs, such as Dongfeng, FAWER Automobile Parts[1229] and SAIC.[1230]

ZF Friedrichshafen opened four companies in China in 2005, and a new Technical Center in Shanghai in 2006. The Asia-Pacific region accounted for around EUR 1.115 million of sales in 2006, which represents 10 percent of total group sales. In 2005, ZF Friedrichshafen employed about 1,900 people in the region. The company gained most new business from carmakers moving into new markets. China is the biggest market for ZF Friedrichshafen in the region, accounting for about two-thirds of the company's Asia-Pacific sales.[1231] ZF Friedrichshafen is well-established there with a big manufacturing presence, as it entered the Chinese market more than a decade ago. Altogether, since the end of 2006, ZF Friedrichshafen has been operating 20 plants in China.[1232]

Delegations of German Industry and Commerce in Beijing and Shanghai:

The Delegations of German Industry & Commerce, and German Industry & Commerce Co. Ltd. belong to the worldwide network of 110 overseas German Chambers of Commerce, Delegations, Representative Offices and Service

[1228] Refer to ZF Friedrichshafen AG (2007), "Geschäftsbericht 2006", Internet Edition, reviewed 29.06.2007.

[1229] FAWER is a wholly-owned subsidiary of FAW.

[1230] Refer to Global Insight (2006), "Bosch Company Profile", Internet Edition, reviewed 29.06.2007.

[1231] Refer to ZF Friedrichshafen AG (2007), "Geschäftsbericht 2006", Internet Edition, reviewed 29.06.2007.

[1232] Ibidem.

Companies in more than 70 countries under the umbrella of the Association of German Chambers of Industry and Commerce in Berlin. The offices and subsidiaries of the chamber of foreign trade and commerce, and GIC in Beijing and Shanghai support German companies in establishing and extending their activities in China on a bilateral basis. In addition, GIC helps Chinese companies to develop their business in Germany.[1233]

Association des Constructeurs Européens d'Automobiles:

ACEA represents the thirteen major European car, truck and bus manufacturers, and is a key interlocutor with the EU institutions in Brussels and Strasbourg.[1234] In Beijing, it bundles the interests of its European members, conducts research, and compiles information on the development of the Chinese auto industry for the European Commission and the Chinese central government. It lobbies for its members in Chinese institutions, and provides its members with information on regulations etc. of the Chinese auto market.

China Association of Automobile Manufacturers:

The CAAM promotes nationally and internationally the interests of the entire Chinese auto industry in all fields of the motor transport sector, e.g. in economic, transport and environmental policy, technical legislation, standardization and quality assurance, and participates in the central government's industrial planning. It is responsible for investigation and research work for industrial economic development, and makes proposals about economic policy and legislation to government departments. Located in Beijing, it conducts industrial statistics surveys, sets up data collection systems, and engages in data analyses, study and information release.[1235]

State Information Center:

The State Information Center, under the State Development and Reform Committee, provides comprehensive and basic economic information and consultant services. It is a Chinese government think tank located in Beijing. It has a thousand regional offices and information centers in the country. It carries out strategic economic development research, monitors the country's economic development, and provides consultant services for government departments.[1236]

1233 Refer to German Industry of Commerce (n.d.), "About us", Internet Edition, reviewed 20.07.2006.

1234 Refer to ACEA (n.d.), Internet Edition, reviewed 20.07.2006.

1235 Refer to CAAM (n.d.), Internet Edition, reviewed 20.11.2006.

1236 Refer to State Information Center (2006), Internet Edition, reviewed 20.11.2006.

Appendix III: Topic overview for interviewees

May 22, 2006

Dear Ladies and Gentlemen,

The focus of my Ph.D. thesis at the University of Hohenheim, Germany, is on the Chinese automobile industry. I am analyzing how the central government and the governments of the municipalities in Beijing and Shanghai have promoted the development of this sector. In this respect, your assessment of the following categories is of great importance for my analysis.

1. **Company Information**

- Automotive business activities
- German-Chinese partnership and government participation

2. **Location**

- Advantages of location
- Government's investment incentives

3. **State - Industrial Policy**

- Investment and economic climate, Foreign participation (FDI)
- Organization and coordination of central – local government policy/automotive industrial policy
- Trade system (import substitution, export-oriented industrialization, WTO)

4. **Financial System**

   Banking and financial services

5. **Bureaucracy**

- Structure and organization of the bureaucracy (central - local agencies involved in automotive business development)
- Coordination of auto industry promotion

6. **State-Business Relationship**

   Information sharing and institutionalized state-business cooperation (business associations etc.)

I am looking forward to seeing you in China. Thank you in advance for your participation!

With kind regards,

Nicola Meier

Appendix IV: Questionnaire for company representatives

Name of the German company: ______________________

Interviewees: ______________________

Date: ______________________

ABOUT YOUR COMPANY

Automotive business activities:

1. What percentage of your sales comes from the automotive business line?
2. What are your automotive business activities in China (import, export, license contracts, representative office, production)?

Information on the JV:

3. How many JVs do you have in China?
4. Where are they located and when did you set them up?
5. What percentage of the JV is owned by the Chinese partner?
6. Who are the main shareholders of your Chinese partner?
7. How did you find the Chinese partner?

Information on the location:

8. What were the major factors that influenced the decision regarding your current production location?
   a) **DaimlerChrysler:** Why did you choose to produce the C- and E-Class in *Beijing*?
   b) **VW:** Why is your holding in Beijing while your production sites are located in other provinces /municipalities (Shanghai with SAIC and Changchung with FAW)?
   c) **Bosch:** Why is your holding located in Shanghai and not in Beijing, as many others are? Why do you produce locally in subsidiaries as well as in JVs with Chinese partners?
   d) **ZF:** Is there a reason why you are located in Shanghai, and not in Beijing?
9. How many people does your company employ in China?
10. What is the investment volume of your current projects in China?
11. What are the challenges to your investment in China, and especially in Beijing/Shanghai?

Government subsidies:

12. Did your company receive any investment incentives or subsidies (tax breaks, cheap credit…) from the local or national government at the time the JV was built?
13. Does your company currently receive any subsidies (e.g. tax breaks) from the local or national government?
14. Are subsidies generally restricted to any requirements (such as exports, local content etc.)?
15. Do government subsidies and tax breaks favor specific companies, activities, regions or industries?
16. Does the government distort competition by granting subsidies to specific companies?

Bureaucracy's engagement to set up JV:

17. Was the central/local bureaucracy involved in your JV negotiations?
18. How long did the negotiations with the local bureaucracy and the national partner take until the JV was finally set up (from the initial contact to the final approval)?
19. Did you have to fulfil any requirements of the Chinese state to be able to set up the JV in China?

INDUSTRIAL POLICY

Investment climate:

20. How content are you with the following aspects of the investment climate in your municipality and in China?
    a. Quality of the economic policy
    b. Economic and business climate
    c. Import/export restrictions
    d. Quality of the financial policy
    e. Possibility of raising local capital
    f. Timeframe and consistency of economic reform (and implementation)
21. Has the investment climate in China and in your locality changed over the last years?

Economic climate:

22. How content are you with the cooperation with public institutions at your locality?
23. How content are you with the cooperation with financial institutions at your locality?

Auto industry policies / Reforms:

24. The automotive industry has been declared a "pillar" industry by the Chinese central government. Is the automotive industry given due consideration/priority compared with other sectors, when the government decides policy on investment and development?
25. Is the government's policy direction consistent? Has the central/local government's auto industrial policy changed over the years?
26. Are firms usually informed clearly by the government on changes in policies and regulations affecting your industry?
27. Is the compliance with administrative requirements (permits, regulations, reporting) issued by the government burdensome?
28. Do you think there are any important reform measures with regard to the automotive industry that have not been implemented so far?

Effectiveness of policy-making in the auto industry policy:

29. Does industrial policy for the automotive sector effectively promote competition?
30. What has caused your company the greatest competitive threat (SOEs; domestic large enterprises; foreign firms producing in the domestic market, imports etc.)?
31. How many competitors for your major product do you have in the domestic market?
32. Is the central government's capacity to promote and direct the development of the auto industry impaired by conflicts between the central government and local governments or conflicts between local governments of different jurisdictions?

Trade policy – Import substitution and export promotion:

33. To what extent do tariff and non-tariff barriers influence the conduct of your business and your competitiveness in the Chinese market?
34. What percentage of your firm's sales are
    a. sold domestically
    b. exported

35. To which countries/regions do you export from China?
36. Do central/local bureaucrats promote your business sector in exporting (e.g. with tax reductions, "cheap" credits, majority stakes in JVs etc.) today, and did they before WTO?

FINANCIAL SYSTEM

State influence on the banking system / Credit allocation:

37. How would you assess the state's intervention (central and local) in the banking system (state and private banks)?
38. Does allocation of credit have a positive impact on economic development (future technologies)?
39. Do you receive credit from local Chinese banks?
40. Do the banks have certain state-initiated programs (such as special interest rates for credits) to support the development of the automotive industry?
41. Has the credit policy of local banks for automotive projects changed over the years?
42. Does the Chinese central government influence sales growth through its regulations for companies' leasing activities?
43. Did the credit tightening measures imposed by the central government in 2003/4 cause decelerating sales growth for the automotive industry, and particularly for your company?
44. Which financing issues do you face that impact the conduct and growth of your business (e.g. lack of available money for banks to lend (low net equity), high interest rates, collateral requirements of banks and financial institutions, paperwork, necessity of special connections with banks, lack of access to foreign banks, corruption of bank officials, lack of access to export finance, lack of access to long term bank loans).

BUREAUCRACY

Effectiveness / Depolitization / Meritocracy:

45. How much time does your firm's senior management spend on obtaining and maintaining licenses, permits and regulatory requirements?
46. How would you estimate the influence of the CCP on central/local bureaucrats?
47. Do high-ranking/low-ranking bureaucrats strive to advance their career in the public or private sector?
48. Do bureaucrats in your municipality usually have a high level of education?

Salaries (and illegal payments) in the private / public sector:

49. How would you estimate the salaries (and perquisites, not including bribes or other extra-legal sources of income) of higher officials in relation to those of private sector managers with roughly comparable training and responsibilities?
50. What was the development of legal income in these agencies compared with salaries in the private sector over the period in question (roughly 1980-2005)?
51. Do other firms' illegal payments influence government policies, laws or regulations that negatively affect your firm?
52. Are government officials usually neutral, or do they favor well-connected firms when they decide upon policies and contracts?

Agencies responsible for the auto industry:

53. Is the development of the auto industry in the locality coordinated and monitored by one agency responsible for the automotive industry, or by different agencies responsible for different aspects of the auto enterprises' engagement?
54. Which organizations at the central or local level are responsible for the development of the automotive industry?
55. Is the division of competence of central agencies (ministries, commissions etc.) and local ones organized well?

GOVERNMENT-BUSINESS RELATIONSHIP

Bureaucrats posts in the private sector / Membership in business associations:

56. How often do local bureaucrats occupy posts in the public and private sector at the same time?
57. What channel do you typically use to affect the outcome of laws, rules, regulations and decrees that affect your business (business association, direct ties to public officials etc.)?
58. Is your firm a member of a business association or chamber of commerce in China?
59. What services do you receive from the association or associations to which you belong (lobbying government, market information, information on new laws...)?
60. How much influence does your firm/business association have on the central or local bureaucracy when a new law, rule, regulation, or decree is being discussed?

Appendix V: Statistics of the 2001 World Bank survey

Table A45: Descriptive Statistics: Reasons for location of plant for companies in the residual sectors, 2000.

		Reasons the plant was located here when plant was established				Advantages for locating plant here now			
		Local market size	Proximity to other firms in the same line of business	Low rents or cost of buying property	Fewer regulatory requirements and taxes based on government's assignments	Local market size	Proximity to other firms in the same line of business	Low rents or cost of buying property	Fewer regulatory requirements and taxes based on government's assignments
N	Valid	473	256	518	362	455	262	481	242
	Missing	811	1028	766	922	829	1022	803	1042
Median		2	2	2	1	2	2	2	1

Source: Data compiled from World Bank survey "Competitiveness, Technology and Firm Linkages in Manufacturing Sectors" (2001).

Table A46: Descriptive Statistics: Reasons for location of plant for companies in the electronics sector, 2000.

		Reasons the plant was located here when plant was established				Advantages for locating plant here now			
		Local market size	Proximity to other firms in the same line of business	Low rents or cost of buying property	Fewer regulatory requirements and taxes based on government's assignments	Local market size	Proximity to other firms in the same line of business	Low rents or cost of buying property	Fewer regulatory requirements and taxes based on government's assignments
N	Valid	111	78	149	129	108	79	137	78
	Missing	284	317	246	266	287	316	258	317
Median		2	2.5	2	1	2	3	2	1

Source: Data compiled from World Bank survey "Competitiveness, Technology and Firm Linkages in Manufacturing Sectors" (2001).

Table A47: Descriptive Statistics: Reason for location of manufacturing plant in the auto and the electronics sector, 2000.

	Group autosec electronicssec	N	Mean Rank	Sum of Ranks
Proximity to other firms in the same line of business as an advantage for locating manufacturing plant here now	Auto sec	52	57,20	2974,50
	Electronics sec	79	71,79	5671,50
	Total	131		

Source: Data compiled from World Bank survey "Competitiveness, Technology and Firm Linkages in Manufacturing Sectors" (2001).

Table A48: Mann-Whitney U-Test: Reason for location of manufacturing plant in the auto and the electronics sector, 2000.

	Proximity to other firms in the same line of business as an advantage for locating manufacturing plant here now
Mann-Whitney U	1596,500
Wilcoxon W	2974,500
Z	-2,213
Asymp. Sig. (2-tailed)	,027

Source: Data compiled from World Bank survey "Competitiveness, Technology and Firm Linkages in Manufacturing Sectors" (2001).

Table A49: Descriptive Statistics: Government agency's or official's assistance in locating foreign technology to license in the auto sector and in the residual sectors, 2000.

			Government agency's or official's assistance in locating foreign technology to license			Total
			Yes	No	N.A.	
Group_autosec_ressec	Auto sec	Count	13	172	30	215
		% within Group_ autosec_ressec	6,0%	80,0%	14,0%	100,0%
	Residual sec	Count	37	980	267	1284
		% within Group_ autosec_ressec	2,9%	76,3%	20,8%	100,0%
Total		Count	50	1152	297	1499
		% within Group_ autosec_ressec	3,3%	76,9%	19,8%	100,0%

Source: Data compiled from World Bank survey "Competitiveness, Technology and Firm Linkages in Manufacturing Sectors" (2001).

Table A50: Chi-Square Test: Government agency's or official's assistance in locating foreign technology to license in the auto sector and in the residual sectors, 2000.

	Value	df	Asymp. Sig. (2-sided)
Pearson Chi-Square	10,204[a]	2	,006
Likelihood Ratio	9,734	2	,008
Linear-by-Linear Association	9,017	1	,003
N of Valid Cases	1499		

a. 0 cells (,0%) have expected count less than 5. The minimum expected count is 7,17.

Source: Data compiled from World Bank survey "Competitiveness, Technology and Firm Linkages in Manufacturing Sectors" (2001).

Table A51: Descriptive Statistics: Government agency's or official's assistance in identifying potential foreign clients in the auto sector and in the residual sectors, 2000.

			Government agency's or official's assistance in identifying potential foreign clients			Total
			Yes	No	N.A.	
Group_ autosec_ressec	Auto sec	Count	21	166	28	215
		% within Group_ autosec_ressec	9,8%	77,2%	13,0%	100,0%
	Residual sec	Count	88	941	255	1284
		% within Group_ autosec_ressec	6,9%	73,3%	19,9%	100,0%
Total		Count	109	1107	283	1499
		% within Group_ autosec_ressec	7,3%	73,8%	18,9%	100,0%

Source: Data compiled from World Bank survey "Competitiveness, Technology and Firm Linkages in Manufacturing Sectors" (2001).

Table A52: Chi-Square Test: Government agency's or official's assistance in identifying potential foreign clients in the auto sector and in the residual sectors, 2000.

	Value	df	Asymp. Sig. (2-sided)
Pearson Chi-Square	7,093[a]	2	,029
Likelihood Ratio	7,384	2	,025
Linear-by-Linear Association	7,054	1	,008
N of Valid Cases	1499		

a. 0 cells (,0%) have expected count less than 5. The minimum expected count is 15,63.

Source: Data compiled from World Bank survey "Competitiveness, Technology and Firm Linkages in Manufacturing Sectors" (2001).

Table A53: Descriptive Statistics: Introduction of new products into the plant by licensing technology from a foreign firm in the auto sector and in the electronics sector since 1998.

			Licensed technology from foreign firm		Total
			Yes	No	
Group_autosec_ electronicssec	Auto sec	Count	40	93	133
		% within Group_autosec_ electronicssec	30,1%	69,9%	100,0%
	Electronics sec	Count	57	214	271
		% within Group_autosec_ electronicssec	21,0%	79,0%	100,0%
Total		Count	97	307	404
		% within Group_autosec_ electronicssec	24,0%	76,0%	100,0%

Source: Data compiled from World Bank survey "Competitiveness, Technology and Firm Linkages in Manufacturing Sectors" (2001).

Table A54: Chi-Square Test: Introduction of new products into the plant by licensing technology from a foreign firm in the auto sector and in the electronics sector since 1998.

	Value	df	Asymp. Sig. (2-sided)	Exact Sig. (2-sided)	Exact Sig. (1-sided)
Pearson Chi-Square	3,998[b]	1	,046		
Continuity Correction[a]	3,518	1	,061		
Likelihood Ratio	3,903	1	,048		
Fisher's Exact Test				,048	,031
Linear-by-Linear Association	3,988	1	,046		
N of Valid Cases	404				

a. Computed only for a 2x2 table

b. 0 cells (,0%) have expected count less than 5. The minimum expected count is 31,93.

Source: Data compiled from World Bank survey "Competitiveness, Technology and Firm Linkages in Manufacturing Sectors" (2001).

Table A55: Descriptive Statistics: Introduction of new process improvements into the plant by licensing processes from a foreign firm in the auto sector and in the residual sectors since 1998.

			Licensed process from foreign firm		
			Yes	No	Total
Group_autosec_ressec	Auto sec	Count	35	98	133
		% within Group_autosec_ressec	26,3%	73,7%	100,0%
	Residual sec	Count	82	501	583
		% within Group_autosec_ressec	14,1%	85,9%	100,0%
Total		Count	117	599	716
		% within Group_autosec_ressec	16,3%	83,7%	100,0%

Source: Data compiled from World Bank survey "Competitiveness, Technology and Firm Linkages in Manufacturing Sectors" (2001).

Table A56: Chi-Square Test: Introduction of new process improvements into the plant by licensing processes from a foreign firm in the auto sector and in the residual sectors since 1998.

	Value	df	Asymp. Sig. (2-sided)	Exact Sig. (2-sided)	Exact Sig. (1-sided)
Pearson Chi-Square	11,889[b]	1	,001		
Continuity Correction[a]	11,009	1	,001		
Likelihood Ratio	10,768	1	,001		
Fisher's Exact Test				,001	,001
Linear-by-Linear Association	11,872	1	,001		
N of Valid Cases	716				

a. Computed only for a 2x2 table

b. 0 cells (,0%) have expected count less than 5. The minimum expected count is 21,73.

Source: Data compiled from World Bank survey "Competitiveness, Technology and Firm Linkages in Manufacturing Sectors" (2001).

Table A57: Descriptive Statistics: New process improvement by licensing processes from foreign firms in the auto and electronics sector since 1998.

			Licensed process from foreign firms		Total
			Yes	No	
Group_autosec_ electronicssec	Auto sec	Count	35	98	133
		% within Group_autosec_ electronicssec	26,3%	73,7%	100,0%
	Electronics sec	Count	47	224	271
		% within Group_autosec_ electronicssec	17,3%	82,7%	100,0%
Total		Count	82	322	404
		% within Group_autosec_ electronicssec	20,3%	79,7%	100,0%

Source: Data compiled from World Bank survey "Competitiveness, Technology and Firm Linkages in Manufacturing Sectors" (2001).

Table A58: Chi-Square Test: New process improvement by licensing processes from foreign firms in the auto and electronics sector since 1998.

	Value	df	Asymp. Sig. (2-sided)	Exact Sig. (2-sided)	Exact Sig. (1-sided)
Pearson Chi-Square	4,440[b]	1	,035		
Continuity Correction [a]	3,903	1	,048		
Likelihood Ratio	4,308	1	,038		
Fisher's Exact Test				,048	,025
Linear-by-Linear Association	4,429	1	,035		
N of Valid Cases	404				

a. Computed only for a 2x2 table

b. 0 cells (,0%) have expected count less than 5. The minimum expected count is 27,00.

Source: Data compiled from World Bank survey "Competitiveness, Technology and Firm Linkages in Manufacturing Sectors" (2001).

Table A59: Descriptive Statistics: Days for consignments of a major input experienced before clearing local customs in the auto sector and the electronics sector, 2000.

	Group_autosec_electronicssec	N	Mean	Std. Deviation	Std. Error Mean
Days for consignments of a major imported raw material to clear local customs	Auto sec	77	11,8312	19,08871	2,17536
	Electronics sec	194	6,6649	8,96025	,64331

Source: Data compiled from World Bank survey "Competitiveness, Technology and Firm Linkages in Manufacturing Sectors" (2001).

Table A60: Independent Samples T-Test: Days for consignments of a major input experienced before clearing local customs in the auto sector and the electronics sector, 2000.

		Levene's Test for Equality of Variances		t-test for Equality of Means						
									95% Confidence Interval of the Difference	
		F	Sig.	t	df	Sig. (2-tailed)	Mean Difference	Std. Error Difference	Lower	Upper
Days for consignments of a major imported raw material to clear local customs	Equal variances assumed	20,291	,000	3,027	269	,003	5,16622	1,70665	1,80613	8,52631
	Equal variances not assumed			2,277	89,604	,025	5,16622	2,26849	,65920	9,67324

Source: Data compiled from World Bank survey "Competitiveness, Technology and Firm Linkages in Manufacturing Sectors" (2001).

Table A61: Descriptive Statistics: Approximate shares of capital from different sources in the auto sector and in the electronics sector (in percent), 2000.

	Group_autosec_electronicssec	N	Mean	Std. Deviation	Std. Error Mean
Retained earnings/internal funds	Auto sec	215	43,0372	37,48718	2,55660
	Electronics sec	390	51,4795	38,22459	1,93558
Bank loans	Auto sec	215	27,0884	31,95816	2,17953
	Electronics sec	390	21,4974	27,78144	1,40677
Loan from other financial institution (e.g. credit union, finance company etc.)	Auto sec	215	2,4744	9,82692	,67019
	Electronics sec	390	,9590	5,96376	,30199
Loan from parent or partner company	Auto sec	215	5,2651	18,73149	1,27748
	Electronics sec	390	9,1821	25,93159	1,31310

Source: Data compiled from World Bank survey "Competitiveness, Technology and Firm Linkages in Manufacturing Sectors" (2001).

Table A62: Independent Samples T-Test: Approximate shares of capital from different sources in the auto sector and in the electronics sector (in percent), 2000.

		Levenes Test for Equality of Variances		t-test for Equality of Means						
									95% Confidence Interval of the Difference	
		F	Sig.	t	df	Sig. (2-tailed)	Mean Difference	Std. Error Difference	Lower	Upper
Retained earnings/internal funds	Equal variances assumed	,246	,620	-2,618	603	,009	-8,44228	3,22481	-14,77550	-2,10905
	Equal variances not assumed			-2,633	448,558	,009	-8,44228	3,20666	-14,74422	-2,14033
Bank loans	Equal variances assumed	8,989	,003	2,244	603	,025	5,59094	2,49153	,69781	10,48407
	Equal variances not assumed			2,155	392,017	,032	5,59094	2,59410	,49085	10,69102
Loan from other financial institution (e.g. credit union, finance company etc.)	Equal variances assumed	18,371	,000	2,359	603	,019	1,51544	,64251	,25361	2,77728
	Equal variances not assumed			2,062	302,854	,040	1,51544	,73509	,06892	2,96197
Loan from parent or partner company	Equal variances assumed	13,865	,000	-1,952	603	,051	-3,91694	2,00710	-7,85868	,02481
	Equal variances not assumed			-2,138	560,737	,033	-3,91694	1,83199	-7,51533	-,31854

Source: Data compiled from World Bank survey "Competitiveness, Technology and Firm Linkages in Manufacturing Sectors" (2001).

Table A63: Descriptive Statistics: Representation of members' views to the government as one function the most important business associations perform on a regular basis for companies in the auto sector and in the electronics sector, 2000.

			Representation of members' view and concerns to the government		
			Yes	No	Total
Group_autosec_ electronicssec	Auto sec	Count	53	80	133
		% within Group_autosec_ electronicssec	39,8%	60,2%	100,0%
	Electronics sec	Count	109	115	224
		% within Group_autosec_ electronicssec	48,7%	51,3%	100,0%
Total		Count	162	195	357
		% within Group_autosec_ electronicssec	45,4%	54,6%	100,0%

Source: Data compiled from World Bank survey "Competitiveness, Technology and Firm Linkages in Manufacturing Sectors" (2001).

References

Abele, C. (2006): Jagd nach Innovationen, in: MARKETS (bfai), Vol. 05, pp. 8-13.

Abrenica, J. (1998): The Asian Automotive Industry: Assessing the roles of state and market in the age of global competition, in: Asian Pacific Economic Literature, Vol. 12, No. 1, pp. 12-26.

ACEA (n.d.): Homepage retrieved from http://www.acea.be/ on 20.07.2006.

ADAC (2005): "Das erste chinesische Auto im ADAC-Crashtest", retrieved from http://www.adac.de/Tests/Crash_Tests/jiangling_landwind/default.asp?TL=2 on 13.09.2006, last update September 2005.

Agricultural Bank of China (2007): "Annual Report 2006", retrieved from http://www.abchina.com/content/56/1200046/1/001.pdf on 22.08.2007.

Ahrens, J. / Mengeringhaus, P. (2006): Institutional Change and Economic Transition: Market-Enhancing Governance, Chinese-Style, in: The European Journal of Comparative Economics, Vol. 3, No. 1, pp. 75-102.

Akamatsu, K. (1962): A historical pattern of economic growth in developing countries, in: The Developing Economies, Vol. 1, No. 1, pp. 3-25.

Alexander, R. (1987): The Import Substitution Strategy of Economic Development, in: Dietz, J. / Street, J. (Eds.): Latin America's Economic Development. Institutionalist and Structuralist Perspectives, Boulder, CO, Lynne Rienner Publishers, pp. 118 - 127.

Alston, L. / Libecap, G. / Mueller, B. (1999): Titles, Conflict, and Land Use: The Development of Property Rights and Land Reform on the Brazilian Amazon Frontier, Ann Arbor, MI: University of Michigan Press.

Alt, J. / Shepsle, K. (1990): Perspectives on Positive Political Economy, Cambridge, UK: Cambridge University Press.

Amsden, A. (1989a): Asia's next giant - South Korea and Late Industrialization, New York, NY: Oxford University Press.

Amsden, A. / Kim, L. (1989b): A Comparative Analysis of Local and Transnational Corporations in the Korean Automobile Industry, in: Kim, D.-K. / Kim, L. (Eds.): Management Behind Industrialization: Readings in Korean Business, Seoul, Korea University Press, pp. 579-596.

Amsden, A. / Hikino, T. (2000): The Bark is Worse Than the Bite: New WTO Law and Late Industrialization, in: The Annals of the American Academy of Political and Social Science, Vol. 570, No. 1, pp. 104-114.

Amsden, A. (2001): The Rise of "The Rest": Challenges to the West from Late-Industrializing Economies, New York, NY: Oxford University Press.

Amyx, J. (The International Centre for the Study of East Asian Development) (2005): "Reforming Government-Backed Financial Institutions: The battle for postal savings reform in Japan", retrieved from http://www.icsead.or.jp/7publication/workingpp/wp2005/2005-17.pdf on 01.05.2007, last update November 2005.

Aoki, M. / Murdock, K. / Okuno-Fujiwara, M. (1997): Beyond the East Asian Miracle: Introducing the Market-Enhancing View, in: Aoki, M. / Murdock, K. / Okuno-Fujiwara, M. (Eds.): The Role of Government in East Asian Economic Development, Oxford, UK, Clarendon Press, pp. xv-xxi.

Arendt, H. (1951): The Origins of Totalitarianism, New York, NY: Harcourt Brace Jovanovich.

Asia Times Online (2002): "China: Banking on bank reform", retrieved from http://www.atimes.com/china/DF01Ad05.html on 10.09.2006, last update 01.06.2002.

Asia Times (2006): "China's extra-special zones", retrieved from http://www.atimes.com/atimes/China_Business/HI12Cb03.html on 17.01.2007.

Asia Times Online (2007): "Taxing times for China's foreign firms", retrieved from http://www.atimes.com/atimes/China_Business/IJ12Cb01.html on 12.10.2007, last update 12.10.2007.

Asian Development Bank Institute (2006): "The Internal Environment and Input Conditions", retrieved from http://www.adbi.org/discussion-paper/2006/09/26/2006.prc.innovation.system/the.internal.environment.and.input.conditions/ on 27.04.2007, last update 26.09.2006.

AT Kearney (together with European Union Chamber of Commerce and Auto Components Working Group) (2005): China Auto Policy-Making - Development Process and Opportunities for Foreign Participation, 21.11.2005, Beijing, pp. 1-35.

Atteslander, P. / Cromm, J. / Grabow, B. / Maurer, A. / Sieger, G. / Zipp, G. (2000): Methoden der empirischen Sozialforschung, Berlin: de Gruyter Studienbuch.

Aufrecht, S. / Li, S. (1995): Reform with Chinese characteristics: the context of Chinese civil service reform, in: Public Administration Review, Vol. 55, No. 2, pp. 175-182.

Auty, R. (1996): Industrial Policy and Market Structure: Korean Auto Assembly, in: Tijdschrift voor Economische en Sociale Geografie, Vol. 87, pp. 419-430.

Bai, C.-E. / Du, Y. / Tao, Z. / Tong, S. (2004): Local Protectionism and Regional Specialization: Evidence from China's Industries, William Davidson Working Paper, No. 565, pp. 1-33.

Bain, J. (1968): Industrial Organization, New York, NY: John Wiley.

Balassa, B. (1981a): The Newly Industrializing Countries in the World Economy, New York, NY: Pergamon Press.

Balassa, B. (1981b): The process of industrial development and alternative development strategies, in: Haggard, S. (Ed.): The International Political Economy and the developing countries, Vol. I, Brookfield, VT, Edward Elgar Publishing Limited, pp. 445-483.

Bank of China (2007): "Annual Report 2006", retrieved from http://www.bank-of-china.com/en/static/investor.html on 22.08.2007.

Bardhan, P. (2002): Decentralization of governance and development, in: Journal of Economic Perspective, Vol. 16, No. 4, pp. 185-205.

Barnett, S. (2004): Banking Sector Developments, in: Prasad, E. (Ed.): China's Growth and Integration into the World Economy, Occasional Paper 232, Washington D.C., International Monetary Fund, pp. 43-50.

Beamish, P. / Banks, J. (1987): Equity Joint Ventures and the Theory of the Multinational Enterprises, in: Journal of International Business Studies, Vol. 18 No. 1, pp. 1-16.

Beeson, M. (2004): "Politics and Markets in East Asia: Is the developmental state compatible with globalisation?" retrieved from http://eprint.uq.edu.au/archive/00000885/01/mb_cwo_04.pdf on 04.06.2004.

Beijing Municipal Bureau of Industrial Development (n.d.): "Auto Manufacturing Industry - Development Advantages", retrieved from http://www.bjid.gov.cn/english/auto/autoAdv3.jsp on 21.07.2007.

Beijing Municipal Bureau of Statistics: various issues of "Beijing Statistical Yearbook", retrieved from http://www.bjstats.gov.cn/esite/.

Beijing Review (1992): Party Congress Introduces Market Economy, in: Beijing Review, Vol. 35, No. 42, pp. 5-6.

Beijing Review (2006): "Getting Out of First Gear", retrieved from http://www.bjreview.com.cn/ml-zhong/Index-2006-10-z.htm on 08.08.2006, last update 09.03. 2006.

Beijing Review (2006): "Growing Pains or Growing Gains?" retrieved from http://www.bjreview.com.cn/backgrounder/txt/2006-12/23/content_51899.htm on 16.07.2007, last update 21.12.2006.

Belaisch, A. / Zanello, A. (2006): Deepening Financial Ties, in: Finance and Development, Vol. June 2006, pp. 16-19.

Belke, A. / Spies, J. (2007): Die Außenhandelspolitik der EU gegenüber China, in: Wirtschaftsdienst, Vol. 7, pp. 458-466.

Belke, A. (2007): "Wirtschaftliche Macht als Instrument der Außenpolitik am Beispiel Chinas", Fachgespräch der Bundestagsfraktion Bündnis 90 / Die Grünen, Berlin, retrieved from http://www.makro.uni-essen.de/_lehre/pdfs/Berlin_19_Sept_07.pdf on 10.11.2007, last update 19.09.2007.

Bennett, A. (1999): Causal Interference in Case Studies: From Mill's Methods to Causal Mechanisms. Paper presented at the annual meeting of the American Political Science Association. Atlanta, GA, pp. 1-28.

Benninghaus, H. (2002 and 2005): Deskriptive Statistik - Eine Einführung für Sozialwissenschaftler, Wiesbaden: VS Verlag für Sozialwissenschaftler.

Berglas, E. / Razin, A. (1974): Protection and Real Profits, in: The Canadian Journal of Economics, Vol. 7, No. 4, pp. 655-664.

Bian, Y. / Logan, J. (1996): Market Transition and the Persistence of Power: The Changing Stratification System in Urban China, in: American Sociological Review, Vol. 61, pp. 739-758.

Bitsch, V. (2000): Die Fallstudie als Forschungsansatz: Konjunktur für eine vernachlässigte Strategie der Erkenntnisgewinnung, in: Gartenbauwirtschaft, Vol. 65, No. 6, pp. 229-236.

Blackaby, F. (1979): De-Industrialisation, London, UK: Heinemann Educational Books.

Blomström, M. / Kokko, A. (1998): Multinational Corporations and Spillovers, in: Journal of Economic Surveys, Vol. 12, No. 2, pp. 1-31.

Bonoma, T. (1985): Case Research in Marketing: Opportunities, Problems, and a Process, in: Journal of Marketing Research, Vol. 22, No. 2, pp. 199-208.

Borensztein, E. / De Gregorio, J. / Lee, J.-W. (1998): How Does Foreign Direct Investment Affect Economic Growth?, in: Journal of International Economics, Vol. 45, pp. 115-135.

Bortz, J. (2005): Statistik für Sozialwissenschaftler, Berlin: Springer.

Bosworth, B. / Collins, S. (1999): Capital Flows to Developing Economies: Implications for Saving and Investment, in: Brookings Papers on Economic Activity, Vol. 1, pp. 143-169.

Brander, J. / Spencer, B. (1985): Export subsidies and international market share rivalry, in: Journal of International Economics, Vol. 18, pp. 83-100.

Breslin, S. (1996): China: developmental state or dysfunctional development?, in: Third World Quarterly, Vol. 17, No. 4, pp. 689-706.

Breslin, S. (1999): The politics of Chinese trade and the Asian financial crises: questioning the wisdom of export-led growth, in: Third World Quarterly, Vol. 20, No. 6, pp. 1179-1199.

Brobak, J. / Nye, J. (1997): The Frontiers of the New Institutional Economics, San Diego, CA: Academic.

Brzezinski, Z. / Friedrich, C. (1956): Totalitarian Dictatorship and Autocracy, Cambridge, MA: Harvard University Press.

Buchanan, J. (1980): Rent Seeking and Profit Seeking, in: Buchanan, J. / Tollison, R. / Tullock, G. (Eds.): Toward a Theory of the Rent-Seeking Society, College Station, TX, College Station, pp. 3-16.

Bühl, A. / Zöfel, P. (2000): SPSS - Einführung in die moderne Datenanalyse unter Windows, München: Addison-Wesley.

Bureau of Foreign Trade and Economic Cooperation of Guangzhou Municipality (2005): "Guangzhou - An Automotive Industry Base with the Strongest Competitiveness in the World", retrieved from http://www.gz.gov.cn/vfs/subsite/QFZZQNCH-UEYR-RYE4-CQEP-PO0PXEO7LORY/content/content.jsp?contentId=257824&catId=3371 on 07.09.2007, last update 25.11.2005.

Bureau of Foreign Trade and Economic Cooperation of Guangzhou Municipality (2005): "Guangzhou Honda Automobile Export Base project", retrieved from http://www.gzboftec.gov.cn/articles/2005-10/15118.htm on 07.09.2007, last update 25.11.2005.

Burki, S. / Perry, G. / Dillinger, W. (1999): Beyond the Center: Decentralizing the State, Washington D.C.: World Bank.

Burns, J. (1987): China's nomenklatura sytem, in: Problems of Communism, Vol. 36, pp. 36-51.

Burns, J. (1989a): Chinese civil service reform: the 13th Party Congress proposals, in: The China Quarterly, Vol. 120, pp. 739-770.

Burns, J. (1989b): The Chinese Communist Party's Nomenklatura System: A Documentary Study of Party Control of Leadership Selection, 1979 - 1984, Armonk, NY: M.E. Sharpe.

Burns, J. (1993): Administrative reform in China: issues and prospects, in: International Journal of Public Administration, Vol. 16, No. 9, pp. 1345-1369.

Business and Industry Advisory Committee to the OECD (BIAC) (2007): "BIAC Priorities for Regulatory Reform in China", retrieved from http://www.biac.org/statements/nme/07-02_Regulatory_Reform_Review.pdf on 28.07.2007, last update 07.02.2007.

Businessweek (2003): "Navigating China's Standards Regime", retrieved from http://www.chinabusinessreview.com/public/0305/weeks.html on 19.07.2007, last update 09.05.2003.

Businessweek (2006): "China's Booming Car Market Defies Pundits", retrieved from http://www.businessweek.com/globalbiz/content/jul2006/gb20060711_947833.htm?chan=autos_autos+index+page_news on 18.07.2007, last update 11.07.2006.

Businessweek (2006): "China's Drive for Local Car Brands", retrieved from http://www.businessweek.com/print/globalbiz/content/may2006/gb20060530_676262.htm on 08.08.2007, last update 30.05.2006.

Businessweek (2007): "The Quality Drag on China's Car Industry", retrieved from http://www.businessweek.com/globalbiz/content/jun2007/gb20070629_028900.htm on 18.07.2007, last update 29.06.2007.

Cabestan, J. (1992): Civil service reform in China: the draft provisional order concerning civil servants, in: International Review of Administrative Sciences, Vol. 58, No. 3, pp. 421-436.

Cai, H. / Fang, H. / Xu, L. (2005): Eat, Drink, Firms and Government: An Investigation of Corruption from Entertainment and Travel Costs of Chinese Firms, National Bureau of Economic Research Working Papers, Vol. 11592, No. September 2005.

Callon, S. (1995): Divided Sun: MITI and the Breakdown of Japanese High-Tech Industrial Policy, 1975-1993, Stanford: Stanford University Press.

CAND (2007a): CAND Weekly Digest, 01.09. – 07.09.2007, pp. 1-24, Beijing.

CAND (2007b): CAND Weekly Digest, 20.10. – 26.10.2007, pp. 1-42, Beijing.

Carr, J. / Landa, J. (1983): The Economics of Symbols, Clan Names and Religions, in: The Journal of Legal Studies, Vol. 12, No. 1, pp. 135-156.

Carreno, E. (2001): Latin America's 1980's and Asia's 1990's debt crisis: a comparison, in: MACLAS Latin American Essays, Vol. March 01, pp. 1-5.

Central Committee of the Communist Party of China (1991): Major Documents of the People's Republic of China - Selected Important Documents Since the Third Plenary Session of the Eleventh Central Committee of the Communist Party of China (December 1978-November 1989), Beijing: Foreign Langugage Press.

Chan, S. (1990): East Asian Dynamism - Growth, Order, and Security in the Pacific Region, Boulder, CO, Westview Press.

Chan, H. / Suizhou, E. (2007): Civil Service Law in the People's Republic of China: A Return to Cadre Personnel Management, in: Public Administration Review, Vol. May/June 2007, pp. 383-398.

Chang, H.-J. (1994): The Political Economy of Industrial Policy, New York, NY: St. Martin's Press.

Chaudhuri, B. (1989): Trade Policies, Development Strategies, and Technological Capabilities: A Study of the Automotive Industry in India, Brazil and South Korea, Inaugural Dissertation, University of California, Berkeley, CA.

Che, J. / Qian, Y. (1998): Institutional Environment, Community Government, and Corporate Governance: Understanding China's Township-Village Enterprises, William Davidson Institute Working Papers Series, Vol. 59, pp. 1-30.

Che, J. (2002): Rent Seeking and Government Ownership of Firms: An Application to China's Township–Village Enterprises, in: Journal of Comparative Economics, Vol. 30, pp. 787–811.

Chen, J. (2003): Capital adequacy of Chinese banks: Evaluation and enhancement, in: Journal of Banking Regulation, Vol. 4, No. 4, pp. 320-327.

Chew, D. (1990): Recent developments in civil service pay in China, in: International Labour Review, Vol. 129, No. 6, pp. 773-782.

China Association of Automobile Manufacturers (n.d.): Homepage retrieved from http://www.caam.org.cn/ on 20.11.2006.

China Association of Development Zones (2002): "World Top 500 in ETDZs", retrieved from http://www.cadz.org.cn/en/zgkfq/500.asp on 25.10.2006.

China Auto (2006): News, in: China AUTO, Vol. December 2006, pp. 1-22.

China Auto (2007): News, in: China AUTO, Vol. January 2007, pp. 1-22.

China Automotive Technology & Research Center (2004): Automotive Industry of China - China Auto Supplementary Issue, Tianjin: China Automotive Technology & Research Center.

China Banking Regulatory Commission (2005): "Loan conditions of major banking institutions", retrieved from http://www.cbrc.gov.cn/mod_en00/jsp/en004002.jsp?infoID=722&type=1 on 06.04.2006.

China Business Infocenter (2005): "FAW posts big loss, government tries to help", retrieved from http://www.cbiz.cn/NEWS/showarticle.asp?id=2328 on 27.08.2007, last update 11.07.2005.

China Business Review (1998): "Shifting Gears", retrieved from http://www.chinabusinessreview.com/public/9711/xing.html on 16.10.2006, last update 07.01.1998.

China Business Review (2004): "WTO: China enters year three", retrieved from http://www.chinabusinessreview.com/public/0401/01.html on 03.10.2006.

China Construction Bank (2007): "Annual Report 2006", retrieved from http://www.ccb.com/portal/uploadFiles/annualreport2006.1177728546000.pdf on 22.08.2007.

China Daily (2001): "Tenth Five-Year Plan of Banking Industry and its Development (Yearbook of China Financial Market 2001)", retrieved from http://bizchina.chinadaily.com.cn/guide/industry/industry1.htm on 28.03.2006.

China Daily (2003): "Focus: China embarks on civil service reforms", retrieved from http://www.chinadaily.com.cn/en/doc/2003-09/23/content_266501.htm on 23.03.2006, last update 23.09.2003.

China Daily (2005): "US lawmakers meddle in CNOOC's Unocal bid", retrieved from http://www.chinadaily.com.cn/english/doc/2005-07/06/content_457677.htm on 17.11.2006, last update 06.07.2005.

China Daily (2006): "Regulations of Qinghai Provincial People's Government on Encouragement of Foreign Investment", retrieved from http://www.chinadaily.com.cn/bizchina/2006-05/18/content_594292.htm on 10.07.2007, last update 18.05.2006.

China Daily (2007): "Beijing Benz may break even in 2007", retrieved from http://www.china.org.cn/english/BAT/208965.htm on 13.09.2007, last update 26.04.2007.

China Daily (2007): "Central bank raises interest rates, reserve requirements", retrieved from http://www.chinadaily.com.cn/china/2007-05/18/content_876031.htm on 23.10.2007, last update 18.05.2007.

China Economic Net (2007): "SVW to develop new model for Chinese and US markets", retrieved from http://en.ce.cn/Industries/Auto/200707/19/t20070719_12223438.shtml on 11.08.2007, last update 19.07.2007.

China Export-Import Bank (n.d.): "The Export-Import Bank of China", retrieved from http://english.eximbank.gov.cn/profile/introduction.jsp on 27.08.2007.

China Export Import Bank (2006): "Export Seller's Credit", retrieved from http://english.eximbank.gov.cn/business/credit.jsp on 06.07.2006.

China Gate (n.d.): "The System of Civil Servant", retrieved from http://www.chinagate.com.cn/english/1120.htm on 13.07.2007.

China.org (2000): "Law of the People's Republic of China on Chinese-Foreign Contractual Joint Ventures; adopted on 13.04.1988, revised on 31.10.2000", retrieved from http://www.china.org.cn/english/government/207090.htm on 17.7.2007.

China.org (2006): "Law of the People's Republic of China on Enterprise Bankruptcy", retrieved from http://www.china.org.cn/english/features/Legislations%20from%202002-2006/199768.htm on 25.10.2007, last update 27.08.2006.

China.org (2007): "Political system and state structure", retrieved from http://www.china.org.cn/e-china/politicalsystem/stateCouncil.htm on 09.09.2007, last update 13.07.2007.

China Regulatory Commission (2007): "Annual Report 2006", retrieved from http://zhuanti.cbrc.gov.cn/subject/subject/nianbao/english/ywqb.pdf on 09.11.2007, last update 29.06.2007.

China-Singapore Suzhou Industrial Park Development Co. Ltd (2007): "Preferential Policies", retrieved from http://www.cssd.com.cn/tzzn1.shtml on 17.01.2007.

Chinese Academy of Engineering and National Research Council (2003): Personal Cars in China, Washington D.C.: The National Academics Press.

Chinese Government (2005): "Economic System", retrieved from http://www.gov.cn/english/2006-02/08/content_182584.htm on 28.03.2006.

Chinese Government (2005): "New and high-tech development zones", retrieved from http://english.gov.cn/2006-02/09/content_184039.htm on 17.11.2006.

Chinese Government (2006): "National programs for science and technology", retrieved from http://www.gov.cn/english/2006-02/09/content_184156.htm on 28.03.2006, last update 09.02.2006.

Chinese Government (2006): "Reform of Financial System", retrieved from http://www.gov.cn/english/2006-02/08/content_182579.htm on 28.03.2006, last update 08.02.2006.

Chou, B. (2005): Implementing the Reform of Performance Appraisal in China's Civil Service, in: China Information, Vol. 19, No. 1, pp. 39-65.

Chou, B. (2006): Downsizing Administrative Licensing System and Private Sector Development in the PRC: A Preliminary Assessment, ADB Institute Discussion Paper, Vol. 52, pp. 1-30.

Clifford, L. (1994): Troubled Tiger: Businessmen, bureaucrats and generals in South Korea, New York, NY: M.E. Sharpe.

Coase, R. (1937): The Nature of the Firm, in: Economica, Vol. 4, No. 16, pp. 386-405.

Coase, R. (1960): The problem of social cost, in: The Journal of Law & Economics, Vol. 3, pp. 1-44.

Coase, R. (1992): The Institutional Structure of Production, in: American Economic Review, Vol. 82, pp. 713-719.

Collier, D. / Mahoney, J. (1996): Insights and Pitfalls: Selection Bias in Qualitative Research, in: World Politics, Vol. 49, pp. 56-91.

Collignon, S. / Pisani-Ferry, J. / Park, Y. (1999): Exchange Rate Policies in Emerging Asian Countries, New York, NY: Routledge.

Congressional-Executive Commission on China (2005): "Annual Report, V. Development of Rule of Law and the Institutions of Democratic Governance", retrieved from http://www.cecc.gov/pages/annualRpt/annualRpt05/2005_5f_commercialrol.php on 27.08.2007, last update 07.12.2005.

Cooke, F. (2003): Seven Reforms in Five Decades - Civil service reform and its human resource implications in China, in: Journal of the Asia Pacific Economy, Vol. 8, No. 3, pp. 380-404.

Cox, A. (1986): State, Finance, and Industry in Comparative Perspective, Brighton, UK: Wheatsheaf Books.

Crespo, N. / Fontoura, M. (2007): Determinant Factors of FDI Spillovers - What Do We Really Know?, in: World Development, Vol. 35, No. 3, pp. 410-425.

Creswell, J. (2003): Research Design - Qualitative, Quantitative, and Mixed Methods Approaches, Thousand Oaks, CA: Sage Publications.

Cullis, J. / Jones, P. (1987): Microeconomics and the Public Economy: A Defence of Leviathan, Oxford, UK: Basil Blackwell.

DaimlerChrysler AG (2004): "Fertigung von Mercedes-Limousinen in China durch Staatsrat genehmigt", retrieved from http://www.daimlerchrysler.com on 22.05.2006, last update 03.05.2004.

DaimlerChrysler AG (2005): Facts - DaimlerChrysler in China, pp. 1-31.

DaimlerChrysler AG (2007): "Annual Report 2006", retrieved from http://www.daimlerchrysler.com/Projects/c2c/channel/documents/1003904_DCX_2006_Geschaeftsbericht.pdf on 29.06.2007.

de Vaus, D. (2001): Research Design in Social Research, London, UK: Sage Publications.

Demsetz, H. (1967): Toward a Theory of Property Rights, in: Demsetz, H. (Ed.): Ownership, Control, and the Firm - The Organization of Economic Activity, Oxford, UK, Basil Blackwell, pp. 104-116.

Deng, X. (1978): "Speech at the opening ceremony of the national conference on science", retrieved from http://english.peopledaily.com.cn/dengxp/vol2/text/b1170.html on 29.05.2006, last update 18.03.1978

Deng, X. (1979): "Some Comments on Economic Work", retrieved from http://english.people.com.cn/dengxp/vol2/text/b1330.html on 19.03.2006, last update 04.10.1979.

Deng, X. (1984): "Building a socialism with a specifically Chinese character", retrieved from http://english.people.com.cn/dengxp/vol3/text/c1220.html on 19.03.2006, last update 30.06.1984.

Deng, X. (1984): Selected Works of Deng Xiaoping (1975-1982), Beijing: Foreign Languages Press.

Deng, X. (1985): "Special Economic Zones should shift their economy from a domestic orientation to an external orientation", retrieved from http://english.peopledaily.com.cn/dengxp/vol3/text/c1440.html on 19.03.2006, last update 01.08.1985.

Deng, X. (1992): "Excerpts from talks given in Wuchang, Shenzhen, Zhuhai and Shanghai", retrieved from http://english.people.com.cn/dengxp/vol3/text/d1200.html on 19.03.2006, last update 18.01.-21.02.1992.

Denzin, N. (1978): The Research Act, New York, NY: McGraw-Hill.

Deyo, F. (1987): Coalitions, Institutions and Linkage Sequencing - Toward a Strategic Capacity Model of East Asian Development, in: Deyo, F. (Ed.): The Political Economy of the New Asian Industrialism, Ithaca, NY, Cornell University Press, pp. 227-248.

Doleys, T. (2000): Member states and the European Commission: theoretical insights from the new economics of organization, in: Journal of European Public Policy, Vol. 7, No. 4, pp. 532-553.

Dorn, J. (1989): Economic Reform in China, in: Cato Journal, Vol. 8, No. 3, pp. 563-566.

Downs, A. (1957): An Economic Theory of Democracy, New York, NY: Harper.

Duchêne, F. / Sheperd, G. (1987): Managing Industrial Change in Western Europe, London, UK: Frances Pinter.

Duckitt, J. (1989): Authoritarianism and group identification: A new view of an old construct, in: Political Psychology, Vol. 10, No. 9, pp. 63-84.

Dunning, J. (1993): Multinational Enterprises and the Global Economy, London, UK: Addison Wesley.

Easterly, W. (2001): The Elusive Quest for Growth: Economists' Adventures and Misadventures in the Tropics, Cambridge, MA: MIT Press.

The Economist (2005): "From T-Shirts to T-bonds", retrieved from http://economist.com/displaystory.cfm?story_id=4221685 on 18.09.2006, last update 28.07.2006.

The Economist (2005): "The insidious charms of foreign investment", retrieved from http://www.economist.com/surveys/displaystory.cfm?story_id=3689274 on 12.12.2006, last update 03.03.2005.

Economist Intelligence Unit (2007): "China Economy: Critical Issues - The renminbi", retrieved from http://www.viewswire.com/index.asp?layout=VWArticleVW3&article_id=962044681 on 10.07.2007, last update 28.03.2007.

Economist Intelligence Unit (2007): "China Economy: Pushing Past Germany", retrieved from http://www.viewswire.com/index.asp?layout=VWArticleVW3&article_id=892710874 on 02.11.2007, last update 25.10.2007.

Economist Intelligence Unit (2007): "China: Automotive Profile", retrieved from http://www.viewswire.com/index.asp?layout=iwArticleVW3&article_id=1381797723&refm=&country_id=1800000180&industry_id=20000002&channel_id=&category_id=1399893725&page_title=Profile on 15.07.2007, last update 14.01.2007.

Edin, M. (2000): Market Forces and Communist Power - Local institutions and economic development in China, Inaugural Dissertation, Political Sciences, Uppsala, Sweden.

Editorial Board of the Progress of China Industry Modernization (1999): The Progress of China Industry Modernization, Beijing: China Intercontinental Press.

Eisenhardt, K. (1989a): Agency theory: An assessment and review, in: Academy of Management Review, Vol. 14, No. 1, pp. 57-74.

Eisenhardt, K. (1989b): Building Theories from Case Study Research, in: Academy of Management Review, Vol. 14, No. 4, pp. 532-550.

Ellram, L. (1996): The Use of the Case Study Method in Logistics Research, in: Journal of Business Logistics, Vol. 17, No. 2, pp. 93-116.

Elson, A. (2006): What Happened?, in: Finance and Development, Vol. June 2006, pp. 37-40.

European Central Bank (2005): "The next dimension for EU-China relations", retrieved from http://www.ecb.int/press/key/date/2005/html/sp050419.en.html on 26.02.2007, last update 19.04.2005.

European Commission (2006): "WT/DS339 - Measures affecting imports of automobile parts", retrieved from http://trade-info.cec.eu.int/wtodispute/show.cfm?id=290&code=1 on 25.07.2007, last update 21.04.2006.

European Commission (2007): "Market Access Database", retrieved from http://mkaccdb.eu.int/madb_barriers/barriers_details.htm?barrier_id=060007&version=2 on 11.07.2007, last update 10.01.2007.

Evans, P. (1979): Dependent Development: The Alliance of Multinational, State, and Local Capital in Brazil, Princeton, NJ: Princeton University Press.

Evans, P. (1989): Predatory, Developmental, and other Apparatuses: A comparatice political economy perspective on the Third World State, in: Sociological Forum, Vol. 4, No. 4, pp. 561-587.

Evans, P. (1995): Embedded Autonomy - States and Industrial Transformation, Princeton, NJ: Princeton University Press.

Evans, P. / Rauch, J. (1999): Bureaucracy and Growth: A Cross-National Analysis of the Effects of "Weberian" State Structure on Economic Growth, in: American Sociological Review, Vol. 64, No. 5, pp. 748-765.

Evans, P. / Rauch, J. (2000): Bureaucratic structure and bureaucratic performance in less developed countries, in: Journal of Public Economics, Vol. 75, pp. 49-71.

Fan, G. / Zhang, X. (2003): The Chinese Reform Agenda, in: Teunissen, J. (Ed.): China's Role in Asia and the World Economy - Fostering Stability and Growth, FONDAD, pp. 11-32.

Feigenbaum, E. (1999): Who's behind China's high technology "revolution"? - How bomb makers remade Beijing's priorities, policies and institutions, in: International Security, Vol. 24, No. 1, pp. 95-126.

FERI Online Explorer: Economic Databases, Bad Homburg.

Fernandez-Stembridge, L. / Huchet, J.-F. (2006): What's next for China's SOEs, in: Far Eastern Economic Review, Vol. 169, No. 5, pp. 32-36.

Fewsmith, J. (2001a): Formal Structures, Informal Politics and Political Change in China, in: Fewsmith, J. (Ed.): Elite Politics in Contemporary China, Armonk, NY, M.E. Sharpe, pp. 35-61.

Fewsmith, J. (2001b): The Dengist Reforms in Historical Perspective, in: Fewsmith, J. (Ed.): Elite Politics in Contemporary China, Armonk, NY, M.E. Sharpe, pp. 3-34.

Fewsmith, J. (2001c): The Impact of Reform on Elite Politics, in: Fewsmith, J. (Ed.): Elite Politics in Contemporary China, Armonk, NY, M.E. Sharpe, pp. 86-117.

Fields, K. (1995): Enterprise and the State in Korea and Taiwan, Ithaca, NY: Cornell University Press.

Figueiredo, R. / Weingast, B. (2005): Self-Enforcing Federalism, in: Journal of Law, Economics, and Organization, Vol. 21, No. 1, pp. 103-135.

Financial Times Deutschland (2007): Daimler krempelt China-Strategie um, 22.05.2007, p. 7.

Findlay, M. (1999): Independence and the Judiciary in the PRC: Expectations for Constitutional Legality in China, London, UK: Routledge.

Flick, U. / Kardorff, E. / Keupp, H. / Rosenstiel, L. / Wolff, S. (1991): Handbuch Qualitativer Sozialforschung - Grundlagen, Konzepte, Methoden und Anwendungen, München: Psychologie Verlags Union.

Flick, U. (1995): Qualitative Forschung. Theorie, Methoden, Anwendungen in Psychologie und Sozialwissenschaften, Reinbeck: Rowohlt.

Flick, U. (2002): An Introduction to Qualitative Research, London, UK: Sage Publications.

Flick, U. (2004a): Triangulation – eine Einführung, Wiesbaden: VS-Verlag.

Flick, U. (2004b): Triangulation in Qualitative Research, in: Flick, U. / Kardorff, E. /Steinke, I. (Eds.): A Companion to Qualitative Research, London, UK, Sage Publishers, pp. 178-183.

Flick, U. (Forum: Qualitative Research) (2005): "Qualitative Research in Sociology in Germany and the US - State of the Art, Differences and Developments", retrieved from http://www.qualitative-research.net/fqs-texte/3-05/05-3-23-3.htm on 5.02.2006.

Fong, G. (1998): Follower at the frontier: international competition and Japanese industrial policy, in: International Studies Quarterly, Vol. 42, pp. 339-366.

FOURIN Inc. (2005a): Auto Industry Development by Region, in: FOURIN China Auto Weekly, 24.01.2005, pp. 1-19.

FOURIN Inc. (2005b): China's Vehicle Production Capacity: Passenger Cars Take the Lead, in: FOURIN China Auto Weekly, 03.10. 2005, pp. 1-19.

FOURIN Inc. (2006): China's Independent Automakers, in: FOURIN China Auto Weekly, 08.05.2006, pp. 1-15.

FOURIN Inc. (2007): Passenger Car Launches in China, in: FOURIN China Auto Weekly, 22.01.2007, pp. 1-23.

Frankfurter Allgemeine Sonntagszeitung (2005): Post oder Partei?, 14.08.2005, p. 11.

FRBSF Economic Letter (2001): "Japan's New Prime Minister and the Postal Savings System", retrieved from http://www.frbsf.org/publications/economics/letter/2001/el2001-15.html on 22.10.2006, last update 18.05.2001.

Frye, T. / Shleifer, A. (1997): The Invisible Hand and the Grabbing Hand, in: American Economic Review, Vol. 87, No. 2, pp. 354-358.

Fu, J. (2000): Institutions and Investments: Foreign Direct Investment in China during an Era of Reforms, Ann Arbor, MI: The University of Michigan Press.

Gabriele, A. (2001): Science and Technology Policies, Industrial Reform and Technical Progress in China - Can socialist property rights be compatible with technological catching up?, UNCTAD Discussion Paper, No. 155, August 2001, pp. 1-60, retrieved from http://www.unctad.org/en/docs/dp_155.en.pdf on 01.05.2007.

Gabriele, A. (2002): S&T policies and technical progress in China's industry, in: Review of International Political Economy, Vol. 9, No. 2, pp. 333–373.

Gallagher, K. (2006): China Shifts Gears - Automakers, Oil, Pollution, and Development, Cambridge, MA: MIT Press.

Gallagher, K. (n.d.): Foreign Technology in China's Automobile Industry: Implications for Energy, Economic Development and Environment, in: China Environment Series, No. 6, pp. 1-17.

García-Herrero, A. / Santabarbara, D. (2004): Where is the Chinese Banking System Going with the ongoing reforms?, in: Banco de Espana Documentos Ocasionales, Vol. 0406, pp. 1-44.

General Administration of Customs, the National Development and Reform Commission, the Ministry of Finance and the Ministry of Commerce (2005): "Measures for the Administration of Import of Automobile Components and Parts Featuring Complete Vehicles", retrieved from http://www.fdi.gov.cn/ltlaw/lawinfodisp.jsp?id=ABC00000000000010943 on 09.10.2006, last update 28.02.2005.

German Industry of Commerce (n.d.): "About us", retrieved from http://www.china.ahk.de/gic/aboutus/ on 20.07.2006.

Gerschenkron, A. (1962): Economic Backwardness in Historical Perspective, Cambridge, MA: Belknap.

Gilboy, G. (2004): The Myth Behind China's Miracle, in: Foreign Affairs, Vol. July/August, pp. 33-48.

Glass, G. (1976): Primary, Secondary, and Meta-Analysis of Research, in: Educational Researcher, Vol. 5, No. 10, pp. 3-8.

Global Business Forum (2006): Conference on "Sourcing Asia", Hannover, 27.04.2006, retrieved from http://www.localglobal.de/sixcms/detail.php?template_id=4174 on 06.06.2007.

Global Insight (2002): Asian Automotive Industry Forecast Report, December 2002, pp. 1-58, Boston, MA.

Global Insight (2002): Asian Automotive Industry Forecast Report - China, March 2002, pp. 137-182, Boston, MA.

Global Insight (2002): Asian Automotive Industry Forecast Report - South Korea, March 2002, pp. 101-136, Boston, MA.

Global Insight (2004): World Car Sales Forecast Report, April 2004, pp. 1-92, Boston, MA.

Global Insight (2006): Asian Automotive Industry Forecast Report, August 2006, pp. 1-146, Boston, MA.

Global Insight (2006): Asian Automotive Industry Forecast Report, December 2006, pp. 1-164, Boston, MA.

Global Insight (2007): Asian Automotive Industry Forecast Report, April 2007, pp. 1-176, Boston, MA.

Global Insight (2007): Asian Automotive Industry Forecast Report, September 2007, pp. 1-186, Boston, MA.

Global Insight (2007): "Bosch Company Profile", retrieved from http://www.globalinsight.com/ on 29.06.2007, last update 05.04.2006.

Global Insight (2007): World Car Sales Forecast Report, April 2007, pp. 1-40, Boston, MA.

Gong, T. (2006): Corruption and local governance: the double identity of Chinese local governments in market reform, in: The Pacific Review, Vol. 19, No. 1, pp. 85-102.

Grossman, S. / Hart, O. (1983): An Analysis of the Principal Agent Problem, in: Econometrica, Vol. 51, No. 1, pp. 7-46.

Haggard, S. (1990): Pathways from Periphery - The Politics of Growth in the Newly Industrializing Countries, Ithaca, NY: Cornell University Press.

Haidian Science Park: "Zhongguancun (Haidian) Science Park", retrieved from http://www.zhongguancun.com.cn/en/overview/default.asp.htm on 02.10.2006.

Hamel, J. / Dufour, S. / Fortin, D. (1993): Case Study Methods, Newbury Park, CA: Sage Publications.

Hamrin, C. / Zhao, S. (1995): Introduction: Core Issues in Understanding the Decision Process, in: Hamrin, C. / Zhao, S. (Eds.): Decision-Making in Deng's China - Perspectives from Insiders, Armonk, NY, M.E. Sharpe, pp. xxi-xlviii.

Harwit, E. (1992): Foreign Passenger Car Ventures and Chinese Decision-Making, in: The Australian Journal of Chinese Affairs, Vol. 28, pp. 141-166.

Harwit, E. (1995): China's Automobile Industry - Policies, Problems and Prospects, Armonk, NY: M.E. Sharpe.

Harwit, E. (2001): The Impact of WTO Membership on the Automobile Industry in China, in: The China Quarterly, Vol. 167, pp. 655-670.

Hawes, G. / Liu, H. (1993): Explaining the Dynamics of the Southeast Asian Political Economy: State, Society and the Search for Economic Growth, in: World Politics, Vol. 45, No. 4, pp. 629-660.

Hayek, F. (1945): The use of knowledge in society, in: American Economic Review: Papers and Proceedings, Vol. 35, No. 4, pp. 519-530.

Hayek, F. (1976; reprinted in 1994): The Road to Serfdom, Chicago, IL: University of Chicago Press.

He, J. / Yang, Y. (1999): The political economy of trade liberalisation in China, Asia Pacific School of Economics and Management Working Paper, Vol. 99-1, pp. 1-24, retrieved from http://dspace.anu.edu.au/bitstream/1885/40385/1/cep99-1.pdf on 27.04.2005.

Hebei Provincial Department of Commerce (2002): "The Provisions of Hebei Province Concerning Further Optimizing of the Investment Environment and the Encouragement of Foreign Investment", retrieved from http://english.hebiic.gov.cn/Policy/PolicyDetail.aspx?id=591 on 27.08.2007, last update 24.09.2002.

Heiler, S. / Michels, P. (1994): Deskriptive und Explorative Datenanalyse, München, Wien: R. Oldenbourg Verlag.

Heilmann, S. / Kirchberger, S. (2000): The Chinese *Nomenklatura* in Transition, in: China Analysis, Vol. No. 1, pp. 1-13.

Heilmann, S. (2002 und 2004): Das politische System der Volksrepublik China, Wiesbaden: VS Verlag.

Hewstone, M. / Fincham, F. (1996): Attributionstheorie und -fragestellung: Grundlegende Fragen und Anwendungen, in: Stroebe, W. / Hewstone, M. / Stephenson, G. (Eds.): Sozialpsychologie - Eine Einführung, Vol. 3, Berlin, Springer, pp. 177-218.

Hirschman, A. (1958): The Strategy of Economic Development, New Haven, CT: Yale University Press.

Holmstrom, B. (1979): Moral Hazard and Observability, in: The Bell Journal of Economics, Vol. 10, No. 1, pp. 74-91.

Holweg, M. / Luo, J. / Oliver, N. (2005): The Past, Present and Future of China's Automotive Industry: A Value Chain Perspective, The Cambridge-MIT Institute Working Paper, Vol. August 2005, pp. 1-79.

Holz, C. / Lin, Y.-M. (2001): Pitfalls of China's industrial statistics: Inconsistencies and specification problems, in: The China Review, Vol. 1, No. 1, pp. 29-71.

Holz, C. (2002): Institutional constraints on the quality of statistics in China, in: China Information, Vol. 16, No. 1, pp. 25-67.

Hong Kong Trade Development Council (2007): "Honda to create brand for China auto market", retrieved from http://my.tdctrade.com/airnewse/index.asp?id=31948 on 11.08.2007, last update 20.07.2007.

Howell, J. (1991): The Impact of the Open Door Policy on the Chinese State, in: White, G. (Ed.): The Chinese State in the Era of Economic Reform - The Road to Crisis, Armonk, NY, M.E. Sharpe, pp. 119-148.

Hu, X. (2007): China's Approach to Reform, in: Finance and Development, Vol. September 2007, pp. 36-37.

Huang, Y. (1996): Inflation and Investment Controls in China - The Political Economy of Central-Local Relations during the Reform Era, Cambridge, UK: Cambridge University Press.

Huang, Y. (2002a): Between two coordination failures: automotive industrial policy in China with a comparison to Korea, in: Review of International Political Economy, Vol. 9, No. 3, pp. 538-573.

Huang, Y. (2002b): Managing Chinese Bureaucrats: An Institutional Economics Perspective, in: Political Studies, Vol. 50, pp. 61-79.

Huang, Y. (2003): Selling China - Foreign Direct Investment during the Reform Era, Cambridge, UK: Cambridge University Press.

Humphrey, J. (2000): Assembler - supplier relations in the auto industry: globalization and national development, in: Competition and Change, Vol. 4, pp. 245-271.

IMD (2006): World Competitiveness Yearbook 2006, Lausanne: Institute for Management Development.

IMD (2007): World Competitiveness Yearbook 2007, Lausanne: Institute for Management Development.

Industrial and Commercial Bank of China (2007): "Annual Report 2006", retrieved from http://www.icbc.com.cn/download/nb/2007/ICBC_H%20share%20engi-as%20printed%20Final.pdf on 22.08.2007.

International Bank of Reconstruction/World Bank (2006): "A Decade of Measuring the Quality of Governance", retrieved from http://siteresources.worldbank.org/INTWBIGOVANTCOR/Resources/1740479-1150402582357/2661829-1158008871017/booklet_decade_of_measuring_governance.pdf on 10.10.2007.

International Herald Tribune (2007): Chrysler deal to help Chery enter US market, 07.04.2007, p. 14.

Ito, T. (2001): Growth, Crisis and the Future of Economic Recovery in East Asia, in: Stiglitz, J. / Yusuf, S (Eds.): Rethinking the East Asian Miracle, Washington D.C., World Bank and Oxford University Press, pp. 55-94.

Iwagaki, M. (1986): The State of China's Automobile Industry, in: JETRO China Newsletter, Vol. 63, pp. 9-16.

Jacquemin, A. (1984): European Industry: Public Policy and Corporate Strategy, Oxford, UK: Clarendon Press.

Janelli, R. (1993): Making Capitalism: The Social and Cultural Construction of a South Korean Conglomerate, Stanford, CA: Stanford University Press.

Japan Automobile Manufacturers Association: "Japan's Motor Vehicle Statistics", retrieved from http://www.jama.org/statistics/motorvehicle/sales/mv_sales_year.htm on 22.06.2007.

Japan Automobile Manufacturers Association: "Japan's Motor Vehicle Statistics (Production and Exports)", retrieved from http://www.jama.org/statistics/motorvehicle/exports/mv_exports_year.htm on 07.09.2007.

J. D. Power (2007): Global Truck and Car Forecast, Second Quarter 2007, pp. 1-300, Troy, MI.

Jefferson, G. (2004): R&D and Innovation in China: Has China Begun Its S&T Takeoff?, Working Paper prepared for the Harvard China Review, pp. 1-12.

Jensen, M. / Meckling, W. (1976): Theory of the firm: Managerial behavior, agency costs, and ownership structure, in: Journal of Financial Economics, Vol. 3, No. 4, pp. 305-360.

Jick, T. D. (1979): Mixing Qualitative and Quantitative Methods: Triangulation in Action, in: Administrative Science Quarterly, Vol. 24, No. 4, pp. 602-611.

Jin, H. / Qian, Y. (1998): Public Ownership of Firms: Evidence from Rural China, in: Quarterly Journal of Economics, Vol. 113, No. 3, pp. 773-808.

Johnson, C. (1981): Introduction: The Taiwan Model, in: Hsiung, J. (Ed.): Contemporary Republic of China. The Taiwn Experience, 1950-1980, New York, NY, Praeger, pp. 9-18.

Johnson, C. (1982): MITI and the Japanese Miracle - The Growth of Industrial Policy, 1925-1975, Stanford, CA: Stanford University Press.

Johnson, C. (1987): Political Institutions and Economic Performance: The Government-Business Relationship in Japan, South Korea and Taiwan, in: Deyo, F. C. (Ed.): The Political Economy of the New Asian Industrialism, Ithaca, NY, Cornell University Press, pp. 136-164.

Kassim, H. / Menon, A. (2003): The principal–agent approach and the study of the European Union: promise unfulfilled?, in: Journal of European Public Policy, Vol. 10, No. 1, pp. 121–139.

Kaufmann, D. / Kraay, A. / Mastruzzi, M. (2007): "Governance Matters VI: Governance Indicators for 1996-2006", retrieved from http://web.worldbank.org/WBSITE/EXTERNAL/WBI/EXTWBIGOVANTCOR/0,,contentMDK:20771032~menuPK:1976990~pagePK:64168445~piPK:64168309~theSitePK:1740530,00.html on 01.10.2007.

Keefer, P. (2007): Governance and Economic Growth, in: Winters, L. / Yusuf, S. (Eds.): Dancing with Giants - China, India and the Global Economy, Washington D.C., International Bank for Reconstruction and Development/World Bank and Institute of Policy Studies (Singapore), pp. 211-242.

Kemmelmeier, M. / Burnstein, E. / Krumov, K. / Genkova, P. / Kanagawa, C. / Hirshberg, M. / Erb, H.-P. / Wieczorkowska, G. / Noels, K. (2003): Individualism, Collectivism, and Authoritarianism in Seven Societies, in: Journal of Cross-Cultural Psychology, Vol. 34, No. 3, pp. 304-322.

Ken'ichi, I. (2003): Five year plans and industrial policy, in: Chinese Industry Handbook, 2003-2004, Marukawa Tomoo, Tokyo, pp. 1-3.

Kennedy, S. (2005): The business of lobbying in China, Cambridge, MA: Harvard University Press.

Kesavatana, W. (1989): Political Economy of Direct Foreign Investment in Thailand: A Case Study of the Automobile Industry, Inaugural Dissertation, Political Science, University of Michigan, Ann Arbor.

Kiewiet, D. / McCubbins, M. (1991): The Logic of Delegation: Congressional Parties and the Appropriations Process, Chicago, IL: University of Chicago Press.

Kim, E. M. (1998): The Four Asian Tigers - Economic Development and the Global Political Economy, San Diego, CA: Academic Press.

Kim, K. / Leipziger, D. (2000): Korea: A Case of Government-Led Development, in: Leipziger, D. M. (Ed.): Lessons from East Asia, Vol. 4, Ann Arbor, MI, The University of Michigan Press, pp. 155-212.

Kirzkowski, H. (1984): Monopolistic Competition and International Trade, Oxford, UK Oxford University Press.

Klitgaard, R. (1988): Controlling Corruption, Berkeley and Los Angeles, CA: University of California Press.

Knell, M. / Radosevic, S. (2000): FDI, technology transfer and growth in economic theory, in: Hunya, G. (Ed.): Integration Through FDI: Making Central European Industries Competitive, Cheltenham, UK, Edward Elgar, pp. 28-49.

Kokko, A. / Blomström, M. (1995): Policies to encourage inflows of technology through foreign multinationals, in: World Development, Vol. 23, No. 3, pp. 1-10.

Kornai, J. (1986): The Soft Budget Constraint, in: Kyklos, Vol. 39, No. 1, pp. 3-30.

Kornai, J. (1990): The affinity between ownership forms and coodination mechanisms: The common experience of reform in socialist countries, in: The Journal of Economic Perspectives, Vol. 4, No. 3, pp. 131-147.

Kornai, J. (1992a): The Socialist System - The Political Economy of Communism, Oxford, UK: Clarendon Press.

Kornai, J. (1992b): The postsocialist transition and the state: Reflections in light of Hungarian fiscal problems, in: The American Economic Review, Vol. 82, No. 2, pp. 1-21.

Kornai, J. (1998): The place of soft budget constraint syndrome in economic theory, in: Journal of Comparative Economics, Vol. 26, pp. 11-17.

Kornai, J. (2001): Hardening the Budget Constraint: The Experience of the Post-socialist Countries, in: European Economic Review, Vol. 45, No. 9, pp. 1573-1600.

Krueger, A. (1974): The political economy of the rent seeking society, in: American Economic Review, Vol. 64, pp. 291-303.

Krueger, A. (1980): Trade Policy as an Input to Development, in: The American Economic Review, Vol. 70, No. 2, pp. 288-292.

Krugman, P. (1988): Strategic Trade Policy and the New International Economics, Cambridge, MA: MIT Press.

Krugman, P. (1991): Increasing Returns and Economic Geography, in: Journal of Political Economy, Vol. 99, pp. 483-499.

Krugman, P. (1998): Saving Asia: It's time to get radical, in: Fortune, Vol. 138, No. 5, pp. 74-80.

Krugman, P. / Obstfeld, M. (2004): Internationale Wirtschaft - Theorie und Politik der Außenwirtschaft, München: Pearson Studium.

Kvale, S. (1996): InterViews - An Introduction to Qualitative Research Interviewing, Thousand Oaks, CA: SAGE Publications.

Kwong, C. / Lee, P. (2005): Bad loans versus sluggish rural industrial growth: A policy dilemma of China's banking reform, in: Journal of the Asia Pacific Economy, Vol. 10, No. 1, pp. 1-25.

Lampton, D. (1987a): The Implementation Problem in Post-Mao China, in: Lampton, D.M. (Ed.): Policy Implementation in Post-Mao China, Berkeley, CA, University of California Press, pp. 3-24.

Lampton, D. (1987b): The Bargaining Treadmill, in: Issues & Studies, Vol. 23, No. 3, pp. 11-41.

Lan, Z. (1999): The 1998 Administrative Reform in China: Issues, Challenges and Prospects, in: Asian Journal of Public Administration, Vol. 21, No. 1, pp. 29-54.

Lardy, N. (1998): China's Unfinished Economic Revolution, Washington, D.C.: Brookings Institution Press.

Lavoie, D. (1985): Rivalry and Central Planning, Cambridge, UK: Cambridge University Press.

Lee, C. (2003): The impact of globalisation on the Chinese automobile undustry: Policy assessments and typology of strategies, in: Hozumi, T./ Wohlmuth, K. / Knedlik, T. (Eds.): After the Asian Crisis - Schumpeter and Reconstruction, Vol. 9, Münster, Institut für Weltwirtschaft und Internationales Management, pp. 283-304.

Lee, H. (1991): From Revolutionary Cadres to Party Technocrats in Socialist China, Berkeley, CA: University of California Press.

Lee, K. / Lim, C. (2001): Technological Regimes, Catching-Up and Leapfrogging: Findings from the Korean Industries, in: Research Policy, Vol. 30, No. 3, pp. 459-483.

Lee, K.-P. (2006): Clans for Markets: The Social Organization of Inter-Firm Trading Relations in China's Automobile Industry, Working Paper accepted for publication at The China Quarterly (forthcoming), May 24, 2006, pp. 1-32.

Leftwich, A. (1995): Bringing Politics back in - Towards a model of the developmental state, in: The Journal of Development Studies, Vol. 31, No. 3, pp. 400-427.

Leung, M.-K. / Mok, V. (2000): Commercialization of Banks in China: institutional changes and effects on listed enterprises, in: Journal of Contemporary China, Vol. 9, No. 23, pp. 41-52.

Levi-Faur, D. (1998): The Developmental State: Israel, South Korea, and Taiwan Compared, in: Studies in Comparative International Development, Vol. 33, No. 1, pp. 65-93.

Li, C. (2001): China's Leaders - The New Generation, New York, NY: Rowman & Littlefield Publishers, Inc.

Li, D. (1998): Changing Incentives of the Chinese Bureaucracy, in: The American Economic Review, Vol. 88, No. 2, pp. 393-397.

Li, H. / Meng, L. / Zhang, J. (2006): Why Do Entrepreneurs Enter Politics? Evidence from China, in: Discussion Paper of the Chinese University of Hong Kong, Department of Economics, Vol. 00009, pp. 1-50.

Li, P. (1986): Resolutely Carry Out the Principles of Improvement, Rectification and Deepened Reform - Report on the Work of the Government, in: Beijing Review, Vol. 32, No. 16, pp. I-XXIV.

Li, P. (1991): Report on the Outline of the Ten-Year Programme and of the Eighth Five-Year Plan for National Economic and Social Development, in: Beijing Review, Vol. 34, No. 15, pp. I-XIV.

Li, P. (1993): Report on the Work of the Government - Delivered at the First Session of the Eighth National People's Congress on March 15, 1993 by Li Peng, Premier of the State Council, in: Beijing Review, Vol. 36, No. 15, pp. I-XVI.

Li, P. (1996): Report on the Outline of the Ninth Five-Year Plan for National Economic and Social Development and the Long-Range Objectives to the Year 2010, in: Beijing Review, Vol. 39, No. 15, pp. I-XVI.

Li, R. (2003): "Continuously adjusting the layout and structure of China's state economy, propelling Chinese SOEs to participate in international competition and cooperation - Keynote speech by Chairman of State-Owned Assets Supervision and Administration Commission of the State Council (SASAC) at the International Mergers and Acquisition Summit in Beijing", retrieved from http://www.sasac.gov.cn/eng/new/new_0007.htm on 10.09.2006, last update 19.11.2003.

Li, S. / Lian, P. (1999): Decentralization and coordination: China's credible commitment to preserve the market under authoritarianism, in: China Economic Review, Vol. 10, pp. 161-190.

Liang, G. (2004): New Competition - Foreign Direct Investment and Industrial Development in China, Inaugural Dissertation, Erasmus Research Institute of Management, Erasumus University Rotterdam, Rotterdam.

Liao, K.-J. (2001): The Developmental State, Economic Bureaucracy and Financial Crisis in Asian Societies, in: Journal of Contingencies and Crisis Management, Vol. 9, No. 1, pp. 36-45.

Libecap, G. (1989): Contracting for Property Rights, New York, NY: Cambridge University Press.

Lieberthal, K. / Oksenberg, M. (1988): Policy Making in China - Leaders, Structures and Processes, Princeton, NJ: Princeton University Press.

Lieberthal, K. (1991): China's Political System in the 1990's, in: Journal of Northeast Asian Studies, Vol. X, No. 1, pp. 71-77.

Lieberthal, K. (1992): Introduction: The "Fragmented Authoritarianism" Model and Its Limitations, in: Lieberthal, K. / Lampton, D. (Eds.): Bureaucracy, Politics and Decision Making in Post-Mao China, Berkley and Los Angeles, CA, University of California Press, pp. 1-32.

Lieberthal, K. (1995): Governing China - From Revolution Through Reform, New York, NY: W. W. Norton & Company, Inc.

Lieberthal, K. (1997): China's Governing System and its Impact on Environmental Policy Implementation, in: China Environment Series, Vol. 1, No. 2, pp. 3-8.

Lin, J. / Cai, F. / Li, Z. (1996): The China Miracle - Development Strategy and Economic Reform, Hong Kong: The Chinese University Press.

Lin, Y.-M. (2001): Between Politics and Markets - Firms, Competition, and Institutional Change in Post-Mao China, Cambridge, UK: Cambridge University Press.

Linz, J. (1995): Autoritarismus, in: Drechsler, H. / Hilligen, W. / Neumann, F. (Eds.): Gesellschaft und Staat - Lexikon der Politik, Vol. 9., neu bearbeitete und erweiterte Auflage, München, Vahlen Verlag, pp. 40-43.

Liou, K. (1997): Issues and lessons of Chinese civil service reform, in: Public Personnel Management, Vol. 26, pp. 505-514.

List, F. (1885; reprinted in 1966): The National System of Political Economy, New York, NY: Sentry Press.

Little, I. / Scitovsky, T. / Scott, M. (1970): Industry and trade in some developing countries: a comparative study, London, UK: Oxford University Press.

Liu, M. (2001): Administrative Reform in China and its Impact on the Policy-Making Process and Economic Development After Mao, Lewiston, NY: The Edwin Mellen Press.

Liu, W. / Dicken, P. (2006): Transnational corporations and "obligated embeddedness": foreign direct investment in China's automobile industry, in: Environment and Planning A, Vol. 2006, No. 38, pp. 1229-1247.

Lo, D. (1997): Market and Institutional Regulation in Chinese Industrialization, 1978-1994, New York, NY: St. Martin's Press, Inc.

Lu, D. (2000a): Industrial Policy and resource allocation: implications on China's participation in globalization, in: China Economic Review, Vol. 11, No. 4, pp. 342-360.

Lu, D. (2000b): "Prospect of industrial policy regime after the WTO". Paper presented at the conference on "China's Accession to the WTO: An Overview of Recent Analyses", Beijing, China, 19.-20.11.2000, retrieved from http://www.cpb.nl/nl/research/sector6/afgeronde_projecten/wto/papers/c-indpol-wto.pdf on 17.11.2006.

Lu, D. (2006): China's Banking Sector Meeting the WTO Agenda, University of Nottingham, China Policy Institute, Discussion Paper 5, pp. 1-23.

Luiz, J. (2000): The politics of state, society and economy, in: International Journal of Social Economics, Vol. 27, No. 3, pp. 227-243.

Luo, Y. (1998): Joint Venture Success in China: How Should We Select a Good Partner, in: Journal of World Business, Vol. 33, No. 2, pp. 145-166.

Luo, J. (2005): "The Growth of Independent Chinese Automotive Companies", retrieved from http://imvp.mit.edu/downloads/The%20Growth%20of%20Independent%20Chinese%20Auto%20Companies-05.06.pdf on 02.08.2007, last update 06.05.2005.

Ma, K. (2006): "The Eleventh Five-Year Plan: Targets, Paths and Policy Orientation", retrieved from http://english.gov.cn/2006-03/23/content_234832.htm on 14.11.2006, last update 19.03.2006.

Manion, M. (1985): The cadre management system, post-Mao: the appointment, promotion, transfer and removal of party and state leaders, in: China Quarterly, Vol. 102, pp. 203-233.

Mann, J. (1989): Beijing Jeep: How Western Business Stalled in China, New York, NY: Simon & Schuster.

Mansfield, E. / Romeo, A. (1980): Technology transfer to overseas subsidiaries by US-based firms, in: Quarterly Journal of Economics, Vol. 95, No. 4, pp. 737-750.

Marshall, A. (1920): Principles of Economics, New York, NY: MacMillan.

Matthews, R. / Sargent, J. (1983): Contemporary Problems of Economic Policy: Essays from the Clare Group, London, UK: Methuen.

McCubbins, M. / Noll, R. / Weingast, B. (1989): Structure and process, politics and policy: administrative arrangements and the political control of agencies, in: Virginia Law Review, Vol. 75, pp. 431-483.

Meuser, M. / Nagel, U. (1991): Experteninterviews - vielfach erprobt, wenig bedacht. Ein Beitrag zur qualitativen Methodendiskussion, in: Grarz, D. / Kraimer, K. (Eds.): Qualitativ-empirische Sozialforschung, Opladen, Westdeutscher Verlag, pp. 441-468.

Miles, M. / Huberman, A. (1994): Qualitative data analysis: A sourcebook of new methods, Newbury Park, CA: Sage.

Miller, H. (1996): Science and Dissent in Post-Mao China: The Politics of Knowledge, Seattle, WA: Washington University Press.

Ministry of Commerce (1990): "Law of the People's Republic of China on Chinese-Foreign Equity Joint Ventures; adopted on 01.07.1979; revised on 04.04.1990", retrieved from http://www.fdi.gov.cn/resupload/epdf/e02739.pdf on 17.04.2006, last update 1990.

Ministry of Commerce (1991): "Income Tax Law of the People's Republic of China on Enterprises with Foreign Investment and Foreign Enterprises", retrieved from http://fdi.gov.cn/pub/FDI_EN/Laws/law_en_info.jsp?docid=51522 on 17.07.2007, last update 01.07.1991.

Ministry of Commerce (2002): "The Commitments to the WTO and the International Practices of the Automotive Industry", retrieved from http://www.fdi.gov.cn/common/info.jsp?id=ABC00000000000001972 on 23.03.2006, last update 17.11.2002.

Ministry of Commerce (2003): "Law on Enterprise Bankruptcy (Trial Implementation)", retrieved from http://english.mofcom.gov.cn/aarticle/topic/lawsdata/chineselaw/200303/20030300074803.html on 17.07.2006.

Ministry of Commerce (2003): "Policies and Preferences", retrieved from http://www.fdi.gov.cn/common/info.jsp?id=CENSOFT0000000007158 on 10.07.2006.

Ministry of Commerce (2004): "Analysis on the Current Situation of Government Management System Adapting Itself to the Market Economy", retrieved from http://www.fdi.gov.cn/common/info.jsp?id=ABC00000000000017367 on 23.03.2006, last update 13.10.2004.

Ministry of Commerce (2004): "Announcement of the Ministry of Commerce on the Issue of Replacing and Issuing Automatic Import Permit of Automobile Import Quota", retrieved from http://www.fdi.gov.cn/ltlaw/lawinfodisp.jsp?id=ABC00000000000011259 on 09.10.2006.

Ministry of Commerce (2005): "Chinese Government's Administrative Mode Transformation", retrieved from http://www.fdi.gov.cn/common/info.jsp?id=ABC00000000000022520 on 23.03.2006, last update 19.07.2005.

Ministry of Commerce (2005): "The Status Quo of Foreign Investment in the Automotive Industry", retrieved from http://www.fdi.gov.cn/common/info.jsp?id=ABC00000000000021839 on 23.03.2006, last update 01.07.2005.

Ministry of Commerce/International Property Protection (2006): "Chinese auto joint ventures go their own way", retrieved from http://www.ipr.gov.cn/ipr/en/info/Article.jsp?a_no=28994&col_no=927&dir=200611 on 29.08.2007, last update 15.11.2006.

Ministry of Commerce (2006): "IPR disputes in China's automobile industry", retrieved from http://english.ipr.gov.cn/ipr/en/info/Article.jsp?a_no=22827&col_no=927&dir=200610 on 23.07.2007, last update 23.10.2006.

Ministry of Commerce (2006): "MOFCOM Holding a Symposium with Industry Associations", retrieved from http://english.mofcom.gov.cn/aarticle/counselorsreport/internationalorganization/200603/20060301691302.html on 28.03.2006, last update 15.03.2006.

Ministry of Commerce (2006): "Tax Policies Concerning Foreign Enterprises in China's Development Zones", retrieved from http://www.fdi.gov.cn/common/info.jsp?id=ABC00000000000003486 on 23.03.2006.

Ministry of Commerce (2007): "China's taxation authorities promise to well advance corporate income tax reform", retrieved from http://big5.mofcom.gov.cn/gate/big5/fec2.mofcom.gov.cn/aarticle/news/200701/20070104311396.html on 21.02.2007, last update 25.01.2007.

Ministry of Commerce (2007): "Mission - Main Mandate of the Ministry of Commerce", retrieved from http://english.mofcom.gov.cn/mission/mission.html on 15.01.2007.

Ministry of Commerce (n.d.): "China's Absorption of Foreign Investment", retrieved from http://www.fdi.gov.cn/lteconomy/index.jsp?currentPage=1&category=10&app=0000000000000000005&language=en on 17.04.2006.

Ministry of Science and Technology (1998): "Reform Program for State Council Departments (S&T Newsletter No. 153)", retrieved from http://www.most.gov.cn/eng/newsletters/1998/200411/t20041125_17517.htm on 22.01.2007, last update 2004.

Ministry of Science and Technology and Ministry of Commerce (2006): "Catalogue of Encouraged Hi-Tech Products for Foreign Investment (2003)", retrieved from http://www.fdi.gov.cn/ltlaw/lawinfodisp.jsp?id=CENSOFT000000009119&appld=1 on 17.04.2006.

Ministry of Science and Technology: various years of "S&T Statistics Data Books", retrieved from http://www.most.gov.cn/eng/statistics/2006/200703/t20070309_42004.htm on 10.11.2007.

Ministry of Science and Technology (2007): "Output Indicators", retrieved from http://www.most.gov.cn/eng/statistics/2006/200703/t20070309_42000.htm on 09.11.2007.

Minns, J. (2001): Of miracles and models: the rise and decline of the developmental state in South Korea, in: Third World Quarterly, Vol. 22, No. 6, pp. 1025 - 1043.

Moe, T. (1984): The new economics of organization, in: American Journal of Political Science, Vol. 28, pp. 739-777.

Montinola, G. / Qian, Y. / Weingast, B. (1995): Federalism, Chinese Style - The Political Basis for Economic Success in China, in: World Politics, Vol. 48, pp. 50-81.

Mu, Z. (2001): Building a Contingent of High-Quality Leading Officials, in: Beijing Review, Vol. 1, pp. 20-23.

Naseem, S. (2003): Rethinking the East Asian Miracle, in: Journal of Economic Studies, Vol. 30, No. 6, pp. 636-644.

National Bureau of Statistics of China (2005): China Compendium of Statistics 1949-2004, Beijing: China Statistics Press.

National Bureau of Statistics of China (2006): China Automotive Industry Yearbook 2006, Beijing: China Statistics Press.

National Bureau of Statistics of China: various issues of "China Statistical Yearbook", retrieved from http://www.stats.gov.cn/english/statisticaldata/yearlydata/.

National Bureau of Statistics of China (Department of Trade and External Economic Statistics) (2005): China External Economic Statistical Yearbook, Beijing: China Statistics Press.

National Bureau of Statistics and Ministry of Science and Technology (2005): China Statistical Yearbook on Science and Technology 2005, Beijing: China Statistics Press.

National Development and Reform Commission (2004): "Automobile Industry Development Policy No. 8 decree of the State Development and Reform Commission", retrieved from http://china.tdctrade.com/content.aspx?data=CHINA_content_en&contentid=170215&src=CN_LawReg&w_sid=194&w_pid=630&w_nid=9927&w_cid=170215&w_idt=1900-01-01&w_oid=180 on 11.04.2006, last update 28.06.2004.

National Development and Reform Commission and Ministry of Commerce (2004): "Catalogue of Priority Industries for Foreign Investment in the Central-Western Region (Amended in 2004)", retrieved from http://www.fdi.gov.cn/ltlaw/lawinfodisp.jsp?id=ABC00000000000010442&appId=1 on 22.04.2006.

National Development and Reform Commission and Ministry of Commerce (2004): "Interim Measures for the Administration of Examining and Approving Foreign Investment Projects", retrieved from http://www.fdi.gov.cn/common/info.jsp?id=ABC00000000000018596 on 24.04.2006, last update 15.12.2004.

National Development and Reform Commission and Ministry of Commerce (2005): "Catalogue of Industries for Guiding Foreign Investment (Revised 2004)", retrieved from http://www.fdi.gov.cn/common/info.jsp?id=ABC00000000000022203 on 22.04.2006.

National Development and Reform Commission (2005): "Major Measures to Promote the Adjustment of Industrial Structure", retrieved from http://en.ndrc.gov.cn/newsrelease/t20051222_54289.htm on 18.12.2006, last update 22.12.2005.

National Development and Reform Commission (2006): "Outline of the Eleventh Five-Year Plan", retrieved from http://ghs.ndrc.gov.cn/15ghgy/t20060529_70793.htm on 14.11.2006, last update 09.11.2006.

National Development and Reform Commission (2006): "Strengthen the Integration of Science, Technology and Economy Enhance Independent Innovation Capability", retrieved from http://en.ndrc.gov.cn/newsrelease/t20060313_62763.htm on 18.12.2006, last update 13.03.2006.

National Development and Reform Commission (2007): "Main Functions of the NDRC", retrieved from http://en.ndrc.gov.cn/mfndrc/default.htm on 16.01.2007.

National Economic and Technological Development Zones (2003): "Tax Policies Concerning Foreign-Funded Enterprises and Foreign Enterprises in National ETDZs", retrieved from http://www.china.org.cn/english/difang/76259.htm on 08.08.2006, last update October 2003.

National People's Congress (1982): "Constitution of the People's Republic of China", retrieved from http://english.people.com.cn/constitution/constitution.html on 11.09.2006, last update 04.12.1982.

Naughton, B. / Segal, A. (2001): Technology Development in the New Millenium: China in Search of a Workable Model, MIT Japan Program Working Paper, Vol. 01.03, pp. 1-24.

Naughton, B. (2003a): The State Asset Commission: A Powerful Government Body, in: China Leadership Monitor, Vol. 8, pp. 1-10.

Naughton, B. (2006): "Top-Down Control: SASAC and the Persistence of State Ownership in China". Paper presented at the conference on "China and the World Economy", Leverhulme Centre for Research on Globalisation and Economic Policy (GEP), University of Nottingham, 23.06.2006.

Nee, V. (1989): A Theory of Market Transition: From Redistribution to Markets in State Socialism, in: American Sociological Review, Vol. 54, pp. 663-681.

Nee, V. / Sijin, S. (1990): Institutional Change and Economic Growth in China: The View from the Villages, in: The Journal of Asian Studies, Vol. 49, No. 1, pp. 3-25.

Nee, V. (1992): Organizational Dynamics of Market Transition: Hybrid Forms, Property Rights and Mixed Economy in China, in: Administrative Science Quarterly, Vol. 37, pp. 1-27.

Nee, V. / Lian, P. (1994): Sleeping with the enemy: A dynamic model of declining political commitment in state socialism, in: Theory and Society, Vol. 23, pp. 253-296.

Nee, V. (2000): The Role of the State in Making a Market Economy, in: Journal of Institutional and Theoretical Economics, Vol. 156, pp. 64-88.

Nee, V. / Opper, S. / Wong, S. (2005): Politicized Capitalism: Developmental State and the Firm in China, in: Economy & Society, January 27, 2005, pp. 1-53, retrieved from http://www.economyandsociety.org/publications/NeeOpperWong07JAN05.pdf on 27.11.2006.

Nee, V. / Opper, S. / Wong, S. (2007): Developmental State and Corporate Governance in China, in: Management and Organization Review, Vol. 3, No. 1, pp. 19-53, retrieved from http://www.economyandsociety.org/publications/wp35_NeeOpperWong_07.pdf. 11.08.2007.

Nee, V. / Opper, S. (2007): On Politicized Capitalism, in: Nee, V. / Swedberg, R. (Eds.): On Capitalism, Stanford, Stanford University Press, pp. 93-127, retrieved from http://www.economyandsociety.org/events/NEE_OPPER_China_Capsm.pdf on 18.06.2007.

Nelson, R. / Winter, S. (1982): An Evolutionary Theory of Economic Change, Cambridge, MA: Harvard University Press.

Ng, C / Sudo, S. / Crone, D. (1992): The Strategic Dimension of the "East Asian Developmental States", in: ASEAN Economic Bulletin, Vol. 9, No. 2, pp. 219-233.

Niskanen, W. (1971): Bureaucracy and Representative Government, Chicago, IL: Aldine Publishing Company.

Niskanen, W. (1973): Bureaucracy: Servant or Master? Lessons from America, London, UK: Institute of Economic Affairs.

Noble, G. / Ravenhill, J. / Doner, R. (2005): Executioner or Disciplinarian: WTO Accession and the Chinese Auto Industry, in: Business and Politics, Vol. 7, No. 2, pp. 1-33.

Noble, G. (2006): "Overcapacity, Contract Design and the Emergence of Independent Auto Firms in China". Paper presented at the "Yale China Conference", New Haven, April 21-22, 2006.

Nolan, P. (1993a): China's Post-Mao Political Economy: A Puzzle, in: Contributions to Political Economy, Vol. 12, pp. 71-87.

Nolan, P. (1993b): State and Market in the Chinese Economy - Essays on Controversial Issues, London, UK: The Macmillan Press Ltd.

Nolan, P. (1995b): China's Rise, Russia's Fall - Politics, Economics and Planning in the Transition from Stalinism, London, UK: Macmillan Press Ltd.

Nolan, P. (2001): China and the global economy - National champions, industrial policy and the big business revolution, New York, NY: Palgrave.

North, D. (1981): Structure and change in economic history, New York, NY: Norton.

North, D. (1990): Institutions, Institutional Change and Economic Performance, New York, NY: Cambridge University Press.

North, D. (1997): The Contribution of the New Institutional Economics to an Understanding of the Transition Problem, Stockholm: UNU World Inst. for Development Economics Research, Annual Lecture.

Norton, R. (1986): Industrial Policy and American Renewal, in: Journal of Economic Literature, Vol. 24, No. 1, pp. 1-40.

Norusis, M. (1988): SPSS-X Introductory Statistics Guide (for SPSS-X Release 3), Chicago, IL: SPSS Inc.

OECD (2002): Foreign Direct Investment for Development: Maximizing Benefits, Minimizing Costs, Paris: OECD.

OECD (2003): "Objectives of the Competition Law of PRC and the Optimal Design of Competition Authorities", retrieved from http://www.oecd.org/dataoecd/58/25/2485968.pdf on 02.10.2006, last update 09.01.2003.

OECD (2005): "Economic Survey of China 2005: Improving the productivity of the business sector", retrieved from http://www.oecd.org/document/54/0,2340,en_2649_201185_35350582_1_1_1_1,00.html on 02.01.2007.

OECD (2006a): Regional Development and Multi-Level Governance in China: Background Paper, in: GOV/TDPC, Vol. 2006, No. 3, pp. 1-29.

OECD (2006b): Financial System Reform in China: Discussions with Chinese Authorities, in: Financial Market Trends, Vol. 91, pp. 63-224.

Oi, J. (1992): Fiscal Reform and the Economic Foundations of Local State Corporatism in China, in: World Politics, Vol. 45, No. 1, pp. 99-126.

Oi, J. (1995): The Role of the Local State in China's Transitional Economy, in: The China Quarterly, Vol. 144, Special Issue: China's Transitional Economy, pp. 1132-1149.

Oi, J. (1999): Rural China Takes Off - Institutional Foundations of Economic Reform, Berkeley, CA: University of California Press.

Okazaki, T. (1997): The Government-Firm Relationship in Postwar Japanese Recovery: Resolving the Coordination Failure by Coordination in Industrial Rationalization, in: Aoki, M /Kim, H.-K. / Okuno-Fujiwara, M. (Eds.): The Role of Government in East Asian Economic Development, Oxford, UK, Clarendon Press, pp. 74-100.

Okimoto, D. (1989): Between MITI and the Market: Japanese Industrial Policy for High Technology, Stanford, CA: Stanford University Press.

Oksenberg, M. / Tong, J. (1991): The Evolution of Central-Provincial Fiscal Relations in China, 1971-1984: The Formal System, in: China Quarterly, Vol. 125, No. March 1991, pp. 1-32.

Olson, M. (1965): The Logic of Collective Action, Cambridge, MA: Harvard University Press.

Önis, Z. (1991): The Logic of the Developmental State, in: Comparative Politics, Vol. 24, No. 1, pp. 109-126.

Opper, S. (1999): Wirtschaftsreform und Beschäftigungswandel in der VR China, Inaugural Dissertation, Schriftenreihe zur Ostasienforschung, Vol.11, Baden-Baden: Nomos Verlagsgesellschaft.

Opper, S. (2001): Dual-track Ownership Reforms: Lessons from Structural Change in China, 1978-1997, in: Post-Communist Economies, Vol. 13, No. 2, pp. 205-227.

Opper, S. (2005a): Inefficient property rights and corruption: the case of accounting fraud in China, in: Graf Lambsdorff, J. / Taube, M. / Schramm, M. (Eds.): Corruption and the New Institutional Economics, London, UK, Routledge, pp. 198-217.

Opper, S. (2005b): "The giant graduates: China's strive for high-technology", in: CESifo Forum, Vol. 3/2005, pp. 43-48.

Pack, H. / Westphal, L. (1986): Industrial Strategy and Technological Change: Theory Versus Reality, in: Journal of Development Economics, Vol. 22, pp. 87-128.

Panagariya, A. (2003): China's Export Strategy: What Can We Learn From It, in: International Trade, Vol. 0309014, pp. 1-16.

Park, A. / Sehrt, K. (2001): Tests of financial intermediation and banking reform in China, in: Journal of Comparative Economics, Vol. 29, pp. 608-644.

Pavlinek, P. / Smith, A. (1998): Internationalization and embeddedness in East-Central European transition: the contrasting geographies of inward investment in the Czech and Slovak Republics, in: Regional Studies, Vol. 32, No. 7, pp. 619-638.

Pazos, F. (1987): Import Substitution Policies, Tariffs, and Competition, in: Dietz, J. / Street, J. (Eds.): Latin America's Economic Development - Institutionalist and Structuralist Perspectives, Boulder, CO, Lynne Rienner Publishers, pp. 147 - 155.

Pearson, M. (1991): Joint Ventures in the People's Republic of China, Princeton, NJ: Princeton University Press.

Pearson, M. (2006): "Regulation and Regulatory Politics in China's Tiered Economy". Paper presented at the conference on "Capitalism With Chinese Characteristics: China's Political Economy in Comparative and Theoretical Perspectives", Bloomington, IN, 19.-20.05.2006.

Pei, M. (2006a): China's Trapped Transition - The Limits of Developmental Autocracy, Cambridge, MA: Harvard University Press.

Pei, M. (2006b): "Has China Fallen into a Trapped Transition?" retrieved from http://www.carnegieendowment.org/events/index.cfm?fa=eventDetail&id=869& &prog=zch on 04.11.2007, last update 30.06.2006.

Pei, M. (2006c): The Dark Side of China's Rise, in: Foreign Policy, Vol. March/April 2006, pp. 1-4, retrieved from http://www.carnegieendowment.org/publications/index.cfm?fa=view&id=18110& prog=zch on 04.11.2007.

Pei, M. (2007): Corruption Threatens China's Future, in: Carnegie Policy Brief, Vol. 55, October 2007, http://www.carnegieendowment.org/files/pb55_pei_china_corruption_final.pdf, reviewed 04.11.2007, retrieved from http://www.carnegieendowment.org/files/pb55_pei_china_corruption_final.pdf on 04.11.2007.

Pempel, T. (1999): The Developmental Regime in a Changing World Economy, in: Woo-Cumings, M. (Ed.): The Developmental State, Ithaca, NY, Cornell University Press, pp. 137-181.

Peng, M. / Luo, Y. (2000): Managerial Ties and Firm Performance in a Transition Economy: The Nature of a Micro-Macro Link, in: Academy of Management Journal, Vol. 43, No. 3, pp. 486-501.

Peng, Y. (2001): Chinese Villages and Townships as Industrial Corporations: Ownership, Governance, and Market Discipline, in: American Journal of Sociology, Vol. 105, No. 5, pp. 1338–1370.

Pennings, P. / Keman, H. / Kleinnijenhuis, J. (1999): Doing Research in Political Science - An introduction to comparative methods and statistics, London, UK: SAGE Publications.

People's Bank of China (2003): "Law of the People's Republic of China on Banking Regulation and Supervision", retrieved from http://www.pbc.gov.cn/english/ on 05.10.2006, last update 27.12.2003.

People's Bank of China (2003): "Law of the People's Republic of China on the People's Bank of China", retrieved from http://www.pbc.gov.cn/english//detail.asp?col=6800&ID=22 on 03.10.2006, last update 27.12.2003.

People's Bank of China (2004): "Administrative Rules for Automotive Loans", retrieved from http://www.pbc.gov.cn/english//detail.asp?col=6800&ID=19 on 27.08.2007, last update 18.08.2004.

People's Daily (2001): "Auto Industry Faces Challenges", retrieved from http://english.peopledaily.com.cn/200111/22/eng20011122_85122.shtml on 16.10.2006, last update 22.11.2001.

People's Daily (2001): "NPC Deputies, CPPCC Members Interpret New Five-Year Plan", retrieved from http://english.people.com.cn/english/200103/05/eng20010305_64129.html on 07.08.2006, last update 05.03.2001.

People's Daily (2001): "Volkswagenwerk AG President Lectures in Shanghai", retrieved from http://english.people.com.cn/english/200102/10/eng20010210_61984.html on 26.08.2007, last update 10.02.2001.

People's Daily (2002): "China's Leading Car Producer Sets up R&D Center", retrieved from http://english.peopledaily.com.cn/200208/05/eng20020805_100889.shtml on 03.09.2007, last update 05.08.2002.

People's Daily (2003): "China's Automobiles to Tap for Overseas Markets", retrieved from http://english.peopledaily.com.cn/200306/02/eng20030602_117574.shtml on 21.07.2007, last update 02.06.2003.

People's Daily (2003): "China Sets to Put Brakes on Auto Industry", retrieved from english.peopledaily.com.cn/200309/10/eng20030910_124091.shtml on 18.10.2006, last update 10.09.2003.

People's Daily (2003): "Economist calls for abolishment of export tax rebate", retrieved from http://english.people.com.cn/200310/05/eng20031005_125408.shtml on 07.08.2006, last update 05.10.2003.

People's Daily (2003): "Exam-based Civil Service Prevails in China", retrieved from http://english.peopledaily.com.cn/200308/16/eng20030816_122412.shtml on 03.10.2006.

People's Daily (2003): "FDI fueling China's economic boom", retrieved from http://english.peopledaily.com.cn/200312/13/eng20031213_130339.shtml on 18.10.2006, last update 13.12.2003.

People's Daily (2003): "Promotion Through Competition - A Major Way for Party & Government Officials", retrieved from http://english.peopledaily.com.cn/200308/13/eng20030813_122261.shtml on 03.10.2006.

People's Daily (2004): "Former land minister expelled from CPC Central Committee", retrieved from http://english.peopledaily.com.cn/200409/20/eng20040920_157566.html on 02.01.2007, last update 20.09.2004.

People's Daily (2004): "GM obtains approval for auto finance", retrieved from http://english.peopledaily.com.cn/200408/06/eng20040806_152057.html on 21.07.2007, last update 06.08.2004.

People's Daily (2004): "Industrial profit growth starts to slow", retrieved from http://english.peopledaily.com.cn/200408/25/eng20040825_154644.html on 15.08.2007, last update 25.08.2004.

People's Daily (2004): "Problems linger in auto parts sector", retrieved from http://www.chinadaily.com.cn/english/doc/2004-07/26/content_351723.htm on 09.10.2006, last update 27.07.2004.

People's Daily (2005): "China aids domestic auto maker for overseas expansion", retrieved from http://english.peopledaily.com.cn/200503/07/eng20050307_175797.html on 19.07.2007, last update 07.03.2005.

People's Daily (2005): "China: Share Wealth With the World", retrieved from http://english.people.com.cn/200505/18/eng20050518_185643.html on 10.07.2007, last update 18.05.2005.

People's Daily (2005): "Full text of Hu Jintao's speech at 2005 Fortune Global Forum", retrieved from http://english.people.com cn/200505/17/eng20050517_185302.html on 10.07.2007, last update 16.05.2005.

People's Daily Online (2006): "China's new policy stresses quality of foreign investment", retrieved from http://english.people.com.cn/200611/09/print20061109_319955.html on 15.11.2006, last update 09.11.2006.

People's Daily (2007): "China's parliament adopts enterprise income tax law", retrieved from http://english.peopledaily.com.cn/200703/16/eng20070316_358252.html on 21.10.2007, last update 16.03.2007.

Perkins, D. (1994): There are at least three models of East Asian development, in: World Development, Vol. 22, No. 4, pp. 655-661.

Perkins, D. (2001): Industrial and Financial Policy in China and Vietnam, in: Stiglitz, J. E. / Yusuf, S. (Eds.): Rethinking the East Asian Miracle, Washington D.C., World Bank and Oxford University Press, pp. 247-294.

Permanent Mission of the People's Republic of China to the United Nations Office at Geneva and Other International Organizations In Switzerland (2005): "Building of Political Democracy in China", retrieved from http://www.china-un.ch/eng/bjzl/t225536.htm on 17.11.2006, last update 09.12.2005.

Pinder, J. (1982): National Industrial Strategies and the World Economy, London, UK: Croom Helm.

Polanyi, M. (1967): The Tacit Dimension, New York, NY: Doubleday.

Pollack, M. (1997): Delegation, agency and agenda setting in the European Community, in: International Organization, Vol. 51, No. 1, pp. 99-134.

Poncet, S. (2005): A Fragmented China: Measure and Determinants of Chinese Domestic Market Disintegration, in: Review of International Economics, Vol. 13, No. 3, pp. 409-430.

Posner, R. (1980): A Theory of Primitive Society, with Special Reference to Law, in: Journal of Law and Economics, Vol. 23, pp. 1-53.

Poulson, B. (1994): Economic Development - Private and Public Choice, St. Paul; Minneapolis, MN: West Publishing Company.

Powell, B. (2003): State Development Planning: Did it create an Asian miracle?, Mercatus Center - George Mason University Working Paper, Vol. 16, pp. 1-45.

Qian, Y. / Weingast, B. (1996b): China's Transition to Markets: Market-Preserving Federalism, Chinese Style, in: Journal of Policy Reform, Vol. 1, pp. 149-185.

Qian, Y. / Roland, G. (1998): Federalism and the Soft Budget Constraint, in: American Economic Review, Vol. 88, pp. 1143-1162.

Qian, Y. (2000): The Process of China's Market Transition (1978-1998): The Evolutionary, Historical, and Comparative Perspectives, in: Journal of Institutional and Theoretical Economics, Vol. 156, No. 2000, pp. 151-179.

Qian, Y. (2003): How Reform Worked in China, in: Rodrik, D. (Ed.): In Search of Prosperity: Analytic Narratives on Economic Growth, Princeton, NJ, Princeton University Press, pp. 297-333.

Qin, J. (2004): WTO regulation of subsidies to state-owned enterprises (SOEs) - A critical appraisal of the China accession protocol, in: Journal of International Economic Law, Vol. 7, No. 4, pp. 863-919.

Ravenhill, J. (2001): "From National Champions to Global Partnerships: The Korean Auto Industry, Financial Crisis and Globalization. The MIT Japan Program, Center for International Studies, Massachusetts Institute of Technology", retrieved from http://mit.edu/mit-japan/outreach/working-papers/WP0104.pdf on 05.09.2007, last update 04.06.2001.

Ravenhill, J. (2005): The Growth of the Chinese Automotive Industry and Its Impact on Production Networks in East Asia, pp. 5-36, Working Paper, retrieved from http://www.kiet.re.kr/kiet/main.files/images/20050701-2/03.pdf on 29.06.2006, last update 01.07.2005.

Rawski, T. (2001): What's happening to China's GDP Statistics, in: China Economic Review, Vol. 12, No. 4, pp. 347-354.

Reuters (2007): "Shanghai license plate pricier than small car", retrieved from http://today.reuters.com/news/articlenews.aspx?type=worldNews&storyid=2007-06-19T070640Z_01_PEK226561_RTRUKOC_0_US-CHINA-CARPLATES xml on 06.09.2007, last update 19.06.2007.

Ricardo, D. (1817): The Principles of Political Economy and Taxation, London, UK: John Murray.

Riker, W. (1964): Federalism: Origins, Operations, and Significance, Boston, MA: Little, Brown.

Robert Bosch GmbH (2005): "Business/Economy - Strong Bosch involvement in China", retrieved from http://www.bosch-presse.de/TBWebDB/en-US/PressText.cfm?id=2516 on 02.02.2007, last update 17.11.2005.

Robert Bosch GmbH (2007): "Annual Report 2006", retrieved from http://www.bosch.com/content/language2/downloads/GB2006_En.pdf on 29.06.2007.

Robert Bosch GmbH (2007): "Bosch in China", retrieved from http://www.bosch.com.cn/new/web/boschinchina/bosch_overview_en.htm on 29.06.2007.

Robins, F. (2002): Industry Policy in East Asia, in: Asian Business & Management, Vol. 1, pp. 291-312.

Rodden, J. (2001): Decentralization and the Challenge of Hard Budget Constraints, Washington D.C.: World Bank.

Rodríguez-Clare, A. (1996): Multinationals, Linkages, and Economic Development, in: American Economic Review, Vol. 86, No. 4, pp. 852-873.

Rodrik, D. (1996): Coordination Failures and Government Policy: A Model with Applications to East Asia and Eastern Europe, in: Journal of International Economics, Vol. 40, pp. 1-22.

Rosen, G. (1992): Contrasting Styles of Industrial Reform. China and India in the 1980s, Chicago, IL: The University of Chicago Press.

Ross, S. (1973): The economic theory of agency: the principal's problem, in: American Economic Review, Vol. 63, No. 2, pp. 134-139.

Rowthorn, B. / Wells, J. (1987): Foreign trade and de-industrialisation, Cambridge, UK: Cambridge University Press.

Rueschemeyer, D. / Evans, P. (1985): The State and Economic Transformation: Toward an Analysis of the Conditions Underlying Effective Intervention, in: Evans, P. / Rueschemeyer, D. / Skocpol, T. (Eds.): Bringing the state back in, Cambridge, MA, Cambridge University Press, pp. 44-77.

Saggi, K. (2002): Trade, Foreign Direct Investment, and International Technology Transfer: A Survey, in: World Bank Research Observer, Vol. 17, No. 2, pp. 191-235.

Schnell, R. / Hill, P. / Esser, E. (1989): Methoden der empirischen Sozialforschung, München: Oldenbourg.

Schramm, M. / Taube, M. (2002): The Institutional Economics of Legal Institutions, Guanxi, and Corruption in the PR China, in: Kidd, J. / Richter, F.-J. (Eds.): Fighting Corruption in Asia - Causes, Effects and Remedies, River Edge, NJ, World Scientific, pp. 271-296.

Segal, A. / Thun, E. (2001): Thinking Globally, Acting Locally: Local Governments, Industrial Sectors, and Development in China, in: Politics & Society, Vol. 29, No. 4, pp. 557-588.

Shambaugh, D. (2000): The Chinese State in the Post-Mao Era, in: Shambaugh, D. (Ed.): The Modern Chinese State, Cambridge, MA; Cambridge University Press, pp. 161-187.

Shanghai Foreign Investment Development Board: "Law of People's Republic of China on Wholly-Foreign Owned Enterprises, adopted 12.04.1986; revised 31.10.2000", retrieved from http://www.fid.org.cn/en/tzsh/p65-2.htm on 17.07.2007.

Shanghai Government (2005): "City seeks better, more spacious cabs", retrieved from http://www.shanghai.gov.cn/shanghai/node8059/City_news/userobject22ai11207.html on 28.07.2007, last update 05.03.2005.

Shanghai Government (2005): "Volkswagen Leading New Way In China-Tribute to the 20th Anniversary of Shanghai Volkswagen", retrieved from http://www.investment.gov.cn/2005-10-27/1130425544083.html on 21.07.2007, last update 27.10.2005.

Shanghai Government (2006): "Examination and Approval Jurisdiction", retrieved from http://www.investment.gov.cn/2005-10-22/1129957271886.html on 10.12.2006, last update 22.10.2005.

Shanghai Government (2006): "Shanghai: car license plate prices set record", retrieved from http://www.gov.cn/english/2006-08/21/content_366801.htm on 14.07.2007, last update 21.08.2006.

Shanghai Foreign Economic Relation and Trade Commission (2006): Homepage retrieved from http://www.smert.gov.cn/gb/2/node498/index.html on 17.01.2006.

Shanghai Foreign Investment Commission: various issues of "Shanghai Statistical Yearbook", retrieved from http://www.stats-sh.gov.cn/2004shtj/tjnj/tjnj2006e.htm.

Shanghai Volkswagen (2005): Homepage retrieved from http://www.csvw.com/csvw/en/ on 29.06.2007.

Shapiro, H. (1993): Automobiles: From Import Substitution to Export Promotion in Brazil and Mexico, in: Yoffie, D. (Ed.): Beyond Free Trade Firms, Governments, and Global Competition, Boston, MA, Harvard Business School Press, pp. 193-250.

Sheatsley, P. (1983): Questionnaire Construction and Item Writing, in: Rossi, P. H. / Wright, J. / Anderson, A. (Eds.): Handbook of Survey Research, New York, NY, Academic Press, pp. 195-230.

Shenkar, O. (2005): The Chinese Century - The Rising Chinese Economy and Its Impact on the Global Economy, the Balance of Power and Your Job, Upper Saddle River, NJ: Wharton School Publishing.

Shirk, S. (1985): The Politics of Industrial Reform, in: Perry, E. J. / Wong, C. (Eds.): The Political Economy of Reform in Post-Mao China, Cambridge, MA, Harvard University Press, pp. 195/222.

Shirk, S. (1992): The Chinese Political System and the Political Strategy of Economic Reform, in: Lieberthal, K. / Lampton, D. (Eds.): Bureaucracy, Politics and Decision Making in Post-Mao China, Berkley and Los Angeles, CA, University of California Press, pp. 59-94.

Shirk, S. (1993): The Political Logic of Economic Reform in China, Berkeley, CA: University of California Press.

Shleifer, A. / Vishny, R. (1994): Politicians and firms, in: The Quarterly Journal of Economics, Vol. 59, pp. 995-1025.

Shleifer, A. / Vishny, R. (1999): The Grabbing Hand, Cambridge, MA: Harvard University Press.

Singh, A. (1977): UK industry and the world economy: a case of de-industrialisation?, in: Cambridge Journal of Economics, Vol. 1, No. 2, pp. 113-136.

Singh, I. (1992): China: Industrial Policies for an Economy in Transition, Washington D.C.: World Bank.

Sit, V. / Liu, W. (2000): Restructuring and Spatial Change of China's Auto Industry under Institutional Reform and Globalization, in: Annals of the Association of American Geographers, Vol. 90, No. 4, pp. 653-673.

Skocpol, T. (1985): Bringing the state back in: Strategies of analysis in current research, in: Evans, P. / Rueschemeyer, D. / Skocpol, T. (Eds.): Bringing the state back in, Cambridge, MA, Cambridge University Press, pp. 3-43.

Smith, A. (1776): The Wealth of Nations, New York, NY: reprinted by Random House (1937).

Smith, H. (1975): Strategies of Social Research: The Methodological Imagination, Englewood Cliffs, NJ: Prentice Hall.

So, A. (2003): Introduction: Rethinking the Chinese Developmental Miracle, in: So, A. (Ed.): China's Developmental Miracle - Origins, Transformations and Challenges, Armonk, NY, M.E. Sharpe, pp. 3-26.

Sohn, Y. (1998): The Rise and Development of the Japanese Licensing System, in: Carlile, L. / Tilton, M. (Eds.): Is Japan really changing its ways?: Regulatory reform and the Japanese economy, Washington, D.C., Brookings Institution Press, pp. 16-32.

Spiegel Online (2007): "Brilliance versagt im Crashtest", retrieved from http://www.spiegel.de/auto/werkstatt/0,1518,489777,00.html on 03.09.2007, last update 21.06.2007.

Spiegel (2007): Prinzip Sandkorn, 27.08.2007 (Vol. 35/2007), pp. 18-34.

Standing Committee of the National People's Congress (1995): "Law of the People's Republic of China on Commercial Banks (Adopted by the 13th Meeting of the Standing Committee of the Eighth National People's Congress on May 10, 1995, Promulgated by Decree No. 47 of the President of the People's Republic of China in May 10, 1995)", retrieved from http://www.chinalaw.cc/lib/banking/02.htm on 18.10.2005, last update 10.05.1995.

State Administration of Taxation (2004): "Circular of the State Administration of Taxation concerning the Tax Preferential Policy Applicable to Enterprises with Foreign Investment with Regard to Technology-Intensive and Knwoledge-Intensive Projects", retrieved from http://www.fdi.gov.cn/common/info.jsp?id=ABC00000000000018627 on 23.03.2006, last update 16.12.2004.

State Council (1994): Industrial policy of China's automobile industry, translated by DaimlerChrysler AG, pp. 1-16.

State Council (1994): "Outline of State Industrial Policies for the 1990s", retrieved from http://www.86148.com/englishlaw/shownews.asp?id=604 and http://www.86148.com/englishlaw/shownews.asp?id=605 on 31.03.2006, last update 25.03.1994.

State Council (1986): "Provisions of the State Council on the Encouragement of Foreign Investment", retrieved from http://www.fdi.gov.cn/resupload/epdf/e00373.pdf on 23.04.2006, last update 11.10.1986.

State Council (2002): "Provisions on Guiding the Orientation of Foreign Investment", retrieved from http://www.fdi.gov.cn/resupload/epdf/e00368.pdf on 18.04.2006.

State Development Planning Commission, the State Economy and Trade Commission, the Ministry of Foreign Trade and Economic Cooperation (2002): "Catalogue for the Guidance of Foreign Investment Industries", retrieved from http://www.fdi.gov.cn/ltlaw/lawinfodisp.jsp?id=ABC00000000000004228 on 18.04.2006.

State Information Center (2006): Homepage retrieved from http://www.sic.gov.cn/web/index.asp on 20.11.2006, last update 20.11.2006.

State-owned Assets Supervision and Administration Commission (2007): "Main Functions and Responsibilities of SASAC", retrieved from http://www.sasac.gov.cn/eng/zyzz.htm on 16.01.2007.

Steers, R. / Shin, Y. / Ungson, G. (1989): The Chaebol, New York, NY: Harper & Row.

Steinfeld, E. (2002): Chinese Enterprise Development and the Challenge of Global Integration. Prepared as a background paper for World Bank Study Innovative East Asia: The Future of Growth, pp. 1-56 and published in: Shahid Yusuf, S. / Altaf, A. / Nabeshima, K. (Eds.), Global Production Networking and Technological Change in East Asia, New York, NY: Oxford University Press.

Stevens, S. (1946): On the theory of scales and measurement, in: Science, Vol. 103, pp. 677-680.

Stigler, G. (1975): The Citizen and the State: Essays on Regulation, Chicago, IL: University of Chicago Press.

Stiglitz, J. (1987): Principal-Agent Problem, in: The Palgrave Dictionary of Economics, Vol. 4, London and Basingstoke, Macmillian Press, pp. 966-972.

Stiglitz, J. (1998): The Role of International Financial Institutions in the Current Global Economy. Address to the Chicago Council on Foreign Relations, retrieved from http://econ.worldbank.org/WBSITE/EXTERNAL/EXTDEC/EXTRESEARCH/EXTPROGRAMS/EXTTRADERESEARCH/0,,contentMDK:20024294~menuPK:64001880~pagePK:210083~piPK:152538~theSitePK:544849,00.html on 25.5.2006, last update 27.02.1998.

Stiglitz, J. (2002): Globalization and Its Discontents, London, UK: Allen Lane The Penguin Press.

Stolper, W. / Samuelson, P. (1941): Protection and Real Wages, in: Review of Economic Studies, Vol. 9, No. 1, pp. 58-73.

Strauss, A. / Corbin, J. (1990): Basics of qualitative research: Grounded theory procedures and techniques, Newbury Park, CA: Sage Publications, Inc.

Su, N. (1993): China's Industrial Policy During Economic System Transformation, in: Harrold, P. / Hwa, E. C. / Lou, J. (Eds.): Macroeconomic Management in China. Proceedings of a Conference in Dalian, June 1993, World Bank Discussion Papers No. 222, Washington, D.C., World Bank, pp. 107-124.

Sun, J. (2006): China: The Next Global Auto Power?, in: Far Eastern Economic Review, Vol. 169, No. 2, pp. 37-41.

Suttmeier, R. / Cao, C. (1999): China faces the new industrial revolution: Achievements and uncertainty in the search for research and innovation strategies, in: Asian Perspectives, Vol. 23, No. 3, pp. 153-200.

Swain, A. (1998): Governing the Workplace: The Workplace and Regional Development Implications of Automotive Foreign Direct Investment in Hungary, in: Regional Studies, Vol. 32, No. 7, pp. 653-671.

Takayama, Y. (1991): The Chinese Automobile Industry, in: JETRO China Newsletter, Vol. 94, No. September - October, pp. 16-21.

Taube, M. (2005): "China - The New Global Player", in: CESifo Forum, Vol. 3/2005, pp. 3-7.

Taylor Wessing China Desk (2004): New Automobile Policy, in: China TIPs, Vol. July/August 2004, pp. 1-10.

Teece, D. (1982): Towards an Economic Theory of the Multiproduct Firm, in: Journal of Economic Behavior and Organization, Vol. 3, No. 1, pp. 39-63.

Tenev, S. / Zhang, C. / Brefort, L. (2002): Corporate Governance and Enterprise Reform in China: Building the Institutions of Modern Markets, Washington, D.C.: World Bank and International Finance Corporation.

Tenev, S. (2006): Why China grows from below, in: Far Eastern Economic Review, Vol. 169, No. 1, pp. 22-25.

Thompson, G. (1989): Industrial Policy: USA and UK Debates, London, UK: Routledge.

Thompson, M. (1996): Late industrialisers, late democratisers: developmental states in the Asia-Pacific, in: Third World Quarterly, Vol. 17, No. 4, pp. 625-647.

Thun, E. (2004a): Industrial Policy, Chinese-Style: FDI, Regulation, and Dreams of National Champions in the Auto Sector,`in: Journal of East Asian Studies, Vol. 4, pp. 453-489.

Thun, E. (2004b): Going local: Foreign Investment, Local Development, and the Chinese Auto Sector, in: Carrillo, J. / Lung, Y. / van Tulder, R. (Eds.): Cars, Carriers of Regionalism?, New York, NY, Palgrave-Macmillian.

Thun, E. (2006): Changing Lanes in China - Foreign Direct Investment, Local Governments and Auto Sector Development, Cambridge, MA: Cambridge University Press.

Tiebout, C. (1956): A Pure Theory of Local Expenditures, in: The Journal of Political Economy, Vol. 64, No. 5, pp. 416-424.

Tong, J. (1989): Fiscal Reform, Elite Turnover and Central-Provincial Relations in Post-Mao China, in: Australian Journal of Chinese Affairs, Vol. 22, No. July 1989, pp. 1-28.

Tong, C. / Straussman, J. / Broadnax, W. (1999): Civil service reform in the People's Republic of China: case studies of early implementation, in: Public Administration and Development, Vol. 19, pp. 193-206.

Tsai, K. (2004): Off Balance: The Unintended Consequences of Fiscal Federalism in China, in: Journal of Chinese Political Science, Vol. 9, No. 2, pp. 7-26.

Tsao, K. / Worthley, J. (1995): Chinese Public Administration: Change with Continuity during Political and Economic Development, in: Public Administration Review, Vol. 55, No. 2, pp. 169-174.

Tsuji, M. (2004): Agglomeration and industrial policy of the Chinese Automotive Industry and Parts Industry, Working Paper of the Osaka School of International Public Policy (OSIPP), Osaka University Toyonaka, Osaka, Japan, 26.04.2004, pp. 1-12.

Tullock, G. / Buchanan, J. (1962): The Calculus of Consent: Logical Foundations of Constitutional Democracy, Indianapolis, IN: Liberty Fund.

Tullock, G. (1985): The Politics of Bureaucracy, Washington, D.C.: Public Affairs Press.

United Nations Conference on Trade and Development (UNCTAD) (2002): "Key Issues in China's Economic Transformation", retrieved from http://www.unctad.org/Templates/Page.asp?intItemID=4064&lang=1 on 12.02.2007.

United Nations Conference on Trade and Development (UNCTAD) (2006): World Investment Report 2006: FDI from Developing and Transition Economies: Implications for Development, New York, NY: United Nations.

United Nations Conference on Trade and Development (UNCTAD) (2007): World Investment Report 2007: Transnational Corporations, Extractive Industries and Development, New York, NY: United Nations.

United Nations Economic and Social Commission for Asia and the Pacific and Korea Maritime Institute (2005): Free Trade Zone and Port Hinterland Development, New York, NY: United Nations.

Unger, J. / Chan, A. (1995): China, Corporatism and the East Asian Model, in: The Australian Journal of Chinese Affairs, Vol. 33, pp. 29-53.

US Embassy Beijing (1996): "PRC State Council 'Decision on Accelerating S&T Development' ", retrieved from http://www.globalsecurity.org/military/library/report/1996/stdec2.htm on 07.09.2006, last update November 1996.

US Department of Commerce - International Trade Administration (2001): "Autos and Auto Parts", retrieved from http://www.mac.doc.gov/China/Docs/industryfactsheets/autos.html on 09.10.2006.

US Government Information (2005): "China's Industrial Policies Conflict with WTO Rules", retrieved from http://usinfo.state.gov/eap/Archive/2005/Jun/02-648829.html on 11.07.2007, last update 02.06.2005.

US Department of Energy (2006): "Major Government-Supported Fuel Cell Vehicle Projects", retrieved from http://www1.eere.energy.gov/hydrogenandfuelcells/pdfs/govt_fc_vehicle_proj.pdf on 26.08.2007, last update 08.03.2006.

US-China Economic and Security Review Commission (2006): "2006 Report to Congress", retrieved from http://www.uscc.gov/annual_report/2006/annual_report_full_06.pdf on 29.07.2007, last update November 2006.

VDA (1990-2007): International Auto Statistics, Frankfurt am Main: VDA.

VDA (2005): Internationale Konjunkturaussichten / Automobilkonjunktur. Paper presented at the "VDA Ausschuss für Internationale Handels- und Weltwirtschaftsfragen (IHW)", 22.11.2005, Frankfurt.

Vogel, E. (1989): One Step Ahead in China - Guangdong under Reform, Cambridge, MA: Harvard University Press.

Volkswagen AG (2004): "Volkswagen and Tongji sign a Memorandum Joining Hands to Develop Fuel Cell Vehicles for the Future", retrieved from http://www.vw.com.cn/publish/en/news/2004_07.htm on 26.08.2007, last update 12.10.2004.

Volkswagen AG (2007): "Annual Report 2006", retrieved from http://www.volkswagenag.com/vwag/vwcorp/info_center/de/publications/2007/03/GB_2006.-bin.acq/qual-BinaryStorageItem.Single.File/GB_2006_d.pdf on 29.06.2007.

Wade, R. (1988a): The Role of Government in Overcoming Market Failure: Taiwan, Republic of Korea and Japan, in: Hughes, H. (Ed.): Achieving Industrialization in East Asia, Cambridge, MA, Cambridge University Press, pp. 129-163.

Wade, R. (1988b): State Intervention in Outward-looking Development: Neoclassical Theory and Taiwanese Practice, in: White, G. (Ed.): Developmental States in East Asia, New York, NY, St. Martin's Press, pp. 30-67.

Wade, R. (1990): Governing the Market - Economic theory and the role of government in East Asian industrialization, Princeton, NJ: Princeton University Press.

Wade, R. (1992): East Asia's Economic Success - Conflicting Perspectives, Partial Insights, Shaky Evidence, in: World Politics, Vol. 44, No. 2, pp. 270-320.

Wade, R. (2003a): What strategies are viable for developing countries today? The World Trade Organization and the shrinking of "development space", in: Review of International Political Economy, Vol. 10, No. 4, pp. 621-644.

Wade, R. (2003b): Governing the Market - Economic theory and the role of government in East Asian industrialization (With a new introduction by the author), Princeton, NJ: Princeton University Press.

Wade, R. (2004): The Reprinting of *Governing the Market*: A Dinner Table Conversation, in: Issues & Studies, Vol. 40, No. 1, pp. 103-134.

Waitt, G. (1993): Say Bye to Hyundai and Hi to Korean Autoparts? Restructuring the Korean Automobile Industry in the 1990s, in: Tijdschrift voor Economische en Sociale Geografie, Vol. 84, pp. 198-206.

Walder, A. (1986): Communist neo-traditionalism, Berkeley, CA: University of California Press.

Walder, A. (1995): Local Governments and Industrial Firms: An Organizational Analysis of China's Transitional Economy, in: The Amercian Journal of Sociology, Vol. 101, No. 2, pp. 263-301.

Wang, H. (1993): China's exports since 1979, New York, NY: St. Marin's Press.

Wang, H. (2001): "Policy Reforms and Foreign Direct Investment: The Case of the Chinese Automotive Industry". Paper presented at the conference on "Ninth GERPISA International Colloquium, Reconfiguring the auto industry: merger & acquisitions, alliances and exit", Paris, 07.-09.06.2001.

Wang, H. (2002): "The coexistence of two automotive systems". Paper presented at the conference on "Dixieme Rencontre internationale du GERPISA - Tenth GERPISA International Colloquium", Paris, 06.-08.06.2002.

Walsh, K. (2003): Foreign High-Tech R&D in China - Risks, Rewards, and Implications for U.S.-China Relations, Washington D.C.: The Henry L. Stimson Center.

Wang, L. / Fewsmith, J. (1995): Bulwark of the Planned Economy: The Structure and Role of the State Planning Commission, in: Hamrin, C. / Zhao, S. (Eds.): Decision-Making in Deng's China - Perspectives from Insiders, Armonk, NY, M.E. Sharpe, pp. 51-65.

Wang, Y. (1997): Investment in China: A Question and Answer Guide on How to Do Business, New York, NY: American Management Association.

Wank, D. (1996): The Institutional Pricess of Market Clientelism: Guanxi and Private Business in a South China City, in: China Quarterly, Vol. 147, pp. 820-838.

Webb, E. / Campbell, D. / Schwartz, R. / Sechrest, L. (1966): Unobtrusive Measures: Nonreactive Research in the Social Sciences, Chicago, IL: Rand McNally.

Weber, M. (1911): Economy and Society, Berkeley and Los Angeles, CA: University of California Press.

Weider, M. (2004): China - Automobilmarkt der Zukunft? - Wie nachhaltig und zukunftsorientiert sind die Strategien der internationalen Automobilindustrie in China?, in: WZB discussion paper, Vol. SP III 2004, No. 105, pp. 1-67.

Weingast, B. (1995): The Economic Role of Political Institutions: Market-Preserving Federalism and Economic Development, in: Journal of Law, Economics and Organization, Vol. 11, pp. 1-31.

Weiss, L. / Hobson, J. (1995): States and Economic Development - A Comparative Historical Analysis, Cambridge, UK: Polity Press.

Weiss, L. (1998): The Myth of the Powerless State - Governing the Economy in a Global Era, Cambridge, UK: Polity Press.

Weiss, L. (2003): Guiding Globalisation in East Asia: new roles for old developmental states, in: Weiss, L. (Ed.): States in the global economy: Bringing domestic institutions back in, Cambridge, MA, Cambridge University Press, pp. 1-18.

Weiss, J. (2005): Export Growth and Industrial Policy: Lessons from the East Asian Miracle experience, ADB Institute Discussion Paper, Vol. 26, pp. 1-35.

Wen, J. (2006): "Report on the work of the government", retrieved from http://www.drcnet.com.cn/DRCnet.common.web/DocViewEnglish.aspx?chnid=1301145&docid=1301145&leafid=929 on 09.05.2006, last update 13.03.2006.

White, G. / Wade, R. (1988): Developmental States and Markets in East Asia: an Introduction, in: White, G. (Ed.): Developmental States in East Asia, New York, NY, St. Martin's Press, pp. 1-29.

Whitley, R. (1999): Divergent Capitalism - The Social Structuring and change of business systems, New York, NY: Oxford University Press.

Williamson, O. (1975): Markets and Hierarchies: Analysis and Antitrust Implications, New York, NY: Free Press

Williamson, O. (1985): The Economic Institutions of Capitalism. Firms, Markets, Relational Contracting, New York, NY: Free Press.

Williamson, O. (1991): Comparative economic organization: The analysis of discrete structural alternatives, in: Administrative Science Quarterly, Vol. 36, No. 2, pp. 269-296.

Williamson, O. (1994): Institutions and Economic Organization: The Governance Perspective, Washington D.C.: World Bank.

Wong, C. (1991): Central-Local Relations in an Era of Fiscal Decline: The Paradox of Fiscal Decentralization in Post-Mao China, in: China Quarterly, Vol. 128, No. December 1991, pp. 691-715.

Wong, C. (1992): Fiscal Reform and Local Industrialization: The Problematic Sequencing of Reform in Post-Mao China, in: Modern China, Vol. 18, No. April 1992, pp. 197-227.

Woo, W.-T. (1999): The real reasons for China's growth, in: The China Journal, Vol. 41, pp. 115-137.

World Bank (1993): The East Asian Miracle, New York, NY: Oxford University Press.

World Bank (1997): World Development Report 1997: The State in a Changing World, Washington D.C.: Oxford University Press.

World Bank (2001): "China's Local Trade Barriers: A Hard Nut to Crack", retrieved from http://www.worldbank.org/html/prddr/trans/JulAugSep01/boxpg11.htm on 25.10.2007.

World Bank (2001): "Competitiveness, Technology and Firm Linkages in Manufacturing Sectors", data sample retrieved from Davidson Data Center & Network.

World Bank (2004): "China: A summary of Implementing GATS Commitments in Main Service Sectors", retrieved from http://siteresources.worldbank.org/INTRANETTRADE/Resources/WBI-Training/288464-1139428366112/SummaryOfTheOpeningProgressOfMainServiceSectors.pdf on 12.07.2007.

World Bank (World Bank Office Beijing) (2005): "China Quarterly Update", retrieved from http://siteresources.worldbank.org/INTCHINA/Resources/318862-1121421293578/cqu08-05.pdf on 17.07.2007, last update August 2005.

World Bank (2006): China Governance, Investment Climate, and Harmonious Society: Competitiveness Enhancements for 120 Cities in China, Report No. 37759-CN, October 8, 2006; available at http://siteresources.worldbank.org/INTCHINA/Resources/318862-1121421293578/120cities_en.pdf, pp. 1-126.

World Bank (2007): "China Quick Facts", retrieved from http://web.worldbank.org/WBSITE/EXTERNAL/COUNTRIES/EASTASIAPACIFICEXT/CHINAEXTN/0,,contentMDK:20680895~pagePK:1497618~piPK:217854~theSitePK:318950,00.html on 21.09.2007.

World Bank (2007): "Governance Matters 2007", retrieved from http://info.worldbank.org/governance/wgi2007/ on 20.10.2007.

World Markets Analysis (2004): China aims to step up auto exports by 2010, 06.04.2004, pp. 1-2.

WTO (1994): "Agreement on Subsidies and Countervailing Measures (SCM Agreement)", retrieved from http://www.wto.org/english/tratop_e/scm_e/subs_e.htm on 18.12.2006.

WTO (1994): "General Agreement on Tariffs and Trade 1994", retrieved from http://www.wto.org/English/res_e/booksp_e/analytic_index_e/gatt1994_04_e.htm on 27.11.2006.

WTO (2001): "Accession documents", retrieved from http://www.wto.org/english/thewto_e/countries_e/china_e.htm on 09.10.2006, last update 11.12.2001.

WTO (2001): "Accession Protocol, (D) Judical Review, Article 7-3", retrieved from http://www.wto.org/english/thewto_e/countries_e/china_e.htm on 09.10.2006.

WTO (2001): "Report of the Working Party on the Accession of China", pp. 1-71, retrieved from http://unpan1.un.org/intradoc/groups/public/documents/APCITY/UNPAN002144.pdf#search=%22Report%20of%20the%20Working%20Party%20on%20the%20Accession%20of%20China%22 on 10.09.2006.

WTO (2004): "Transition period extended for export subsidies of developing countries", retrieved from http://www.wto.org/english/news_e/news04_e/sub_committee_04nov04_e.htm on 08.08.2006.

WTO (2007): "The 128 countries that had signed GATT by 1994", retrieved from http://www.wto.org/English/thewto_e/gattmem_e.htm on 23.09.2007.

WTO Secretariat (2001): Accession of the People's Republic of China - Decision of 10 November 2001, pp. 1-103, retrieved from http://www.wto.org/English/thewto_e/acc_e/completeacc_e.htm#chn on 23.11.2006.

WTO Secretariat (1999): Guide to the Uruguay Round Agreements, London, UK: Kluwer Law International.

Wu, A.-C. (2000): State Capacity in the RoC and PRC: A Comparative Perspective, in: Brodsgaard, K. / Young, S. (Eds.): State Capacity in East Asia - Japan, Taiwan, China and Vietnam, New York, NY, Oxford University Press, pp. 131-156.

Xia, M. (2000): The Dual Developmental State - Development Strategy and Institutional Arrangements for China's Transition, Brookfield, VT: Ashgate.

Xin, K. / Pearce, J. (1996): Guanxi: Connections as Substitutes for Formal Institutional Support, in: Academy of Management Journal, Vol. 39, No. 6, pp. 1641-1658.

Xinhuanet (2006): "A Review of China's Car Industry in Past 5 Years", retrieved from http://www.china.org.cn/english/BAT/191884.htm on 26.07.2007, last update 11.12.2006.

Xinhuanet (2006): "Rule will require SOEs to submit dividends to government", retrieved from http://news.xinhuanet.com/english/2006-09/20/content_5113638.htm on 03.10.2006.

Xinhuanet (2007): "NPC to speed up legislation on social issues in 2007", retrieved from http://news.xinhuanet.com/english/2007-03/11/content_5831053.htm on 21.10.2007, last update 11.03.2007.

Yamamura, K. (1967): Economic Policy in Postwar Japan: Growth Versus Economic Democracy, Berkeley, CA: University of California Press.

Yin, R. / Moore, G. (1987): The use of advanced technologies in special education in: Journal of Learning Disabilities, Vol. 20, No. 1, pp. 60-63.

Yin, R. (1993): Applications of case study research, Beverly Hills, CA: Sage Publishing.

Yin, R. (1994): Case Study Reseach - Design and Methods, Thousand Oaks, CA: SAGE Publications.

Young, A. (2000): The Razor's Edge: Distortions and incremental reform in the People's Republic of China, in: The Quaterly Journal of Economics, Vol. CXV, No. 4, pp. 1091-1135.

Young, M. / Tan, J. (2001): Beijing Jeep at a crossroads: Facing the challenge of China's entry into the WTO, in: Asian Case Research Journal, Vol. 5, No. 1, pp. 1-26.

Young, S. / Lan, P. (1997): Technology transfer to China through foreign direct investment, in: Regional Studies, Vol. 31, No. 7, pp. 669-679.

Yu, Q. (1999): The implementation of China's science and technology policy, Westport, CT and London, UK: Quorum Books.

Yue, C. (1995): Government's role in East Asia's Economic Success, in: Garnaut, R. / Grilli, E. / Riedel, J. (Eds.): Sustaining export-oriented development, Cambridge, UK, Cambridge University Press, pp. 76-105.

Yueh, L. (2006): Patent Laws and Innovation in China, in: University of Oxford - Department of Economics Discussion Paper Series, Vol. 271, pp. 1-37.

Yusuf, S. / Nabeshima, K. / Perkin, D. (2006): Under New Ownership - Privatizing China's State-Owned Enterprises, Washington, D.C.: Stanford University Press and World Bank.

Yusuf, S. / Nabeshima, K. (2006a): Two Decades of Reform: The Changing Organization Dynamics of Chinese Industrial Firms, World Bank Policy Research Paper, Vol. 3806, No. January 2006, pp. 1-45.

Yusuf, S. / Nabeshima, K. (2006b): Under New Ownership - Priviatizing China's State-Owned Enterprises, Washington D.C.: International Bank for Reconstruction and Development/World Bank.

ZF Friedrichshafen AG (2007): "Geschäftsbericht 2006", retrieved from http://www.zf.com/zf_group/daten_und_fakten/Geschaeftsbericht/41341_ZF_GB06_D.pdf on 29.06.2007.

Zhang, K. / Song, S. (2000): Promoting exports - The role of inward FDI in China, in: China Economic Review, Vol. 11, pp. 385-396.

Zhang, W. / Taylor, R. (2001): EU Technology Transfer to China - The automotive industry as a case study, in: Journal of the Asia Pacific Economy, Vol. 6, No. 2, pp. 261-274.

Zhang, X. / Long, G. (1997): China's Industrial Policy in the Process of Marketization, in: Masuyama, S./ Vandenbrink, D. / Yue, C. (Eds.): Industrial Policies in East Asia, Tokyo, Club Foundation for Global Studies, pp. 255-292.

Zhao, S. (1995): The Structure of Authority and Decision-Making: A Theoretical Framework, in: Hamrin, C. / Zhao, S. (Eds.): Decision-Making in Deng's China - Perspectives from Insiders, Armonk, NY, M.E. Sharpe, pp. 233-245.

Zheng, S. (1997): Party vs. State in Post-1949 China - The Institutional Dilemma, Cambridge, MA: Cambridge University Press.

Zheng, Y.-N. (1995): Institutional Change, Local Developmentalism and Economic Growth: The Making of Semi-Federalism in Reform China, Inaugural Dissertation, Department of Politics, Princeton University, Ann Arbor, MI.

Zhu, J. (2004): Local Developmental State and Order in China's Urban Development during transition, in: International Journal of Urban and Regional Research, Vol. 28, No. 2, pp. 424-447.

Zhu, T. (1999): China's Corporatization Drive: An Evaluation and Policy Implications, in: Contemporary Economic Policy, Vol. 17, pp. 530-539.

Zhu, T. (2003): Building Institutional Capacity for China's New Economic Opening, in: Weiss, L. (Ed.): States in the global economy: Bringing domestic institutions back in, Cambridge, MA, Cambridge University Press, pp. 1-18.

Zhou, X. (2001): Political Dynamics and Bureaucratic Career Patterns in the People's Republic of China, 1949-1994, in: Comparative Political Studies, Vol. 34, No. 9, pp. 1036-1062.

HOHENHEIMER VOLKSWIRTSCHAFTLICHE SCHRIFTEN

Band 1 Walter Deffaa: Anonymisierte Befragungen mit zufallsverschlüsselten Antworten. Die Randomized-Response-Technik (RRT). Methodische Grundlagen, Modelle und Anwendungen. 1982.

Band 2 Thomas Michael Baum: Staatsverschuldung und Stabilisierungspolitik in der Demokratie. Zur neoinstitutionalistischen Kritik der keynesianischen Fiskalpolitik. 1982.

Band 3 Klaus Schröter: Die wettbewerbspolitische Behandlung der leitungsgebundenen Energiewirtschaft. Dargestellt am Beispiel der Fernwärmewirtschaft der Bundesrepublik Deutschland. 1986.

Band 4 Hugo Mann: Theorie und Politik der Steuerreform in der Demokratie. 1987.

Band 5 Max Christoph Wewel: Intervallarithmetische Dependenzanalyse in der Ökonometrie. Ein konjekturaler Ansatz. 1987.

Band 6 Heinrich Pascher: Die U.S.-amerikanische Deregulation Policy im Luftverkehrs- und Bankenbereich. 1987.

Band 7 Harald Lob: Die Entwicklung der französischen Wettbewerbspolitik bis zur Verordnung Nr. 86-1243 vom 01. Dezember 1986. Eine exemplarische Untersuchung der Erfassung der Behinderungsstrategie auf der Grundlage des Konzepts eines wirksamen Wettbewerbs. 1988.

Band 8 Ulrich Kirschner: Die Erfassung der Nachfragemacht von Handelsunternehmen. Eine Analyse der ökonomischen Beurteilungskriterien und der wettbewerbsrechtlichen Instrumente im Bereich der Verhaltenskontrolle.1988.

Band 9 Friedhelm Herb: Marktwirtschaftliche Innovationspolitik. 1988.

Band 10 Claus Schnabel: Zur ökonomischen Analyse der Gewerkschaften in der Bundesrepublik Deutschland. Theoretische und empirische Untersuchungen von Mitgliederentwicklung, Verhalten und Einfluß auf wirtschaftliche Größen. 1989.

Band 11 Jan B. Rittaler: Industrial Concentration and the Chicago School of Antitrust Analysis. A Critical Evaluation on the Basis of Effective Competition. 1989.

Band 12 Thomas Märtz: Interessengruppen und Gruppeninteressen in der Demokratie. Zur Theorie des Rent-Seeking. 1990.

Band 13 Andreas Maurer: Statistische Verfahren zur Ermittlung von oligopolistischen Strukturen. 1990.

Band 14 Peter Mendler: Zur ökonomischen und politisch-institutionellen Analyse öffentlicher Kredithilfen. 1992.

Band 15 Heinrich J. Engelke: Die Interpretation der Rundfunkfreiheit des Grundgesetzes: Eine Analyse aus ökonomischer Sicht. 1992.

Band 16 Thomas Fischer: Staat, Recht und Verfassung im Denken von Walter Eucken. Zu den staats- und rechtstheoretischen Grundlagen einer wirtschaftsordnungspolitischen Konzeption. 1993.

Band 17 Stefan Elßer: Innovationswettbewerb. Determinanten und Unternehmensverhalten. 1993.

Band 18 Reinhard Scharff: Regionalpolitik und regionale Entwicklungspotentiale. Eine kritische Analyse. 1993.

Band 19 Karin Beckmann: Probleme der Regionalpolitik im Zuge der Vollendung des Europäischen Binnenmarktes. Eine ökonomische Analyse. 1995.

Band 20 Bernd Nolte: Engpaßfaktoren der Innovation und Innovationsinfrastruktur. Eine theoretische und empirische Analyse für ländliche Wirtschaftsräume in Baden-Württemberg. 1996.

Band 21 Klaus-Rainer Brintzinger: Die Nationalökonomie an den Universitäten Freiburg, Heidelberg und Tübingen 1918 - 1945. Eine institutionenhistorische, vergleichende Studie der wirtschaftswissenschaftlichen Fakultäten und Abteilungen südwestdeutscher Universitäten. 1996.

Band 22 Steffen Binder: Die Idee der Konsumentensouveränität in der Wettbewerbstheorie. Teleokratische vs. nomokratische Auffassung. 1996.

Band 23 Alexander Burger: Deregulierungspotentiale in der Gesetzlichen Rentenversicherung. Reformnotwendigkeiten versus Reformmöglichkeiten. 1996.

Band 24 Burkhard Scherer: Regionale Entwicklungspolitik. Konzeption einer dezentralisierten und integrierten Regionalpolitik. 1997.

Band 25 Frauke Wolf: Lorenzkurvendisparität. Neuere Entwicklungen, Erweiterungen und Anwendungen. 1997.

Band 26 Hans Pitlik: Politische Ökonomie des Föderalismus. Föderative Kompetenzverteilung im Lichte der konstitutionellen Ökonomik. 1997.

Band 27 Stephan Seiter: Der Beitrag Nicholas Kaldors zur Neuen Wachstumstheorie. Eine vergleichende Studie vor dem Hintergrund der Debatte über den Verdoorn-Zusammenhang. 1997.

Band 28 André Schmidt: Ordnungspolitische Perspektiven der europäischen Integration im Spannungsfeld von Wettbewerbs- und Industriepolitik. 1998.

Band 29 Bernd Blessin: Innovations- und Umweltmanagement in kleinen und mittleren Unternehmen. Eine theoretische und empirische Analyse. 1998.

Band 30 Oliver Letzgus: Die Ökonomie internationalen Umweltschutzes. 1999.

Band 31 Claudia Hafner: Systemwettbewerb versus Harmonisierung in Europa. Am Beispiel des Arbeitsmarktes. 1999.

Band 32 Jürgen Kulle: Ökonomie der Musikindustrie. Eine Analyse der körperlichen und unkörperlichen Musikverwertung mit Hilfe von Tonträgern und Netzen. 1998.

Band 33 Michael Ganske: Intertemporale Aspekte von Staatsverschuldung und Außenhandel. 1999.

Band 34 Margit Ströbele: Die Deregulierungswirkungen der europäischen Integration. Das Beispiel der Sondermärkte. 1999.

Band 35 Marion Benesch: Devisenmarktinterventionen in Theorie und Praxis. Eine umfassende Analyse ihrer Zielsetzungen, Wirkungsweisen und wirtschaftspolitischen Bedeutung. 1999.

Band 36 Torsten Gruber: Unterschiedliche geldpolitische Transmissionsmechanismen und Stabilitätskulturen als mögliche Ursachen geldpolitischer Spannungen in der Europäischen Währungsunion. 2000.

Band 37 Bertram Melzig-Thiel: Arbeit in der Informationsgesellschaft. Chancen und Risiken neuer Informations- und Kommunikationstechnologien für die Beschäftigung. 2000.

Band 38 Annette Fritz: Die Entsorgungswirtschaft im Spannungsfeld zwischen Abfallpolitik und Kartellrecht. Eine industrieökonomische Branchenstudie. 2001.

Band 39 Harald Strotmann: Arbeitsplatzdynamik in der baden-württembergischen Industrie. Eine Analyse mit amtlichen Betriebspaneldaten. 2002.

Band 40 Dietrich Benner: Qualitätsungewißheit bei Gütern mit Vertrauenseigenschaften. Entwicklung und Anwendung eines entscheidungstheoretisch fundierten Analyserahmens. 2002.

Band 41 Jürgen M. Schechler: Sozialkapital und Netzwerkökonomik. 2002.

Band 42 Kay-Uwe May: Haushaltskonsolidierung durch Ausgabekürzungen. Restriktionen und Strategien. 2002.

Band 43 Peter Kühnl: Der Wechselkurs als Zwischenziel der Geldpolitik im Aufholprozess. Die monetärkeynesianische Entwicklungsstrategie der Berliner Schule vor dem Hintergrund der makroökonomischen Entwicklung ausgewählter Länder Mittel- und Osteuropas. 2003.

Band 44 Steffen Wirth: Nichtparametrische Analyse von Bildungsertragsraten. Neuere Entwicklungen und Anwendungen. 2003.

Band 45 Bernhard Holwegler: Innovation, Diffusion und Beschäftigung. Die ökonomische Theorie der Technologiediffusion und ihr Beitrag zur Erklärung technologischer Arbeitslosigkeit. 2003.

Band 46 Guntram R. M. Hepperle: Zukunftsorientierte Industriepolitik. Möglichkeiten und Grenzen. 2004.

Band 47 Udo Vullhorst: Stabilisierungspolitik bei supranationaler Geldpolitik und nationaler Fiskalpolitik. Eine spieltheoretische Betrachung. 2004.

Band 48 Matthias Rösch: Die Bedeutung von Investivlöhnen und Gewinnbeteiligungen für Einkommensverteilung und Beschäftigung. 2004.

Band 49 Michael Bubik: Erfolgskriterien für Unternehmenszusammenschlüsse. Eine theoretische und exemplarische Analyse. 2005.

Band 50 Jörg Weltin: Internationale Unternehmensbesteuerung. Allokation der Besteuerungsrechte unter veränderten Rahmenbedingungen. 2005.

Band 51 Susanne Reichart: Zum Konvergenzprozess der mittel- und osteuropäischen EU-Beitrittsländer. 2005.

Band 52 Daniel Hartmann: Geldpolitik und Beschäftigung. Die geldpolitische Strategie der Federal Reserve: Vorbild oder Auslaufmodell? 2005.

Band 53 Marc Peter Radke: Explaining Financial Crises. A Cyclical Approach. 2005.

Band 54 Katja Hölsch: Umverteilungseffekte in Europa. Eine Analyse für ausgewählte Länder. 2006.

Band 55 Ulrike Lehr: Contingent Valuation Daten und Bayes'sche Verfahren. Ein Vorschlag zur Verbesserung von Umweltbewertung und Nutzentransfer. 2006.

Band 56 Jutta Maute: Hyperinflation, Currency Board, and Bust. The Case of Argentina. 2006.

Band 57 Michael Knittel: Geldpolitik und Stabilität des Bankensystems. Das Liquiditätsproblem aus Sicht der Theoriegeschichte und der gegenwärtigen Finanzmarktentwicklung. 2007.

Band 58 Oliver Frör: Rationality Concepts in Environmental Valuation. 2007.

Band 59 Jochen Gert Arend Wiegmann: Produktivitätsentwicklung in Deutschland. 2008.

Band 60 Nicola Meier: China – The New Developmental State? An Empirical Analysis of the Automotive Industry. 2009.

www.peterlang.de

Peter Lang · Internationaler Verlag der Wissenschaften

Francesco Garibaldo / Philippe Morvannou / Jochen Tholen (eds.)

Is China a Risk or an Opportunity for Europe?

An Assessment of the Automobile, Steel and Shipbuilding Sectors

Frankfurt am Main, Berlin, Bern, Bruxelles, New York, Oxford, Wien, 2008.
125 pp., 2 fig., num. tab. and graph.
Labour, Education & Society. Edited by Francesco Garibaldo. Vol. 11
ISBN 978-3-631-57474-4 · pb. € 29.60*

China's industrial growth has been the unexpected event of the beginning of the 21st century owing to its impact on the entire global economy. The aim of the book is to get a common understanding of China's economic future and its consequences for Europe based on the situation in three metal sectors chosen as examples, namely steel, shipbuilding, and automotive. That assessment can then serve as a basis for describing and evaluating the importance of the factors enabling Chinese industry to be globally competitive. Finally, this research will endeavour to pinpoint the relevant issues and establish ways of internationally regulating the growth of China's metal industries, making them compatible with international standards regarding sustainable development and social responsibility.

Contents: China's industrial growth · Global competitiveness · US debt · Investments by multinationals · Relocation · A new international division of labours · Weakening of European industries · Unfair competition · Lisbon strategy · European social model

www.ingramcontent.com/pod-product-compliance
Ingram Content Group UK Ltd.
Pitfield, Milton Keynes, MK11 3LW, UK
UKHW021843100926
8556IPUK00019B/1017

9 783631 582848